To Mary Lou —

Best of luck in your
new career!

Julia Silvers

9/28/06

Professional Event Coordination

The Wiley Event Management Series

SERIES EDITOR: DR. JOE GOLDBLATT, CSEP

Special Events: Twenty-First Century Global Event Management, Third Edition
by Dr. Joe Goldblatt, CSEP

The International Dictionary of Event Management, Second Edition
by Dr. Joe Goldblatt, CSEP, and Kathleen S. Nelson, CSEP

Corporate Event Project Management
by William O'Toole and Phyllis Mikolaitis, CSEP

*Event Marketing: How to Successfully Promote Events,
Festivals, Conventions, and Expositions*
by Leonard H. Hoyle, CAE, CMP

Event Risk Management and Safety
by Peter E. Tarlow, Ph.D.

Event Sponsorship
by Bruce E. Skinner, CFE, and Vladimir Rukavina, CFE

Professional Event Coordination
by Julia Rutherford Silvers, CSEP

Professional Event Coordination

Julia Rutherford Silvers, CSEP

WILEY

JOHN WILEY & SONS, INC.

Copyright © 2004 by John Wiley & Sons, Inc. All rights reserved.

Published by John Wiley & Sons, Inc., Hoboken, New Jersey
Published simultaneously in Canada.

For general information on our other products and services or for technical support, please contact our Customer Care Department within the United States at (800) 762-2974, outside the United States at (317) 572-3993 or fax (317) 572-4002.

Wiley also publishes its books in a variety of electronic formats. Some content that appears in print may not be available in electronic books. For more information about Wiley products, visit our web site at www.wiley.com.

Library of Congress Cataloging-in-Publication Data:

Silvers, Julia Rutherford.
  Professional event coordination / Julia Rutherford Silvers.
    p. cm. — (The Wiley event management series)
Includes index.
  ISBN 0-471-26305-2
  1. Special events—Planning. 2. Special events—Management. I.
Title. II. Series.
  GT3405.S55 2004
  394.2—dc21   2003012936

Printed in the United States of America.

10 9 8 7 6 5 4 3 2 1

To Larry, my husband, my sailor, my best friend—the one who has made any and all moon hanging possible.

Contents

Foreword

In 1976 the president of the university where I was teaching asked me to take over the direction of a tourism program that was losing enrollment. His charge was to make the program grow or sign its death certificate. I began researching all aspects of tourism for a program that would use our teaching resources, appeal to our students, and give them some leverage in the job market after graduation.

Our research discovered a subset of tourism called meetings, events, conventions, and expositions. At that time this industry was contributing $32.5 billion to the gross national product, but there appeared to be no formal educational path for young people wishing to enter the industry.

On closer examination we discovered that most of the people working in the industry had gravitated to it by chance. Some of the most influential people in the industry at that time had been assigned the task of producing great events and outstanding meetings by a boss who did not want to do it himself. We were amazed at the size of the budgets for many of these events. In some cases they exceeded the annual budgets of small companies and divisions of large firms. With little or no formal training available, these people produced creative and memorable events. Over time, and with much trial and error, a recognizable profession gradually took shape. We pondered, "Was everything they did intuitive?"

Many of the profession's leading practitioners were surveyed to determine what they considered to be their educational weaknesses and what subjects they wish they had studied in school. The information we collected helped us to define our curriculum.

As we grew closer to the launch of our program, we discovered two things:

- Most professionals thought that we were embarking on a fool's journey. This was one profession that could not be taught in a classroom.
- There were no books that could be used in the classroom to teach these courses.

Times have changed. Meetings, exhibitions, events, and conventions (MEEC) courses now appear in the curriculum of more than 200 universities worldwide. In fact, postgraduate course work in these fields is taught at many of the world's leading universities. It is quite common for employers to contact universities to request students who have MEEC degrees. Clearly, there is a demand for college-trained professionals in an industry that has tripled in size in the last 27 years.

However, the greatest cause of near failure of our educational program in the late 1970s was lack of books for our courses. As in any emerging industry, codification of rules, techniques, and guidelines is a critical step in the educational process.

Over the years I have been impressed when I heard that someone was getting ready to publish a new book for the industry. It meant that someone like Julia Rutherford Silvers was going to add to her personal workload the task of creating a book about the events industry. In the case of this book, it is a selfless effort to help others understand the dynamic and exciting events industry.

I am pleased to have the honor of introducing this book. It represents another milestone in the educational process. It is a concise guide for seasoned professionals and will serve as an excellent classroom resource for students trying to understand the dynamics of this industry. It will allow students to grasp the complexities that thousands of industry professionals accept as a regular part of their jobs.

Julia Rutherford Silvers has taken a no-nonsense approach to a "fun" industry. She has put another important building block in place to help event management to be better recognized as a fully developed industry.

What book dedicated to this complex business would not include checklists? I believe that this book contains some of the clearest, most concise, and extremely useful lists that have been developed to date.

I know you will enjoy this valuable resource. It will be a great adventure for the novice and yet serve as an effective guide for the seasoned professional.

Let the event begin!

Edward G. Polivka

Foreword

Pulitzer prize–winning historians Will and Ariel Durant described *education* as "the transmission of civilization." In this important and comprehensive volume, Julia Rutherford Silvers, CSEP, has transmitted literally hundreds of ideas that will dramatically improve the coordination of your events.

Ms. Silvers is a leading force in the field of event management education and has distilled her many years of professional experience into an easy-to-use compendium of best practices for modern event coordinators. "On-Site Insights" are presented throughout the chapters, which immediately enable you to apply her theories through real-world anecdotal examples. Furthermore, this valuable book has dozens of checklists, tables, figures, and other proven strategies for future success.

Whether you are coordinating a small function for ten guests or a major exposition or festival with 10,000 attendees, this book and the wisdom within can serve as a reliable guide to ensure seamless coordination. From the opening chapter, which conducts a thorough study of the anatomy of professional events, to the closing final strategies for success, this book will soon be among the most important resources you will use and recommend to others.

One of the best features of this book is the comprehensive appendix (Appendix 5) citing the numerous resources and texts that were used to compile this work. This alone is worth the price of the book and much more.

Julia Rutherford Silvers is one of the leading practitioners, authors, educators, and consultants in the event management industry. This book allows you to tap her expertise as often as you wish so as to continually improve your event coordination practices.

Although the Durants defined education as the transmission of civilization, the *American Heritage Dictionary* further defines *civilization* as "an advanced state of cultural and material development in human society marked by political and social complexity and progress in the arts and sciences." Ms. Silvers's book is an extraordinary work of both art and science that enables you to rapidly and consistently advance and develop your professional career in this field. Throughout human history major developments, such as the creation of tools, have marked the development of humankind. History will soon record that Julia Rutherford

Silvers, CSEP, provided us with a major development in our industry with this book, the foremost resource to produce more civilized events now and in the future.

Dr. Joe Goldblatt, CSEP
Series Editor

Preface

*In all chaos there is a cosmos, in all disorder a
secret order.*

—CARL JUNG (1875–1961)

The modern event industry has grown from a subset of administrative
duties and creative individuals in a variety of fields into a full-fledged
profession that is practiced globally, with all the responsibilities and proficiency expectations of a modern profession. The tasks and techniques
that have been developed through trial and error over the years have
been quantified, which serves us by providing a clear path of training toward event excellence—mastering that chaos by understanding the secret
order and transforming the "priesthood" of secrets into a recognized and
accessible body of knowledge. I wrote this book to bring together the
hundreds of years of collective experience of that priesthood so that it
will be accessible to you.

Although the industry has identified the skills and competency domains required of an event professional, we have not yet standardized
the titles we go by. In different companies and different parts of the
world we are called event coordinators, event planners, event managers,
event producers, event directors, event designers, account executives,
and countless other monikers. My former business partner and I had our
own unique titles; I was the Grand Poohbah and she was the Vice Em-
press. The titles may be different, but we are all engaged in the business
of creating event experiences that serve the needs of the client or host
and fulfill the expectations of the guest or attendee. This requires due
diligence—the investigation and consideration of all the requirements
and possibilities, both good and bad, for the event.

Whether you are preparing to enter this profession, preparing for advancement within it, or preparing for certification as a professional, this

book will provide you with a comprehensive overview of the competencies required of a professional event coordinator. I hope that it will also become a reference tool you may use throughout your professional career. The scope of competencies addressed herein is based on the Tourism Standards of Western Canada for Special Events Coordinator and Special Events Manager, and the Tourism, Hospitality & Sport Education & Training Authority (THETA) National Qualifications Framework for Event Support in South Africa, as well as the event management competencies outlined in the Exam Blueprint for the International Special Events Society Certified Special Events Professional (CSEP) certification program.

Each chapter examines a variety of competency points, outlined in the objectives at the beginning of each chapter, and there are numerous checklists you may use to refine your skills as a professional event coordinator. **On-Site Insights,** by various industry professionals around the world, provide examples to put the content in a real-life context, and **Technology Tips** direct you to relevant technology to enhance the efficiency and effectiveness of event coordination, operations, and opportunities. At the end of each chapter you will find **Exercises in Professional Event Coordination** to perform that will reinforce the concepts and competencies in practical applications, as well as help to prepare you for taking the CSEP certification exam.

The book starts by examining the anatomy of an event to establish the different layers of an event experience and the general process of professional event coordination. Based on this foundation, it considers the assessment of the various elements of an event, which can allow the event coordinator to visualize, organize, and synchronize the event's resources and operations through project management techniques. Next it explores the critical aspects of site selection and development to ensure that the location and layout of the event meet its needs. Inviting attendees and providing them with the appropriate access to the event site is considered from the perspective of customer service as the event coordinator plans to accommodate the event's audience. Although not particularly glamorous, it is important to arrange for the essential services that provide the necessary infrastructure for the event, as well as mitigate the event's impact on its neighbors and the environment. It is also necessary to make plans for the safety and security of the event's guests and organize the services and strategies to ensure safe operations before, during, and after the event.

As the book moves to a discussion of event design, it examines the creative, as well as practical, aspects of coordinating the event environment through theme design, décor, and numerous other staging considerations. It also delves into the fundamentals of technical productions and entertainment possibilities that set the stage for the event experience. The discussion provides a taste of food and beverage possibilities and practicalities by investigating catering operations, menu design, and food service styles. The various opportunities for adding value and meaning to the event experience are explored, such as the selection and presentation of gifts and amenities, as well as the various ancillary programs and mini-events that not only entertain and enrich, but also support the objectives of the event.

An event is all about people—people coming together to create, operate, and participate in an experience. In that vein, the book explores the supplier solicitation and selection process, as well as vendor relations, and discusses human resources management issues as they relate to staffing, volunteers, and participants. Finally, it examines performance reviews, evaluation techniques, and knowledge management strategies that help the professional event coordinator to continually improve his or her performance and operations.

It is important to understand that professional event coordination is a complex job, and the topics covered in this book are what you must consider for each and every event you undertake. It is also important to understand that each topic represents an entire course of study in and of itself, many representing distinct industries within the overall event management industry. You are not expected to be an expert in each field, nor could one book provide the entire body of knowledge for each field, but as a professional event coordinator, you are expected to know enough to be able to effectively procure, organize, implement, and monitor all the products, services, and service providers that will bring an event to life.

Creating and producing events is an exhilarating and sometimes exhausting occupation, but it is always rewarding, emotionally, spiritually, and often economically. The professional event coordinator must be flexible, energetic, well organized, detail-oriented, and a quick thinker. As a professional event coordinator, you must understand the integrated processes, plans, and possibilities specific to each event you coordinate so that you will be a better planner, producer, purchaser, and partner in delivering the special event experience that exceeds expectations. We must always remember that although not every event is a milestone for us, it is for the client or guest. From festivals and fairs to meetings and conventions, fund-raising events to familial occasions, civic celebrations to athletic competitions, or parades to theme parties—every event is special. We, as professional event coordinators, make dreams come true.

Acknowledgments

I shall know that your good is mine; ye shall know that my strength is yours.

—RUDYARD KIPLING (1865–1936)

When asked how long it has taken me to design something, I always answer, "All my life." When asked how I was able to write this book, I will always have to answer, "All my friends."

My deepest thanks to my former business partner Virginia Huffman of Expo Events, Inc., with whom, for more than a decade, I was privileged to have the opportunity to create fantastic memories for thousands and thousands of guests at the themed events and special occasions we designed and produced for attendees from all over the world. We came to this profession from different backgrounds and shared the joy of discovering each other's talents and gifts as together we grew personally and professionally.

My appreciation and admiration to Dr. Joe Goldblatt, CSEP, an icon, inspiration, mentor, coach, colleague, nudge, cheerleader, and true friend, with whom I have been privileged to work on numerous educational projects and programs to prepare professionals for this exciting and demanding industry.

My sincerest gratitude goes to my family of friends and colleagues in the International Special Events Society (ISES) who have been unfailing in their support and eagerness to share their experience, experiences, and expertise, not only with me, but also with the industry as a whole. My special thanks to:

- James Decoulos, Esq., for his contributions and advice regarding event insurance in Chapter 2
- Robert Estrin, for his insights on event safety for Chapter 6 and laced throughout the book

- Ralph Traxler, CSEP, for his assistance with the content on technical production in Chapter 8
- Robert Sivek, CSEP, CERP, Deborah Borsum, CSEP, CMD, and Connie Riley, CSEP, for providing me with access to many proprietary internal documents and policies used to benchmark best practices
- And to those who took the time and effort to personally contribute to this book:

Ruda Anderson	Jessica Levin
Aimee V. Brizuela	Dani Mulhern
Kendall Collier, CSEP	Kathy Nelson, CSEP, CMP
Trevor Connell	Bill O'Toole
John J. Daly Jr., CSEP	Romaine Pereira
Patrick Delaney, CITE	Ed Polivka
David DeLoach	Mike Rudahl
Karla Grunewald	Brenda Schwerin, CSEP
Robert Hulsmeyer, CSEP	Mark Sonder, CSEP
Bob Johnson	David Spear, CSEP
Steve Kemble	Tony Timms
Cal Kennedy, CSEP	Mary Tribble, CSEP
Ginger Kramer	Benjamin Wax
Janet Landey, CSEP	Sally Webb
Glen Lehman, CSEP	Dana Zita, CSEP

- I must also express my appreciation to those who have contributed so much to the leadership of and the body of knowledge for this industry and, therefore, my ability to write this book.

Richard Aaron, CSEP, CMP	Sandra Khoury
Stan Aaronson, CSEP	Bill Knight, CSEP
John Baragona	Amy A. Ledoux, CMP
Suzanne Bristow, CSEP (deceased)	Tim Lundy, CSEP
	Lena Malouf, CSEP
Nigel Collin	Nancy Matheny, CSEP
Alice Conway, CSEP	Carol McKibben, CSEP
Patti Coons, CSEP	Mona S. Meretsky, CSEP
Paul Creighton, CSEP	Patricia Merl, CSEP
Duncan Farrell, CMP	Andrea Michaels
Kenny Fried	Phyllis Mikolaitis, CSEP
Robyn Hadden, CSEP	James Monroe, CSEP, CMP
Linda Higgison	Dan Nelson, CSEP, CMP
Lisa Hurley	Lisa K. Perrin
Klaus Inkamp, CSEP (deceased)	David Peters
	Garland L. Preddy
Steve Jeweler	Pat Schaumann, CSEP, CMP, DMCP

Steve Schwartz
Patti J. Shock
David Sorin, CSEP
David Tutera

Josh Waldorf
Harith Wickrema
Betsy Wiersma, CSEP
Joseph Yaffe

Professional
Event
Coordination

CHAPTER 1

Anatomy of an Event

Consumers [will] begin to collect experiences as consciously and passionately as they once collected things.

—ALVIN TOFFLER, FUTURE SHOCK, *1970*

IN THIS CHAPTER YOU WILL LEARN HOW TO:

- Recognize the economic, social, cultural, and political value of an event.
- Identify the dimensions and elements of an event.
- Understand the interdependence of event elements to forecast potential gaps and discrepancies in an event plan.
- Develop a strategy for creating and coordinating a comprehensive event experience.

An event is an experience, carefully crafted to deliver an impact on the person in attendance. The activities, environment, and layers of multisensory effects are integrated into an event design that is staged and choreographed with precision and polish. The best event experience is one in which the mechanics are imperceptible to the attendee and the intended impact is delivered effectively and invisibly.

The Role and Scope of Professional Event Coordination

Professional event coordination is the integrated implementation of all the operational and logistical requirements of an event, based on the scope of event elements included in the event design. An event, any type of event, is held for a purpose. Public or private, commercial or charitable, celebratory or commemorative—events bring people together to share an experience and produce a measurable outcome. The event experience may be a civic celebration or a charity fund-raiser, an anniversary or a wedding, a corporate product introduction or incentive program, a sports event or a convention event. It may be a company picnic, a hospitality reception, a grand opening, or a family reunion. It is the job of the professional event coordinator to package and manage that event experience.

Event Solutions Event Types	Goldblatt Event Management Subfields
Association Meetings/Events	Civic Events
Attraction Events (Amusement Parks)	Conventions
Business Incentive Events	Expositions
College/University Events	Fairs & Festivals
Concerts	Government
Corporate Meetings/Events	Hallmark
Exposition Events	Hospitality
Fairs or Festivals	Incentive Travel
Fund-raising Events	Meetings & Conferences
Government/Political Events	Retail Events
Military Events	Reunions
Social Events	Social Life-Cycle
Sporting Events	Sport Events
Weddings	Tourism

Source: 2002 Fact Book: A Statistical Analysis of the Event Industry, Event Solutions Magazine, *p. 20.*

Source: Joe Goldblatt (2002), Special Events: Twenty-first Century Global Event Management, *3d ed. (New York: John Wiley & Sons, Inc.), p. 15.*

Figure 1-1
Special Event Genres

Figure 1-1 provides an overview of the scope of the event genre applicable to the event coordination profession. As a professional event coordinator, you may specialize in specific types of events and event clientele, focusing on one or two primary event genres. However, you should have an understanding of the role and scope of all types of events to better serve your target market through the thoughtful and comprehensive analysis of the needs, resources, and physical requirements for an event. In other words, you may not need to incorporate all the facets and elements discussed in this book for every event, but you should analyze and consider each one for every event. You may discover a serious gap in your event plan. You may find a strategy for improving the event experience. You may find a feature that will facilitate a value-added experience.

Event design and coordination is a comprehensive process. Janet Landey, CSEP, of Party Design CC in Johannesburg, South Africa, expresses her amazement at many customers' lack of understanding of the scope of an event: "What did you expect, a couple of balloons in the boot [trunk] of my car?" You must consider administrative matters, logistics issues, marketing implications, legal questions, and risk management ramifications. You are managing time, money, people, and information.

To paraphrase Robert C. Lewis, author of *Instructor's Manual to Accompany Cases in Hospitality Marketing and Management,* you are serving both "users"—attendees and guests—and "customers"—clients and sponsors—creating an event that delivers the expected experience.

The professional event coordinator uses a sequential process to consistently produce events of any genre or scope that deliver the intended event experiences:

- Conduct the necessary research to determine expectations and create a customer profile of the event attendees or participants.
- Conceptualize the event, assessing the scope of the event required to meet expectations.
- Determine which event elements and components will provide the features of the desired experience.
- Visualize how all these event components will and must fit together, and design the strategy for implementation.
- Select the best products and providers available and affordable.
- Finally, monitor the delivery of the experience.

DETERMINE THE EXPECTATIONS

Start with the basic information: who, what, where, when, and, most important, why. Create a customer profile of the guests. What are the demographics? How many are expected? What type of function is it? What is the history of the event? What has worked before and what hasn't? What did the guests or attendees like and dislike?

When will the event take place? What date or dates, and at what times? What else will be happening concurrently and in conjunction with the event? Where is the event to be held? Where have the guests attended events in the past? Where are they from? What type of experience will fit their personalities and preferences?

Why is the event being held? The professional event coordinator must have a clear understanding of the purpose of the event, as well as the goals and objectives of the event. The goal or objective may be to express appreciation for a job well done or to celebrate a cultural heritage. It may be to increase sales or increase awareness. It does not matter whether the event experience is paid for with cash or with the investment of time and effort; the experience must have value.

Develop your evaluation strategy from the very beginning by specifying the measurements that will indicate success. Draw this information out of the client. Such measurements may be attendance figures, revenues, perceptions, or publicity. Even a family reunion, surprise birthday party, or wedding will have measurable objectives: having special people in attendance, guest enjoyment levels, or having an event more lavish than that of a colleague, neighbor, or rival. Some clients will be very explicit about what they want to achieve with the event; others may not be able to articulate their expectations.

DEVELOP THE CONCEPT

The professional event coordinator must put together an overall picture of the final event, the concept, to be able to incorporate all the necessary elements and components, as well as to merge the logistical and operational parameters and practices into the event plan. We need to consider ourselves, to quote Alvin Toffler, as "experiential engineers." Some professional event coordinators prefer to start with the concept, developing the theme or event name, in a manner similar to composing the title of a book or a film. Then they start filling in all the details, like roots growing from the base of a tree. Others begin with the event elements, building a pyramid with all the details until the complete picture or vision of the event emerges. Still others use both an inductive and deductive approach. It is critical to realize that the entire event must be envisioned and implemented in your head, and on paper, before the first step is taken.

DESIGN THE EXPERIENCE

Remember that you are packaging and managing an experience. This means that you must envision that experience, from start to finish, from the guests' point of view. Imagine every minute of their experience. Identify event elements and components that will enhance that experience. Identify elements that will build on previous successes, elements that will take advantage of opportunities and strengths, and elements that will mitigate challenges, weaknesses, and threats.

On-Site Insight

Event designer John J. Daly Jr., CSEP, always begins an event installation by conducting a read-through of the event description from his proposal with the entire event team, sharing his vision and the experience he has sold to his client. He has found that when the setup crew hears that "the guests will enter through a lush tropical entryway," it has a positive effect on the crew's being able to install the eight potted palm trees, 24 potted ferns, 20 yards of silk, and two bamboo screens listed on the order form according to his vision.

DELIVER THE DREAM

Choreograph the experience by anticipating attendee needs, wants, and expectations, then arranging the elements and adding layers of detail that will provide a memorable experience. Think of everything so they don't have to. The best compliment a professional event coordinator can receive is that no one asked for directions or questioned what was happening. The best tribute a professional event coordinator can receive occurs when the host or client can take a bow for a fantastic and hugely successful event.

Virtually all events include six dimensions to the experience. To deliver the dream—that value-added event experience—the professional event coordinator must incorporate these six dimensions into a cohesive whole, each one supporting the others, each integrated into a progressive experience: anticipation, arrival, atmosphere, appetite, activity, and amenities.

Anticipation

It is human nature to want something to look forward to. The first dimension of the event experience is the anticipation created with the announcement of the event. You may create the foundation for an entire marketing strategy, such as with an incentive program, or set the stage for a spectator spectacle such as an entertainment or sports event. You are thereby establishing expectations and building excitement for the event through the initial communications.

The invitations, notices, brochures, publicity, advertising, and/or promotions that will create this anticipation must be planned from the very inception of the event and incorporated into the budget and the timeline (see Figure 1-2). These materials must be designed to prepare the individual for the event experience. They must be timed appropriately to reach the recipient in enough time to inform, yet should not be so early that the anticipation wanes. Sometimes numerous impressions will be required to build and sustain anticipation.

MARKETING THE EXPERIENCE

You are always selling something—a product, a service, an idea—trying to create interest and desire so another person will want it, accept it, or invest in it, and in this case it is an event and an event experience you are selling. In designing an invitation to a charity gala or a brochure for a conference, you must create interest in the event, enticing the guest or

❏ Advertising	❏ E-mail	❏ Notices/Memos
❏ Agendas	❏ Flyers	❏ Posters
❏ Brochures	❏ Instructions/Directions	❏ Promotions
❏ Cards/Letters	❏ Internet Web Site	❏ Public Relations
❏ Catalogs	❏ Invitations	❏ Registration Materials

Figure 1-2
Anticipation Elements Checklist

attendee to invest time, and probably money, to attend the event. Whether sending out handcrafted invitations for a bar mitzvah, direct mail flyers for a civic festival, or agendas for a meeting, the principle is the same. You must influence the targeted customer to make the decision to attend or participate.

To provide effective pre-event communications, you must understand what will motivate the guests or attendees—why they would or should want to attend—and incorporate those inducements into a compelling format. You must understand their purchase decision processes. Remember that the decision to purchase relates not only to exchanging money for a product. It refers to exchanging resources, such as time and emotional investment, for the event experience—"buying into" the purpose of the event.

A COMMUNICATIONS ISSUE

Determine where, when, why, and how these purchase decisions are made so you can develop the appropriate strategy to create interest and anticipation for the event. Does the first conference brochure need to reach attendees prior to their annual budget process so that costs can be incorporated into that budget? Does the first poster or flyer for the community arts festival need to be prepared a month prior to the event, or a year before the event, so these materials can be distributed through the local tourism agencies to potential visitors and commercial tour operators?

Provide the information required to facilitate successful participation in the event experience. Communicate the basics—who, what, when, where, why, how, and how much. Prepare the attendees or guests for the experience, furnishing the directions, instructions, and recommendations that will enhance their experience. Convey and reinforce the purpose of the event, the reason the event is being held and the reasons the guests will benefit from attending. Find ways to intensify the anticipation factor, building the excitement and commitment to attend, participate, and enjoy the event experience.

Arrival

From the moment the decision is made to attend an event, the journey begins. Plans are formed, tickets are purchased, reservations are made, schedules are established, and hundreds of other personal and professional details are put in motion in order for the attendee to arrive at the right time and place for the event.

As the professional event coordinator, you may or may not be responsible for arranging such details for the attendee or guest, but you should consider all these aspects to determine what you can do to facilitate the logistics of the arrival (see Figure 1-3).

TRAVEL AND TRANSPORTATION

The guest or attendee may be traveling across town or around the world to attend the event. How can the professional event coordinator enhance and improve this facet of the event experience? Understand the resources that will be available and how the attendee will likely utilize them. When looking at travel to an event site, particularly from another country, city, or locale, consider the options the traveler might use: trains, airplanes, boats, buses, and/or private automobiles.

Analyze the potential arrival schedules and evaluate the arrival facilities to determine what attendees will likely encounter. Will they need rental cars? Will they need directional maps sent to them prior to their departure? Do you need to prepare a fact sheet on passports, visas, and customs regulations? Provide the information they will need to have as smooth a travel experience as possible, preparing them for what to expect. Arrival patterns must also be taken into account. Are all the attendees expected to arrive at the same time? What will be needed to make certain they will be accommodated efficiently and effectively? Do you need more entrances to the event site? Can you arrange for more personnel at the check-in desk at the hotel? Should you alert the taxi and

---

❏ Decorations	❏ Instructions/Maps	❏ Security
❏ Entertainment	❏ Interpreters/Translators	❏ Signs
❏ Ground Transportation	❏ Meet and Greet	❏ Support Staff
❏ Guides/Ushers	❏ Parking Facilities/Services	❏ Traffic Services
❏ Housing	❏ Registration	❏ Travel Arrangements

Figure 1-3
Arrival Elements Checklist

rental car companies so they will be appropriately staffed and their inventory sufficient?

Ground transportation must be considered for attendees arriving at their destination. How will they transfer from place to place? You must know the customer. Some people wish to be in complete control of their comings and goings, others may expect to be chauffeured and shuttled. If all persons attending the event are expected to provide their own transportation to the event site, you must still anticipate and facilitate that experience, perhaps by providing traffic control, parking facilities, or valet parking services. You may need to arrange for motor coaches or shuttle buses. You may need to organize limousine services or a fleet of motorcycles, or even antique automobiles.

MEETING AND GREETING

Travel, both to and at an event location, can set the tone for the attendee's experience. The professional event coordinator must understand that no matter how excited the guest or attendee is or how intense the anticipation may be, travel is hard work. It is fraught with potential minor and major disasters and distractions. Lost luggage, long lines, and tedious layovers can quickly turn anticipation into frustration, which is not the way an event coordinator wants the experience to be remembered.

You may mitigate many aspects of a frustrating travel experience with a warm welcome. This can include anything from welcome signs and banners at the airport and around town to receptive guides and ushers, or a welcome basket in a guest's hotel room. You want to communicate that the travelers are in the right place and you are glad they are here. Theme entertainment or decorations at the point of entry can pull the traveler back into a positive experience. Friendly staff at the registration counters can redefine that first impression. An ample number of ticket windows can relieve a crowded entrance and the perception that the event experience is going to take too much effort to be enjoyable.

NAVIGATION AND DIRECTIONAL SIGNS

The professional event coordinator must ensure that the attendees or guests can navigate their way to and through the event site. Such help should start with the information provided in the invitation or instructions, including maps and directions (see Figure 1-4), but it usually must be supplemented with on-site signs. It is, again, a matter of anticipating the attendee's needs and providing answers to questions before they have to be asked.

Assume that you are new to the city, and consider how you would find your way from the train station to the event grounds. How will you

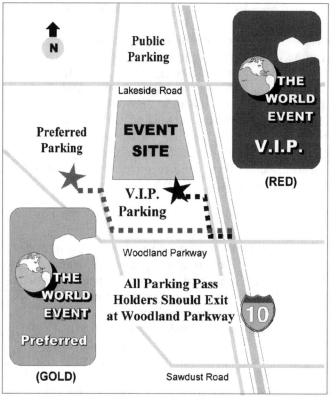

Figure 1-4
VIP and Preferred Parking Pass Directions

find your way if you do not speak or read the language? How will you find your way to the first aid station at an outdoor festival or to your assigned table in a gigantic banquet hall? How will you find your way to the right meeting room in a huge convention center? At every point along the route where a decision can or must be made, determine how you can communicate the information needed for the attendee or guest to make the right directional choice.

WELCOMING ENTRANCES

Welcoming entrances will reestablish the expectations of event attendees. A brightly decorated entrance to the festival grounds will bring attendees back into the excitement and anticipation felt when the decision was made to attend. A well-designed registration area will communicate to conference-goers that the event will be well run and worthwhile. A themed entryway will help guests at a theme party to make the transition from the real world outside into the fantasy world to be experienced inside.

Sometimes decorations and signs alone are not enough. The professional event coordinator should also consider incorporating personnel and performers into the entrance design. According to Anton Shone, author of *Successful Event Management: A Practical Handbook,* people arriving at an unfamiliar location will first seek a person to ask directions from before referring to signs. It is important always to provide someone who can answer questions about the event and the event site, either at the entrance or at a well-positioned hospitality desk or information station. Costumed characters, sight acts or variety performers, hosts and hostesses, and other individuals can add that human connection between the guest and the event experience.

DON'T FORGET THE DEPARTURE

Give the same consideration to the departure as you do to the arrival. The same requirements apply—signs, instructions and directions, transportation and travel. The last impression of an event experience will be just as powerful as, if not more than, the first impression. It is often said that most guests remember the entrance and the dessert. Consider the memories you are creating if there are long lines of cars trying to get out of the parking lot or crowded shuttles to the airport or if attendees have no idea where it is safe to go to dinner after the conference program ends that afternoon. The event experience must be considered from start to finish, and it is not finished until the attendees or guests are back home safe and sound. Exercise the same care and creativity for their departure as you do for their arrival.

Atmosphere

The atmosphere of an event relies on the physical environment, both inherent in and imposed on the venue or event site. Each component of the physical site, from theme décor and props to the location of the toilet facilities, will have an impact on the experience (see Figure 1-5).

THE PHYSICAL ENVIRONMENT BASICS

The environment of an event is developed to meet and serve the physical needs of the attendee while enhancing the style and substance of the event experience. Temperature will affect comfort levels and enjoyment. The actual space allotment per person will affect the satisfaction level. The physical layout of venue features and furnishings can contribute to the achievement of event goals and objectives.

❑ Audiovisual Equipment	❑ Heating/Cooling	❑ Soundscaping
❑ Dance Floor	❑ House Lighting/Controls	❑ Special Effects
❑ Decorations/Props	❑ Lighting—Theatrical	❑ Staging
❑ Equipment Rentals	❑ Linens/Napery	❑ Table and Chairs
❑ Floor/Ceiling Décor	❑ Potable Water	❑ Tents/Shelters
❑ Flowers	❑ Seating Systems	❑ Toilet Facilities
❑ Furnishings	❑ Site Selection	❑ Waste Control

Figure 1-5
Atmosphere Elements Checklist

The layout of the event should promote the desired choreography of the event experience. If guests are expected to mingle, fewer chairs will be required than for a spectator event where everyone is to be seated. If attendees are expected to move through the event space, such as at an exposition or street fair, the positioning of event elements can facilitate traffic flow. The guests must be able to see and hear what is going on, and this can require technical augmentation such as lighting and sound systems. Lighting and sound can also be used to create a new reality for an event space, establishing a particular ambiance or fantasy setting.

The professional event coordinator must consider all the physical needs of the guest or attendee. Drinking water should always be available, especially in a hot climate. Sheltered areas should be provided at outdoor events in any weather. A coat check area should be considered for any event at which the guests will be arriving wearing bulky outerwear. Of course, toilet facilities must be sufficient for the volume of guests or attendees expected and should be fully accessible to those with disabilities. Safety and security must be considered in terms of ingress, access, and egress. Guests and attendees must be able to get in, get around, and get out of a venue quickly and safely. Entrances and exits must be visible and obvious; often they must be protected from unlawful or unauthorized entry.

THE VENUE—EMBRACE THE PLACE OR SURPRISE THEIR EYES

The venue, the site of an event, has an inherent atmosphere. This may be an asset or a liability. Some venues are fully functional and others require extensive site development. It is incumbent upon the professional event coordinator to arrange for everything needed to create the desired ambiance and meet the physical requirements.

Unusual or unique venues offer numerous creative opportunities and challenges. For example, hosting a high school reunion in the school gymnasium reinforces the nostalgia of the event. However, you may face restrictions on what equipment may be placed on the gymnasium floor and whether alcoholic beverages may be served on school property.

There are two approaches to the utilization of an event venue. You can "embrace the place," highlighting its intrinsic features, or you can "surprise their eyes," completely transforming the facility or site into a totally unexpected environment. To embrace the place, you might use dramatic lighting to enhance architectural features of a building's interior or exterior for a grand opening, or perhaps create sculptural buffet displays on pedestals for a charity reception in a museum. To surprise their eyes, you might transform an empty warehouse with draping, props, and furnishings to create a trendy nightclub atmosphere, or turn a hotel ballroom into a hot, steamy jungle.

FORM FOLLOWS FUNCTION

The dictum *form follows function* was coined by American architect Louis Sullivan in 1896. "All things in nature have a shape, that is to say, a form, an outward semblance, that tells us what they are . . . form ever follows function, and this is the law." The event site must be functional, meeting the requirements for fulfilling the function of the event—its purpose, goals, and objectives. Educational events require appropriate learning environments. Entertainment and spectator events require sufficient and controlled seating systems. Gala dinner dances require enough space for dining tables, a dance floor, and a stage for an orchestra.

Yet this perspective does not preclude creative use of a traditional event space or unique venues. With a little imagination, and sometimes a lot of logistical expertise, a site can accommodate nearly any function. Assorted tables can be fashioned into unusual configurations to create an effective schoolroom setting in a cocktail lounge or an elegant dinner along the passageways of an office building. You should also keep in mind that with today's tent technology, you can create an event space practically anywhere.

On-Site Insight

A gala awards celebration for event professionals designed by David Tutera and hosted by an event industry magazine in Dallas, Texas, included an awards presentation, to be followed by a

(Continued)

banquet and dancing. It was held in a concert hall, with the awards ceremony held in the auditorium and the dinner in the massive lobby area. To mask off the banquet setting, which by necessity had to have been completely set and dressed prior to the start of the event, Tutera created a long, winding tunnel of white spandex shapes from the building entrance to the auditorium entrance. This spandex tunnel was backlit with various colors while the overhead lights in lobby area were turned off. This prevented any view of the tables just on the other sides of the tunnel. During the awards ceremony in the auditorium the tunnel was removed and, upon exiting the auditorium, the guests found an unexpected banquet area, fully decorated in a lush enchanted forest setting.

FINDING THE BEST FIT

The event site selected should fit the character of the event as well as the character of the host. Selecting the best destination and the best venue is a matter of understanding the goals and objectives for the event, as well as the budgetary and regulatory constraints. You may think that an exotic island may be the best place for an executive retreat or a destination wedding, but can the attendees or guests afford to get there? The question may not be a matter of money, but time away from the office or the public relations impact. You may think that a football stadium is the perfect venue for the political rally or rock concert you are coordinating, but will the facility management allow you to roll extensive and extremely heavy staging onto their precious turf? You may be looking at expensive field insurance or replacement costs.

The great outdoors, whether urban, rural, or extremely remote, can provide interesting settings for a broad variety of events. The professional event coordinator must carefully assess all the functional needs of the event and event attendees to be sure that the experience is appropriate. Festivals, fairs, fun runs, and family or company picnics are natural events to be staged outdoors, but the event coordinator might also consider a gala banquet or hospitality reception under the stars on the rooftop of a corporate headquarters. What about the top level of a parking garage, or the apple orchard on the host's property?

Appetite

Food and beverage constitute an integral part of a event experience—any event experience. There is always some type of refreshment at an event, even if it is simply a water station in a meeting room or at an outdoor

❏ Alcohol and Beverages	❏ Concession Equipment	❏ Rental Service Ware
❏ Bar Setups and Bartenders	❏ Dinners	❏ Serving Equipment
❏ Breakfasts	❏ Disposable Service Ware	❏ Specialty Foods
❏ Buffet Displays	❏ Ice and Ice Sculptures	❏ Staffing/Labor
❏ Coffee and Energy Breaks	❏ Lunches	❏ Water Stations

Figure 1-6
Appetite Elements Checklist

athletic event (see Figure 1-6). Food service must be incorporated into the event plan so that it meets the needs of the guests and serves the purpose of the event. It should never be an afterthought. Consider the comment of a disgruntled guest leaving a hospitality reception after seeing the long lines at the buffet: "Even free food is only worth so much."

NUTRITION, NURTURING, AND HUMAN NATURE

As Margaret Visser asserts in *The Rituals of Dinner*, "Eating together is a potent expression of community." Food is a symbol of nurturing. It is synonymous with most social gatherings. The food and beverages served at an event should be nutritious, but they must feed both the body and the soul. Despite the current emphasis on a healthy lifestyle, it seems everyone still wants a luscious and rich dessert at a banquet. Jeff Rasco, CMP, explained in an MPI Institutes presentation on the Fundamentals of Food and Beverage Planning, "The trend toward healthier food continues, but people are still 'eating out' when they attend meetings."

The event experience relies on utilizing all five senses. This provides an opportunity to heighten the sense of taste and smell through the menu design for any event. However, you should not discount the importance of how the food looks and sounds. The presentation should be pleasing to the eye as well as the palate, and the textures of the food should be consistent with freshness and form—a fresh apple should be crunchy and a chocolate mousse should be smooth.

Certain aromas bring back intense memories for people, often associated with previous events. Think about the smell of popcorn or cotton candy, and you will probably think of a movie house or carnival. The taste and aroma of certain spices can conjure up images of exotic destinations. It is a well-known fact that many cafés and diners keep some onions cooking on the back of the grill and vent the smells out into the dining area, and even to the street, to stimulate the appetite of those who happen by. Pastry shops employ the same technique. The professional event coordinator can utilize this strategy to the advantage of the event experience.

It is critically important to pay attention to the physical needs and restrictions that accompany food and beverage selection. You must determine whether any of the guests or attendees have particular food allergies or dietary restrictions—physical, philosophical, or religious. The last thing you want is to have someone rushed to the hospital in anaphylactic shock because a life-threatening allergy to nuts was triggered by the peanut oil used in a recipe. Collect the information you need, from both the attendees and the chef, and be prepared to offer appropriate options. Also keep in mind that water and fluids should always be available at any and every event and that alcohol service will usually have regulatory requirements.

MEALS TO MATCH THE OCCASION

Menu selection is a dimension in which the professional event coordinator can exercise considerable creativity. The menu can influence the entire theme or tone of an event. Hot dogs, hamburgers, and beans would signify a casual atmosphere; chateaubriand and Cherries Jubilee suggest a formal dining experience. The fun part is that these two menus can be switched to add a surprising twist to an event.

The type and style of an event will determine the direction to be taken in planning the menu. Athletes at a sports event will probably require different foods than guests at a wedding reception. Attendees at a multiday conference, having all their meals on-site, will want something different for lunch and dinner each day. Incentive winners enjoying an exotic destination expect to try the local cuisine. Menus based on an ethnic cuisine or historical record can add authenticity to a theme event. Indigenous ingredients will add a flavorful feature for those experiencing a new locale. Certain food items are closely associated with specific occasions, such as wedding and birthday cakes, or certain rituals, such as matzo at the Seder dinner at Passover.

CONCESSIONS, CATERING, OR BRING YOUR OWN

Different events require different food and beverage purveyors. Concession stands are completely appropriate for public festivals, but probably not for an upscale hospitality reception, unless, of course, they fit with a theme. Concessionaires may operate out of permanent facilities within a venue or from temporary facilities at an event site. They may have exclusive or specific licensing or franchise agreements with a venue. However, the professional event coordinator should make certain that any purveyor is fully licensed and carries appropriate insurance.

Caterers can provide anything from a lavish 12-course banquet to a backyard barbecue. Many facilities, particularly hotels and convention centers, have exclusive in-house food service providers that the professional event coordinator must use. Other facilities may have preferred caterers, usually catering firms that have provided excellent references to the facility and excellent service to their users. Again, the professional event coordinator must verify that the caterer is <u>fully licensed and insured, as well as qualified to handle</u> the scope and type of event being planned.

Most facilities and professional caterers have restrictions on what the client or guest may bring to the event for consumption, because of liability concerns, but compromise is often possible. Of course, picnics, socials, and private events are a natural for the "potluck," with guests bringing their favorite dishes to share with everyone, but make sure you have <u>removed yourself from legal liability.</u>

Beverages are another matter. The serving of <u>alcohol is strictly regulated</u> in most places. The professional event coordinator must become familiar with the rules and regulations in a jurisdiction before making any arrangements regarding alcohol service. Some places are more restrictive than others regarding licenses and liability issues; some locations prohibit alcohol altogether.

If serving alcohol, the professional event coordinator can incorporate the drink menu into the theme or event experience. Martini bars serving flavored martinis or drinks poured through an elaborate ice sculpture can become an interesting and decorative focus to an event. Wine tasting can be the main attraction for a fund-raiser. Serving local wines at a banquet can celebrate the site and may be an opportunity for sponsorship.

Other beverages present occasions for creativity as well. Fruit smoothies are fun for tropical themes or health-oriented events. Restaurant patrons are often offered a selection of flavored teas, so why not at an event? Flavored coffees and coffee drinks are very popular at a broad spectrum of events; in fact, such fare has become an experience industry unto itself.

SERVING WITH STYLE

How the food and beverages are served can significantly affect the event experience. *(Even free food is only worth so much.)* There are countless ways to serve food and beverages: massive or minuscule buffet stations, cafeteria lines, waitpersons placing course after course in front of diners, platters placed family-style on the table, buckets of shellfish and barrels of beer, or hors d'oeuvres placed on cascading levels of a Southern belle's hoop skirt.

Food service can determine and improve the choreography and flow of an event. A variety of food stations can help move guests through an event space and encourage networking. A food court can create trade show traffic in a remote area of an exhibition hall. Butlers passing trays of edibles and champagne add glamour to a charity reception without taking up floor space for food stations. Gourmet box lunches can accompany participants on a tour of the destination or feed executives in a strategic planning meeting. Certain civic festivals are all about food, and attendees wander from booth to booth tasting the best a city's restaurant community has to offer.

PALATE AND POCKETBOOK

Food choices are based on the palate and the pocketbook. The professional event coordinator must establish the budgetary and dietary param-eters with the host or client. Certain groups will be hungry for a gastronomical adventure, whereas others may not respond to a locality's spicy cuisine and subdued choices will have to be offered. The chef should be able to design a menu full of flavor that will delight the taste buds and still reflect the theme cuisine.

Kendall Collier, CSEP, of Legendary Events in Atlanta, Georgia, puts it quite succinctly: "Pasta is cheap; people are expensive." She notes that the style of service requested and the location of the event will determine the number of requisite waitstaff, and menu items requiring a great deal of preparation will be far more expensive than those more easily prepared and served. To save money at a welcome reception, you might select fewer hors d'oeuvre items but in greater volume. Perhaps you will eliminate the dessert from the luncheon at the conference and serve it during the afternoon break. You might choose the food vendors for a street fair so that there will be a variety of food and beverage choices as well as price points. There are always options to overcome the challenges of a tight budget or a finicky palate.

Activity

Without exception, there is always something to do at an event. There is always some sort of action or activity (see Figure 1-7). It may be as simple as conversation with fellow guests or as complex as a showy multimedia production incorporating music, dancing, laser shows, ceremonies, and interactive demonstrations. It may be passive, with the attendees or guests as spectators, or it may be active, with the guests participating in the entertainment. The task for the professional event coordinator is to incorporate and choreograph the appropriate activities so they increase the value of the event experience.

❏ Acrobats	❏ Dancers	❏ Pageants
❏ Aerialists	❏ Demonstrations	❏ Parades
❏ Animal Acts	❏ Disc Jockey	❏ Photo Stations
❏ Astrologers	❏ Drumming Groups	❏ Pyrotechnic Shows
❏ Bands	❏ Emcee	❏ Recorded Music
❏ Barbershop/Sweet Adeline	❏ Exhibits	❏ Rides
❏ Caricaturists	❏ Film/Video	❏ Rhythmic Ensembles
❏ Carnival Games	❏ Flag Dancers	❏ Robots
❏ Casino Games	❏ Handwriting Analysts	❏ Singers
❏ Celebrities	❏ Heraldic Horns	❏ Speakers
❏ Celebrity Look-alikes	❏ Human Floats	❏ Sports and Games
❏ Ceremonies	❏ Inflatable Games	❏ Stiltwalker Puppets
❏ Charity Projects	❏ Interactive Media	❏ Storytellers
❏ Choirs—Gospel or Youth	❏ Laser/Light Shows	❏ Strolling Musicians
❏ Circus Performers	❏ Lectures	❏ Tableau Characters
❏ Cirque-Style Performers	❏ Karaoke	❏ Temporary Tattoo Artists
❏ Comedians	❏ Magicians/Illusionists	❏ Tournaments
❏ Cooking Demonstrations	❏ Mentalists	❏ Tours
❏ Contortionists	❏ Multimedia Shows	❏ Variety Acts
❏ Costumed Characters	❏ Orchestras	❏ Ventriloquists
❏ Craft Activities	❏ Operatic Soloists	❏ Virtual Reality

Figure 1-7
Activity Elements Checklist

COLLECTABLE EXPERIENCES

As the Alvin Toffler quote at the beginning of this chapter suggests, this is the business of providing experiences consumers want to collect. Event experiences must have value to the customers. They must worthwhile—worth their time and money. You must go back to the customer profile to determine what the customer wants, needs, and expects in order to determine what, where, when, and how entertainment and activities should be incorporated into the event plan.

Agendas are used to plan and monitor the activity of a meeting. Variety entertainment is employed to direct and redirect attendee focus. Special effects are utilized to add emphasis to an awards presentation. Pyrotechnics create an electrifying finale to a hallmark event. Kiddie craft areas and inflatable bounce cages allow children to enjoy a civic celebration. Opening and closing ceremonies enhance the spirit of sports events. Dramatic light shows and multimedia productions intensify the impact of a product introduction. The right activity will increase the value of the experience.

ALL THE WORLD'S A STAGE—AN EVENT IS THEATER

Designing an event is similar to writing a theatrical play or movie screen-play. It requires a plot (goals and objectives), a message (theme), and characters (event components). The action, activities, and entertainment at an event must be carefully scripted. There should be a strong opening, peaks and respites, surprises and discoveries, and an exciting finale—all advancing at the appropriate pace and in a natural progression. There is always a beginning, a middle, and an ending to an experience, which must be clear to the attendee or guest.

The event experience should have multiple dimensions and layers, providing something of interest for each attendee or participant. Live en-tertainers might be incorporated into the environment, such as "talking heads" on a buffet table or costumed characters providing walk-around local color. Recorded music or sounds might be used to establish a theme environment, such as a flamenco guitar to suggest a Spanish cantina at-mosphere or the sound of crickets to reinforce a nightscape.

Carnival or casino-style games (such as a ring toss, balloon darts, roulette table, or wheel of fortune) can be the focus of a charity fund-raiser. A strolling violinist might add just the right touch to a foundation fête. Strolling mariachis might be used to direct guests from the pre-function area to a bright Mexican fiesta. A comedian might emcee a corporate employee training presentation. Whatever entertainment and activities are selected, they should contribute to the event choreography, moving the experience through its required progression.

PARTICIPATORY VERSUS SPECTATOR

In order to accomplish the purpose of an event, the professional event coordinator must determine whether the attendees or guests are partici-patory or passive. Would it be advisable to force active types to sit and watch something? Perhaps. Would it be appropriate to go against type and provide interactive attractions for a usually passive audience? If done correctly, this can be an exciting and effective approach.

You might slowly introduce action into passive entertainment, such as having dancers at a '50s rock-and-roll theme party start with an exhi-bition of jitterbug dancing, then move into the crowd and draw guests as partners onto the dance floor. You might provide some participatory aspects to a spectator event, such as bringing audience members up onstage to assist a magician or into the arena to compete in a chicken wrangling event at an exhibition rodeo. The spectators may become par-ticipants, such as in performing "card tricks" in which the audience in the grandstands hold up various colored cards to form a massive mosaic picture.

Consider the entirety of the event when developing the entertainment agenda. Incentive planners do not schedule an important program or expansive entertainment spectacle the first night of the incentive trip, because the guests are probably tired and may be affected by jet lag. If normally energetic attendees have been in a classroom setting all day at a conference, the evening event will probably need some sort of active options to allow them to expend some of their pent-up energy.

DIVERSION AND RECREATION

Interactive activities and amusements are often used to please both the guest and the guest's guest, such as companion programs during a convention or optional tours and sports activities during an incentive program. Recreational activities are usually included at company picnics, corporate team-building programs, and reunion outings. Fairs and festivals frequently include interactive games and rides interspersed with the food stalls, exhibits, and other entertainment.

Active people such as Baby Boomers and Generation Xers want activity and adventure. They want something to do. It is important to arrange for suitable recreational activities and meaningful diversions. You might consider incorporating a charitable project into a corporate training conference, such as organizing the painting of a community center during the free afternoon. You can add cultural enrichment to the optional tour offerings by organizing a visit to an artist's studio or an exhibition planning session at an anthropology museum. Help the attendees to become immersed in the experience, and it will become truly memorable.

Amenities

Once the event is over, all that is left are the memories. These memories can be enhanced through the employment of layers of detail and numerous tokens of acknowledgment and appreciation (see Figure 1-8). These details do not necessarily need to be costly; they just need to be thoughtful. These are the niceties and features of the event experience that add to the comfort of the guest and provide a physical reminder of the experience after the event.

WALK-AWAY VALUE

An event is an ephemeral thing. There is no lasting substance to it without something physical one walks away with, so the professional event coordinator should always find something for the attendees or guests to

❏ Albums	❏ Custom Label Beverages	❏ Prizes
❏ Arts and Crafts	❏ Flowers	❏ Programs
❏ Audio/Videotapes	❏ Food/Beverage Items	❏ Restroom Upgrades
❏ Awards	❏ Imprinted Items	(soaps, colognes, etc.)
❏ Badge Holders	❏ Logo Merchandise	❏ Souvenir Items
❏ CD-ROM of Program	❏ Luggage Tags	❏ Speaker Gifts
❏ Certificates	❏ Memorabilia	❏ Table Gifts
❏ Clothing Items	❏ Menus/Place Cards	❏ Tote Bags
❏ Commemorative Pins	❏ Photographs	❏ T-Shirts
❏ Conference Binders	❏ Pillow Gifts	❏ Welcome Baskets

Figure 1-8
Amenities Elements Checklist

take away. Meeting and conference attendees should be given handouts and conference materials. Visitors to a tourism event can be given programs with information on the destination. Guests at a corporate hospitality function can be given logo-imprinted mementos. Award winners should be given customized trophies, certificates, or plaques.

These walk-away items may be given away or may be revenue-generating products. Many conferences and conventions provide audio-tapes of the various sessions for sale at and after the events. Many also provide or sell custom-imprinted tote bags for the session materials and marketing materials collected at a trade show. Name badge holders have become fashion items, featuring zippered pockets for event tickets, room keys, and business cards. Lanyards for badges are woven with a sponsor's logo or the event name and date.

TANGIBLE MEMORIES

Prizes, gifts, mementos, and souvenirs are the physical items that the attendee or guest will keep to remember the event experience. The more substantial and appropriate the item, the longer the legacy will be. Most sporting events offer an expansive assortment of team-oriented souvenirs for sale at the venue and year-round at sporting goods outlets. Nearly all festivals sell commemorative clothing or posters, and some sell or give out commemorative drinking cups to support recycling objectives.

Volunteers may be given jackets, caps, or commemorative lapel pins to show appreciation for their contribution to the success of an event. Incentive winners are treated to expensive pillow gifts, indigenous to the locale, each night of their trip. Participants in a marathon or walk-a-thon receive T-shirts emblazoned with the event name and sponsor logos. Anniversary dinner guests may find a framed menu at their place settings, or the napkins may be imprinted with a photo of the happy couple.

SHOWING YOU CARE

There are thousands of ways you can show you care about the guest or attendee's experience. Full-size logo-imprinted tablets and pens on the tables at a meeting or educational session show attention to detail. Speakers and special guests appreciate welcome baskets with some tasty treats and simple souvenirs in their guest rooms. Souvenir sunglasses are great for a beach party. Colorful imprinted hand towels are a wonderful touch for a golf tournament. Something as simple as bottled water with a custom label will be noted and appreciated by participants in a parade or on a photo safari. Custom labels on wine bottles will add a special touch to a charity banquet; they can even be engraved with the event logo.

You may have noted that many of these amenities are excellent candidates for sponsorship and opportunities for sponsor recognition. As a professional event coordinator, you should always find ways to integrate the event's marketing objectives into the event elements.

match need

PERSONALIZE THE EXPERIENCE

Capturing and incorporating the attendee's or guest's image in a souvenir or memento will put the person in the context of the experience. A photographer strolling through an event is standard at social gatherings and virtually mandatory at any marketing event. The photograph of the company president presenting the Employee of the Year with his or her award will go in the company newsletter, and a framed copy will go on the winner's wall.

Many theme events include a photo station where guests can have their images inserted into an appropriate setting via a digital camera or have their portraits done, dressed in appropriate slip-on costumes. Caricature artists are always popular. Commemorative newspapers or magazine covers can be printed with funny headlines or posed pictures taken with a video camera. How about hopping on a Harley Davidson motorcycle to have a picture taken at a Route 66 reception or in the winner's circle at a road rally?

Technology Tip

Web-cam Wanted Posters—A Web camera (the type used for Web conferencing) may be used to digitally capture the guest's image and then electronically paste it into a customized poster designed with a space for the digital desperado's image. This can be printed on a color printer on-site while the guest waits. All the operator on-site needs is a Web-cam on a tripod, a laptop computer, and a color printer (and a little creativity in designing the Wanted Poster in a standard graphics program). Provided you have the equipment, the posters can cost as little as 50 cents apiece for materials.

Many private life-cycle events such as birthday parties, anniversaries, and casual wedding events provide a disposable camera at every table for guests to take candid photos during the festivities. These and other photographs may be scanned and put up on a private, controlled-access event Web site for all the guests to see and download as desired. Conference photographers often have their work processed quickly and offer the pictures for sale at events. Trade show exhibitors sponsoring a convention reception may have the photos taken at the party available for pickup at their exhibit the following day, ensuring that the guests will come by and see their displays.

Target Competency Review

The professional event coordinator must conduct the necessary research to determine the purpose, goals, and objectives of an event. He or she must examine all potential elements of an event to determine which are necessary, appropriate, or advantageous, and which should be incorporated into the event plan.

The professional event coordinator will work with the host or client to develop a strategy for creating and coordinating a comprehensive event experience. Every event should be designed to incorporate the six critical dimensions of an experience, including anticipation, arrival, atmosphere, appetite, activity, and amenities.

All facets, components, and elements of an event are interdependent. The professional event coordinator merges each component and its inherent logistics together with all the others and facilitates a smooth and seamless operation. Each dimension of the event experience is crafted to support the whole and designed to meet the needs, wants, and expectations of the consumer.

EXERCISES IN PROFESSIONAL EVENT COORDINATION

Design and write a description for each of the following events, incorporating the six critical dimensions of an event experience.

1. The local art museum foundation wants a fund-raising gala for 300 patrons held in the sculpture garden on the grounds of the museum.
2. A couple wants their wedding on a remote tropical island, and they will be inviting 100 of their family and friends to this three-day celebration.
3. A pharmaceutical company exhibiting at a medical convention trade show in your city wants to host an off-site evening hospitality reception for 200 of their best customers, featuring a theme that celebrates the local culture.

CHAPTER 2

The Event Element Assessment

We think in generalities, but we live in detail.

—ALFRED NORTH WHITEHEAD

IN THIS CHAPTER YOU WILL LEARN HOW TO:

- Determine the purpose and prioritized goals and objectives of an event.
- Assess the needs, available resources, and time restrictions of an event project.
- Identify the event elements, determine their logical sequencing, and develop efficient schedules.
- Identify problem areas in the event plan, evaluate available options, devise appropriate contingency plans, and procure proper insurance coverage.

As the event coordinator and her husband were walking through a large festival, enjoying the sights and sounds, watching the action and the audience, her husband commented on the sheer size of the event, marveling at what it must have taken to put all this together. The event coordinator smiled at her husband and said, "Honey, it's just a longer list."

Event coordination is all about "the list"—what goes on the list and why. Event coordination is the visualization, organization, and synchronization of the event elements and the tasks required to implement them. To create that list, you, as the professional event coordinator, must define the purpose of the event and analyze all the desires, demands, assumptions, and constraints involved to determine the products, materials, services, activities, and suppliers to be included in the event project. You will not need to include every component discussed in this book in every event, but you should consider each to ensure you deliver an event that meets the needs and expectations of those attending and investing in the experience.

Think of the event element assessment in terms of three "tents"—the in*tent* (purpose), the ex*tent* (scope), and the con*tent* (program). In the world of project management, conducting the needs assessment is part of Project Scope Management. The event scope definition is derived from the identified need, request, or requirement for the event (purpose of the event and outcome/benefit expectations), the product description (type of event), the product analysis (event components), and the feasibility analysis (balance of resources), resulting in a Work Breakdown Structure and Activity Schedule. There are references to project management throughout this chapter, because using project management as a discipline will help you consistently coordinate events of any size or context efficiently and effectively.

Needs Assessment

Need is a complex term. People do not buy an airline ticket because they *need* an airline ticket—what they *need* is to be in Pittsburgh on Friday or in Paris on Tuesday. You must remember that you are not just taking an order. You are crafting a solution to what the client truly needs.

Defining needs is a critical component of the ability to deliver a successful event. Needs, however, are not always apparent or fully considered. "I need a wedding reception" is certainly not enough to direct your design and delivery of a reception event for this client. It is definitely not enough to ensure that the event you coordinate will be a success, even if you have coordinated hundreds of other wedding receptions. Marketing consultant Robert Middleton advises, "You cannot assume what success would look like. You have to ask. You have to get specific answers." A needs assessment should provide these answers. A feasibility study then shows the viability of achieving success—the outcome envisioned by the client—by defining the event elements and requirements and putting them into the context of reality. (See Figure 2-1.)

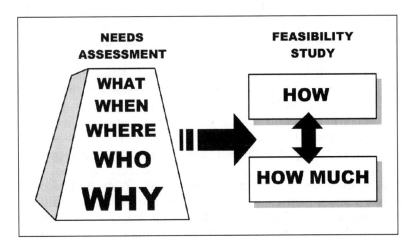

Figure 2-1
The Needs Assessment and Feasibility Study

Answers to Rudyard Kipling's "six honest serving men"—why, who where, when, what, and how—provide the information needed.

- WHY—the purpose of the event is the foundation that drives all other decisions about its scope and the event elements to be included.
- WHO—provides the audience or guest profile.
- WHERE and WHEN—provide the logistical parameters as well as creative opportunities.
- WHAT—determines the event context, content, and mandate.
- HOW determines HOW MUCH—how much in the way of resources will be required.
- HOW MUCH determines HOW—how the resources will be allocated.

CUSTOMERS, CAPABILITIES, AND COMPETITION

The marketing mantra "know your customer" is as applicable in event design and coordination as in any marketing realm. There are, however, many different customers you must serve during an event. There will be clients, users (guests and attendees), and numerous other stakeholders and influencers to consider. Each will have an impact on the event elements to be included.

Customers

Create a customer profile for each constituency you will need to serve, including demographics, lifestyle and life stage, purchase stimulus, and benefits sought. The profile of each of these customer groups will reveal needs and desires that should be factored into the event element analysis and plan. For example, you might use a generational marketing consumer profile, such as shown in Figure 2-2, when determining the features and activities for a tourism festival or convention program.

The Travel Industry Association of America (TIA) and the National Geographic Traveler sponsored a large-scale national study of the current and potential consumer market for geotourism, defined as "tourism that sustains or enhances the geographical character of the place being visited—its environment, culture, aesthetics, heritage, and the well-being of its residents" (www.tia.org/Press/pressrec.asp?Item=176). The results indicate that Traditionalists are conservative in their travel choices, looking for predictability and high levels of cleanliness, safety, and security. Baby Boomers show a distinct preference for culturally and socially related travel, and many are looking specifically for upscale travel experiences. Gen-Xers and Millennials want to be very busy and active when they travel and are seeking to be entertained and to have fun.

Generational Names	Traditionalists Silent Generation Matures	Baby Boomers "Me" Generation	Baby Busters Gen-Xers 13th Generation	Echo Boomers Millennials Generation Y
Approx. Birth Year	–1945	1945–1960	1960–1980	1980–
Character	Adaptive	Idealistic	Optimistic	Empowered
Values	Conservative	Driven	Risk-takers	Tenacious
Focus	Family	Civilization	Environment	Community
Thrive on	Rewarding social experiences	Individual growth and improvement	Truth and flexibility	Speed, change, and information
Technology	Telephone	Mainframe computers	Fax and personal computers	Wireless and handheld
Media	Radio	Television	Cable TV	The Internet
Entertainment	Nightclubs	Coffee shops	Action/adventure	Extreme/authentic
Learning Style	Avoid jargon and show respect	Q & A time important	Stimulating and relevant	Short duration and hands-on
Fashion	Formal	Sexual	Asexual	Androgynous
Music	Swing/Big Band	Rock and Roll	Disco/Pop/Heavy Metal	Rave/Grunge/Rap

Sources: Graeme Codrington (1997), Generations: From Silent, through Boomer and X, to Millennial, *www.youth. co.za/generations.htm; Robin E. Craven and Lynn Johnson Golabowski (2001),* The Complete Idiot's Guide to Meeting and Event Planning *(Indianapolis: Alpha Books); Ann Fishman (2001),* Generational Targeted Marketing, *www. annfishman.com; Donald Getz (1997),* Event Management and Event Tourism *(New York: Cognizant Communications Corp.), 28–32; Philip Kottler, John Bowen, and James Makens (1999),* Marketing for Hospitality and Tourism, *2d ed. (Upper Saddle River, NJ: Prentice-Hall); Walker J. Smith and Ann Clurman (1977);* Rocking the Ages: The Yankelovich Report on Generational Marketing *(New York: Harper Business), www.uiowa.edu/~commstud/adclass/ research/ages1.html; The Gail Tycer Company,* Generational Marketing, *www.gailtycer.com/articles/generate.htm.*

Figure 2-2
Silvers Event Guest Profiler

Capabilities

The capabilities you must consider include your ability to handle the event in its proposed scope and context, the availability of products and services, and the features of the event site. Although the core processes remain the same, coordinating a large festival for a civic celebration is different from producing a multicity product launch for a major corporation or the perfect wedding celebration. Each event context will have its own set of parameters and a specialized body of knowledge. You need to be completely honest with yourself and your client about your ability to deliver the event required and desired.

The world has gotten much smaller through the various forms of new communications technology, and vendors and suppliers to the event industry have embraced this opportunity by expanding their geographic markets. However, not all products and services are available or affordably accessible in all parts of the world. You must know what you can and cannot reasonably obtain in your area and through your supplier resources.

The site selected for the event also involves capabilities that must be examined. These present a set of constraints, as well as creative possibilities, to be incorporated into your event design and implementation strategy. Site issues and implications are discussed in depth in Chapter 3; the event site and/or venue is a key component of a needs assessment, and in determining the elements that must, should, and could be included in the event.

Competition

Considering the competition includes a determination of what will be competing with your event for the time, money, and emotional investment of the attendees or guests. If you are coordinating a fund-raising event, you will want to ensure that it is not scheduled at the same time as other charity functions competing for the same patrons. If you are coordinating a festival designed to increase tourism to your area, you will need to evaluate the assets of other tourism destinations and events. If you are coordinating an incentive event for General Motors at an exotic destination, you can be assured that the company does not want it in the same place and at the same time when Toyota is there.

You may also need to consider the situation of a single event within an entire event program. What else will be happening before, concurrently, and after the event? If the event you are coordinating is a hospitality reception in conjunction with a conference or convention, you will want to know what other receptions will be taking place and when, as well as where this reception fits into the overall agenda. You may be responsible for only this one reception, but you want it to become part of the overall event experience, as well as achieve the attendance expectations of the host client.

PRIORITIZE GOALS AND OBJECTIVES

A needs assessment helps you determine expectations so that you can define the scope and the specifications that result in an event that satisfies the customer's needs and desires—the project deliverables. It is critical that you work with your client to specify the goals and objectives for the event and to put them in a prioritized hierarchy (see Figure 2-3). You must clarify what the client is trying to attain, achieve, or accomplish. The client may not be able to articulate this immediately or succinctly. You may need to probe for the stated objectives, the unstated objectives, the hard objectives, and the soft objectives.

On-Site Insight

Patrick Delaney, CITE, partner and CEO of Ovation Group, an award-winning Destination Management Company in Dublin, Ireland, specializing in incentive events, notes that hard objectives for incentive programs include increased sales, increased profits, product awareness, and raised productivity. Soft objectives include camaraderie and team bonding, peer recognition, company loyalty, and education or training. For incentive programs, the hard objectives are linked to very specific and measurable targets that the winner must have met in order to receive the incentive travel award. Therefore, the events included in the incentive travel program must be worthy of the effort required to win; they must be exceptional and something the winners could not have orchestrated on their own.

Wouldn't it be great if all event goals and objectives were so precise and the expectations so well defined as Patrick Delaney notes in the On-Site Insight above? Unfortunately, this is not usually the case. More often the task is to help clients put their needs and desires into words, probing to determine what they mean by what they say. Return on investment (ROI) applies to the corporate world as well as to associations,

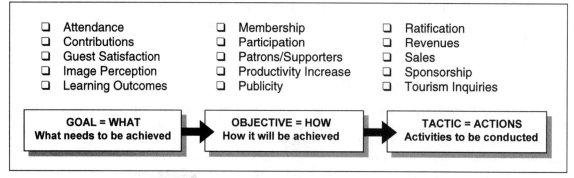

- ❏ Attendance
- ❏ Contributions
- ❏ Guest Satisfaction
- ❏ Image Perception
- ❏ Learning Outcomes
- ❏ Membership
- ❏ Participation
- ❏ Patrons/Supporters
- ❏ Productivity Increase
- ❏ Publicity
- ❏ Ratification
- ❏ Revenues
- ❏ Sales
- ❏ Sponsorship
- ❏ Tourism Inquiries

GOAL = WHAT
What needs to be achieved

OBJECTIVE = HOW
How it will be achieved

TACTIC = ACTIONS
Activities to be conducted

Figure 2-3
Goals, Objectives, and Tactics

governments, charitable organizations, leisure and entertainment organizations, and private individuals. You must seek a definitive description of the return expected for the investment made.

If you are coordinating a 50th birthday celebration, does your client want specific people in attendance? If you are coordinating a corporate event, are there measurable areas of market share growth expected? If you are coordinating a festival or association event, are there particular constituencies that must be served? If you are coordinating a sponsored event, what are the sponsors' marketing objectives?

To put this in perspective, suppose you are coordinating a conference for your professional association. The costs to a delegate may include a registration fee of $600, an airline ticket at $500, a hotel room at $600 (4 nights × $150/night), and meals, business center services, and other incidentals may add up to $400. Add to that $900 for a week away from work (a factor all too many organizers ignore), and the cost to the delegate is $3000. To achieve a positive ROI, the delegate will have to come away from that conference with a $3000 idea.

Goals and objectives must not only be defined, they must be measurable. (How will you know if you have delivered that $3000 idea?) The acronym SMART, devised by George Doran for an article on writing management goals and objectives for *Management Review* in 1981, illustrates the qualities required of goal and objective statements.

Specific	Must be specific in targeting an objective
Measurable	Must have a measurable indicator(s) of progress/ success

Assignable   Must be capable of being assigned to someone to
                  accomplish
Realistic   Must be realistic within allotted resources
Time-related   Must have a specified duration

Without the goals and objectives specified, you will not be able to describe the results expected. You will not be able to define the scope of
the project, specify the scope of your responsibilities, control the extent
of your obligations, nor evaluate your success.

Event coordinators invariably encounter the "could-you-just" syn-
drome—"Could you just add candles to the centerpieces?" "Could you
just have your people put up these flags behind the dais?" "Could you
just change those table linens from red to blue?" The client keeps adding
or changing one more thing, and one more thing, and one more thing, expecting there to be no change in the resources provided. (Changing the
linen color, even if feasible, can involve numerous telephone calls, various pieces of paperwork, perhaps even additional costs.) In project
management this is called *scope creep*—the scope of the project keeps
creeping outward. Without establishing clear parameters and objectives,
you will not be able to identify the appropriate event elements, sequence
the tasks efficiently, or effectively manage the resources for the event.

How do you determine the prioritized goals and objectives? You ask.
You probe. You listen. Using a comprehensive Client Interview Form (see
Appendix 1) and a consultative selling process, you keep challenging the
client, in a nice way, to define the guest reaction and/or results expected.
Once the list of goals and objectives is established (with the measurement of success defined), you must work with the client to rank them in
order of precedence and preference. You need to determine which event
elements are absolutely necessary, which will enhance the event significantly, and which would simply be nice to have. This information will
be critical when you begin to analyze feasibility and find that you must
ask the client, who wants the sun, the moon, and the stars, to decide
whether he or she wants the sun, the moon, *or* the stars.

FEASIBILITY, PRIORITY, AND IMPACT

Once needs are identified and the prioritized goals and objectives established, you must blend creativity with practicality. You must identify the
resources and any obstacles to determine the practicality of the project
and the potential for success. Resources include time, money, humanpower, information, space, and service availability. Each one of these can
be an advantage or become an obstacle. You must make sure that you
have a reasonable balance of resources to allocate to achieve the event
requirements.

Michael C. Thomsett, author of *The Little Black Book of Project Management,* states, "True creativity demands a methodical, organized approach," and recommends getting the answers to these questions:

- What is the purpose of this project [event]?
- What will the outcome look like?
- What is my responsibility?
- What is my authority?
- What is my budget?

As noted earlier, the event must meet the prioritized needs and goals and objectives of the client and other constituents. Therefore, another set of questions you should ask that will help to prioritize the event elements to be included might be the following:

What must be done?	Is it doable?
What should be done?	Is it affordable?
What can be done?	Is it meaningful?

It is critical to remember that in considering each potential event element, there are conditions and consequences that come with each choice. Each element has or can have an impact on virtually every other element. As when pebbles are dropped into a still pool of water, there are ripples that expand out in all directions. Selecting a theme for a party will drive decisions about the invitations, site selection, décor, food and beverages, entertainment, and party favors. Selecting pin spots to highlight the centerpieces on the banquet tables will affect the timing of when the tables can and must be positioned and dressed (the lights must be rigged before the tables are positioned, and then focused after the tables have been positioned and dressed).

COMPREHENSIVE PERSPECTIVE

The event experience must be considered from threshold to threshold and considered from the guests' point of view. Drawing on your experience with previous and similar events, as well as the history of this or comparable events, you identify the event elements that will deliver the required results to the client and the desired benefits to the attendee. You then examine the implications of each element within the overall plan. (See Figure 2-4.)

An event does not happen in a vacuum. You must include a comprehensive perspective of your different customers, plus the internal and external stakeholders, in analyzing their needs, wants, and mandates. Depending on the event type, the stakeholders or influencers you can be dealing with may include corporate executives, boards of directors, sponsors, family members, public bureaucrats, or regulatory officials. You

CONTENT (column headers): Invitations/Brochures · Printed Collateral · Promotions/Advertising · Public Relations/Media · Protocol/Etiquette · Sponsorship · Intellectual Property · Transportation/Travel · Parking/Services · Housing/Services · Handicap Services · VIP/Guest Services · Traffic/Crowd Control · Registration/Admission · Signage · Theme Design/Decor · Seating/Credentials · Tents/Equipment · Environment Control · Security · Medical/Emergency Srvs · Communications · Storage/Prep/Admin · Power/Utilities · Load-in/out · Staging · Lighting · Sound / PA / AV · Special Effects · Labor Unions · Food & Beverage · Waste Management · Recycling · Entertainment · Speakers/Presenters · Participants/Performers · Ceremonies/Emcee · Companion Programs · Sightseeing Tours · Sports/Tournaments · Exhibits · Ancillary Events · Prizes & Gifts · Souvenirs/Mementos · Hospitality · Recognition

INTENT & EXTENT (rows):

SCOPE MANAGEMENT
- Assessment
- Definition/Design
- Change Control
- Evaluation Specs

SITE MANAGEMENT
- Specifications
- Inspection/ADA
- Selection/Contract
- Layout/Diagrams

TIME MANAGEMENT
- Task Definition
- Sequencing
- Duration Estimation
- Schedule Dev.
- Schedule Control

FINANCIAL MANAGEMENT
- Resource Definition
- Cost Estimating
- Budgeting
- Cost Control

HUMAN RESOURCES MANAGEMENT
- Stakeholders
- Org. Structure
- Support Staffing
- Labor Needs
- Volunteers
- Mgmt./Leadership

COMMUNICATIONS MANAGEMENT
- Definition/Planning
- Info Acquisition
- Info Distribution
- Reporting
- Documentation

RISK MANAGEMENT
- Identification
- Analysis
- Response Planning
- Monitoring/Control
- Compliance
- Insurance

PROCUREMENT MANAGEMENT
- Definition
- Solicitation
- Selection
- Quality Control
- Contract Admin.

CLOSEOUT & EVALUATION
- Performance Review
- Evaluations
- Financial Reports

Figure 2-4

The Silvers Event Coordination Matrix

must conduct a situational assessment of the macro- and microenvironments in which the event takes place. Macroenvironments include the economy, community and constituent sociocultural demographics, and governmental influence. Microenvironments include industry-specific factors, competitive forces, and supply and demand. Failure to scan these environments and identify the needs of internal and external stakeholders can cause problems when it comes time move in and set up, not to mention contributing significantly to *scope creep.*

Analyzing Resources

Management is allocating, directing, and controlling resources to achieve objectives, and resources, by definition, are limited. The professional event coordinator must balance the "need" with the "have," making sure that what must be done can be done with the resources available for the event project. (See Figure 2-5.)

TIME, MONEY, AND HUMANPOWER

Of all the resources at your disposal, time is the one resource that is finite. When clients really want something that is not included in the budget, there are usually ways to find more money to make it happen. When money is short, volunteer humanpower can often fill in the gap. When

Resource		Project Management Process		Event Output
Time	➡	Time Management	➡	Schedules
Money	➡	Financial Management	➡	Budget
Humanpower	➡	Human Resources Management	➡	Organizational Chart
Information	➡	Communications Management	➡	Production Book
Space	➡	Site Management	➡	Site Plan
Suppliers	➡	Procurement Management	➡	Requests for Proposal and Bid Specifications

Figure 2-5
Controlling Resources through Event Project Management

space is limited, creative options such as adding a tented area are often possible. But when you have run out of time, you have run out of time. You cannot beg, borrow, or steal more.

This is the primary difference between event project management and other realms of project management. The event's date, which is virtually always fixed, not flexible, is the starting point of project time management, rather than the project management process determining the completion date. Time restrictions will determine the tempo of the event project.

Monetary resources must be allocated carefully. It is important to remember that everything will cost something. Goods and services require labor and raw materials. Volunteers and donated items will incur administrative and hospitality costs. Securing more money through sponsorships, gifts, and grants will have costs attached. Even assessing needs and analyzing event resources take time, and time is money. Nothing is free. The more limited the budget, the more focused you must be on the event goals, but a quality event does not depend on a large budget.

Your humanpower resources may include part-time or full-time paid staff, casual or temporary labor, or a volunteer corps. Depending on the type of event, these human resources may be secured through recruitment, hired through various agencies, or provided by the sponsoring organization. Your human resources must be assessed based on experience and expertise, as well as their availability within the schedule requirements.

CALCULATING REALITY

You must be brutally realistic about the quantity and quality of the resources committed to the event project. Insufficient resources in one area may be mitigated by additional resources of another type—for example, less time = more humanpower, insufficient number of volunteers = more money for support staffing. However, if there are insufficient resources all around, the scope of the event may have to be reduced.

You must validate the budget and the availability of additional money if required. You must specify the Work Breakdown Structure and analyze the schedule to be certain that what needs to be accomplished can be accomplished within the time constraints. You must assess the capabilities and availability of volunteers and vendors. You must verify the facilities and capabilities of the site selected. And you must calculate the realistic likelihood of achieving the level of success expected.

DELEGATION AND DIRECTION

The professional event coordinator must always work within a team, even if he or she is a sole, independent practitioner. There are always vendors, suppliers, support staff, and volunteers or helpers involved in an event project. Their numbers can range from a few family members and a couple of suppliers to the hundreds of vendors and 26,000+ volunteers and staff included for the 2002 Winter Olympic Games in Salt Lake City, Utah.

Big jobs are accomplished by completing small tasks. Utilizing these humanpower and vendor resources requires delegation and proper direction. The professional event coordinator maintains the focus on the big picture and delegates the task assignments. Project management consultant James P. Lewis, author of *Fundamentals of Project Management,* notes, however, that "delegation does not mean abdication." Well-trained, experienced personnel may be utilized because they are usually more cost-effective, yet everyone, including professionals, will need direction. There will be lots of pieces to the puzzle, and the event coordinator is the one who knows what the final picture should look like.

Logical Sequencing

Two of Stephen Covey's *Seven Habits of Highly Effective People* are to "begin with the end in mind" and to "put first things first." These could arguably be the essence of the logistics and logical sequencing of the event elements. There will be a natural order and a necessary order in which the various event elements (and the tasks associated with them) will have to be chronologically organized. Certain event elements and tasks will have to be sequential and others may be simultaneous, and many of the controlling and monitoring processes of event coordination are iterative.

Logical sequencing follows a critical path, meaning that some tasks will be dependent on other tasks having already been completed, and some tasks will be affected by the way in which others have been done. Developing the logical sequencing for an event depends on sound reasoning, collecting the specifications, and understanding the interdependencies. In project management, this is Activity Sequencing, which will depend on the activity list, mandatory dependencies, external dependencies, and milestones (the completion of major and requisite deliverables or tasks).

IDENTIFYING EVENT COMPONENTS

The components of an event project will, of course, depend on the type and scope of the event. As you envision the Six Dimensions of an Event Experience in Figure 2-6 and scan the elements in the Content column of Figure 2-4, you will identify the features, activities, supplies, products, services, and vendors that must go on your list. Each dimension, each

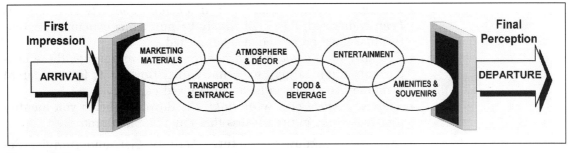

Figure 2-6
The Six Dimensions of an Event Experience

feature, each product or service will indicate certain characteristics and options, as well as additional operational requirements.

For example, if you decide to include colorful fabrics, spandex, or vinyl stretched from a high ceiling to the centers of the buffet displays to indicate their positioning within a cavernous space, you will probably need to secure a scissor lift or high jacker to install them. You will also have to ensure that the material used complies with the fire codes of the particular jurisdiction. In certain jurisdictions (e.g., Las Vegas, Nevada), you must have the installation done by a professional rigger from a specific labor union.

As you visualize the event experience, from threshold to threshold, itemize the elements that will or should be included. Then analyze each of these elements to determine the products and/or services that will be required for implementation, as well as the likely impact they will have on the other elements. You will also have to consider the administrative issues, marketing implications, and risk management ramifications.

FLOWCHARTS, OUTLINES, AND STORYBOARDS

A time line can serve as your event flowchart, illustrating the flow of the tasks necessary to produce the event. In project management, this begins with the Work Breakdown Structure (decomposing the event into its elements and components), which facilitates creating the Activity List (the tasks associated with each element). You then identify the interdependencies to create the Activity Sequencing and estimate the duration of each activity. Thomsett suggests the following flowchart rules:

- *Always use the precedence method;* what fits where and when according to what precedes it and what follows it.
- *Make sure the path of activities and events makes sense;* the path works when it is arranged logically.

- *An activity cannot occur until a preceding activity or event has been completed;* there will likely be numerous concurrent activities that must be precedence-connected.
- *Carefully plot, explain, and control concurrent events;* these concurrent activities may have individual flowcharts (and different team members) that must be supervised carefully.
- *Exercise control over weak links;* the flowchart helps you identify the weak links in the process that must be monitored.

The Work Breakdown Structure, Activity List, and Activity Sequencing may be composed in an outline form, either a Harvard or numerical outline, or can be generated via a mind-mapping technique or a scalar organization (see Figure 2-7). Some find the storyboard method effective—creating a card for each task and arranging the cards in groups and chronological order. You should lock in the most important items first, incorporating the chronology, priority, and flexibility of each.

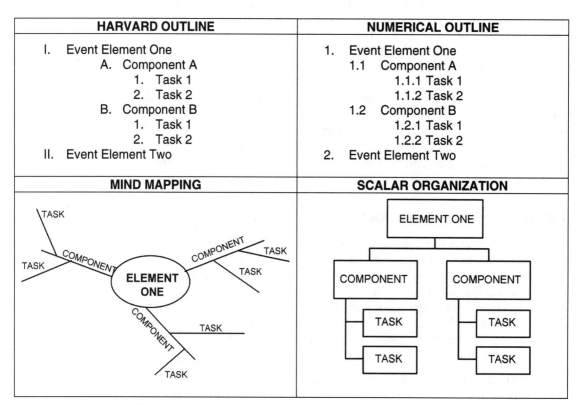

Figure 2-7
Flowchart Styles

COLLECT SPECIFICATIONS AND DIRECTIONS

Once the list of event elements is prepared, the specifications must be determined. Consider the quality level or type of product or service that will be appropriate for the event style and context. For example, name badges can be handwritten on paper badges with sticky backs, printed on card stock and inserted in plastic holders, or embossed on plastic cards (like credit cards) with large amounts of data imbedded in a magnetic strip on the back, and can cost anywhere from a few cents apiece to double-digit dollar amounts each.

Ascertain the installation or implementation requirements for each element. You must thoroughly understand what resources (time, money, humanpower, and space) will be required for each product or service. For event elements, products, or services associated with disciplines with which you are unfamiliar, collect this information through research, your colleagues on the event team (i.e., scenic designer, catering manager, or graphic designer), or directly from the vendors and suppliers you will be contracting (remember, they should also be practicing consultative selling). Include the following specifications.

- **Product**—quantity, quality, features, or brand specifications
- **Time**—fabrication/installation/removal duration; sequence restrictions; materials and/or information dependencies (what a vendor needs you to provide before it can begin)
- **Space**—dimensions; proximity requirements and/or restrictions
- **Humanpower**—number of people required to install/operate/remove (number to be included by provider and/or number to be provided by event organization)
- **Accessibility**—number and type of delivery vehicles; proximity requirements and/or restrictions
- **Other**—power requirements and other utility needs; installation equipment requirements; special permits, compliance instruments, and/or insurance requirements

RECOGNIZING BOTTLENECKS AND OUTSIDE INFLUENCES

You must understand what each provider will do, what equipment or materials each needs to be able to do it, how much time is needed to do it, and what impact that may have on other providers. Of particular note, you will have to integrate and synchronize those tasks and those providers who will need to be occupying the same or contiguous space or time in the sequence in the schedule. When setting up an event on-site, the activity will be fast and furious and you must carefully choreograph this delicate dance of possibly hundreds of people coming together in the same space at the same time to create, operate, and participate in the event experience.

The event elements must be arranged in order of priority, logistics, and chronology. Tap into your own experience and the experience of others to recognize, anticipate, and alleviate potential congestion and conflict before it can result in financial or productivity problems. In project management this is called Project Integration Management, which includes Project Plan Development, Project Plan Execution, and Integrated Change Control.

LOGISTICS OF A PROGRESSIVE EXPERIENCE

A progressive event experience is an event program that follows a natural or designed progression from start to finish or threshold to threshold. Not everything happens at once, at least for the individual at the event. At a public festival, for example, there may be different activities and amusements scheduled continuously throughout the day, and the visitor will be experiencing these attractions one after the other. At a conference or convention, there may be numerous concurrent sessions, but the delegate can attend only one at a time. During an incentive travel program, there will be a balance of sightseeing, social events, free time, and rest.

This progression, or flow, of the event will indicate additional operational elements that must be sequenced logically as well. The professional event coordinator must supervise vendors as they replenish supplies and materials, monitor volunteer arrivals and activities, and arrange everything performers or participants will need for their arrival, preparations, waiting, performance, and departure throughout the duration of the event program. This may necessitate dressing rooms, a green room, and/or break areas for staff, volunteers, cast, and crew.

The months of preplanning culminate in an event that is often over in just a few hours. But the party does not end there. You must remember that the breakdown and move-out is an essential component of the event production. It must have sufficient resources allocated (i.e., time, money, humanpower) and must be choreographed as carefully as the move-in and the event itself. So I just smile and nod when an admiring guest comes up to me during an event and bubbles, "Oh, you do parties . . . what fun!" I know that all the hard work was truly invisible to the guest.

Timelines and Schedules

You have identified the event elements, collected the specifications for each product or provider, and identified the interdependencies. Now you must integrate this into a project schedule that includes tracking systems and control points to ensure that the schedule is effective. Timelines, production schedules, running orders, and scripts should reflect the necessary chronological sequence of the delivery and implementation of the goods, services, tasks, and performances required to produce the event experience.

TIMELINE VERSUS PRODUCTION SCHEDULE

The project schedule or timeline should be presented in a chronological format, which may be a scroll list or a graphical or schematic chart. The scroll list format may be a simple numerical sequence by date (see Figure 2-8). The graphical format may be a bar chart (often called a Gantt chart, named for Henry Gantt, who developed a complete notational system for showing progress with bar charts in the late 1950s) or a network diagram, often an arrow diagram. (See Figure 2-9.) The graphical format may also simply be a calendar. To facilitate monitoring functions, either the scroll list or graphical format should include the name of the person, vendor, or team responsible for each task listed.

The style or format you use will depend on the complexity of the event project and what best communicates the schedule to your event project team. In many cases a combination of formats will be needed for different event elements, such as printing, catering, décor and entertainment. The key for any of these formats is to ensure that Task A is done before Task B as needed, and that it is clear which tasks must be sequential, which are simultaneous, which are conditional, and which are iterative.

Date	Activity	Responsibility	Interdependency Notes
02 Jan 2004	ACTIVITY 1	FRED	
10 Jan 2004	ACTIVITY 2	GINGER	Must have information from Fred's research
16 Feb 2004	ACTIVITY 3	ADAM	Cannot proceed without client deposit
14 Mar 2004	ACTIVITY 4	EVE	Client must approve prior to final order

Figure 2-8
Scroll List Timeline Format

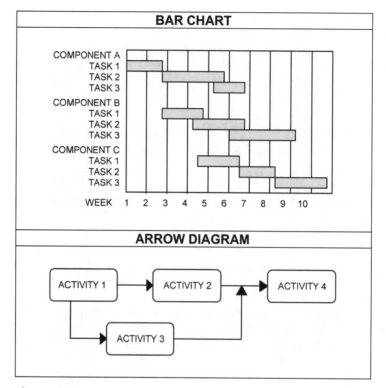

Figure 2-9
Graphical Timeline Formats

Technology Tip

For larger, complex events, the use of project management software will facilitate the event coordination process. This type of software includes the ability to provide the project network diagrams, flowcharts, schedules, and monitoring checkpoints (e.g., Gantt charts, PERT charts, precedence diagrams, arrow diagrams, network loops, GERT diagrams, and system dynamics models). For smaller or onetime events, project management software may be too expensive—both the investment for purchasing the software and the investment of learning/training time to be able to master it. Standard software will likely suffice for organizing and integrating timelines, address files, personal scheduling, word processing, spreadsheets, budgeting, basic reports, and graphics.

As the day of the event nears, the project schedule will shift from the broader calendar perspective to a daily and hourly (or even minute-by-minute) version. This agenda is called a production schedule and is most often presented in the scroll list format, arranged in a table displayed in columns. The number of columns will depend on the type or scope of the event and the information necessary to monitor the schedule. Each column will include a qualifying factor such as starting and ending times, event element or activity, location, person responsible (with contact numbers), and other specifications or notes as required (see Figure 2-10).

For multiday, complex, or mega-events, the production schedule may be dozens or hundreds of pages long and/or require versions specific to individual vendors or event team members. You may create customized schedules that include only the information required by each vendor or group. You might wish to print daily versions for each day of a multiday festival, or you might omit certain elements, such as the arrival time of a specific dignitary that should be confidential for security reasons. However, as changes are made to the master schedule, these updates must be included in the customized versions as well. Also remember that you want your entire team to have a clear understanding of the event as a whole.

The schedule may be printed a variety of ways. It can be printed horizontally or vertically on standard stationery, which would facilitate inclusion in the Production Book (discussed further in Chapter 14) and/or on a clipboard at the receiving dock or registration table. It can be enlarged to poster size and mounted on the wall in the on-site headquarters office. It can be downloaded into a PDA (personal digital assistant) or posted on a company intranet. Again, form follows function; the format should facilitate effective communications.

REVERSE PLANNING TO ACHIEVE REALISTIC SCHEDULING

How do you ensure that you will have all the information required to print the conference brochure or trade show directory on time? How long can you wait to order a customized stage backdrop? How do you establish the entry deadline for participants in a road rally? Professional event coordinators learn to *plan backward.* You collect the specifications data and duration estimations for all the event elements, integrate the critical path of interdependencies into the Activity Sequence, and establish a deadline for each task. With the deadline noted on the calendar or schedule, you move backward on the schedule the amount of time it will take to accomplish a particular task to establish the start date or time.

When estimating the time required for each task defined, you must consider all constraints, assumptions, capabilities, historical information, and mandatory dependencies (the tasks that must be completed

When	Who	What	Where
05h30	SAGC	Driving range set, golf carts staged	@ Cart staging area
06h00	CSS	Start installation for lunch	East lawn
06h30	CSW	Shuttles from hotel begin	Hyatt ABQ lobby
06h30	SAGC	Registration table set	Banquet entry foyer
06h45	All	Breakfast ready	Banquet room
06h45	ASA	Native American flute player ready	Banquet room
07h00	**All**	**Breakfast begins**	**Banquet room**
07h00	*CSS*	*Rain decision re: outdoor events if needed*	
07h30	SAGC	Service attendant ready, shuttle carts ready	@ Cart staging area
07h45	SAGC	Bagpipe march	Putting green
08h15	All	Strike buffet breakfast	Banquet room
08h20	SAGC	Gather guests for announcements	@ Cart staging area
08h30	SAGC	Shotguns sound to start play	
08h45	SAGC	Stage carts for 2nd shotgun	@ Cart staging area
10h20	SAGC	Service/pro shop traffic directors	@ Cart staging area
10h30	ASA	Native American flute player until 11h10	Portal @ putting green
11h00	SAGC	Transfer of clubs to new carts complete	@ Cart staging area
11h05	SAGC	Guests report to new carts	@ Cart staging area
11h15	SAGC	2nd shotgun start	
12h45	ASA	Disc jockey set	East lawn
13h00	All	Lunch ready	East lawn
13h05	SAGC	Service/pro shop traffic directors	@ Cart staging area
13h15	**All**	**Lunch begins**	**East lawn**
13h35	SAGC	Transfer of clubs to new carts complete	@ Cart staging area

Figure 2-10
Production Schedule for One Day of a Familiarization Trip for
Incentive Planners at a Golf Resort

When	Who	What	Where
14h00	SAGC	Final shotgun start	
14h15	All	Strike lunch	East lawn
15h00	TRI	Pavilion tent & chairs set	@ 4th hole
15h00	RR	Hot air balloons arrive, start to inflate	@ 4th hole
15h45	ASA	Native American dancers arrive, get into costume	Resort conference room
16h00	SAGC	Sevice/pro shop traffic directors	@ Cart staging area
16h00	ASA	Band begins setup	South lawn
16h15	ASA	Native American dancers ready	Resort entrance
16h15	HYT	Tours of resort facility begin	Resort
16h30	SAGC	Cleaned clubs into storage	Clubhouse
16h30	ASA	Native American dancers begin	Resort entrance
17h00	ASA	Native American dancers transfer to 4th hole	Resort entrance
17h15	ASA	Native American dancers begin—until 17h45	@ 4th hole
17h15	SAGC	Shuttles from resort to 4th hole	Resort entrance
17h30	SAGC	Closest to pin contest	@ 4th hole
18h00	All	Dinner set	South lawn
18h15	ASA	Band ready	South lawn
18h30	**All**	**Dinner begins**	**South lawn**
19h30	SAGC	All carts back to SAGC	Cart staging area
21h00	CSW	Guests depart	South lawn
21h00	CSS	Strike dinner	South lawn
21h15	HYA	Hospitality suite	Hotel
24h00	CSS	Finish setup for breakfast	Banquet room

Figure 2-10
(Continued)

before another task can begin). You need to determine, from your prior experience and a healthy measure of optimistic pessimism, how much time it will actually take to complete a task. Although the industry trend is shorter lead times for event preparation, try to build plenty of flexibility into your schedule. You should be very conservative when estimating productivity and very generous when anticipating problems.

Once you have the initial drafts of both your timeline and production schedule, you should distribute these to your staff, vendors, and/or key stakeholders for review and comment. These draft schedules should be distributed as early as possible to allow time for any changes or concerns to be addressed and incorporated into the final version.

TRACKING AND CHANGE CONTROLS

A carefully crafted schedule is a thing of beauty, but unless it incorporates tracking and control mechanisms, it is next to worthless. In project management you use the Project Schedule with Critical Path Milestones, Performance Reports, and Change Orders to develop the Schedule Control System.

The timeline and production schedule should have the critical milestones and deadlines highlighted, including those tasks or activities that must be completed before another task may begin. With the responsibility for each task assigned to an individual (remember the "A" of SMART objectives), regular performance updates should be plotted into the schedule, including written reports and in-person meetings. These reports and meetings must be scheduled to allot sufficient time to take corrective action if required. Incorporate a Tickler System (to "tickle" your memory) into your timeline, computer scheduler, and/or personal scheduler system.

Change controls include the manner of and documentation required for making any changes to the project scope or the project schedule. The professional event coordinator should develop and utilize a Change Order Form (see Appendix 2) for changes to the scope of the event project. Change notification protocols must be developed to ensure that schedule updates are communicated efficiently and effectively.

Not only are these tracking and change control mechanisms important for keeping the event project on time and on track, they will provide valuable information when coordinating your next event project. This is why you should analyze and document the causes of any variances, the reasons behind the corrective actions selected, and other lessons learned. You should be creating a historical database for this event as well as other event projects so that you may continuously improve your processes and procedures.

On-Site Insight

Robert Hulsmeyer, CSEP, senior partner with Empire Force Events, Inc., in New York City, describes the production schedule as your roadmap to a successful event. He suggests creating a fax cover sheet including a notice requesting each team member to review the schedule, input any necessary changes or additions, and return fax by a certain date. If the schedule is acceptable as is, the team member signs the cover sheet and faxes that back as a record of his or her approval. For updates, Hulsmeyer recommends a schedule be dated as to its last revision, using "As of" or "Revised," plus the date, on the first page of the schedule. When a schedule has gone through numerous revisions, as happens when an event takes place over several days or has extended load-in and rehearsal days, it is important that all of the team members are working from the most recent version. Empire Force Events, Inc., prints the final production schedule on a colored paper stock, allowing easy monitoring of which version each team member is working from.

Contingency Plans

There are never unlimited resources. There are no guarantees in life. The only constant is change. Stuff happens! Given all of these caveats, it is clear that there will always be a certain amount of risk associated with any event project. The professional event coordinator must carefully identify, analyze, plan for, and manage these risks by examining problem areas and available options to develop suitable contingency plans for identified risks. This task may include anything from an Event "Survival" Kit (see Appendix 3) to a full-blown alternate production plan.

Risk, as defined by the Project Management Institute, Inc., is "an uncertain condition that, if it occurs, has a positive or negative effect on a project objective. Each risk has a cause, and if it occurs, a consequence." Note that risk is not exclusively negative. There may be a risk that your Concert in the Park fund-raiser is more popular than your wildest dreams and you are selling tickets at an unprecedented rate. At a certain point, you must implement your contingency plan to secure more portable toilet facilities or bring in several more food stalls. This risk can be a good thing.

However, most risk management efforts are directed at the potential hazards associated with an event. In testimony conducted at the Coronial Inquest in conjunction with the crowd collapse death during the Limp Bizkit performance at the Big Day Out 2001 festival in Sydney, Australia, it was determined that there are no international minimum standards for crowd safety or management (www.crowdsafe.com), but there are numerous factors that have been identified as specific to special events, as outlined in Figure 2-11, that may increase the degree of risk but do not necessarily mean the event will be "risky." (For more on crowd collapse, see Figure 6-7.)

It is important to understand that risk management is an ongoing, integrated, and iterative process. Resources must be allocated, plans must be devised, and a commitment must be made to manage the uncertainties and vulnerabilities surrounding your event. You must examine the worst-case scenarios and the best-case scenarios in order to be prepared with the appropriate contingency plans. (Force majeure risks—earthquakes, floods, civil unrest, and terrorism—generally require disaster recovery actions rather than contingency plans.)

RISK IDENTIFICATION

There are several categories of risk the professional event coordinator should examine: safety, security, capability, internal, and external. Safety risks include physical harm, violence, sanitation issues, and health issues. Security risks include physical or intellectual property loss, property damage, theft, and fire. Capability risks include processes, technology, unrealistic goals, and unrealistic projections. Internal risks include resource allocation, scope creep, and changing priorities. External risks include legal and/or regulatory environments, labor issues, weather, and competition.

Risks are identified by reviewing historical information and industry standards; interviewing subject matter experts; conducting brainstorming sessions with the event team, vendors, and key stakeholders; and sometimes through simulation and scenario forecasting. You should also conduct a SWOT (strengths, weaknesses, opportunities, and threats) analysis, as well as a gap analysis (identifying the gaps in the planning process) to mitigate exposure and any disparities between what the vision is and what will be deliverable.

The professional event coordinator should continuously be developing checklists to serve as the starting point for the risk identification sessions. As the coordinator goes through the event element list item by item, he or she should question all assumptions and consider options as they relate to the cost, schedule, scope, and quality of the activities, products, and services included in the event plan. The causal influences

Organization	
Staffing	Insufficient number, inadequate training, incorrect deployment
Planning	Insufficient time, accelerated tempo, unprepared decision making
Structure	Unclear chain of command and control, unsanctioned leadership
Event Time/ Duration	Unauthorized camping, temporary marketplaces, late night exiting
Audience	
Audience/ Event Type	Open to public—ticketed/free, young/old, sports/music fans
Crowd Size	Crowd crushes, crowd collapses, crowd movement and dispersal, crowd rushes ("Virtually all crowd deaths are due to compressive asphyxia."—Fruin)
Crowd Density	Insufficient dimensions, access and segregation, crowd mobility
Behavioral Patterns	Mosh pits, heterogeneous groups with different acceptable behaviors, performer behavior, flight responses, mass craze
Unauthorized	Ticketless gate crashers, drug trafficking, picketing and protests
Site	
Venue and Layout	Public or private, private with proximity to public, barrier layout, overoccupancy, traffic proximity, unfenced open space
Arrival	Traffic density, parking facilities, insufficient and congested entrances
Departure	Insufficient routes for mass exodus at close of event
Structures & Facilities	Temporary or unsafe construction, slip and trip hazards ("Wet floors account for 90% of slip and trip injuries."—agency.osha.eu.int)
Lighting	Inadequate lighting increases the risk of a crowd losing its sense of orientation and lessens social control; electricity usage—cables and cords slip and trip hazards, illuminated pathways/hazards
Environment	Heat exhaustion, dehydration, wet and muddy (frolic behavior), hazardous waste disposal, litter and debris, pollution

Figure 2-11
Silvers Event Risk Factor Analysis

Communications	
Internal	Insufficient communications equipment, lack of centralized command center, inadequate crisis management plans
External	Insufficient public address capabilities and/or protocols, lack of community support, poor media relations
Promotional	Promoting unrealistic expectations, insufficient directions, cancellation
Signage	Insufficient directional and locator signs
Activities	
Arrival	Queue pressure, security searches for weapons/projectiles, mixed-sex search
Hazardous Activities	Thrill rides, unusual/untried tricks, fireworks, special effects—lasers, strobe lights, fog/smoke machines
Entertainment or Program	Concerts—particularly those with festival or general admission seating Content—meetings-cum-demonstrations
Consumption	Alcohol and euphoric substance use
Public Safety	
Antisocial Behavior	Terrorism, theft, violence, sexual assault ("Open spaces where people congregate are very vulnerable to terrorist shootings, bombings, and assaults of other types."—www.crowdsafe.com)
Authorities	Insufficient police presence, ineffective identification of safety personnel
Emergency Planning	Insufficient procurement, planning, placement, and practice of evacuation and medical assistance services, fire prevention, detection and control

Sources: Alexander Berlonghi (1990), The Special Event Risk Management Manual *(Dana Point, CA: Berlonghi); Peter Tarlow (2002).* Event Risk Management and Safety *(New York: John Wiley & Sons, Inc.); Danish Government Ministry of Culture,* Rock Festival Safety, *www.kum.dk; William O'Toole,* Event Project Management System—Risk Management, *http://www-personal.usyd.edu.au/~wotoole/EPMS_Control/Control_Areas/risk.html;* Crowdsafe News, *www.crowdsafe.com; John J. Fruin,* The Causes and Prevention of Crowd Disasters, *www.crowdsafe.com; Greater London Authority Carnival Review Group,* Notting Hill Carnival Review: Interim Report and Public Safety Profile Recommendations for 2001, *www.london.gov.uk/mayor/carnival; Greater London Authority,* Future Major Events in London, *www.london.gov.uk; Public Events Planning Group,* Event Safety: A Guide for Organisers, *www.nelincs.gov.uk; National Fire Protection Association,* Glossary of Terms, *www.nfpa.org*

Figure 2-11
(Continued)

associated with each risk identified should also be considered to determine whether there will be several risks driven by a common cause.

RISK ANALYSIS

Once the potential risks are identified, you must assess the likelihood and impact of each. Peter E. Tarlow, author of *Event Risk Management and Safety,* notes, "All event risk analyses should be based on the principle that there is no object, person, or reputation that cannot be stolen, damaged, or destroyed." You must also prioritize risk based on the potential impact on the event as well as the impact on the resources for the event. Using an evaluation tool such as the Event Probability/Impact Risk Rating Matrix (Figure 2-12), determine which risks can and/or must be avoided and which may be mitigated with additional event elements such as redundant equipment or other contingency planning, based on your event organization's threshold of tolerance.

As you are considering each identified risk, you must identify and evaluate the available options and their impact on the event's quality and resources. You must remember one of Norman R. Augustine's "Laws": No change is a small change. There will likely be a cost—in money, time, humanpower, or quality—for any contingency plan option selected. Reserving an indoor site or a tent for an outdoor wedding reception in case of inclement weather will likely require nonrefundable deposit money. Securing a portable generator as a backup power supply will incur rental

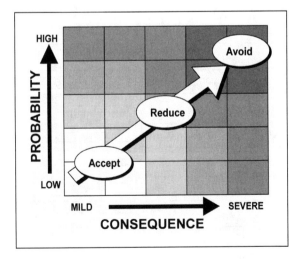

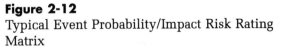

Figure 2-12
Typical Event Probability/Impact Risk Rating Matrix

costs, and the equipment must be plotted into the site plan. Obtaining specialty insurance, such as in the case of the Albuquerque International Hot Air Balloon Fiesta (insuring the airspace above the launch field), may be expensive or available through only one or two providers in the world.

To create a list of potential responses, you might use a Decision Tree (Figure 2-13) to analyze your contingency plan options. (The Decision Tree and the Rating Matrix are common tools used by a wide range of project management scholars and practitioners.) There will often be more than one alternative to any contingency plan option, and each alternative will have its own set of implications, including costs, rewards, and potential residual risks. For example, if you are having a big-name rock-and-roll band playing at a fund-raiser concert, you may need to construct a barrier between the stage and the audience. This barrier could be made of fencing (wire, mesh, or wood), or you could use security personnel lined up along the edge (uniformed guards, off-duty law enforcement officers, or volunteers in event T-shirts).

The fencing option will have costs associated with fabrication and/or installation. It will have an impact on the look of the stage. It may have an impact on the event grounds, depending on the type of fencing and the installation procedures. The security guard option will have costs associated with it as well, either for hiring or subcontracting personnel or for T-shirts for the volunteers. Uniformed security or off-duty law enforcement personnel may create an offensive or militaristic feel to the event, yet untrained volunteers may not be sufficient if the audience is likely to be aggressive about approaching the stage. Clearly, each option and its alternatives must be considered from a variety of perspectives.

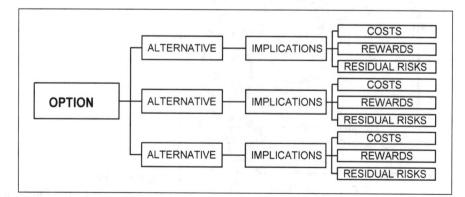

Figure 2-13
Typical Event Decision Tree Analysis

DEVELOPING RESPONSE PLANS

There are four ways to handle risk: avoidance, transference, mitigation (loss control), and acceptance (retention). Avoidance means you do not take the risk at all. Transference means you transfer the risk through insurance, performance bonds, warranties, guarantees, or contractual liability. Mitigation includes incorporating redundancies into your plan and targeting the linkages or causes that control and prevent the potential severity of the impact. Acceptance includes your contingency plans.

With your options identified, communication will be the foundation of the success of your contingency plans. You must specify your reporting format, including how and when decisions will be made to implement any portion of your plans and how this will be communicated to the event team. The triggers, actions, and individuals involved must be determined. Your list of potential responses must be linked with the threshold of tolerance that will trigger the response. You must specify what action steps will be taken. (Robert Hulsmeyer, CSEP, of Empire Force Events, Inc., recommends that a weather contingency production schedule should take the same form as, and be attached to, your fair weather production schedule.) You must also specify those individuals empowered to make the decision to implement a response. To eliminate any false alarms, only one person should be authorized to change, move, or cancel an event element, or the event itself. These roles and responsibilities should be documented and communicated to the entire event team.

You must verify and validate your contingency plans with the host organization or your client so that the resources required to implement a risk response or contingency plan are fully funded and supported. The host or client must be informed of the triggers, actions, and individuals involved and must be included in the communications surrounding response implementation.

TIMELINE INTEGRATION

The contingency plans must be integrated into your timeline so that you will be able to monitor situations and/or conditions and act as required and appropriate. This will include periodic risk reviews, performance reviews, taking corrective action when necessary, implementing change controls, and continuously updating your plan. What happened, why it happened, and when it happened must be included in your documentation procedures.

The professional event coordinator must be proactive rather than reactive. Decisions made in a panic are rarely cost-effective or efficient and often lead to more risk and unpleasant consequences. If at all possible, incorporate a generous response time into your schedule so that your contingency plans may be integrated into the event plans and implemented smoothly if required. It is better to have the wedding reception weather tent installed and beautifully decorated, but not be required, than to have the bride's lasting memory be a muddy and miserable wedding day.

INSURANCE

As noted, there are four ways to handle risk, one of which is to transfer risk by purchasing insurance coverage. Of course, insurance will not prevent something from happening; it will only lessen the financial impact should it happen. An insurance policy is a legal agreement for transferring risk that defines what will be paid for, in the event of a defined loss, in exchange for a defined amount of money (the premium). The professional event coordinator will work with an insurance broker to identify and purchase the appropriate insurance coverage for the type and size of event that is being produced.

Most purpose-built and commercial venues will require specific levels of insurance coverage, primarily Commercial General Liability (CGL), also known in countries other than the United States as Public Liability Insurance, which usually protects your organization if a volunteer, employee, or other individual, supervised, directed, or whose duties are controlled by the organization, makes a mistake and a patron is injured or has his or her property damaged. This coverage is not universal, however, and you must always check the exclusions in your policy because not all persons injured and all property damaged may be covered. You should always secure Certificates of Insurance from your vendors, particularly those providing their goods and services on-site at the event.

Onetime (often called "one-off") and annual events often require Event Liability Insurance, often called Spectator Insurance, which will be priced according to the type of event and the capacity of the audience, and perhaps the event elements to be included. James N. Decoulos, a Massachusetts lawyer and insurance broker specializing in legal and insurance services for special events, explains that an event liability policy is really a CGL policy issued on an industry standard form, but rather than for the usual one-year term, it is issued for the duration of the event. Decoulos advises that there are basically four kinds of losses that should be addressed with the procurement of insurance coverage, as illustrated in Figure 2-14.

Decoulos notes,

These products apply not so much to the type of event, but rather to the type of business that the event professional conducts. Also, the client bears potential loss and the planner may

RISK OF LOSS		INSURANCE PRODUCT
PROPERTY	Loss of tangible property, such as equipment, intangible property, such as a copyright, or real property such as a building. A loss can even exceed the value of what is lost, for example, the costs associated with removing a building destroyed by fire.	Homeowners Renters Commercial Package Policy (CPP) Building and Personal Property (BPP) Business Owners Policy (BOP) Commercial Crime Inland Marine
LIABILITY	This is imposed, by law, on an individual who causes damage to another individual.	
Tortious	Pertaining to a wrongful act for which a civil lawsuit can be brought; negligence—that is, not acting as a reasonably prudent person would under the circumstances, as a result of which somebody was hurt.	Commercial General Liability (CGL) Liquor Liability Business Owners Policy (BOP) Spectator, Volunteer, Participant Liability
Contractual	Breach of a contract or failure to perform a contract.	None
Professional	Not performing a contract according to the standards of the profession.	Errors and Omissions (E&O) Directors and Officers (D&O)
Statutory	Determined by legislation and legally punishable	Workers' Compensation Automobile Employment Practices
PERSONNEL	A loss to a business when a key person is disabled or dies.	Key Man Life and Disability
NET INCOME	The loss of revenues or increase of expenses when a business is interrupted because of damage to its property or another business upon which the first business relies to operate its business, such as a supplier.	Business Income Coverage (BIC) Business Owners Policy (BOP) Commercial Crime Event Cancellation Nonappearance Weather Prize Indemnification Bonds

Figure 2-14
Decoulos Insurance Analysis

have a duty to advise the client about the risk of that loss and methods to reduce it. For example, if an outdoor event is being planned in the Southeast during hurricane season, a planner, being the professional and thus having certain higher standards of performance, may have a duty to advise the client to get weather insurance or to forgo the event altogether, especially if the client is not from the Southeast and is not aware of the hurricane season. The weather insurance would likely be quite expensive or unavailable, but the risks should be discussed. Failure to discuss the risks could lead to a professional liability claim for which the planner may want insurance coverage to finance any liability that may arise due to damages incurred by the client if the event is canceled or the risk is not otherwise properly managed.

The event professional must also become familiar with various insurance-related documents such as a certificate of insurance, declarations page, binder, policy, and endorsement, as well as the meaning of terms that appear in them such as additional named insured, policy limitations, exclusions, *and* duties in the event of loss. *Insurance is a tool by which risk management is financed. An event professional shouldn't employ that tool without knowing what it does and doesn't do, any more than an audiovisual technician employs a soundboard, or a pyrotechnician employs a detonating device.*

Risk is an uncertainty about whether a loss will occur, what peril will cause that loss, and what damage may be done as a result. Once all the efforts have been exhausted at managing the risk by preventing it altogether, reducing the likelihood of its happening, and reducing the severity of it, one purchases insurance to finance it when it does happen [see Figure 2-15].

Target Competency Review

The professional event coordinator conducts an assessment to determine the purpose of and expectations for an event in order to be able to visualize, organize, and synchronize the elements and actions required to deliver the desired event experience. Using the principles and discipline of project management, the professional event coordinator will be able to identify, prioritize, and sequence event elements in a comprehensive and

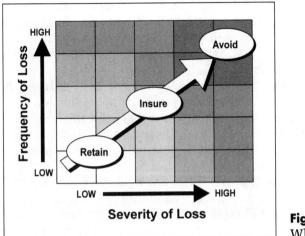

Figure 2-15
When to Insure

successful manner, as well as allocate and control resources to achieve the event objectives.

The professional event coordinator must create realistic time lines and production schedules that incorporate the interdependencies and critical path of activities, as well as manage the risks associated with them. These schedules must be validated and verified by the event stakeholders and then distributed to all appropriate personnel and providers. Timely and efficient communications are critical to the successful achievement of the event goals and objectives.

The professional event coordinator also performs risk assessment and analysis to identify problem areas, evaluate available options, and create contingency plans that will mitigate the consequences should an incident occur. These contingency plans should include the triggers to indicate implementation, the actions to be taken if implemented, and the individuals who will be responsible, as well as the procurement of the appropriate insurance coverage.

EXERCISES IN PROFESSIONAL EVENT COORDINATION

Determine the event elements and create a time line and production schedule for each of the following events. Be sure to include the research, design, planning, implementation, and evaluation phases.

1. Your professional association will be holding its annual convention in your city two years from now. It will consist of four days, including 36 concurrent seminars, a trade show, a welcome reception, an awards banquet, and three days of leadership meetings before the convention begins.

2. Your Convention and Visitors Bureau wants to hold a three-day Familiarization Tour for 50 meeting planners in conjunction with your city's famous cultural heritage festival six months from now. The tour should include a visit to the festival, site visits to ten hotel properties and attractions, and meal functions at at least six other hotel or resort properties.

3. The city elections took place yesterday, and the newly elected mayor just called and wants to hold an impressive investiture ceremony and inaugural ball six weeks from now. The ceremony will be in the afternoon and the inaugural ball that evening, and both are to include elements that recall the campaign issues of supporting youth programs, strong law enforcement, and community pride.

Facing Page

Events often take place in unusual and exciting locations, such as this natural history museum. *Photograph by Mike Rudahl, courtesy of Expo Events, Inc.*

CHAPTER 3

Developing the
Event Site

Small rooms discipline the mind; large ones distract it.

—*Leonardo da Vinci (1452–1519)*

IN THIS CHAPTER YOU WILL LEARN HOW TO:

- Identify potential event sites and evaluate their suitability to select the best fit for an event.
- Develop site plans that utilize the space in an efficient and effective manner to meet the goals and objectives of an event.
- Determine and implement strategies to ensure full accessibility of the event site in compliance with the Americans with Disabilities Act (ADA) and other special needs.
- Ensure that the use of the event site is in compliance with all federal, state or provincial, and local legislation, health and safety ordinances, and other jurisdictional regulations.

The event coordinator was standing in a corner watching the action at the client hospitality reception she had designed and organized for a décor rental company. She had transformed its cavernous warehouse into a fantasy environment by having the space emptied (the stock was loaded into the company's large delivery trucks for the duration of the event), draping the walls and perimeter storage racks from floor to ceiling in black, and installing lush carpeting throughout. Props, lighting, decorated buffets, and well-dressed tables and chairs created various theme areas that illustrated the décor company's capabilities. A colleague approached the coordinator in awe and, in all seriousness, asked, "How can I rent this nightclub for my client's company party?"

Every event is held *somewhere*—a specific space and place. Events can be held in almost any place imaginable, from purpose-built facilities to unique or off-premise sites, even in industrial real estate masquerading as a trendy nightclub. Large public events can be held outside in public parks or in the streets, or inside in convention facilities, town halls, or shopping malls. Private or corporate events can be held in hotel function spaces, stately homes, or out in the middle of a desert.

Some events such as annual festivals are held in a specific place year after year. Others, such as hospitality functions and incentive events, seek new and unusual sites. The event site may be predetermined, or the professional event coordinator may be charged with securing a venue from a world of possibilities (see Figure 3-1). He or she must blend the needs and wants of the host and guests with the realities of availability, capability, affordability, and accessibility.

Site Selection and Inspection

Site selection is both a science and an art—part investigation and part intuition. The professional event coordinator will select a site based on the purpose, role, goals, and objectives of the event, as well as the capabilities, desirability, and safety of the venue or location. The site where an event is held can have a significant impact on the shape and style of the event, and vice versa, and may or may not require additional development to make it ready to welcome the guests. Many professional event coordinators prefer to select the site prior to establishing a theme in order to capitalize on the intrinsic features of the venue or destination.

An event site is an environment that includes physical surroundings, atmosphere, facilities, activities, and the people in attendance. To elicit inspiration, the professional event coordinator needs to "feel the place"

Figure 3-1
Silvers Hierarchy of Site Selection

by experiencing the venue. A hotel brochure is no substitute for the inspirational act of physical immersion, such as experienced by a floral designer in a visit to a flower wholesaler or a chef at a farmer's market. The manner in which the space is used can help to control movement, direct attention, enhance interactions, and facilitate the smooth progress of individuals within and through it, as well as the progression through the event experience.

ESTABLISH EVENT SPECIFICATIONS

Selection starts with the needs assessment, which will identify the requirements of the event host or client, the needs and desires of the audience or attendees, and the specifications associated with the event elements. The results of the assessment, which are used to create the event profile or prospectus, include the event objectives (why), attendee expectations (who), event format and scope (what), physical requirements (where), and dates and schedules (when).

The professional event coordinator often has many different options; however, a site evaluation may be conducted, rather than a selection, if only one site is possible or preselected. Several factors affect the search for potential sites or venues that can accommodate the event profile.

- **Availability**—date(s) and duration, including move-in and move-out requirements, and acceptable service levels
- **Location**—accessibility by air and ground transportation, proximity to other attractions, and the surrounding environment
- **Rates**—rental fees, costs for site development, food and beverage prices, and surcharges
- **Attendance**—occupancy capacity, anticipated behaviors, arrival and departure modes, and ancillary activities before, during, and after the event
- **Function type**—educational, spectator, ceremonial, social, political, etc.
- **Event elements**—room dimensions, spatial requirements, activities, access logistics, storage, and administrative functions
- **Style or personality**—conservative, adventurous, youthful, mature, rustic, luxurious, unique, traditional, theme-specific, etc.

DEVELOP SELECTION CRITERIA

Site selection focuses on the area, atmosphere, and attraction of the potential site or venue. Selection criteria include location, cost, space, facilities, and personnel. The professional event coordinator works with the client or event organization to establish the prioritized criteria for each event.

Location

For many association and corporate meetings, the destination or site may be affected by internal policies, such as mandated regional rotation of annual meetings or the requirement that there be a host chapter. Other conference, business, or event tourism factors are marketing-driven, such as the attractiveness of and attractions available at a destination. Local attractions include cultural sites, museums, restaurants, shopping, recreation, theaters, and festivals or other events. A local convention and visitors bureau or tourism authority should be able to provide a list of coinciding events, attractions, and activities that may enhance the overall event. Environmental factors include weather, scenic beauty, convenience, economic health, community spirit, and the friendliness of the local people.

Numerous studies have shown that the number one criterion in selecting a destination, for both tourism and events, is safety. A survey conducted by the Travel Industry Association of America showed that nearly 44 percent of the respondents believed that safety was the main concern among international travelers to the United States (http://www.tia.org/tiaweb/ivis/oldivis/pollresults.asp). Peter Tarlow, author of *Event Risk Management and Safety*, notes that site selection is both a marketing issue and a risk-management issue, as "people now use safety and security as one of the reasons for choosing a particular site." Therefore, the area surrounding an event site should be evaluated based on safety and security conditions in addition to its physical appeal. Political unrest, crime-ridden areas, extensive roadway construction, or other potentially hazardous conditions must be evaluated carefully. These do not necessarily prevent a site from being considered, but additional precautions may need to be implemented to make it feasible.

The proximity and accessibility of the location may be important to the event, including such considerations as the distance to the airport, routes and access to adjacent parking areas, routes and access to public transportation (trains, buses, subways, etc.), and even access to the event grounds. When producing an off-premise conference event in an air and space museum on a military base, I had to provide a complete guest list to the facility 30 days prior to the event in order to be issued a security clearance allowing the guests on base.

Cost

The cost criteria include not only the rates to rent a facility, but the costs of getting and staying there for the attendees. Hotel room rates, travel distance and transportation costs, parking fees, and numerous other expenses will affect the desirability of an event site or destination. The amount of site development or improvement will also have a budgetary impact. The facility or site may be beautiful and capable of accommodating the event's guests and activities, but there may be insufficient parking areas, unsuitable toilet facilities (in regard to quantity, quality, or ADA accessibility), or inadequate kitchens or food preparation areas. Such conditions can necessitate securing additional equipment and services to bring the site up to your standards.

When negotiating for space with a hotel, the professional event coordinator must understand that hotels make their profit on the sleeping rooms. Therefore, the rental rates for function space that is not linked to room nights will obviously be higher than for space that is. In Europe function space is often not found in hotels, and if it is, it may not be linked with sleeping room revenues at all. In negotiating for exclusive use of a restaurant, the projected income from the event will be weighed against the lost business from regular restaurant patrons. When considering use of a property open to the public, such as a museum or historical site, note that the setup time may be restricted to a period after the facility closes to the public, and this can entail additional installation labor to ensure that the event is ready on time.

Space

Spatial considerations include the dimensional requirements for both the people and the equipment necessary to produce the event, as well as a variety of proximity issues. I once presented a to-scale floor plan to a client hosting a company party for 6000, and when she saw how much remaining floor space there was on the drawing, she wanted to add more space-eating activities. I quickly prepared a floor plan that included an illustration of the amount of space 100 people would use, and the client finally understood that we had already reached our capacity. Depending on the type and scope of the event you are coordinating, you may need sleeping rooms, function rooms, administrative space, storage space, exhibit space, hospitality suites, staff and volunteer lounges, green rooms, dressing rooms, media lounges, and numerous other types of space.

There may be allied groups that want or need to convene in tandem with your event, such as for leadership meetings prior to an annual conference, hospitality functions conducted by sponsors during the event, or leisure or recreational activities after the event. Such an activity must be considered, either as a mandated inclusion in the scope of the overall event or as a feature that increases the value of the event. Some organizations exercise strict control over these ancillary activities; for instance, there may be a policy that hospitality suites may be booked only with prior approval of the sponsoring organization to control ambush-marketing tactics of companies that are not sponsors or exhibitors.

Facilities

The features and attributes of an event site include appearance, furnishings, equipment, and amenities. Every site or venue has particular capabilities and constraints. The professional event coordinator should consider the public areas (including the grounds), the décor, the equipment, services available, cleanliness, and congested areas. Other physical considerations include elevators (particularly freight elevators), kitchen facilities, public toilet facilities, recreational facilities, loading docks and storage facilities, safety and security features, plus electrical and heating, ventilation, and air-conditioning (HVAC) capabilities.

You may also have to confirm the technological abilities of a venue or site. Depending on the event elements, you may need a certain infrastructure and services such as fiber-optic cables, analog and digital communications lines, wireless communications capability, Internet access or intranet capability, closed-circuit television, electronic marquee messaging, satellite uplink and downlink capability, and closed-circuit digital recording security systems. Be sure to check the security cameras at a facility you are considering; they may not be functional or monitored by anyone. You may be able to overcome potential problems by bringing in equipment and/or outside services that will meet your standards.

Personnel

Many professional event coordinators consider the personnel and level of service at a facility as important as the physical property itself. Service personnel in purpose-built facilities may include a general manager, convention services manager, account representative or event supervisor; chef and banquet staff; banquet setup manager; janitorial or housekeeping, security, and engineering staff; and recommended or exclusive vendors. Excellent service can overcome many weaknesses of a facility, just as poor service can destroy the value of an excellent venue.

When faced with a list of exclusive, certified, or recommended vendors that you must use, understand that these vendors often have extensive experience in the particular venue and can disclose hidden limitations and obscure opportunities. These vendors must often adhere to a specific set of facility regulations, and sometimes they must pay the facility a fee or commission on sales. At some venues, you may negotiate the ability to use an outside vendor or provider; however, this may incur a commission fee to the exclusive or in-house provider.

UNIQUE VENUES—BECOME A LOCATION SCOUT

According to survey results in the *Event Solutions 2002 Fact Book,* the top three types of sites where events are held in the United States are (1) a hotel or resort property, (2) a convention center, and (3) a tent. These are followed closely by outdoor venues without a tent, corporate facilities, and private residences. Certified Fund Raising Executive James S. Armstrong, author of *Planning Special Events,* notes, "Attendance may benefit from the magnetic power of a unique and exclusive locale" and recommends "locations that not just anyone could rent or access."

When looking for a unique venue, you must be like a location scout for a film, viewing virtually any space or place as a potential event venue. Some professional event coordinators simply knock on the door of a property that looks promising and start talking. Unusual space within a purpose-built facility might be the unique venue you have been looking for, such as an area that has not been used for events before, or a traditional space you might develop in a new way. Note, too, that a tent or marquee may be set up almost anywhere, either as a stand-alone venue or as extra space to increase the capacity of an existing site.

On-Site Insight

Ralph Traxler, CSEP, president and senior designer of RTx inc., an event design and production firm with offices in Atlanta and the United Kingdom, shares his experience with using unique venues for events:

The commercial real estate industry exploded in the mid 1980s in Atlanta. Several high-rise buildings were planning on having grand opening events on the top floor. As it developed, the floors were not leased and the developers continued to hold special events such as New Year's Eve parties. The most unique event I staged was a concert with Smokey Robinson. The room was shaped like a square donut, with restrooms, utilities, and elevators in the middle of the room. The ceilings were only 11 ft high. The stage was placed in one corner of the building, so Smokey literally had two audiences wrapping around the building's 50th floor. We installed extensive lighting and audio for Smokey as per his rider. We designed the room for 50 rounds of eight for dinner guests and lighted the room carefully so that the reflections were not a problem and guests could see out of the windows that wrapped the entire room.

Indianapolis hosted the NCAA men's Final Four basketball tournament in 1997, and a special event for a corporate sponsor was planned for a rooftop ballroom of a historic downtown theater. No freight elevators were available. The only way to get the equipment up to the ballroom was to transfer the equip-

ment from a trailer to a van and then bring it up to the parking deck adjacent to the ballroom. The theme included a jungle and Moroccan desert set for a takeoff of Indiana Jones. *Trees as tall as 25 ft tall and two live camels were brought in for décor and atmosphere. The camels were walked up four levels of the parking garage.*

A unique venue should be carefully examined to determine its capabilities and challenges. You should be looking at accessibility for the vendors providing the goods and services for the event, as well as accessibility for the guests, workable space for preparations and event activities, power and parking capabilities, safety and sanitation issues, and, of course, protection of the property and property rights of the venue as well as of its neighbors—for example, in regard to noise, light, and other forms of disturbance or pollution. (A historic conference center, now surrounded by a quiet rural neighborhood, was prohibited from hosting any social functions whatsoever because neighbors had had too many incidents of drunken guests wandering onto their properties and befouling the bushes.)

Do not let the potential logistical challenges posed by a unique venue deter you from considering it as a site for your event. Depending on the type and scope of the event, the unusual can be the difference between a rewarding or routine event experience. Talk with your colleagues, suppliers, industry organizations, local convention and visitor bureaus or destination management companies (DMC), tourism authorities, friends, and relatives, and search the Internet for creative alternatives such as those listed in Figure 3-2.

On-Site Insight

David DeLoach, event manager for the Magic Kingdom Park at Walt Disney World in Lake Buena Vista, Florida, shares his insight on site selection from the venue's point of view. "We want the event to be successful even more than the client does, because if it isn't a perfect experience, it tarnishes the Disney reputation." David and his 15-person production team know that the park ticket is what it is all about—when they create a memory with a legacy for a special event, it will bring the event guests back with their families as park guests.

(Continued)

Abbeys	Clubhouses	Halls of Fame
Airplanes	Coliseums	Haunted Houses
Airport Hangars	Colleges	Health Clubs
Amphitheatres	Community Colleges	Historic Homes
Amusement Parks	Community Rooms	Historic Landmarks
Aquariums	Concert Halls	Historic Neighborhoods
Arboretums	Conference Centers	Industrial Lofts
Archaeological Sites	Conservatories	Inns
Arenas	Corporate Dining Rooms	Islands
Armories	Country Clubs	Laboratories
Artists' Studios	Courthouses	Labyrinths
Atriums	Courtrooms	Lagoons
Auditoriums	Courtyards	Lakes
Aviaries	Coves	Libraries
Ballparks	Cruise Ships	Lighthouses
Bandshells	Cruise Terminals	Living Museums
Banqueting Halls	Cultural Centers/Parks	Manor Houses
Barns	Dance Halls	Mansions
Beach Clubs	Depots	Marinas
Beaches	Deserts	Markets
Bed-and-Breakfasts	Empty Buildings/Floors	Masonic Temples
Botanical Parks	Entertainment Centers	Military Bases
Boutiques	Equestrian Centers	Mines
Bowling Alleys	Estates	Monasteries
Breweries	Factories	Monuments/Memorials/
Bridges	Fairgrounds	Shrines
Building Lobbies	Farms	Movie Sets
Cafeterias	Ferries	Mountaintops
Campgrounds	Festival Grounds	Museums
Camps	Fisheries	Music Halls
Campuses	Forests	National Parks
Canyons	Forts	Nightclubs
Carriage Houses	Fraternal Lodges	Observation Lounges
Casinos	Galleries	Observatories
Castles	Game/Nature Preserves	Office Buildings
Caves/Caverns	Garages	Open Fields
Celebrity Homes	Gardens	Opera Houses
Cellars	Ghost Towns	Orchards
Chateaus	Golf Courses	Palaces
Churches/Synagogues	Government Buildings	Parks
Cinemas	Guest/Dude Ranches	Parking Lots/Structures
Civic Squares	Guesthouses	Pastures
City Streets	Gymnasiums	Pavilions

Figure 3-2
Alternative Venue Possibilities

Performing Arts Centers	Roller/Ice Rinks	Tennis Courts
Picnic Areas	Rooftops	Theaters
Piers	Sailing Vessels	Theater Stages
Planetariums	Scenic Outlooks	Theme Parks
Plantations	Schools	Tourist Sites
Playgrounds	Science Centers	Town Halls
Plazas	Sculpture Gardens	Trading Floors
Pools and Patios	Seminaries	Trails
Private Clubs	Shopping Malls	Training Centers
Private Homes	Ski Lodges	Universities
Public Buildings	Skyboxes	Village Greens
Pump Houses	Speedways	Villas
Racetracks	Sports Domes	Volcanoes
Railway Cars	Sports Fields	Warehouses
Railway Stations	Sports Team Training Camps	Waterfalls
Ranches	Stables	Water Parks
Recording Studios	Stadium Clubs	Wharves
Restaurants	Stadiums	Wildlife Refuges/Sanctuaries
Retail Stores	Stockyards	Wineries
Retreats	Storefronts	Yachts
Riverboats	Symphony Halls	Zoos
River Walks	Taverns	
Rodeo Grounds	Television Studios	

Figure 3-2
(Continued)

David handles up to 500 events per year and has accommodated groups of as many as 18,500 people. Depending on the time of year, his team can set up a party in less than 90 minutes after the park's closing time. Because of Florida's unpredictable weather, he always builds an event with a rain plan in mind. David notes that his only real problem arises when clients have "ballroom expectations." A theme park is not a ballroom—there is no back hall, storage areas can be quite a distance away, and there is a definite limit on installation capabilities. "We will often start setup prior to closing, but we will not disturb the park customer."

The Magic Kingdom Park is available for special events only for the local social market, groups staying at a Disney hotel property, or groups using the Orange County Convention Center.

When approaching a new venue to schedule an event, particularly if events have not been held at that location before, the professional event coordinator should explain the project—describing the purpose of the event, the program and activities, and the type of guests attending. He or she must always respect the venue's concerns regarding damage, security, structural or environmental impact, and the loss of privacy, and do whatever it takes to address and alleviate these concerns. This may require special insurance, moving furnishings into a storage facility, protecting or replacing vegetation, providing security personnel, blocking off streets or changing traffic routes (which must be coordinated with the local transportation authority), or even making a substantial donation to the facility's foundation or its owner's favorite charity.

Technology Tip

Finding distinctive venues in another country begins with a click—searching the Internet with a search engine or discovering links through the tourism authority of the country or destination.

- The European Castle Group can provide information on fortresses, castles, and old monasteries (www.european-castle.com).
- Austria and Switzerland offer the possibility of renting an entire village (www.rentavillage.com, www.destinationaustria.at).
- The Icehotel in Sweden (www.icehotel.com) and the Igloo Village Hotel in Greenland (www.greenland-guide.dk/gt/visit/events-05.htm) offer the "coolest" accommodations in the world, and historical elegance can be found on the Venice Simplon-Orient-Express (www.orient-expresstrains.com).
- For other venues around the world, check out the Meeting Venues Web site (www.venues-on-the-web.com), Conworld.net (www.conworld.net), or Worldwide Conference Cities (www.worlddmc.com).

STRUCTURAL AND ENVIRONMENTAL IMPACT

The professional event coordinator must carefully consider the potential structural or environmental impact of the event elements on the event site. If a new automobile or piece of heavy farm equipment is to be showcased, the floor load limit will have to be verified with the venue management or engineer. The surface of the floor may be tile, which may be damaged by heavy equipment rolling over it. There may be a need for rigging points in a ceiling for installing décor or lighting, and these rigging points may have specific weight tolerances.

Many, if not most, facilities will restrict attaching or taping anything to the walls in order to reduce maintenance costs. Even a quickly drawn meeting sign taped to a door may damage the paint or wood when pulled off. A certain décor company was presented with a hefty bill for replacing the carpet of an entire meeting space when a careless employee did some quick touch-up on the props with a can of spray paint. Another company had to foot the bill for having a hand-painted floor redone because the carpet tape used to install a red-carpet entry lifted chunks of paint when removed.

Outdoor sites should be considered in terms of the impact on the surrounding grounds, vegetation, and ecosystem. Waste management is discussed further in Chapter 5; other environmental impacts include light and sound pollution, equipment access and installation (damaging vegetation, disturbing fauna), and the effect of hundreds, even thousands of people trampling on the grass or ground. You may need to plan for turf replacement, tree trimming, surface grading, or, as shown in the film *Pretty Woman,* making divot replacement at a polo match part of the event activities.

SITE INSPECTION STRATEGIES

Site inspections should be conducted to confirm the best fit. Unless it is completely impossible, the professional event coordinator should personally examine a site prior to signing a contract. Glossy brochures, Web sites, and other marketing materials are designed to show a property in its best light. In addition, capacities and dimensions listed in a brochure may be misleading. The capacities will be based on the maximum occupancy allowed by local code, but if all those space eaters such as a dance floor, stage, or rear screen projection are added in, the maximum number quickly shrinks. And although the dimensions may be accurate, there may be obstructions that could encumber your design possibilities. The ceiling height in one brochure referred to the uppermost point in a ballroom for which I was designing a screen surround; however, the tracks for the air wall were 12 in. lower. This had a significant effect on the size of the prop that would be custom-made for this event.

You should come prepared to view every part of the venue that might have an impact on the ability to produce your event, using a site inspection checklist designed to allow you to rate and evaluate the selection criteria and specifications important to the event (see Appendix 4). There is no one perfect site inspection checklist appropriate for all events; you must customize a list for each event, based on the requirements of that event.

Many event professionals suggest that site inspection visits should be conducted at approximately the same time of year that the event is to take place so as to get an accurate judgment of the conditions for the actual event. Others suggest "secret shopping"—arriving at the property unannounced and as a regular guest. This allows you to view the property as your guests or attendees would and experience the actual services provided by the property. You should also search for hidden problems, such as zoning restrictions and union requirements, which could affect your ability to produce the event as designed or increase the costs for doing so.

Designing the Site Plan

Once a site has been selected and contracted for, you must determine how best to allocate the space. Space, like time, is finite. You cannot simply pretend that tables and chairs are smaller than they actually are, or that there is a door where there is none, or that a doorway is wider than it is. The site begins either as a blank canvas on which you can "paint" the event elements, or a puzzle requiring you to fit the pieces together. You must consider placement, proximity, and accessibility, and position the activities, equipment, and service areas according to the needs of the event and the constraints of the space. Your site plan must also include the logistics of setting up, servicing, and clearing the event site.

IDENTIFY SPATIAL REQUIREMENTS

The professional event coordinator must incorporate into the site plan the spatial requirements of all the equipment and elements needed, including both the "footprint" (the actual space on the floor or ground) and the area required around a particular piece of equipment or event activity. For example, a double-sided buffet station may be 8 ft long by 30 in. wide; however, the space required around it may indicate blocking out a space 14 ft by 10 ft to allow for guests and service personnel. This is why there may appear to be lots of floor space available on a floor plan and why people are tempted to squeeze more into the plan.

Virtually any element of an event will require space, from arrival to departure of the attendees and guests, participants and performers, and the vendors and volunteers. You must consider each of these individuals and their needs and expectations when designing the site plan. Review the items in Figure 3-3 to create a checklist of what should be included when developing the site or floor plan for your particular event.

❏ Administrative Areas
❏ Air Walls
❏ Aisles
❏ All Exits
❏ Audiovisual Equipment
❏ Barricades/Ropes and Stanchions
❏ Busing Stations
❏ Carpet
❏ Catering Areas/Kitchens
❏ Closets and Coatrooms
❏ Command Center
❏ Dance Floor
❏ Décor Elements, Props and Drops
❏ Electrical Outlets
❏ Emergency Access
❏ Entertainment and Equipment
❏ Environmental Controls (HVAC)
❏ Equipment—Miscellaneous
❏ Exhibits and Exhibitors
❏ First Aid and Medical Services
❏ Food and Beverage Stations/Concessions
❏ Fountains and Floral Displays
❏ Furnishings
❏ Games and/or Rides
❏ Green Room/Dressing Rooms
❏ Hallways and Pathways
❏ Hazards (bodies of water, etc.)
❏ Hospitality Areas
❏ Information Station
❏ Lighting (house and decorative)
❏ Loading Dock or Area
❏ Lost and Found (incl. "Lost Parents")
❏ Main Entrance

❏ Media Areas or Lounges
❏ Obstructions (pillars, posts, chandeliers)
❏ Parking Areas and Designations
❏ Participant Lounges/Facilities
❏ Pipe and Drape
❏ Platforms and Risers
❏ Power Outlets/Generators
❏ Prep Areas
❏ Registration/Admissions Areas
❏ Rigging Points
❏ Roads and Routes
❏ Seating
❏ Security Areas
❏ Sound Equipment
❏ Special Effects
❏ Staff/Volunteer Lounges
❏ Stages and Backstage Areas
❏ Staging/Marshaling Areas
❏ Stairs
❏ Storage Areas
❏ Tables
❏ Tech Booth
❏ Telephones
❏ Tents and Marquees
❏ Ticket Booths/Tables
❏ Toilet Facilities
❏ Utility Lines/Connections (power drops)
❏ Vegetation (permanent or potted)
❏ Vehicle Drop-Off Zone
❏ Vendor or Service Access
❏ Waste Control
❏ Water Outlets
❏ Windows

Figure 3-3
Site or Floor Plan Elements

UNDERSTAND PROXIMITY ISSUES

Certain elements must be next to certain other elements, and some elements should not be next to other particular elements. Safety and sanitation issues must be carefully considered: the juxtaposition of food service areas and toilet facilities; slip and trip hazards posed by cords, cables, wires, hoses, lines, and connections associated with power or water; and ventilation or container security requirements for petrol, propane, natural or other gases used for cooking, heating, filling balloons, or portable generators.

The professional event coordinator must also anticipate potential areas of congestion. Retail anthropologists have found that as people enter a shopping mall or retail establishment, they slow down to get a navigational scan and orient themselves to the new environment. This movement pattern indicates that the entrance to an event or event site should be spacious and uncluttered. Food stations and bars should be readily visible, but never positioned directly adjacent to the entrance. However, information stands or concierge tables should be near an entrance.

All the logistical requirements of the production and servicing of the event must be scrutinized from the perspective of proximities as well. Catering tents or kitchens may have to be a specific distance from the function space, or holding and preparation areas provided adjacent to the room. Exhibitor parking for an outdoor craft fair may have to be contiguous with the exhibit stalls, or you may find craftspeople parking their vehicles on the grass next to their stalls so they can quickly replenish stock.

STORAGE CONSIDERATIONS

Storage areas and facilities must be identified and positioned to ensure a clean, sanitary, and attractive event space. Items requiring storage may include equipment, excess inventory, materials and supplies, packing cases, and personal items. You may need to provide storage rooms that can be locked to protect valuable equipment or personal items. You might include storage areas that are masked with pipe and drape for excess inventory or packing cases. You might select furnishings, such as registration counters, with shelves underneath for administrative supplies. You may determine that packing cases should be stored in a delivery van next to the event site. There will be numerous spaces within a floor plan that are usable for storage because they are behind, below, or beside an event element, but they must be accessible as required and protected from unauthorized access.

ACCURATE DIAGRAMS CRITICAL TO SUCCESS

An accurate diagram of the event space is crucial to the planning and production of the event, as well as for securing approvals and permits from a fire marshal or municipal authorities. The diagram should include all the features and constraints of the site, such as doors, windows, electrical outlets, and posts or pillars within a function room, or the buildings, roads, and vegetation at an outdoor site. A site or floor plan is a map of where everything included in the event will be placed, and as a map, it should always indicate the scale and the universal reference direction, north.

This diagram may be created by computer, using simple graphics software or sophisticated computer-aided design (CAD) programs, hand-drawn on graph paper, or created by a graphic designer. Many décor companies have measured and drafted accurate site plans for the venues in which they work, and you may wish to work with them to create a floor plan diagram for your event. Hotels and convention centers may have this CAD capability as well, but many rely on their vendors, either decorators or in-house audiovisual providers, to provide floor plans for an event.

Granted, there are plenty of planners and venue personnel who work from a sketch on a notepad or paper napkin, but the professional event coordinator uses an accurate, to-scale diagram not only to plan and control efficient operations, but also to communicate his or her abilities and professionalism to the client, venue management, and regulatory officials (see Figures 3-4 and 3-5). Accurate and detailed site and floor plans become exponentially critical as the size and scope of an event increases.

VERIFICATION, VIABILITY, AND VERSATILITY

According to William O'Toole, designer of *The Event Project Management System*, the site plan or floor plan is a "cartographic communication" tool. It illustrates the use of the space to clients, vendors, staff, participants, and authorities. It is a valuable planning tool in determining the usage of the site and verifying the viability of the logistics. Therefore, a draft of the diagram should be circulated to key stakeholders for their review and recommendations. Once any necessary revisions have been made, the final draft should be distributed to all those who will use it to create, fabricate, assemble, deliver, install, operate, replenish, and remove the goods and services associated with the event production. You must still be prepared, however, for last-minute changes on-site at the time of the event.

It may be appropriate to create several versions of the diagram. Not everyone needs to know where absolutely everything will be on-site. For example, the storage area for expensive equipment or materials should not be identified to anyone except those requiring access. O'Toole suggests, "It may be preferable to have a master map and a number of derivative maps—one for the suppliers, one for the public, and another for use on the Web . . . so that attendees and suppliers may familiarize themselves with the layout. A number of outdoor events use an aerial map as a basis for this."

The site or floor plan may also be used in a variety of marketing functions, such an enlarged floor plan used as a seating chart or a map in a

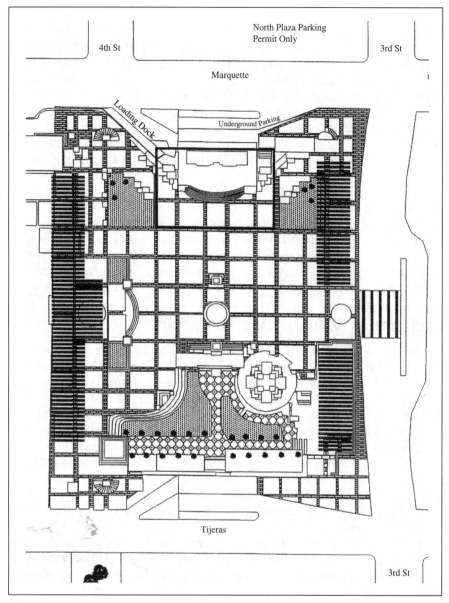

Figure 3-4
Architectural Rendering of Albuquerque Civic Plaza Used to Create Site
Plan Diagram. *Courtesy of The FMSM Design Group, Inc.*

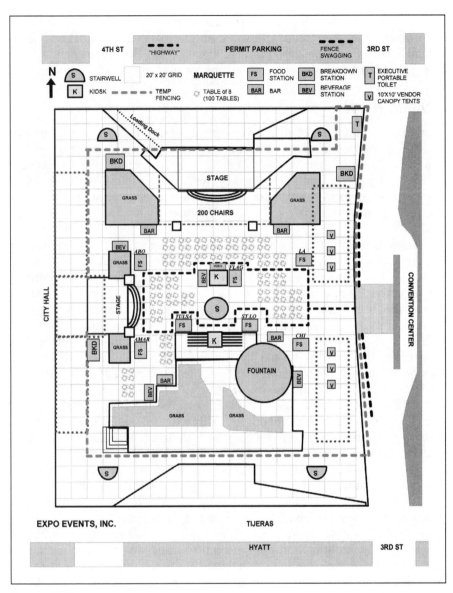

Figure 3-5

Site Plan Diagram for Event on Albuquerque Civic Plaza Devised from Architectural Rendering. *Courtesy of Expo Events, Inc.*

festival program showing where entertainment and food concessions are. You might use a version of the site map to create "You Are Here" directional signs at an extensive outdoor event or the floor plan printed in a program for a trade show listing all the exhibitors.

TRAFFIC FLOW

Designing a site plan also involves the direction and control of human and vehicular traffic flow—the movement to, through, around, within, and away from the event site. There must be sufficient space allotted to allow access, egress, and easy passage within the event. Traffic flow considerations include safety and security, crowd control, arrival and departure modes, queuing patterns, deliveries, and loading/unloading needs.

Human traffic flow may be managed through the use of barricades, fencing, or rope and stanchions to help direct and control the flow entering or departing the event or at activities within the event. Positioning of activities or event elements may help reduce congestion in certain areas and build traffic in others, such as positioning concessions or demonstrations in the least accessible areas of a trade show to increase traffic to those exhibitors. The position of an event element or activity may affect the profit potential for the organizer; trade show space is often priced based on proximity to the entrance or whether it is end-of-aisle space, center island space, or other desirable space.

The layout can also affect service flow. The tables at a large banquet function should be set in quadrants, with wider aisles between the quadrants to facilitate efficient serving and clearing. Popular activities or entertainment should be allocated additional space for queues, and to prevent them from obstructing access to service areas. Special routes should be established for deliveries and maintenance activities.

The professional event coordinator should become familiar with queuing theories (the mathematical principles of moving people or objects through queues and portals) in order to manage the use of space appropriately. Long registration and buffet lines are often the most frustrating to the event attendee. A snaking line, established with a rope and stanchions, may be used, or the number of portals or buffets may be increased. The cultural implications should also be considered—some societies naturally form queues, whereas others do not. The start of a queue should be obvious and should not obstruct other event activities.

Vehicular traffic considerations include zones for passenger drop-off and pickup, taxis or motor coaches, loading and unloading materials, service vehicles used to replenish supplies, and the vehicular traffic that normally surrounds an event site. You must exercise great care whenever pedestrians and vehicles are likely to occupy the same space, particularly in urban settings. Even crossing the street should be a factor in your site plan.

You may need to establish staging or marshaling areas where people and/or equipment may gather or line up prior to the start of the event. For a parade, there may be hundreds of people in marching bands, elaborate floats, equestrian groups, motorcycle clubs, and dignitaries in all sorts of vehicles, which must all be assembled and sent off in order. For sports events, there may be opening and closing ceremonies, including a parade of athletes and numerous entertainers or entertainment features. For large exhibitions, there may be a fleet of large trucks, with their drivers checking in and waiting for further instructions before delivering freight to an exhibit hall.

THINKING OUTSIDE THE BOX

When designing the layout of the event, the professional event coordinator should endeavor to merge the spatial needs and traffic flow with a creative approach to the use of the space. Particularly in unique or unusual spaces, you may need to devise unconventional configurations and space usage. Unique dining table shapes may be created using serpentine or half-moon tables. Video screens may be used to broadcast the entertainment into various rooms or to various floors. Nooks and crannies may be draped to block off bussing or prep areas for the caterer. The main stage may be hidden by a balloon wall that will explode when the speeches are over and the dancing is to begin.

Constantly exercise your creativity by viewing a space with a fresh perspective, even a space that has "always been set this way." Unless you are in a facility with fixed seating, there are dozens of ways you can configure the chairs and tables to create an out-of-the-ordinary meeting environment, dining environment, or entertainment environment. Risers may be used to provide different levels for tables. Décor and draping may be used to reshape a room. Tents may be used to extend the indoors outdoors. Hallways can become entertainment areas, and driveways can become dining areas. It is all up to you and your ability to see things in a fresh and creative manner.

Accessibility Issues

The event and its site must be accessible to all those invited to attend (guests, delegates, attendees, and/or audience), those required to attend (staff and suppliers), and those expected to attend (participants, performers, and volunteers). It must accommodate people with special needs, sometimes by providing special services, often by ensuring that all obstructions or barriers are minimized or eliminated. Consideration must be given to disabilities such as mobility or dexterity limitations, hearing or sight impairments, and language or literacy limitations (in regard to those who speak a different language or cannot read), as well as to the accommodations each disabled person requires to fully function within the event or environment, (e.g., wheelchairs or mechanical devices, service animals, and assistants or companions). The professional event coordinator must ensure that the event and the site are "user-friendly."

The event and the event site must have sufficient and appropriate ingress, egress, and access not only for the audience, but for the production personnel and equipment as well. Celebrity guests or dignitaries may require special entrances and exits. Media personnel may or may not be provided with access to guests, celebrities, VIPs, or participants (but if the event is news, you can be assured the media *will be there* and angling for access). Preferential entrances and seating may be required for physically challenged individuals, participants, or patrons. Exclusive access to specific areas may be required for vendors or volunteers, and special training may be required for staff or service personnel.

ADA COMPLIANCE

In 1990, the U.S. Americans with Disabilities Act (ADA) was signed into law. The ADA guarantees equal opportunity for individuals with disabilities in public accommodations, employment, transportation, state and local government services, and telecommunications. The law applies to persons who have impairments that substantially limit major life activities such as seeing, hearing, speaking, walking, breathing, performing manual tasks, learning, caring for oneself, and working.

Compliance with the ADA can affect the professional event coordinator in a number of ways, primarily in site selection and development and the provision of auxiliary aids. The ADA covers public accommodations (i.e., private entities that own, operate, lease, or lease to places of public accommodation), commercial facilities, and private entities that offer certain examinations and courses related to educational and occupational certification. This means that both the facility and the entity sponsoring an event at the facility are responsible for compliance. The event coordinator should ensure that the site selected is architecturally compliant and that the program is communications compliant.

Auxiliary aids to ensure effective communication with individuals with hearing, vision, or speech impairments may include such services or devices as qualified interpreters, assistive listening headsets, television captioning and decoders, telecommunications devices for deaf persons (TDD), videotext displays, readers, taped texts, brailled materials, and large-print materials. Barrier-free building and site elements may include parking, loading zones, accessible routes, ramps, stairs, elevators, doors, thresholds, drinking fountains, bathrooms, controls and operating mechanisms, storage areas, seating and tables, and assembly areas. Visual alarms, visual notification devices, signage, TDD and volume-control telephones, and assisted evacuation areas may also be required. Whether required by law or not, failure to consider and make arrangements for those with ambulatory, auditory, mental, literacy, visual, or other special needs is discrimination by neglect.

SENSE AND SENSITIVITY

Accommodating special needs requires common sense and general sensitivity to the issues surrounding a special need. The best person to help you determine what form an accommodation should take is the person with the special need. Understand that special needs may not be exclusively disability-related. You may receive special requests from the very short, the very tall, or the very large. You should ask for special needs requests and accommodate them in a nondiscriminatory manner.

When planning to accommodate the special needs identified by individuals, make certain that such needs are integrated throughout the event plan, such as by letting speakers or exhibitors know that special handouts will be required, or letting the audiovisual team know that a sign language interpreter will be onstage so they can make certain the interpreter is well lit and visible even if the lights are lowered for the program. You may have to make certain that snow has been removed from accessible parking stalls, curb cuts, building entrances, and ramps just before the start of the event. You may need to scan the environment to make certain that the path of travel from the entrance to the function room is free from obstructions (busy hotel lobbies can quickly fill with mountains of luggage at a premium check-in or checkout time).

Your staff and the venue's staff should have had some sensitivity training regarding interactions with and attitudes about individuals with special needs. You should speak directly to the individual, rather than to his or her sign language interpreter or oral translator. Your tone of voice should be the same as it would be for any other individual—persons who are hard of hearing or visually impaired should not be shouted at or talked to as if they were children. You may be asked to speak more slowly to allow lipreading or a translation to be adapted. A person in a wheelchair should not be pushed unless that person so requests. The staff should *never* be found making jokes or disparaging remarks about a disability or deformity.

Understand, too, that you are not required to provide anything at any time. An accommodation requested may be a financial burden or simply not available. However, you must make a good faith effort to comply with ADA requirements, as well as other special needs. Such compliance starts with by adding a line item to the budget for Accessibility or ADA, followed by familiarizing yourself with the options available. For example, according to *Professional Meeting Management,* edited by Edward G. Polivka, alternate media (i.e., large print, audiotapes, computer disks) are less expensive than sign language interpreters.

You may include a deadline for requesting auxiliary service aids in your marketing materials, giving you sufficient time to arrange for the service requested. A deaf individual registering for your convention a few days before or on-site at the convention should not expect you to have a real-time captioning service provided in each session, but this has happened. The more you know about your attendees, the better you will be able to serve all their needs. For more information about the Americans with Disabilities Act, visit the U.S. Department of Justice Web site (www.usdoj.gov/crt/ada/adahom1.htm).

LOOK AT THE LOGISTICS

Accessibility issues have logistical implications, and this does not apply exclusively to accommodating persons with disabilities. Logistics is the system of applying of the principles of logic and reasoning. In its original milieu logistics was the military science of procurement, distribution, and transportation of troops and matériel. The professional event coordinator must scan the event site and its environment to ensure that goods and services can be transported and delivered efficiently and effectively.

Food service logistics, from replenishing buffet stations to waste disposal, must be anticipated and mapped into the site layout. Décor and equipment may require maintenance during the event. Entertainment and entertainers may have numerous vehicles and huge crews that must move through the event site. Speakers or athletes may require special access, special areas, or special equipment delivered.

Load-in, load-out, loading docks, and loading zones must be plotted and often planned meticulously. Load-in is usually arranged with the largest items going in first, followed by the smaller ones, and load-out is usually in reverse. However, depending on the type of event, the products or vendors, and the venue, this may or may not be the case. The point is that the event and event site must be designed to provide accessibility for all those needing it—to all areas, activities, and aspects.

Permits and Permissions

The site plan or floor plan and the event itself must comply with all applicable legislation, ordinances, and other jurisdictional regulations. Not only is securing the appropriate permits and permissions a legal requirement, it is also a sound risk management practice in ensuring a successful and sustainable event and event organization. Most, if not all, of these regulations have been instituted to ensure a safe environment for and reputable services provided to attendees and personnel working at a venue or site.

It is the responsibility of the professional event coordinator to identify and secure all the necessary permits, approvals, licenses, waivers, certificates, and other compliance instruments in accordance with the type and scope of the event being produced. This may include securing certificates of insurance and copies of licenses from the vendors supplying goods and services to the event, certificates of inspection (for elevators or alarm systems) from the venue, or visas and temporary work permits if the event is being held in another country. Working in a foreign country may also involve securing agricultural permits for bringing in floral supplies, customs clearance for importing décor and supplies, and sales tax recovery (e.g., value-added tax, VAT). The event coordinator should check with local authorities, the venue management, the vendors and suppliers, and legal and financial advisors to determine the standard and customary permits and permissions required for the operations of the event.

LICENSES AND PERMITS

Depending on the size and scope of the event and where it is to take place, the professional event coordinator may need to secure permits or licenses for alcohol service, entertainment (in regard to noise levels), fireworks, food handling, gaming (bingo, lottery, or contests), music use, ocean or lake use, parades or marches, parking, public assembly, signs or banners, street closures, venue or site occupancy, waste management, and numerous other event elements and operations. The event organization may require a business license and tax identification number (national or federal and/or state or provincial).

Some municipalities allow you to secure all necessary permits from one special events office, whereas others may have numerous departments and agencies that must be contacted and worked with independently. Some permissions require forms be filled out, some require copies of site plans and other documentation, and others may require your appearance before a commission, board, or committee to verbally and visually present your event plan. The time required to secure these permissions, often related to the specific bureaucracy of the granting authority, can range from the time it takes to fill out a form and pay a fee to days or weeks to seek out and meet with the proper officials. You must factor this into your timeline.

OCCUPANCY ISSUES

Of particular importance to events are the occupancy regulations regarding fire safety, usually governed by the fire marshal or the local fire brigade/authority. In the United States, fire regulations are based on the Life Safety Code established by the National Fire Protection Association (www.nfpa.org/Home/index.asp). The purpose of the Life Safety Code is to establish minimum requirements that will provide a reasonable degree of safety from fire in buildings and structures. These regulations cover such areas as the number, visibility, and functionality of fire exits, the flammability of décor and exhibit materials, the storage and use of flammable or combustible liquids and gases, sprinkler systems and extinguisher placement, and the use of open flames or cooking devices.

Although fire prevention is paramount, the fire marshal's specific site concerns are that, should a fire occur, those inside or on-site are able to evacuate the area quickly and safely and fire-fighting equipment can access the fire. Understand that a fire in an enclosed space can become lethal in less than two minutes, primarily because of the fumes, and can spread very quickly on the ground in an open space.

The fire marshal may require a copy of the floor or site plan for review prior to the event, but may not issue the final approval until he or she conducts an on-site inspection. Fire inspections may also be conducted during the course of the event. The fire marshal may perform "field flame tests" on the décor and acoustical materials used at the event. You may be asked to install fire extinguishers or "Fire Exit" signs at certain points around the site or venue. You may be asked to move certain equipment or materials to another location. If you have a roof on an exhibit booth, it may require a sprinkler system, and if you are using a simple canopy tent to cover your sound and light control board at an outside venue, you may need a fire extinguisher within the tented area. You may even be asked to install smoke detectors under a stage.

Other occupancy issues may include the construction of bleachers or grandstands to withstand the loads imposed, floor load limits, designated smoking areas, safety of tenting materials and their installation, and, of course, evacuation routes and procedures. These are discussed further in Chapter 6, but the acquisition of the proper permits will affect and be affected by the design and layout of the site.

SAFETY AND SANITATION CODES

Safety and sanitation codes are established to protect the public from harm. These apply to the workplace, which includes an event site as well. In the United States, these workplace regulations are established and governed by the U.S. Department of Labor's Occupational Safety and Health Administration (OSHA) (www.osha-slc.gov). In addition, municipal safety and sanitation regulations may be in force. These may govern such things as temporary food service, noise levels, waste disposal, and numerous other aspects of an event.

The professional event coordinator must analyze the elements to be included in the event, discuss the implications with the providers, and determine the specific licenses and permits that are applicable. For example, special effects such as pyrotechnics require specific minimum distances between fireworks and spectators, and getting fireworks to an event site may be regulated by the Department of Transportation, which controls the transport of all "hazardous materials," including fireworks.

On-Site Insight

Robert Sivek, CSEP, CERP (Certified Event Rental Professional), chief operating officer of The Meetinghouse Companies, Inc., based in Elmhurst, Illinois, and former president of the International Special Events Society, maintains that working with public safety officials is a relationship-building process. The professional event coordinator must work *with* the inspectors or fire marshals, listen to what they say (because there is always a reason for their concern or stance), and dialogue to a solution. In one instance, Sivek was in charge of re-creating a temporary swimming pool to replicate the setting of a commercial, but no one had applied for a permit for this type of thing for more than 50 years. Consequently, all the regulations were antiquated, there were new materials being used, and the inspectors had never inspected this type of structure before. Sivek provided them with all the facts about the construction and composition of materials so that they were able to reach a satisfactory agreement and grant approval.

In another case, during the on-site inspection for a street festival, the fire marshal had two specific concerns that could have prevented the festival from opening to the public. First,

(Continued)

there was a line of cold-air inflated balloons providing the primary décor that the fire marshal wanted to eliminate because they blocked the only viable fire lane into the event site. It was agreed that the fire department had permission to "run over the balloons" if it needed to use the fire lane. Second, the fire marshal wanted the largest stage moved a couple of feet farther away from a fire hydrant. Because the stage was already installed (and next to impossible to break down, move, and reassemble in time for the event to start), it was agreed that several signs would be installed to highlight exactly where the hydrant was.

When dealing with fire marshals, inspectors, and union officials, Sivek notes that you must become a team member with them and approach the task in a positive and proactive manner. "They are trying to protect the public or their members. You will create a self-fulfilling prophecy if you go into this expecting problems."

DOCUMENTATION STRATEGIES

Keep copies of everything! This includes the various drafts of your site or floor plan, the original diagrams provided by the venue (its brochure or a printed copy from its Web site), the spatial dimensions and requirements provided by your vendors, the verifications and approvals from your vendors and authorities, ADA compliance communications, licenses, permits, waivers, approvals, certificates of insurance, and any other documentation that illustrates the decisions you made and why you made them. Some of these documents may have to be displayed on-site at the event (particularly permits or licenses, such as shown in Figure 3-6). Some will need to be accessible on-site and will be included in your Production Book. Some should be copied, and the originals stored securely in your office.

Target Competency Review

The professional event coordinator must identify potential event sites by establishing selection criteria and quantifying spatial requirements. Event sites may include purpose-built facilities, unique venues, or urban, rural, or remote open spaces. The professional event coordinator evaluates the site's capabilities and suitability to select the best fit for the event.

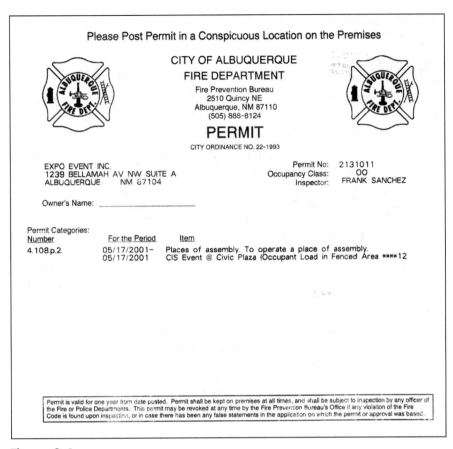

Please Post Permit in a Conspicuous Location on the Premises

CITY OF ALBUQUERQUE
FIRE DEPARTMENT
Fire Prevention Bureau
2510 Quincy NE
Albuquerque, NM 87110
(505) 888-8124

PERMIT
CITY ORDINANCE NO. 22-1993

EXPO EVENT INC.
1239 BELLAMAH AV NW SUITE A
ALBUQUERQUE   NM 87104

Permit No: 2131011
Occupancy Class: OO
Inspector: FRANK SANCHEZ

Owner's Name: _____

Permit Categories:

Number	For the Period	Item
4.108.p.2.	05/17/2001– 05/17/2001	Places of assembly. To operate a place of assembly. CIS Event @ Civic Plaza (Occupant Load in Fenced Area ****12

Permit is valid for one year from date posted. Permit shall be kept on premises at all times, and shall be subject to inspection by any officer of the Fire or Police Departments. This permit may be revoked at any time by the Fire Prevention Bureau's Office if any violation of the Fire Code is found upon inspection, or in case there has been any false statements in the application on which the permit or approval was based.

Figure 3-6
Occupancy Permit. *Courtesy of Expo Events, Inc.*

The professional event coordinator develops site plans that utilize the space appropriately to achieve the goals and objectives of the event and meet the needs of the participants and providers. This includes creating accurate diagrams for use in the planning, production, and promotion of the event.

The professional event coordinator determines the requirements and implements strategies to ensure full accessibility of the event and event site in compliance with the Americans with Disabilities Act and other special needs, including operational and logistical requirements. He or she also makes sure that the use of the event site is in compliance with all federal, state or provincial, and local legislation, health and safety ordinances, and other jurisdictional regulations, and obtains all necessary permits, licenses, and insurance coverage.

EXERCISES IN PROFESSIONAL EVENT COORDINATION

Select sites or venues within your community and create an accurate diagram site plan or floor plan for each of the following events. Be sure to identify all the event elements within the site plan.

1. You are coordinating a four-day arts and crafts fair (indoors or outdoors) that will include 200 exhibitors, three entertainment stages, 12 food and beverage concessions, a youth exhibit, a jurors' exhibit, an information booth, an official souvenir sales booth, and all the appropriate first aid and administrative locations.
2. You are coordinating an all-day outdoor "Wacky Olympics" offsite team-building event for 100 employees of a corporation, including ten track and field events, a catered luncheon under a tent, refreshments, hospitality areas for persons accompanying the attendees, and a means of displaying corporate branding images.
3. You are coordinating the awards celebration for a regional association of special event professionals, including a prefunction reception and banquet for 300, a display area for the awards entries, a silent auction area, and dancing following the awards program. Remember, these are people who have "seen everything before," and you must dazzle these jaded event-goers.

Facing Page
Public events require comprehensive admittance procedures and controls in order to welcome the thousands of guests that attend. *Photograph by RUDA Photography, courtesy of Steve Kemble Event Design.*

CHAPTER 4

Accommodating the Audience

Human action can be modified to some extent, but human nature cannot be changed.

—ABRAHAM LINCOLN (1809–1865)

IN THIS CHAPTER YOU WILL LEARN HOW TO:

- Determine and procure suitable and effective collateral materials that will support the promotional and direct sales marketing strategies of an event.
- Select and organize appropriate registration, admission control, and guest greeting systems for an event.
- Create and implement appropriate event accreditation and credentialing procedures for participants, providers, patrons, and the media.
- Develop effective and efficient seating and ushering systems to accommodate an event audience.
- Identify and coordinate attendee and VIP services and protocol requirements as appropriate.

The event coordinator was checking on the welcome desk during registration for a large employee gathering when she noticed one of her staff and a guest in what appeared to be a heated discussion. The event coordinator asked another staff member to step in and handle the guest's complaint, took the fuming registrar to the staff lounge, sat her down with a cool soft drink, and listened to her recount the unreasonable demands of the guest. Then calmly and quietly, the event coordinator said, "I completely understand your frustration; however, we have to remember we are in the hospitality industry, not the hostility industry."*

Accommodating the event audience depends on customer service, and good customer service is always measured from the customer's point of view. From the first announcement, creating anticipation, to the final departure and afterglow, the professional event coordinator has countless opportunities to create a memorable experience for every customer by considering and controlling "Moments of Truth." According to Kristin Anderson and Ron Zemke, authors of *Delivering Knock Your Socks Off Service,* "a Moment of Truth occurs anytime a customer comes in con-

---

*My thanks to Ginger Kramer for this astute and acute observation.

tact with any part of your organization and uses that contact to judge the quality of the organization." Beginning with initial communications to frontline employees, and continuing with encounters with parking attendants, janitorial staff, service providers, and product suppliers—each interaction with the event, the event team, or the event environment contributes to the event experience and signifies a potential Moment of Truth.

Whether they are called attendees, customers, delegates, festivalgoers, guests, participants, the public, spectators, or visitors, the audience for your event is the reason your event is taking place. No audience— no event. The treatment each individual receives will determine the level of success for the event, because those individual experiences add up to a collective experience that the audience either enjoys or endures. Each person in attendance is likely to interact with others, and with this interaction comes influence; a bad experience will be told and retold, which has the potential for changing another individual's perception of his or her own experience. Bad news travels fast and misery loves company.

Customer service is a critical component of Customer Relationship Marketing (CRM), which entails observing and listening to customers in order to meet their needs and expectations, as well as their perceptions of service quality (see Figure 4-1). If we do not listen to our customers (both clients and guests), we will lose them. If we do listen to and interact with them, we can learn a great deal about their needs, expectations, motives, and perceptions of service quality, which helps us refine our product (the event), our positioning, our sales and service, and our

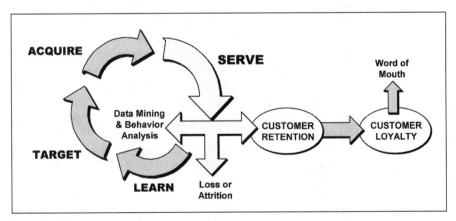

Figure 4-1
Customer Service within Customer Relationship Marketing

service consequences. With each customer interaction, whether in person, in print, or electronically, we have the opportunity to gain customer intelligence, retain that customer and create customer loyalty (which provides the incredibly valuable word-of-mouth advertising), or lose that customer through attrition or by not delivering a sufficient return on expectations.

Creating the Collateral Materials

As marketing gurus have been proclaiming for years, customer satisfaction isn't the main thing; it is the *only* thing. Thus, the professional event coordinator must view the event experience from threshold to threshold and make certain the customer's experience meets (and exceeds) his or her expectations. The critical component of this effort is to establish the appropriate expectations through effective communications and marketing materials. The type, quality, and format of the event's collateral materials will depend on the type, scope, and budget of the event (see Figure 4-2).

INTEREST, INFORM, INVEST

The purpose of an event's collateral materials is to create interest in the event and provide information about the event so that the customer will decide to invest in (attend) the event. In *Best Practices in Customer Service* (edited by Ron Zemke and John A. Woods), Terry G. Vavra and Douglas R. Pruden explain, "It has long been accepted that in making a purchase decision, consumers pass through a series of stages of varying investigation and commitment . . . a buying decision process . . . often defined by the stages of awareness, interest, desire, and action (purchase)." These stages are often described by the acronym AIDA.

The collateral materials for an event provide a medium for communication and must offer sufficient information, in an interesting format, to facilitate the purchase of and participation in the event. These materials may be advertising items, direct mail pieces, publicity materials, or amenities, and may be printed or in digital form. Although the trend is toward the Internet and e-mail for reasons of cost and speed (according to Victor T. C. Middleton, author of *Marketing in Travel and Tourism*), many professional event coordinators and marketers believe that the physical, printed item, such as a brochure or registration packet, provides the tangible evidence of the event experience purchased or to be purchased (according to Susan Briggs, author of *Successful Tourism Marketing: A Practical Handbook*).

Event Collateral	Primary Uses	Cause-Related	Corporate/Incentive	Exposition/Fair	Festival/Tourism	Government	Hallmark	Marketing	Meeting/Conference	Social	Sports
					Typical Event Genre						
Agenda	Outline content and control scope		X			X		X	X		
Brochure	Create awareness, provide information, create desire	X	X	X	X		X		X		X
Card/Letter	Personalized notification, provide information, build excitement	X	X			X		X	X	X	
Catalog	Listing event products available for sale				X		X		X		X
CD-ROM/Video	Create awareness and interest, build excitement and desire, merchandise	X	X		X		X	X			X
Coupon	Call to action, promote purchase			X	X		X	X			X
Directory	Provide contact and locator information, memento	X		X			X		X		
E-mail	Word-of-"mouse" campaign, provide information, create desire, build excitement	X	X	X	X			X	X	X	X
Flyer/Leaflet	Create awareness and provide information	X		X	X	X		X			X
Guidebook	Provide information, instructions and directions, memento				X		X				X
Internet Web Site	Provide and collect information, build excitement, facilitate participation	All events									

Figure 4-2
Typical Event Collateral Materials, Uses, and Event Genre

Event Collateral	Primary Uses	Cause-Related	Corporate/Incentive	Exposition/Fair	Festival/Tourism	Government	Hallmark	Marketing	Meeting/Conference	Social	Sports
		Typical Event Genre									
Invitation	Request attendance and/or participation	X	X	X		X		X	X	X	X
Map/ Directions	Provide navigational information and participant instructions	All events as needed									
Menu	Provide information and recognition, memento	Any event with served food and beverage									
Name Tag	Identification and credentialing		X	X	X	X	X		X		X
Notice/ Memo	Alert and provide information		X			X			X		
Poster	Create awareness and interest, provide information and recognition, merchandise	X		X	X		X				X
Program Book	Provide information and recognition, merchandise, memento	X		X	X	X	X	X	X		X
Registration Material	Collect and provide information	X	X	X	X	X	X	X	X		X
Tickets/ Passes	Authorize admission and/or assign seating	X		X	X		X	X	X		X

Figure 4-2
(Continued)

The style and quality of collateral materials will communicate certain things about the event as well. Glossy brochures may enhance the perceived value of a conference event. Hand-done calligraphy on invitations to a gala fund-raiser may communicate exclusivity and elegance. There is a possible downside as well; the glossy brochure or expensive invitation may suggest that you have spent too much money on it: "Oh, that's why the conference is so expensive" or "You're wasting money that should go to the charity's programs."

ESTABLISHING EXPECTATIONS

Steve Schwartz, director of facility operations at the Washington, D.C., Convention Center and instructor at the George Washington University Event Management Certificate Program, has suggested that people do not measure their experience at an event against their last event experience, but against their *best* event experience. A realistic approach is to establish appropriate expectations with the customer from the beginning—then overdeliver. According to consultant Michael Vandergriff in *Best Practices in Customer Service* (edited by Zemke and Woods), "If the reality of the service exceeds the expectations of the customer, then excitement or even elation can occur." Establishing service expectations and experience expectations may be accomplished through well-designed collateral materials.

Keep in mind that any and all promotional or collateral materials created for an event may be considered part of a legally enforceable contract between the event producer and the attendee. You must be able to provide what you said you would provide, at the price you said it would cost, delivered when you said it would be delivered. Do not make claims you cannot substantiate or promises you cannot keep (or do not intend to keep). If something is "subject to change"—say so. The use of disclaimers will not only protect you and your event organization from unhappy or litigious customers, it will give the customer the "truth" about what to expect and allow the customer to make an informed purchase decision.

BUILDING EXCITEMENT

Many event collateral materials are a form of promotion, meant to stimulate the potential attendee to act—to purchase the event ticket or "buy" the event concept and attend. People's decisions to buy are most often based on emotion rather than logic, and on perception rather than reality; therefore, according to Briggs, the event marketing materials should focus on the benefits of attendance (i.e., fun, status, job security) rather than its features. For example, as reported in the International Events

Group's *Banking on Leisure Transcripts: Event Marketing Seminar Series,* the blue jeans maker Levi Strauss sells apparel, but what it *markets* is comfort, fashion, endurance, fit, and quality—the benefits, real or perceived, of wearing its apparel. The professional event coordinator or marketer must target the potential customer or attendee's wants and desires, matching them to the benefits of the event experience to be had. According to the clever marketing adage, the smart approach is to "sell the sizzle." Identify the benefits or problem solutions your event will deliver and highlight them in your materials.

It usually requires numerous impressions (visual or auditory contacts) for an advertising or promotional message to interest, inform, and instigate action. This is why an integrated and multilevel approach may be necessary to create and build excitement for your event, resulting in audience attendance. Meetings and conventions often use "Save the Date" or "teaser" postcards eight to ten months before an event, followed by a brochure outlining the preliminary program four to six months out, sending the final brochure with the final program outline and list of speakers plus registration forms two to four months out, and, finally, following up with a reminder card, fax, or e-mail two to six weeks before the event. The timing, of course, depends on the timeline and type of conference; annual conventions and conferences may require a different schedule than onetime or periodic congresses or symposiums.

Incentive programs use this multitiered approach with collateral materials to continuously motivate employees throughout the duration of the program, providing encouragement and building excitement. The program may start with an informational brochure outlining the objectives, the incentive trip to be won, and what it will take to win it. This is followed by periodic messages (printed or digital) and advertising specialties to reinforce the participant's objective—to achieve the sales or productivity increase needed to win the travel reward.

Festivals and sports events usually orchestrate a public relations and promotions calendar leading up to an event, including media kits and communiqués, sponsorship solicitation materials, bill stuffers (flyers or brochures included in utility bills or bank statements), souvenir/collectable posters and programs, contests and stunts at which leaflets or coupons are distributed, and numerous other promotions. These efforts are often augmented with paid advertising close to the event to further build awareness, excitement, and urgency to purchase.

These materials and tactics must be designed and planned from the inception of the event to ensure they communicate the correct message in the correct mediums at the correct times so that they will be cost-effective and build excitement at the correct pace. As one advertising executive told me, "You have to be in front of the customer when that customer is ready to make that purchase." This integrated approach also allows the professional event coordinator or marketer to develop an integrated and cohesive "look" or style for the collateral materials to create a repetitive and cumulative impression.

THEME AND LOGO INCORPORATION

Theme development is discussed in depth in Chapter 7, but it is important here to understand that a selected theme should be visually integrated throughout the elements of an event, including the collateral materials. All collateral materials should incorporate the theme or logo of the event with a consistent style and placement. Identifying symbols, logos, or graphic representations associated with the event or an event organization are a form of "branding," projecting an image and linking the product (the event) with an easily recognizable and consistent perception of value to the consumer.

Policies governing the logo and design should be crafted to ensure the integrity of the branding images associated with an event or event organization. The professional event coordinator should create a design checklist that includes the key images and information to be included in all collateral materials (see Figure 4-3), as well as cautions and restrictions. Imagine the branding image conveyed when a local festival was ecstatic to have its logo incorporated into all the city's communications, only to find that a warning memo from the Hazardous Waste Department

Branding	Event Specifics	Content
❑ Event Organization— address, telephone, fax, e-mail, Web site ❑ Event Title ❑ Logo—placement, spacing, color restrictions ❑ PMS Color Specifications ❑ Slogans ❑ Symbols/Emblems/Insignia ❑ Trademarks, Service Marks, Copyright ❑ Typestyle—font and size	❑ Commercial Sponsor Recognition ❑ Date ❑ Deadlines ❑ Fees or Prices ❑ Location ❑ Purchase Mechanism ❑ Return Address ❑ Times—opening/closing, start times, schedule	❑ Captions for Photos ❑ Contact for Further Information ❑ Copy Points ❑ Correct Spelling— particularly for names ❑ Directions ❑ Instructions ❑ Recognition—boards, committees, patrons, etc.

Figure 4-3
Design Elements Checklist for Collateral Materials

faxed to all city employees had a large skull and crossbones linked with its festival name and logo.

The collateral you create for an event may include souvenirs such as pins, printed cups and napkins, place cards, T-shirts, and other promotional items, plus numerous forms, newsletters, business cards, or even Smart Cards (cards with a magnetic strip or chip, similar to a credit card, used in an electronic lead retrieval system). Anything associated with an event that is printed, imprinted, or digitized should have a uniform and recognizable image.

GRAPHIC DESIGN AND PRINTING BASICS

From desktop publishing to Web site design, the graphic design of an event's collateral materials encompasses the layout of words, images, and color. The type and purpose of the collateral will determine the form these communication vehicles will take. The professional event coordinator must work with the graphic designer to achieve the objectives established for each piece or format, based on the typical recipient or receiver's needs and the actions desired of the recipient.

For printed promotional materials, the distribution method may influence the design, such as for festival or event brochures in a display rack where the upper third of the cover must capture attention. Edward G. Polivka, editor of *Professional Meeting Management,* suggests that conference brochures may require testimonials to add credibility and the inclusion of teaser copy on the mailing envelope to ensure that it will be opened. For electronic promotional material, such as Websites and e-mail, the compatibility of the sender's and recipient's capabilities must be considered, including typestyle compatibility and the time required to download complex images and photographs. The core outcome desired is that the collateral must achieve its purpose, and this is accomplished by delivering the necessary information in the best visual context, using effective design techniques and compelling text.

THE PRINTING PROCESS

You must schedule the printing of your collateral materials into your timeline. Printing can take up to eight weeks or more, depending on the complexity of the job, and you should not sacrifice your ability to proof and approve each stage in the process (see Figure 4-4). Proofing is critical. Not only should you be checking for any spelling or grammatical errors early in the process, you should also be checking for consistency in style (i.e., use of capital letters, numbers, abbreviations, ambiguous wording, and complementary lists), placement and proximity, correct captions with photos, and double-checking on the spelling of names. Of course,

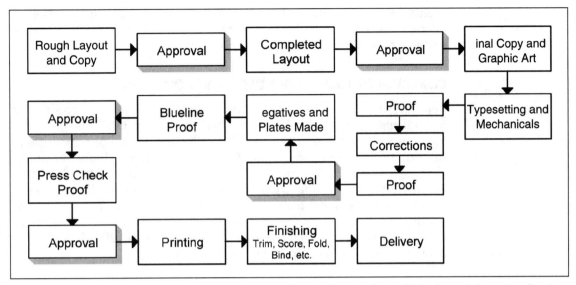

Source: *Adapted from Catherine H. Price (1999),* The Complete Guide to Professional Meeting and Event Coordination, *2nd pub. (Washington, DC: George Washington University Event Management Program, p. 269)*

Figure 4-4
The Printing Sequence

the copy you give the graphic artist or printer must start out well proofed (you pay for your mistakes; the printer pays for printer errors). As you proceed through each step in the printing process, changes become increasingly more expensive. Any changes after the blueline (the final proof copy before printing) stage may be as expensive as starting over.

CREATIVE INVITATIONS GET NOTICED

Invitation design has become an art form. For gatherings ranging from life-cycle to cause-related events, retail events to reunions, invitations are used to personally request the pleasure of an individual's company. The more creative, unusual, or outstanding the invitation, the more likely its recipient will be to consider attendance or participation. It is important to understand that even the most worthy cause or significant celebration is competing for a person's limited time. A creative and persuasive invitation helps to communicate that attendance will be well worth the time (and/or money) invested. This is where the unique, unusual, and extraordinary papers, shapes, packaging, and delivery should be considered. (Avoid any glitter, sprinkles, or other powdery substance as an enclosure.) Exceptional invitations may provide a nonprofit or retail event with a better market share than competing events, or corporate events with an innovative branding opportunity. If truly unique, the invitation may create a high profile for the event and even reap media coverage or publicity as an award-winning design.

COMMUNICATIONS TECHNOLOGY REVOLUTION

The infrastructure of the Internet and other communications and digital technologies have made electronic alternatives to printed collateral the marketing mediums of this millennium. Electronic mediums available to the event marketer now include CD-ROMs, cellular telephone/radios, chat rooms, cybercafés and kiosks, digital video disks (DVDs), digital avatars, digital camcorder video, e-mail, extranets (using the Internet to establish private global networks), the Internet, Internet-enabled cellular phones, limited area networks (LANs)—within a building, live and on-demand Webcasts, pagers, personal digital assistants (PDAs), wide area networks (WANs)—multiple sites, and Web sites.

Technology Tip

Websites are practically mandatory for most public events. An event Web site as a platform may be used as an electronic brochure, to conduct on-line registration, sell tickets and collect fees, sell souvenirs, sign up volunteers, poll delegates, conduct evaluations and marketing surveys, supply maps and directions, provide directories, recognize sponsors, issue coupons, build membership and/or mailing lists, extend the event through postevent highlights and encapsulated proceedings to increase retention, create pre- and postevent discussion forums, conduct interactive sessions with remote audiences, and to perform countless other functions yet to be discovered.

Registration

A registration system will be required for any event at which you need to collect information from the attendee or participant. The most common event genre using a registration system is the conference or convention event, but it may also be used at sports events (athletes and media), expositions (exhibitors and buyers), marketing events (familiarization tours or hospitality suites), government events (security clearances), reunion events, and numerous other gatherings. The professional event coordinator must ensure that the registration procedures and on-site logistics meet the needs of the attendee as well as the event organization.

Efficient and effective systems must be in place to handle the size and type of audience expected and the functions required. You may be conducting preregistration activities prior to the event as well as on-site registration or check-in functions. You may be collecting personal data or distributing collateral materials. You may be serving attendees from the local area or from around the world. Thus, registration is part of customer service.

FIRST IMPRESSIONS

How the registration process is managed—either prior to the event or on-site—gives a lasting first impression of the event, the event organization, and how the attendee can expect to be treated throughout the event experience. The procedure must be well organized, efficient, and easy for the individual registering. The professional event coordinator has numerous techniques and technical equipment options available to accomplish this, including computerized registration systems, integrated database functions, on-site Internet kiosks, and attractive, useful registration collateral.

Registration forms, either physical or digital, must be quick and easy to fill out. They should be designed in such a way that instructions are clear and information is requested in a logical progression. Event branding should be included to reinforce the image of the event, and all rules, regulations, or restrictions should be clearly displayed. Specify what to "do next" by clearly explaining how, where, and when forms must be submitted. Acknowledge receipt of the registrations in some manner, either with an e-mail notification, postcard, letter, receipt, packet, or ticket. On-site, have materials organized and ready to be picked up, as well as systems to handle on-site registrations.

GET THE INFORMATION YOU NEED

The basic information to be collected includes name, mailing and e-mail addresses, phone and fax numbers, special needs or dietary requirements, package or sessions selected, and payment method. Beyond that, depending on the type of event, you can request personal information such as age, income level, education level, food or travel preferences, clothing size (if you are giving out T-shirts or other limited-edition clothing), or opinions about issues or practices to be covered at your event.

The collection of this information must not be intrusive—collect only that information you need and specify how it will be used. You might choose to make some information mandatory for registration, and other requested information optional. All information collected should be considered private and should not be released to outside organizations. If your practice is to sell your information for other direct marketing activities, you must reveal this to the individual in a "disclosure of use" statement. You may or may not be required to develop a privacy policy, but doing so is a sound practice.

STREAMLINE THE DATA MANAGEMENT SYSTEM

Collect registration information in such a way that it streamlines your data management system. Integrate an on-line system to feed directly into your database system so you do not have to reenter information. Use a relational database that allows you to access any piece of information anywhere in your system without having to open a different database or create a report on that sort field. Set up your system to generate automatic e-mail confirmations. Create reports that help you track your progress, including up-to-the-minute reports on session selections to adjust your allocation of space or to determine who has or has not registered yet.

When using on-line registration, design the system to automatically build your database for marketing purposes. Make certain you are able to generate reports that give you market segment and demographic data to better understand and serve your audience. Services such as Cvent.com offer personalized communication, attendee management, and business intelligence reporting to manage and promote meetings and events of all sizes (www.cvent.com).

USE INCENTIVES TO SCULPT BEHAVIOR

When you use an on-line registration system, your database is building itself, which saves you money and time. Encourage your attendees to register on-line by offering incentives to do what is most beneficial to you and your organization. You might offer discounts, rebates, or gifts. You might structure your registration fees for an "early bird" rate if attendees register by a certain deadline (providing you with better cash flow). You might secure sponsored gifts for the first 100, 300, or 500 registrants, such as high-quality tote bags, or hold an on-site drawing from the first 100, 300, or 500 for a complimentary registration for the next conference. People will always act in their own best interests, so make it worth their while to do what you want them to do.

WELCOMING YOUR GUEST

Whether a paid delegate, ticket holder, or invited guest, everyone coming to your event should feel welcomed and treated as a guest. Your registration or check-in area should be clean and attractive. Make certain there are sufficient tables or counters, adequate signs, the appropriate telecommunications equipment (Internet kiosks or registration networks may require ISDN or T1 lines or a DSL connection), all collateral material to be distributed, sponsor and other promotional material, a credit card authorization terminal, petty cash and receipt books, and your registration system and equipment (computers, preprinted badges and packets, badge printers, etc.).

When registration begins and attendees are flowing through the lines, the registration area can begin to look like a madhouse, with boxes stacked about, papers strewn hither and yon, and empty cups piled on tables and counters. It is important to keep this area neat and clean throughout the event so that your efficiency is not questioned because of the condition of the workspace. Use pipe and drape arrangements or other masking to keep the mess out of sight. Restrict eating and drinking to a staff lounge, and when registrars are not on duty, make certain they are not visible. ("Why aren't you helping *me* instead of sitting there with your soda pop!") This will also control the proliferation of cups and napkins contributing to the mess to be managed.

USER-FRIENDLY LAYOUTS

It was reported in the November 2001 issue of *The Customer Service Advantage* newsletter that the most important factor affecting customer satisfaction is how long customers must wait. Anderson and Zemke note, "Dissatisfaction is often the result of uncertainty. Research shows that the most frustrating aspect of waiting is *not knowing how long the wait will be*." And, as Ralph Waldo Emerson said, "We boil at different degrees."

We all hate waiting in lines, but we all have to stand in a queue or line at some point in our lives, and getting into an event is usually one of those times. The professional event coordinator must control these lines to make sure that the waiting is bearable and safe. As shown in Figure 4-5, you will be able to accommodate more people in a limited space by creating a "snake" system with rope and stanchion guides than by simply allowing people to line up in one long queue or, worse yet, in no queue at all. The compression mode, in which people at the back push forward and compress the space (and people) in front, is a recipe for disaster and the cause of most crowd injuries—crowd rushes, crushes, and collapses. A long line winding down the hall or around the corner is an

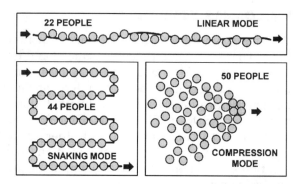

Figure 4-5
Queue (Waiting Line) Types

indication that "this is going to be a nightmare" and can become dangerous as the queue blocks other transit functions.

Take a queue cue from Disney, Universal Studios, and other theme parks. They have made waiting in long lines tolerable by installing signs stating just how long the wait will be at various points along the queue. Of course, you should anticipate the arrival volume, which will differ according your entry system and type of event, and arrange for sufficient registration or check-in desks and personnel. Always have a separate service desk or "courtesy counter" to handle problems or special circumstances, which should be off to the side so that resolving a problem does not impede the progress of the queue.

AN ENTERTAINING EXPERIENCE

Disney, Universal Studios, and other theme parks have also learned to incorporate the wait into the "show," making it part of the experience. At the Back to the Future ride at Universal Studios in Orlando, Florida, guests wind through an intricate snaking queue that is lined with television monitors. As one moves along the queue, the TV monitors display a progression of short videos, synchronized to the time it takes to move a group, of the size that will fit in the ride itself, along the path. By the time a person actually gets to the ride, he or she has seen six or seven parts of a story that culminates with the experience of the ride.

You might adopt and adapt this technique by employing walk-around entertainers, distributing toys and games, and installing interesting displays, or you might provide or sell refreshments along a queue. (Why do you think retailers put racks of impulse items at the checkout counters?) You might make the queue part of the party. I once had a police officer (a friend) actually fingerprint conference attendees as they were waiting to sign up for a murder mystery party, with each fingerprint page emblazoned with the logo of the event's sponsor. Of course, it wasn't a requirement, but because none of these people had ever been fingerprinted before, it was a unique experience and became the talk of the conference (just what the sponsor was hoping for).

PAYMENT, CANCELLATION, AND OTHER ISSUES

When designing your registration collateral and system, establish your payment and cancellation policies and procedures. Clearly state these policies on your materials, including deadlines for special requests (dietary or accessibility needs), prorated refunds, and other terms and conditions. Then make certain you provide the infrastructure to collect fees, disburse refunds, and notify registrants of cancellations or delays. You may also wish to set up separate welcome desks or registration counters for speakers, exhibitors, international delegates, preregistered delegates, and on-site registrations that will involve collecting fees. (Not all your registrars need to handle money.) You must also implement audit procedures to ensure accurate gate counts, ticket sales, and cash controls.

THE SUCCESSFUL STAFF

The staff must be thoroughly briefed on their duties and responsibilities, rules and regulations while on duty, breaks and break areas (the staff lounge), and to whom they report or turn to with questions or service problems. Whether your registration staff is composed of volunteers, personnel of a contracted service, or your own staff, they must receive training on the equipment and procedures of your registration system. They should receive orientation regarding the event, the program schedule, and the location of venue features such as toilet facilities, meeting rooms, dining rooms, on-site emergency services, and adjacent restaurants or attractions. Even if you have a hospitality desk with concierge personnel, the registrars will likely be relied upon to provide this service to attendees.

Other issues to be covered in training include how to recognize accreditation credentials and tickets, follow procedures for complimentary passes, handle monetary transactions and apply admission rates, and enforce security procedures for cash deposits and crowd control. There are two things your staff are never obligated to tolerate—profanity and physical abuse. Make certain that security personnel are available in the registration area and that there is a two-way method of communication (i.e., radios, telephones) between staff and security personnel. Establish guidelines as to when it is appropriate to ask for a supervisor or a security guard, and when it is appropriate to call the police emergency number directly and immediately.

Have all the materials that registrars will need prepared and ready, such as delegate packets at a conference, or T-shirts, athlete numbers, and safety pins for a fun run. Consider the use of uniforms or special clothing items (e.g., shirts, scarves, jackets, vests, or hats) to clearly identify registration staff, and provide name badges to facilitate person-to-person interactions with customers.

Admissions

Admitting an audience member, attendee, or guest into the event is, like registration, a customer service Moment of Truth. The professional event coordinator must anticipate the logistics and operational requirements in order to allocate the appropriate resources (time, money, humanpower, and space) to provide the appropriate guest experience.

ADMISSION CONTROL STRATEGIES

The admittance system is a control point. Most events have an admission control system of some sort, for counting attendance, controlling access, controlling costs, or collecting tickets. You may be checking a guest list, checking badges or wristbands, tearing tickets, distributing amenities, ink-stamping hands, keeping a catering or occupancy count, or preventing the entrance of unauthorized visitors or industrial espionage.

Some events ask invited guests to bring their invitations to show at the door. Others sell tickets in advance and/or at the door. Some require preregistration, and some require special credentials. Some events are free to the public, with access to special areas or seating ticketed. Some events, such as sightseeing tours, may not take place unless a minimum number of tickets have been sold. The type of event and operational requirements will also suggest certain admittance control issues. For example, graduation ceremonies often have limited seating and issue graduates a specific number of tickets, but when the entire proud family wishes to attend, the ticketed event becomes a first-come, first-seated fiasco. (If this is your problem, you should consider a larger venue, staggering parts of the ceremony, or creating a second venue location with closed-circuit coverage of the event.)

ARRIVAL AND DEPARTURE MODES

Arrival and departure modes will dictate the number of portals and personnel required. When guests "trickle" in or out, arriving or departing sporadically throughout the duration of the event, such as at a festival, exhibition, or open house, they are in Trickle Mode. When guests "dump" into or out of the event en masse or within a brief time period, which is particular to events with specific start and end times, they are in Dump Mode. Even with the Trickle Mode, there may be peak and low traffic times that may be anticipated and planned for. In dealing with the Dump Mode, you must make certain that you have sufficient entrances or portals and sufficient personnel to process arrivals in a timely manner. According to Anton Shone, author of *Successful Event Management: A Practical Handbook,* research done in cinemas shows the average time to process a ticket transaction is 20 seconds; multiplied by 1000 guests, this equals about 5½ hours. You should review the history of the event, comparable event statistics, and other forecasting information to determine the probable and predictable mode.

TICKETING ISSUES

Tickets, whether purchased or issued, are used as an admittance control to ensure authorized entry and restrict occupancy. You may issue meal vouchers to conference delegates to ensure that only paid registrants are admitted to a large luncheon or dinner. Tickets may be used to stipulate a specific seat or seating section at a spectator event. A food or wine festival may sell tickets to be used at any concession so as to eliminate cash handling or accounting problems. Event tickets may serve as a proof of payment or as a door prize drawing receipt. Ticketing issues are also pricing issues. A ticket price is determined by the revenue requirements of the event, the desirability or proximity of the seat assignment, and the selling costs—taxes, service or handling charges, venue percentage, and so on (see Figure 4-6). Tickets may be hard tickets (preprinted, preferably by a bonded printer and incorporating a watermark if counterfeiting is a possibility), computer-generated, e-tickets, or tickets on a roll.

Ticket purchase and distribution will be determined by the type and scope of the event, as well as numerous other factors. Advance ticket purchase options include in-person purchase at a box office or ticket outlet, purchase by mail, telephone, fax order, on-line, or by inclusion in the registration fees. If you have several ticketed events or additional admission permits available for sale, sell them all at the same time on one order form or registration form. These can include parking permits, special events, tours or companion programs, RV or campsite permits, and numerous package options such as group discounts, multiday passes, bundled products, and even souvenirs.

When conducting on-site sales, carefully establish your box office or ticket window sales system. A formal box office or sales windows may be available at the venue, or you may need to bring in or construct them, using either a trailer or a secure registration counter arrangement. The

Location Pricing	On-Ticket Information	Other Considerations
❑ Balcony ❑ Box Seat ❑ Dress Circle ❑ Floor Seat ❑ Gallery ❑ General Admission ❑ Mezzanine ❑ Obstructed View ❑ Orchestra ❑ Private Suite ❑ Reserved Seating ❑ Standing Room ❑ Tier/Level/Section ❑ Upper Circle	❑ Aisle ❑ Event Name ❑ Gate ❑ Legal Disclaimers ❑ Month, Date, and Time ❑ Price or Price Category ❑ Row ❑ Seat Number, Letter, Color ❑ Section Number, Letter, Color ❑ Terms and Conditions ❑ Venue	❑ Complimentary Tickets ❑ Discounts—group, promotional, subscriber ❑ One-Day/Multiday Pass ❑ Papering the House ❑ Perforated Stub ❑ Refund/Exchange Policy ❑ Scalping ❑ Watermark or Security Seal ❑ Will Call—CABO (call at box office)

Source: International Ticketing Association (www.intix.org)

Figure 4-6
Ticketing Checklist

box office or ticket counter must have a secure area for storing tickets and money, all the equipment necessary to collect cash and perform credit card transactions, and a secure area for counting and processing transactions. Some event sponsors negotiate and distribute coupons (e.g., on-pack, in-pack, and box tops), which provide a discounted entrance or ticket price. The coupon redemption process must be integrated into your advance and on-site sales procedures. Ticket distribution methods include mailing, pickup at a box office or other point of sale (POS) outlet, will-call windows at the event, an e-mailed confirmation number, or inclusion in a registration packet.

THE GATEKEEPERS

Volunteers, staff, stewards, or security personnel may handle taking tickets or checking credentials. They may need to confirm that the guest is entering through the correct portal, check to ensure that the attendee is registered for a particular session, inspect a ticket to make sure it is authentic, and/or tear a ticket in two and hand the stub to the attendee. Other gatekeeping duties might include counting people as they pass through—either with a hand counter or ensuring people pass through a turnstile, or directing attendees through a magnetometer or security checkpoint.

These functions should be positioned and staffed appropriately to allow rapid accommodation of the volume of admissions expected. As with registration areas, these areas should be incorporated into the décor plan to ensure that they are attractive, efficient, and effective. You might use colorful Airtubes (www.airdd.com) to direct guests to the correct portals, install banners or flags, or create balloon arches in various color schemes. You should prepare the guests for the admission procedure by installing instructional signs describing what they will be asked to do before they reach the entrance. If they will have to show a ticket, identification, or pass, ask them to have it out and ready. If they are prohibited from bringing certain items into the venue (e.g., food or beverages), provide trash receptacles along the path. If they are required to pass through a magnetometer, provide trays for loose change, keys, and other metal items.

Your admissions staff must be provided with the appropriate training so they will recognize and implement the accreditation system effectively and efficiently. They should also be familiar with the layout of the event, the schedule of the event, and the event organization's policies and procedures. If admission to the event is restricted, either to ticket holders or credentialed individuals, you should have security personnel at each entry portal to assist and/or support the other gatekeepers.

CREATING THE "REVEAL"

As the first threshold, admission into an event is an opportunity for the professional event coordinator to enhance the event experience. Many event designers use this opportunity to intensify the special nature of the event by highlighting the difference between the outside environment and the inside setting with an exciting entryway or entrance scenario.

On-Site Insight

Mary Tribble, CSEP, president of Tribble Creative Group in Charlotte, North Carolina, has won numerous awards for creating innovative solutions and exciting event experiences. She shares an example of creating a "reveal" that overcame the challenge of a less-than-exciting venue. As the culmination of an incentive weekend, 150 top producers awaited the highly anticipated awards ceremony. The Ports Authority—the only facility available that could accommodate the party—was a mere

(Continued)

shell of a brick building with no inherent accoutrements. The outside approach was even worse, and the client feared that guests would be disappointed when they arrived at this building for their big event. To solve the dilemma, an elaborate ruse was set up to fool the guests into thinking that things had gone awry.

Motor coaches and VIP limousines first transported guests to the Charleston Visitors Center, where a twenties-themed cocktail party included gangsters, cigar girls, jazz performers, and flappers. The guests were then asked to reboard the buses for their long-awaited four-star dinner. During the weeks and days leading up to the event, the client and Tribble Creative Group dropped some clues about the evening, which traditionally remains a surprise. It was revealed that as a special dispensation for the important audience, the famed Magnolia's restaurant would close its doors for a rare private party. As the motor coaches pulled up, however, something appeared to be amiss!

Representatives from Tribble Creative Group and a local ground operator flagged down and boarded the buses and limos to impart the disappointing news: The mayor of Charleston had held a late afternoon fund-raiser at the restaurant, which was running overtime, but Magnolia's had volunteered to send drinks and hors d'oeuvres to the nearby Ports Authority to await availability for the disturbed guests.

The guests were fooled into thinking they had been dropped off in an empty building. Tribble Creative Group had curtained off a small area and "decorated" it to look as if it hadn't been cleaned after a recent cruise had come through. They hung bare bulbs, brought in trash and equipment, and hired "maintenance workers" to vacuum as the guests entered. The client, pretending to be fed up with this disaster, climbed atop a ladder to get the crowd's attention. In front of the guests, he blamed his assistant, who quit right then and there. As the assistant yelled, "I quit!" the sounds of a snare drum were heard from behind a curtain. Out of a trash pile, an actor emerged, inviting guests to believe that "what is fantasy is reality!" and as a black curtain dropped, a big band orchestra began to play, revealing a 1920s nightclub decorated in black and white feathers and draping, with a troupe of flappers and champagne-carrying waitstaff waiting to cater to the guests. The guests gasped—then laughed—at their own folly as they realized they had been completely fooled.

Accreditation

The International Dictionary of Event Management, second edition, (Goldblatt and Nelson, eds.) defines accreditation as "the process required for receiving credentials for access to an event or a certain area of an event" and defines credentials as "evidence of identity and qualification." Not all events require an expansive or complex accreditation system—a ticket is a credential that *identifies* the ticket holder as *qualified* to enter. The professional event coordinator must determine the appropriate level and type of accreditation system to meet the security needs of the event, event stakeholders, and event audience. The system selected must be integrated into the site plan, the budget, and the operations. Appropriate policies and procedures must be established, materials must be procured, and training for staff must be provided.

AUTHORIZING ACCESS—WHO'S WHO DETERMINES WHERE AND WHEN

Your accreditation system—establishing and issuing credentials—authorizes access to your event and to specific areas at the event site. This means access to the individuals at the event as well, including the guests or attendees, participants, and performers, plus the actions or activities taking place at the event. The type and scope of your system will be determined by the type and purpose of the event, as well as the need to control access to certain areas, people, activities, information, equipment, or materials (see Figure 4-7).

Not everyone needs access to everything at all times. Those who set up the event do not necessarily need to be there during the event. Those who have received special access on a certain day are not necessarily authorized to be there at any time during the run of the event. Volunteers who are helping with the registration do not automatically get into the VIP lounge or get access to the star performer. The media may be welcomed into the stadium, but not necessarily into the locker room (until after the game). The participants or exhibitors do not necessarily get onto the event site at any time of the day or night, or get to participate in all event activities.

ZONES OF NEED AND SECURITY ISSUES

When designing the layout of the event, the professional event coordinator will specify the restricted areas that must have controlled access and determine who should have access to those areas based on the need

Credentials	Individuals	Access
❏ Badge ❏ Button ❏ Laminate on Lanyard ❏ Logo Wear ❏ Name Tag ❏ Pass ❏ Personalized Badge ❏ Photo ID ❏ Printed Invitation ❏ Ribbon/Sash ❏ Smart Card ❏ Stick-on Silks ❏ Wristband	❏ Delegates/Attendees ❏ Exhibitors ❏ Media ❏ Participants/Athletes ❏ Performers ❏ Security ❏ Staff/Volunteers ❏ Suppliers ❏ Vendors/Concessionaires ❏ VIPs ❏ Workers/Laborers	❏ All Access (with/without escorting privileges) ❏ Backstage/Onstage ❏ Date/Time Span-Valid ❏ Exhibit Hall ❏ Locker/Dressing Rooms ❏ Lounges/Suites ❏ Production Areas ❏ Special Parking Areas ❏ Special Seating Areas ❏ Staging/Storage Areas ❏ VIP Hospitality Areas

Figure 4-7
Accreditation Checklist

to be there. As the event coordinator is identifying the event elements and their positioning within the event site and schedule, he or she must confirm the interactions and interdependencies and try to create zones of need. These zones of need must be cordoned off in some manner to facilitate controlled access, either with fencing, enclosures, separate portals, or other perimeter controls. If it cannot be contained, it cannot be controlled.

For example, at a large air show the hospitality tent was restricted to sponsors and their guests (each sponsor received a limited number of ID buttons). The tent had a steward checking buttons at the entrance, but guests were walking out to the patio area on the side of the tent and handing their buttons over the fence to their friends, who were repeating this scenario. Quite soon, the hospitality tent was filled to capacity with unauthorized guests, and the sponsors complained bitterly to the show management that this benefit of sponsorship was not as promised.

Certain credentials may indicate access to specific areas, such as backstage but not onstage, and access at specific times, such as backstage only after the performance. Some venues require that all workers, even a subcontractor's workers, wear identification such as a company name tag or a logo on clothing to prevent theft during setup. Confirm your plan with your stakeholders and security advisors, make any necessary revisions, and then communicate with those who will be responsible for implementing the system.

DISTRIBUTING BADGES OF HONOR

The process of accreditation includes the method of registration and distribution. For large festivals, sports events, and exposition events, you may wish to schedule one or two days prior to the start of the event for registration and manufacture of these credentials. You may conduct this activity by mail or on-line; however, if positive identification is required, this must be done in person. For events using lots of volunteers, you might schedule a pre-event rally to get everyone excited about the job to be done while they are getting their photo IDs processed.

Your options for establishing credentials can range from quick and cheap to involved and costly. As with tickets, you may need to consider a watermark or security seal to prevent counterfeiting. You may issue different-colored passes for different days or different areas. Staff or volunteer badges may be coded by area or function and may include a bar code that must be swiped through a laser reader to bring up the photo IDs on a computer screen. Many events have an "Ask Me" button for staff members and certain volunteers to wear to let guests know to whom they can turn for assistance.

MEET THE PRESS

Depending on the type, scope, or host of the event, the professional event coordinator may have to be cognizant of media relations. You may be coordinating a small wedding ceremony, in which case media will not likely be an issue. But if it is a movie star's wedding, you may have to arrange a "no-fly zone" over the seaside promontory where the ceremony is taking place to prevent paparazzi from dangling from helicopters, trying to get a cover photo for the tabloids. However, in most cases, the media are welcomed into an event for the purpose of generating positive publicity about the event.

Media credentials are issued based on the type of media (broadcast, print, or electronic) and the areas or activities the media will be provided access to. Sometimes the media are courted like royalty, provided with a media hospitality lounge, special media conferences with significant access to celebrities or participants, and a fully equipped media center with everything from fax machines to T1 lines. At other times the media are given only limited access, such as photographer areas behind rope-and-stanchion barriers at the entrance to the event or a specific interview area inside the venue where special guests or spokespersons are brought to the reporters. At some events the media are prohibited from taking any photos or video because the photographic rights have been assigned or sold to an exclusive outlet or individual. And at some events the media are not permitted access of any type. (Contrary to what reporters would have you believe, the media are not guaranteed access to any- and everything.)

Although most public and marketing events are eager to have media coverage, the professional event coordinator must be prepared for the media that will, no doubt, descend on the event if something bad or controversial happens. In their book *Marketing for Hospitality and Tourism,* Philip Kotler, John Bowen, and James Makens advise that a good crisis management plan will include a predetermined spokesperson and space where information and updates will be issued, a communications mechanism for getting the facts to the spokesperson, and specific policies and training for staff to ensure all media inquiries are referred to the official spokesperson. Media coverage may result from a crisis or may be anticipated because of the local, national, or international significance of the event or event participants. You may have to locate or designate areas for the microwave or satellite trucks needed for the electronic feeds to network broadcasts.

Seating and Ushering Plans

Seating and ushering plans are based on the purpose of the event, politics, pricing, protocol, and proximity requirements. The purpose of an event may dictate that attendees be able to see and interact with each other or that they all need excellent sight lines to a main stage. The politics surrounding an event may indicate that certain people or groups should not be positioned next to each other, such as fans of rival teams at a sports event or certain relatives at a social gathering. Pricing issues include ticket prices based on seat location or on investment levels by sponsors or donors. Protocol and etiquette issues relate to rank, precedence, and tradition and may mandate who sits next to whom. Proximity requirements may involve accessibility issues, such as a hearing-impaired person's sight line to a sign language interpreter or an award recipient's movement from seat to stage.

CAPACITY AND CAPABILITY

The seating plan of an event may be influenced by the occupancy regulations for a specific venue or facility. The seating capacity of a venue is established by the local fire and safety codes, depending on the configuration, furnishings, aisle width, and obstructions (see Figure 4-8). The seating equipment at a venue may be stationary and built-in or portable and adaptable, or there may no equipment on-site at all and you will need to rent, build, and/or install it yourself. Many purpose-built facili-

Seating—Theater Style	❑ The center seat in the first row should be no less than 6 ft (1.8 m) from the front of the stage, and no chairs should overlap the front of the stage. ❑ Typical stacking chairs are 20 in. (50 cm) front to back and 17.5 to 18.5 in. (44.5 to 47 cm) wide. ❑ Chairs should be set with at least 3 to 6 in. (7.6 to 15.3 cm) between contiguous chairs. *Note:* Many convention centers and auditoriums require and use chairs that interlock for theater-style seating. ❑ Allot a minimum of 24 in. (61 cm) between rows, and if space allows, 32 in. (81 cm) or more. ❑ Row spacing for wheelchair access rows needs to be 5 ft (1.5 m).
Aisles—Theater Style	❑ There should be aisles on both sides, even if a center aisle is present. ❑ Aisles should be a minimum of 4 ft (1.2 m) wide. ❑ Increase aisle width by 1 ft (31 cm) if more than 400 people. ❑ Wheelchair-accessible aisles must be 6 ft (1.8 m) wide. ❑ Create a midsection aisle after 15 seats in any direction. ❑ Cross aisles should be added after 10 to 15 rows, preferably aligned with an exit door. ❑ If the number of rows in a section exceeds 10 rows, aisles should be a minimum of 6 ft (1.8 m) wide, and if more than 30 rows, 8 ft (2.4 m) wide.
Classroom Setups	❑ Typical tables are 6 or 8 ft (1.8 or 2.4 m) long and 18 or 30 in. (46 or 76 cm) wide. ❑ Allot a minimum of 2 ft (0.6 m) of table space per person and 2½ to 3 ft (0.8 to 0.9 m) per person if attendees will be using large notebooks or laptop computers. ❑ Allot a minimum of 34 in. (87 cm) between table rows for seats and passage. ❑ As wheelchairs require maneuvering space, row space between tables in wheelchair-access rows will require 6 ft (1.8 m) and the table space allotment should be at least 36 to 42 in. (91 to 107 cm). ❑ Rows should be no more than 24 ft (7.3 m) in length and should have aisles on both sides.
Banquet Setups	❑ Typical round banquet tables are 60, 66, or 72 in. (152, 168, or 183 cm) in diameter. The 60 in. (152 cm) table seats 8, the 66 in. (168 cm) seats 9 or 10, and the 72 in. (183 cm) seats 10 or 11 people comfortably. ❑ Wheelchair seating will require 1.5 times as much space per person at the table. ❑ The space between round tables should be 6 to 7 ft (1.8 to 2.1 m) for seats, aisle space, and serving functions.

Figure 4-8
Spatial Considerations for Event Layouts (All spatial requirements must be confirmed to ensure they comply with local fire regulations.)

Other	❏ When using risers, the backs should have a security rail, and steps with handrails should be added for anything over 12 in. (30 cm) high.
	❏ Dance floor size—10 sq ft (0.93 sq m) per couple.
	❏ Average number of couples dancing = 25% of total attendance.
	❏ Exhibit aisles should be 10 ft (3.05 m) wide.
	❏ Rear screen projection allowance—16 to 35 ft (4.9 to 10.7 m) between wall and screen or 1.7 × screen width.
	❏ 2 × 8 principle—No one should be seated closer to the screen than 2 × the screen height nor farther than 8 × the screen height.

Confirm typical setups with venue—unusual configurations and atypical setups may incur additional charges and, because they are unfamiliar to setup crews, supervision may be required.

Sources: Catherine H. Price (1999), The Complete Guide to Professional Meeting and Event Coordination, *2d pub. (Washington, DC: George Washington University Event Management Program); Edward G. Polivka, ed. (1996),* Professional Meeting Management, *3d ed. (Birmingham, AL: PCMA Education Foundation); Patti J. Shock and John Stefanelli (2001),* On-Premise Catering *(New York: John Wiley & Sons, Inc); Sandra L. Morrow (1997),* The Art of the Show *(Dallas: International Association of Exposition Management Education Foundation).*

Figure 4-8
(Continued)

ties have fixed and flexible seating options and equipment, but not all venues have all types and sizes of equipment (i.e., chairs and tables). Some facilities such as theaters, arenas, and stadiums have fixed spectator seating; however many have flexible seating alternatives such as telescopic grandstands or other adjustable seating. For example, the Plenary Hall in the International Convention Centre in Durban, South Africa, has raked seating for 1644 that may be subdivided into two separate 840-seat auditoriums, and sophisticated technology enables the seats to be raised into the ceiling so that a banquet can be set up in the floor space created. Fiber-optic lights on the underside of the seating create a starry night sky when in this configuration.

USHERS ARE AMBASSADORS

Depending on the type and size of the event and its seating plan, ushers may be called stewards, escorts, guides, greeters, or, as at the 2002 Winter Olympics, the Event Services Team, and may be used to guide guests to a seating section, assigned tables, or specific seats. They may also be used to distribute programs and direct traffic flow into (and out of) an event. They may be used to welcome a delegation arriving at an airport or to put dignitaries or athletes in the correct order for a formal entrance. They may be charged with checking tickets or credentials, assisting with shuttle bus loading, or they may simply be there to serve as welcoming faces to greet and guide guests as ambassadors of the event.

Whatever they are called, ushers should be completely familiar with the admissions and seating system (including the guest list if appropriate), the layout and features of the venue, the purpose of the event and program agenda, as well as the policies and procedures regarding guest relations. They should be selected based on their social skills and convivial personalities, and provided with appropriate training to ensure that they will represent the event organization in a positive and productive manner.

Consider providing a distinctive uniform or clothing item so that these individuals are readily identifiable. Many large sports events and entertainment venues use a specific colored suit jacket. Other events use logo-imprinted vests, shirts, T-shirts, aprons, or entire outfits. When ushers are expected to guide or seat guests after the lights have been lowered, they should be provided with small flashlights to illuminate the footpath.

CREATIVE SEAT IDENTIFICATION

Table numbers, seat numbers, color-coded seating sections, row letters or ribbons, or a combination of these means may be used to identify assigned seating. Depending on the type of event and the seating plan, the professional event coordinator may use place cards on the table or place a name card on each seat. Place cards may be laid out alphabetically on a reception table, with party favors linked to a specific table assignment by color or centerpiece. For example, for a baseball-themed bar mitzvah party, the guests' place cards were attached to baseball caps of different teams and each table centerpiece featured a pennant flag of a particular team. For a cartoon-themed bat mitzvah party, each place card included a cartoon character to match the centerpiece, which featured a large stuffed toy of the character (the toys were donated to a children's hospital after the event).

Seating sections may be identified by color by using chair covers or painted chairs, or identified by team, delegation, or department by using flags or banners at the ends of the aisles. The rows or pews at a wedding ceremony might be cordoned off along the center aisle with ribbons or floral garlands, or the front pews reserved for the family adorned with bouquets. Polaroid photos may be taken of incentive guests, scanned, printed on iron-on transfers, and applied to seatback covers. One group of attendees had their photos taken upon arrival, and these were given to a caricaturist to create drawings in time for them to be made into framed place cards for the final dinner.

Attendee Services

Attendee services should be designed to improve the event experience by anticipating the likely needs and making services available to meet them. The type of event, attendee profile, and overall event environment guides the decision on what services should be included. The professional event coordinator also considers the location of the event in proximity to the attendee's home; obviously, for a local event fewer services may be needed than for an event that requires extensive travel to attend.

Attendee service begins with the pre-event communications and collateral materials preparing the guest for the event experience as well as establishing expectations. Local guests may need simple directions. Travelers may need extensive instructions regarding anything from travel routes to cultural customs of the host country. Delegates to a conference may need business center services for connections to their offices or tuxedo rental services for the final night gala. Festival-goers may welcome stroller rentals, and fair exhibitors may appreciate on-site automatic teller machines (ATMs) so that buyers can quickly get cash to complete their purchases. Party guests may need a coat check service for bulky outerwear.

INFORMATION STATIONS

One of the basic services that a professional event coordinator can provide at any type of event is someone to talk to for a guest or attendee who has questions. That human connection is a central component of quality customer service. An information station is appropriate for nearly any type of event; it may be called Guest Services, the Information Booth, or the Welcome Table. It may be staffed with volunteers, members of a host committee, or hospitality personnel from an agency or visitor bureau. An information station should have two-way communication capabilities for contact with event security staff and may have telephones—pay phones and/or courtesy phones.

The information station can have local or area information and event site directions. It may serve as a message center or the Lost and Found and "lost parents" department. It may serve as the place where inebriated guests come to get a safe ride home (from a prearranged taxi service), or it may serve as the location where groups come to make their connections or to board shuttles. It may become an enterprise zone, where publications, souvenirs, office supplies, or sponsor-imprinted items are available for sale (you will need to make certain you are set up to collect and pay local sales tax), or serve as a Resource Center with displays, refreshments, and brochure racks.

HOUSING ISSUES

As professional event coordinator, you may be responsible for the housing needs of an event's guests, staff, participants, VIPs, and/or entertainers. Depending on the type of event, such accommodations may include hotels, university dormitories, guest houses, or host residences. You may be reserving and paying for rooms, negotiating rates for attendees at a headquarters hotel or hotels, or simply identifying accommodation options. For tourism events, such as festivals or sports events, the identification of adequate rooming options may be sufficient. For conference events, specific hotels may be identified, a negotiated room block reserved, and a housing bureau secured to handle individual attendee bookings. Some life-cycle events require that accommodations be identified and reserved for out-of-town family and guests. For incentive travel and corporate events, you might arrange for early check-in and late check-out privileges.

When paying for specific rooms out of the event budget (e.g., for staff, speakers, VIPs, mandated corporate training, or incentive winners), make certain you have clearly specified, both with the room occupant and the hotel, what will and what will not be charged to your master bill. In-room purchases can range from international long distance calls to cleaning out the minibar, even expensive spa treatments or luxury items from the hotel gift shops.

Whether you identify, block, or buy rooms, understand that rates will be negotiated based on availability and volume, and these negotiations take place during your site selection process. Note that delegates who make their own rooming arrangements without identifying their affiliation with your event may compromise tracking the pickup on your room block (crediting rooms to your contracted number of reserved guest rooms). And when negotiating the rates with a hotel, be aware that Internet specials or other discounted rates could jeopardize your room pickup if those rates are lower than the conference rates you advertise in your registration materials, not to mention the dissatisfaction attendees will express when they find someone else has received a lower rate.

TRAVELER AIDS

Meetings and conferences, tourism events, destination weddings, and many other events welcome out-of-town attendees. I have often advised my lecture audiences that when people leave town they get stupid, but Peter E. Tarlow expresses it much better with the term "traveler anomie." *The American College Dictionary* defines *anomie* as "a social vacuum marked by the absence of social norms or values." The ordinary precautions a person would normally take are forgotten when the individual becomes preoccupied with the new and unfamiliar surroundings and expectations of the event experience. Consequently, personal items are lost or stolen, people lose their sense of direction (and often their inhibitions), and attendees find themselves in need of assistance.

The professional event coordinator may anticipate and alleviate some of the distress by locating shopping outlets for lost or left-behind items and providing pre-event tips on traveler safety, wardrobe suggestions, and maps with detailed driving directions. Another idea is to provide a "Welcome Session," an orientation lecture that reviews the event program and the traveler safety tips and highlights the area attractions and amenities.

CHILDREN ARE WELCOME

Current trends suggest that children will be accompanying their parent(s) at events of all types. Children's programming is discussed further in Chapter 12; in the context of attendee services, however, accommodating children must be considered within the scope of accommodating the audience. Festivals may include children's areas and activities, as well as "baby stations"—diaper-changing facilities. Conferences and gate shows may provide crèche or baby-sitting services so that the delegate or visitor is free to attend sessions. Of course, all child care services you provide must be bonded and insured, and any event that welcomes children should arrange for a "lost parent" system.

LOUNGES AND CONCIERGE SERVICES

Special lounges may be appropriate for delegates arriving earlier than the allowed check-in time at a hotel. Cybercafés may be arranged to allow attendees to collect e-mail, or public telephones may be provided to check voice mail. Smoking lounges may be set aside to accommodate smokers within an otherwise smoke-free environment (which will be far more attractive than cigarette butts littering the sidewalk or the area just outside the entrance).

For incentive groups, the professional event coordinator may arrange a concierge desk exclusively for the event's guests, special delivery of specific newspapers or magazines, or reserved tee times at a golf course. If the incentive guests are receiving numerous souvenir items and gifts, a special shipping service might be prearranged so they do not have to carry them home in their luggage. If a conference event has a final night gala scheduled, it may be possible to have a local beauty salon set up a table to take reservations for hairstyling appointments or spa treatments. According to Certified Incentive Travel Executive Patrick Delaney, shopping is the number one activity preferred at incentive and other destination events, so the event coordinator might arrange with a signature retail outlet or shopping center to provide shuttle service for attendees at appropriate times throughout the event program.

Protocol and VIP Services

Protocol, from the Latin *protocollum,* meaning "the first (document) glued into" a book of records (presumably setting the form for others to follow), is the code of conduct and the forms of ceremony and etiquette observed by diplomats and others in a society. In general terms, it means the customs and rules of politeness and courtesy between individuals through which we recognize status and avoid giving offense (see Figure 4-9). For nations and governments, protocol is a system of conventions, procedures, and symbols that govern the relationships between nation-states and within international organizations. The same is true in regard to public or private organizations at formal functions sponsored or held by such organizations.

ROLE AND SCOPE OF PROTOCOL

Protocol covers such areas as procedures for official visits, symbols (flags and other visual emblems, anthems, and uniforms), verbal and written forms of address and salutations (known as Tongue and Quill), Order of Precedence tables, seating arrangements, ceremonial procedures, and guidelines for hospitality. But protocol does not apply to official state visits and functions exclusively. Issues of protocol can affect the order of

Protocol	Etiquette	Principles
❑ Anthems ❑ Ceremonies ❑ Distinguished Visits ❑ Flags and Emblems ❑ Forms of Address ❑ Introductions ❑ Order of Precedence	❑ Color Usage ❑ Dining ❑ Dress Codes ❑ Gestures ❑ Gift Giving ❑ Personal Space ❑ Touching	❑ Courtesy ❑ Cultural Tradition ❑ Historical Custom ❑ Politics ❑ Priority ❑ Religious Rites ❑ Social or Diplomatic Rank

Figure 4-9
Protocol Checklist

speakers at a corporate event, seating at the tables at a wedding banquet, or which team enters the stadium first at a sports event. Societies, whether macro or micro, establish formal and informal rules based on cultural tradition, historical custom, social rank, priority, and politics.

Protocol also includes cultural personal etiquette and social customs such as gift giving, gestures, personal space, alcohol use, eye contact, touching, color usage, and dress codes. Particularly in today's global economy, cultural etiquette facilitates communication and the conducting of business. According to Morrison, Conaway, and Borden, "communication always takes place between individuals, not cultures. Few individuals are perfect representations of their culture." Their book, *Kiss, Bow, or Shake Hands,* includes cultural overviews, behavior styles, negotiating techniques, protocol, and business practices for 60 different countries.

The handling and display of flags and other symbols are also sensitive issues. Oretha D. Swartz, author of *Service Etiquette,* explains: "Laws have been written to govern the use of the flag and to ensure a proper respect for the [U.S. flag]. Custom has decreed certain other observances in regard to its use." Flag protocol extends to the world of events in numerous contexts and has serious implications; there was an international incident in 1992 when, during a World Series game between the Atlanta Braves and the Toronto Blue Jays in Atlanta, the Canadian flag was carried onto the field upside down.

Symbols and emblems may entail similar sensitivities and regulations in the corporate world as well. David DeLoach notes that Disney carefully controls "crossover branding" when it comes to its characters such as Mickey Mouse. Although the Disney characters are regularly present at events held at the MAGIC KINGDOM Park, "Mickey does not hand out company awards at special event functions; it could be perceived as a form of corporate endorsement."

TRADITION, PRECEDENCE, AND POLITICS

Determining order of precedence is the starting point for almost all you do regarding protocol at functions where officials of a government or its representatives are present—from organizing the order of arrival and departure, to seating, to introductions of distinguished guests. The need for a system of precedence may be explained by the fact that we cannot all walk through a door at the same time. The formal order of precedence based on diplomatic rank is a matter of sheer timing. McCaffree and Innis, authors of *Protocol: The Complete Handbook of Diplomatic, Official and Social Usage,* reported, "At the Congress of Vienna in 1815, the nations laid down the rules of precedence based on diplomatic titles. Envoys of equal title were ranked according to the date and hour they presented their letters of credentials rather than the size or influence of the nation the envoy represented." This model for order of precedence has been extended to other milieus as well. For example, the order of precedence for the states of the United States is based on their date of entry into the Union. Other precedence lists for the United States may be found at www.airforcewives.com/protocol/ch08.html.

Formal protocol and tradition usually determine what and who takes precedence, but other factors may impact this determination, such as security needs, the program agenda, a specific corporate culture, or plain old family politics. From state dinners to simple wedding ceremonies, seating plans and entry order ensures that the right person is put first, and next to the right person. Sometimes putting two individuals together is inappropriate—Aunt Jane and Uncle Bud at a family gathering, a feuding mayor and governor at a civic banquet, or heads of state from countries in conflict.

On-Site Insight

Sally Webb of The Special Event Company in London, England, shares this example of a royal visit:

We were engaged in 1996 to arrange a royal visit for Her Majesty Queen Elizabeth II and her husband, the Duke of Edinburgh, to the London town of Croydon, situated south of the City. The sequence of planning included a briefing meeting held with local council representatives where the optimum route, places to visit, and people to meet were decided in principle. This schedule was put to Her Majesty's equerry at a meeting at Buckingham Palace. The places and people were then altered by the royal household to include fewer dignitaries and more local people and places. The task of deciding who should be removed from the list was daunting.

Secondly, each person both royals were to meet needed to have security clearance, which meant obtaining the passport details of over 75 people and passing them on to the Metropolitan Police. Some were rejected without explanation. The Metropolitan Police and the Royal Protection Squad then completed a thorough inspection of each venue, checking escape routes and access to rooftops for armed guards.

(Continued)

Menus for the day were surprisingly easy. We were informed that Her Majesty had no real preferences, but was rather fond of hot desserts with custard. The only request was for Dubonnet (a vermouth) and lemonade to be available. At each venue there was to be a "retiring" room with cloakroom facilities—we now know why the queen believes all restrooms smell of fresh paint!

Prior to the visit, we went to each establishment and briefed everyone they were meeting on the etiquette required.

- *Don't speak unless you are spoken to.*
- *A short bob curtsey or bow is sufficient but not a requirement.*
- *Address the queen as "Your Majesty" on initial introduction and "Ma'am" subsequently; "Sir" is sufficient for the Duke of Edinburgh.*

The day seemed to pass in a flash, and I felt truly sorry for the amount of hand shaking, plaque unveiling, and often inane conversation necessary for the queen to complete her duties—not to mention an omnipresent smile, which we all know is difficult but necessary in the event industry. Midmorning Her Majesty made her first impromptu comment to me. "It seems to be going very well, you must be very pleased," she surprised me by saying out of the blue. "Yes, ma'am," I replied, for we had already been officially "introduced" so we were on Ma'am and Sally terms by this time.

Luncheon went like a dream, with Her Majesty passing her compliments to the chef, and on the way back in the car for the next rendezvous stating, "It seems to be going very well, you must be very pleased." "Thank you, ma'am," with short bob akin to a curtsey was the reply. After a whirlwind tour culminating in a 4:00 P.M. high tea with yet more officials, Her Majesty and the Duke of Edinburgh made their departures. Her Majesty bade farewell, and as relief was ebbing out of every pore in my body, she turned and in a final address said, "It seems to have gone very well, you must be very pleased." "Thank you, ma'am," came my final retort.

Finally, once they had departed, I was asked to give an on-the-spot interview for the local BBC TV channel. "So what was your overall impression of the day?" asked the reporter. "It went very well, we were very pleased" was really the only reply to give.

CEREMONIES AND CEREMONIAL PROCEDURES

Another event context in which protocol, customs, procedures, and precedence are often featured are ceremonies and ceremonial events. Ceremonies may be governmental, celebratory, commemorative, reverent, joyous, or solemn and may include religious rites, traditional rituals, formal emblems, and official or symbolic tasks. They can include investitures or inaugurations, commencements or confirmations, groundbreakings or grand openings, and the rites and rituals associated with christenings or naming ceremonies, weddings, or funerals.

A ceremony within an event should be considered an event unto itself so that it will be a memorable and meaningful part of the event experience. There may be issues of precedence order, religious requisites, and traditions that must be observed. There may be a level of pomp and pageantry expected, or specific event elements mandated. There may be a prescribed agenda, such as the posting of the colors (flags), Pledge of Allegiance, national anthem, invocation, and the order of toasts. Depending on cultural traditions, you may have the beating of drums or heraldic horns to officially open an event, or, as is done at important official occasions in Jakarta, Indonesia, you may have "Mr. and Mrs. Jakarta" (a married couple selected by the government for their attractiveness, charm, and cultural knowledge) in national costume as the official greeters.

Sources of information on protocol will vary according to the type of event. You might consult governmental departments or protocol officers, cultural or ceremonial guidebooks, etiquette books or experts, military protocol manuals, organizational policy manuals, corporate representatives, or family members to determine the protocol issues and requirements for your particular event. Remember that status, rank, and politics exist in virtually any milieu, and failure to consider the issues of protocol may have poor results, ranging from disgruntled dinner guests to a diplomatic disaster (not to mention the loss of your credibility as a professional event coordinator).

SPECIAL SERVICES FOR SPECIAL PEOPLE

Everyone attending an event is important; some people are *very important persons* (VIPs) because of their status, rank, fame, fortune, stature, significance to the event client or host, or significance to the purpose or success of the event. VIPs might include award recipients, celebrities, corporate executives, dignitaries, family members, honorees, politicians, or sponsors. They may be attending the event, participating in the event, supporting the event, or the very reason for the event. VIPs often require special attention and assistance. They must be treated with respect and care commensurate with their rank and importance to the event.

Including and accommodating VIPs can increase the status, stature, and attendance of an event, but special security issues may be involved, which will have costs and special logistics that must be factored into the event's budget, timeline, and site plans. Special routing to, from, and within the event site may be required, including particular drop-off and pickup arrangements. Certain celebrities and public figures may have to be routed through the backstage or back-of-the-house area. Depending on specific security needs, particularly with government dignitaries, several routes may be required. The entire event site or certain portions of it may have to be thoroughly examined by special security personnel and then closed to all until the event starts. The professional event coordinator will work with the booking agent, protocol representative, or security officials early in the planning process to determine the special amenities and arrangements necessary to facilitate attendance, as well as the level of products or services that befits the VIP's position or status.

Target Competency Review

Accommodating an audience is primarily focused on marketing and customer service. The marketing and collateral materials printed and distributed must be designed to create interest, establish expectations, and provide all the necessary information for participation or attendance. Although the printed piece is still standard, new communications technology offers innovative and exciting promotional opportunities.

Admission controls allow the professional event coordinator to regulate attendance for marketing, financial, and security reasons. An efficient and effective registration and credentialing system will automatically build databases while serving the needs of the guest and the hosting organization. The arrival of the audience must be anticipated and arranged to ensure a safe and smooth entrée into the event.

Seating plans are designed to facilitate the appropriate visibility and attendee interactivity specified by the purpose, goals, and objectives of the event. Numerous creative and expressive strategies may be used to direct guests and attendees to their assigned seats. Providing the appropriate services for attendees and VIPs ensures a memorable and meaningful event experience. Attention to protocol issues facilitates the appropriate recognition of rank, tradition, and ceremonial customs associated with many events.

EXERCISES IN PROFESSIONAL EVENT COORDINATION

Outline and describe the collateral materials, admissions control systems, seating plans, attendee services, and protocol requirements you would implement for each of the following events.

1. The national soccer championships are to be held in your city and will include four competitions on four different days. You are hoping to attract 20,000 spectators for each game, and you expect that each game will be sold out. You also anticipate significant media coverage and probably some unruly fans.

2. Your local college is holding an alumni reunion in conjunction with the commencement ceremonies for the upcoming graduating class. The alumni reunion is designed to kick off a major fund-raising drive for a new student union building, and it will be important to attract generous contributions at the reunion. A famous movie star, a former student of the college, has agreed to deliver the commencement address.

3. Your city has been selected as the site for an international summit conference on promoting peace through event tourism. Delegations from 40 different nations will be invited, including high government officials and numerous diplomatic envoys. The six-day conference will include daily plenary sessions, breakout meetings, and poster sessions, culminating in the delivery of a position paper to be circulated to heads of state throughout the world. There will be delegate luncheons each day, but the attendees will be on their own in the evenings. Because of the inclusion of numerous countries with controversial government policies, you are expecting significant media coverage, and the conference may attract demonstrators wishing to gain publicity.

CHAPTER 5

Providing the Event Infrastructure

Americans will put up with anything provided it doesn't block traffic.

—Dan Rather, TELEVISION NEWS ANCHORMAN AND JOURNALIST

IN THIS CHAPTER YOU WILL LEARN HOW TO:

- Coordinate public and private transportation services and other transportation needs as required, and implement sound traffic control strategies.
- Identify parking needs, secure parking services and equipment as required, and ensure compliance with municipal ordinances.
- Organize efficient, effective, and safe waste control plans including recycling strategies to ensure a sustainable event environment.
- Identify and arrange the implementation of all essential power, water, gas, and telecommunications needs.
- Procure an appropriate labor force and ensure that an event complies with labor union jurisdictions and regulations.

The event coordinator was giving a newspaper reporter a tour of the festival site prior to opening, showing him all the entertainment stages, food concessions, hospitality tents, and activity areas. The reporter asked to see the behind-the-scenes operations, so the event coordinator supplied a golf cart and they toured the parking areas, the temporary buildings housing the administrative offices and volunteer headquarters, the portable toilet facilities, the storage areas, and utility hookups to generators and water tanks. The reporter was astounded at the scope of the operations that the festival visitor would take for granted, saying, "You have an entire, fully functioning city here!"

Many an event could qualify as a city unto itself because it must function as a self-contained ecosystem, including a complete infrastructure to support the temporary virtual metropolis created by the event production. Just as a viable infrastructure is vital to the maintenance of a real city, it is critical to an event site as well. In their book *Marketing for Hospitality and Tourism,* Kotler, Bowen, and Makens define infrastructure as hotels, roads, airports, water systems, utility systems, and public services—specifically, public safety, traffic and crowd control, emergency health, sanitation, and street cleaning. Donald Getz, author of

Event Management and Event Tourism, delineates infrastructure in the event context even further:

- Power needs (generators and dedicated lines, amperage for special equipment, protection from weather, outlets, heat and air-conditioning, lighting and sound systems, backup and contingency plans); consultations with suppliers; need for electricians or permits; covers to protect people and lines
- Water: for drinking, food and beverage preparation, washrooms, and participants, legislation and backup supply to be checked
- Sewerage: existing lines and capacity; toilet requirements
- Gas availability

The event site may be its own virtual metropolis situated on a barren plot of land or inside a full-service purpose-built facility, yet it will still require this internal infrastructure as well as the external infrastructure of the surrounding community or destination. Dwight W. Catherwood and Richard L. Van Kirk, authors of *The Complete Guide to Special Event Management,* note that infrastructure, as it relates to special event production, not only includes the physical attributes, services, and venues, "it also means that the most powerful people, whose support and cooperation is vital to getting anything done in the community" are also lined up. They stress that "seeing that it has the proper venues and backing of every necessary group . . . including politicians, civic and community groups, private-citizen influence makers, and the area's governmental bodies" is crucial to successfully attracting or supporting a world-class event. Just as the proper functioning of your municipality of residence provides your quality of life, your temporary event metropolis must have sufficient services and systems capacity to provide the event's quality of life for the participants and visitors (see Figure 5-1).

Transportation

Transportation requirements for an event will depend on the type and size of a particular event, the scope of the professional event coordinator's responsibilities, and the impact the event will have on the surrounding community. The professional event coordinator may be charged with providing travel arrangements for an incentive group, street closures for a parade, a fleet of motor coaches to move a group from a hotel to an off-premise event, or a fleet of limousines for a motorcade.

Getting to an event can be an arduous adventure or an effortless exercise; usually, however, it is something in between. The professional event coordinator can do many things to streamline and simplify the

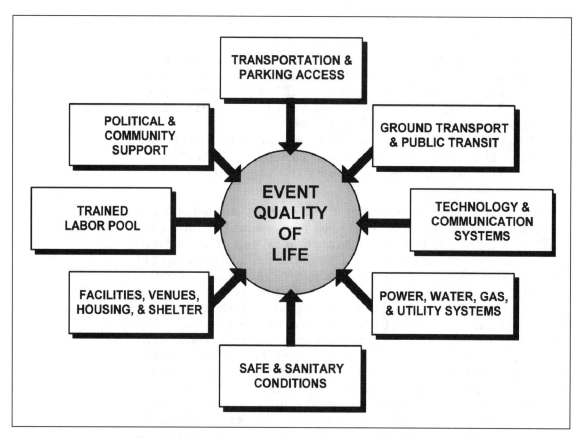

Figure 5-1
Silvers Event Infrastructure Overview

journey, whether across town or around the world. In regard to the transportation options for getting to the event destination and the options for getting around the destination or event site, the professional event coordinator makes the arrangements, selections, and recommendations that will facilitate a smooth travel experience for the guest or attendee (see Figure 5-2).

You may be arranging for an airline to become the official airline for a convention, exposition, or tourism festival and negotiating with the public transit authority for discounted-fare access to public transportation with an admission ticket to the event. You might be selecting a site based on adequate "lift" (the number of flights and airlines flying to the destination) or chartering flights on large airlines or small airplanes to a

Travel Arrangements	Transportation Needs	Transportation Options
❑ Airfare Negotiations ❑ Arrival/Departure Manifests ❑ Chartered Flights ❑ Group Bookings ❑ Infrastructure—air, rail, etc. ❑ Itineraries ❑ Meet and Greet	❑ Equipment and Supplies ❑ Group Transfers ❑ Parking ❑ Public and Private Transit ❑ Specialty Vehicles ❑ Spectators and Participants ❑ Staff and Volunteers ❑ Suppliers and Vendors	❑ Aircraft ❑ Automobiles/Taxis ❑ Buses ❑ Limousines ❑ Ships/Ferries ❑ Trains ❑ Trucks ❑ Vans

Figure 5-2
Transportation Checklist

remote destination. If the event is a multiproperty conference or convention (often designated a "city-wide"), a shuttle service running on a continuous or timed route between hotels and the convention center may be required, or a shuttle to local shopping centers for conference delegates may be needed.

The transport of goods and supplies to the event site must also be factored into the transportation plan. Such transport can involve anything from scheduling deliveries to shipping an entire race car, plus all pit equipment, halfway around the world. Meeting planners ship meeting supplies to the event site. Event designers have décor items shipped in from anywhere around the world. Festival coordinators have entire carnivals transported to their events. And a racing team did indeed ship several cars and all the requisite pit equipment from North Carolina to Australia via FedEx for a single race.

TRAVEL AND TRANSPORTATION—MOVING THE CROWD

For most event genres, the professional event coordinator is called upon to take into account the requirements for travel to the event destination as well as the transportation requirements at the destination (see Figure 5-3). Many air carriers and other transportation options offer group rates, complimentary tickets based on group sales volume, onboard amenities, and assistance with bookings and manifests. However, as with hotel room rates, group members making independent arrangements or securing lower rates through Internet specials will compromise tracking and qualifying for volume rewards.

The professional event coordinator must assess the travel and transportation requirements by identifying the likely needs of the general

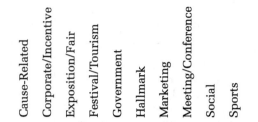

Transportation	Typical Uses	Cause-Related	Corporate/Incentive	Exposition/Fair	Festival/Tourism	Government	Hallmark	Marketing	Meeting/Conference	Social	Sports
		Typical Event Genre									
Airlines	Inbound visitors and attendees		X		X		X		X	X	
Chartered Flights	VIP or group travel, access to remote sites		X			X	X	X	X		
Ferries/Water Taxis	Over-water transfers—group or individual	X	X	X	X		X			X	X
Limousines	Upscale individual transport	X	X			X		X		X	
Motor Coaches	Group transfers, spectator shuttles, sightseeing tours		X		X		X		X		X
Private Cars	Local attendee transport	X		X	X		X	X		X	X
Public/Mass Transit	Individual transport—local and visitor	X		X	X		X				X
Rental Cars	Individual visitor transport		X	X	X	X	X		X	X	X
Shuttle Vans	Airport transfers, remote parking transfers, small group transfers, continuous shuttles	X	X	X	X		X		X		X
Taxicabs	Individual transport		X			X		X	X	X	
Trains	Inbound visitors		X		X	X	X		X		X
Trucks and Vans	Delivery of equipment and supplies	X	X	X	X	X	X	X	X	X	X

Figure 5-3
Typical Transportation Requirements

population of attendees, as well as the special transportation needs of VIPs, performers, providers, and sponsors. This may also include special arrangements with the transportation terminals, such as security-laden arrivals and departures, customs and immigration clearance, and cargo handling of special equipment. The professional event coordinator may be organizing meet-and-greet services, special baggage handling, shuttle services and/or courtesy cars, and, if handling a group of VIPs or dignitaries, possibly securing a fleet of limousines of varying quality and assigning them in order of importance.

The professional event coordinator must also take into consideration how the out-of-town attendees, spectators, or guests will get about once they are at the destination. Obviously, ground transportation needs vary greatly, depending on the type and scope of the event. The Boston Marathon's one million spectators and 20,000 participants will have different challenges than a regional arts and crafts fair that attracts 30,000 visitors primarily from the local population, and a transfer for a conference group of 1,000 will be different from a transfer for 40 VIPs at a corporate management retreat. Recurring or annual events taking place year after year or at the same venue time after time will have fewer operational challenges (it is hoped), as the transportation logistics have been improved with each event. New or temporary event venues or sites need special attention, and perhaps professional consultation, to determine the most appropriate routes and on-site transportation accommodations such as parking areas, ingress and egress, and vehicle capacity and capability.

LEAVE THE DRIVING TO US—SHUTTLING, COACHES, AND LIMOUSINE SERVICE

Ground operators, transportation providers, destination management companies (DMCs), or professional congress organizers (PCOs) may be retained to secure or provide the appropriate equipment, coordination, and supervision of on-site transportation services. With the exception of the transportation provider (the bus equipment rental company itself), these companies offer local transportation coordination and other local travel needs, including group tours, group transfers, shuttle scheduling, and special event arrangements. The professional event coordinator or transportation coordinator will consider the number of people who need to be transferred, the times when transfers are required, and the types of vehicles suitable for the transfer. Group transfer vehicles can include 55-, 47-, or 36-passenger motor coaches, 24-, 15-, or 8-passenger shuttle vans, limousines (regular sedans, stretch, or super-stretch), or a wide range of creative conveyances. When planning a group transfer via bus or motor coach, Robin E. Craven and Lynn Johnson Golabowski, authors of *The Complete Idiot's Guide to Meeting and Event Planning,* note the following factors to be addressed:

- Where—how far away is the off-site location?
- When—what are the required arrival and departure times?
- How many people are being transported?
- Do they all need to arrive/depart at the same time?
- Will it be a single trip or continuous loop?
- Where will the buses stage (line up) for pickup and park when at the off-site location?
- When should vehicles arrive for pickup at both ends?
- Where will the vehicles pick up and drop off passengers at both ends?
- Will the vehicles be accessible but secured during the event?
- Will the drivers need to be fed or are they on their own?

When selecting a transportation provider (ground operator, DMC, PCO, or bus company), the professional event coordinator should confirm the size of the fleet and the condition of the vehicles, appropriate insurance coverage, and contingency plans should a bus or motor coach break down in transit. Motor coaches are available in numerous sizes of differing quality with a broad spectrum of onboard amenities, ranging from toilets and air-conditioning to televisions sets and VCRs. Marilyn J. Reis, author of *The Receptive Operator,* advises,

> *One of the unique characteristics of international visitors is their experience and expectations regarding upscale, modern motor coach equipment (such as MCI, Van Hool, Prevost, and Setra). They are so used to seeing state-of-the-art transportation that they've come to expect it anywhere that they travel. When one travels abroad, especially in Europe, it is amazing to see the level of sophistication found in international buses even when they are used for local transportation. This difference is especially apparent when such buses are compared with most equipment used in the United States, although many American manufacturers are now modeling their equipment after the European vehicles.*

Drivers should always be provided with maps and directions and all necessary parking passes. They should have capability for two-way communication with the dispatcher at all times and, preferably, two-way communication with the event coordinator via cellular phone or radio. All vehicles used for a group transfer should have discreet but visible group identification signs in the front and door-side windows. You may wish to include step-on guides to give a presentation about the destination's culture or geography, provide onboard refreshments, and/or present onboard entertainment.

The professional event coordinator must make certain the loading area is apparent (to both the driver and the riders) and well lit, including the pathway to the loading area. If attendees must have credentials or tickets to enter the event venue or site upon arrival, check these credentials as they load the bus, not when they get to the event, to facilitate a smooth arrival. There should be a staff person from either the event organization or the transportation provider to assist with loading and to confirm qualification to board, as well as to answer any questions guests may have. To get the guests in the spirit of the event to come, theme party favors may be distributed as they board or such items may be put on the seats to save time (assuming the group will be transferred in one move).

TRAFFIC IMPACTS AND IMPLICATIONS

When you have vehicles, you have traffic, and traffic can cause problems for your event, or traffic problems may be caused by your event. Traffic congestion is affected by the time of day (rush hour), and road conditions (an accident or construction) or can be caused by a competing event drawing vehicles to the same site or crossing paths with the route to your event site. Some very large-scale or hallmark events, such as the NFL Super Bowl, necessitate changing traffic direction to facilitate the flow of large crowds into and out of the event site—all lanes are converted to one-way in, then one-way out in the opposite direction. Getz notes that large public events often cause a hardship to the surrounding residential or commercial areas, resulting from reduced accessibility to establishments and thus discouraging local customers from coming near the area. The impact of public inconvenience requires careful consideration in planning a large-scale festival or civic event and may require significant attention to community relations.

The professional event coordinator will work with the appropriate authorities to arrange the proper traffic management and control services and strategies (see Figure 5-4) based on the anticipated arrival and departure patterns—trickle (arriving/departing at various times over the duration of the event) and dump (arriving/departing all at the same time). *Traffic Management for Special Events,* published by the Roads and Traffic Authority of New South Wales, Australia (www.rta.nsw.gov.au/traffic/se_manual_v6.pdf), specifies, "The purpose of the Traffic Control Plan is to inform, control, [and] guide road users and protect the safety of all event participants, spectators, police, marshals and volunteers."

Depending on the size and type of event, the creation of a traffic control plan may be mandated prior to receiving the permits and permissions you require to stage your event. On-road events such as fun runs or parades will be regulated far more strictly than off-road events such as functions inside a purpose-built facility or at a site that will not have a significant impact on the general population, but you must never

Routing	Congestion Mitigation	Equipment and Personnel
❑ Distances and Direction ❑ Transit Duration ❑ Street/Lane Closures ❑ Alternate Routes—accidents, congestion, construction, weather ❑ Regulated Routes—high/heavy vehicles, mass movements, residential/commercial impact, emergency access	❑ Transit Timing ❑ Site Proximity to Traffic Generators—churches, hospitals, industrial areas, schools, shopping centers ❑ Signal Adjustment ❑ Promoting Public Transport ❑ Communication—inform and guide road users	❑ Route Protection—barricades, barriers, cones, signs ❑ Clearways—towing services to clear accidents ❑ Traffic Direction Personnel—police, marshals, flagging personnel ❑ Safety Equipment—high-visibility jackets and helmets

Figure 5-4
Traffic Control Checklist

assume that an event will not require authorization or traffic management assistance from local authorities. The local authorities know the business of traffic control particular to their area. For example, in San Diego, California, the traffic control policy for special events is as follows:

> *Traffic control is to be provided at various locations, such as, narrow road segments, intersections, and starting or ending points. Only properly trained or certificated personnel (by a training program approved by the Commissioner of the California Highway Patrol) are to handle the traffic control responsibilities. Traffic controllers shall wear orange vests and utilize a "Stop/Slow" paddle. Advance warning signs shall be placed, well in advance of any personnel and the event, to alert oncoming vehicles of the supplemental traffic control and the event. Traffic controllers will avoid delays or back up of traffic onto primary County roadways such that "grid-lock" does not happen; waits of more than two minutes are excessive and will not be allowed; and adjacent driveways to neighboring businesses and residences will not be blocked. The Applicant is required to use barricades for the Special Event and event materials such that emergency vehicles and personnel will be able to have unimpeded access to the area. (Reprinted courtesy of San Diego County Department of Public Works, www.sdcdpw.org/event/)*

Signs and route protection equipment, as well as the personnel authorized to direct traffic, must conform to the traffic and transportation codes of the particular jurisdiction. Both national and local governments establish these codes. In the United States, official sign color and shape, as well as regulations for temporary traffic control personnel such as flag persons, are specified in the *Manual on Uniform Traffic Control Devices* (available at mutcd.fhwa.dot.gov/kno-millennium_12.28.01.htm).

The underlying principle of any traffic control plan must be that you safely separate vehicular and pedestrian traffic. This will be particularly important in designing the site plan to accommodate the arrivals and departures of the attendees or visitors to the event, whether by private car, group transport, or public transit. Signage should be designed for the person who has never been to the area or site before, giving highway numbers, exit numbers, clear graphic directions, and event branding. Signage must be plentiful and positioned so it is visible to those driving the vehicles to the event.

Technology Tip

For major events, the event organizers should work closely with the municipal transportation authority to technologically moderate traffic congestion. Many cities employ computerized traffic management systems that discern traffic volume, flow, and congestion and are able to mitigate congestion through signal adjustment (extended signal time and/or flashing yellow or red) and variable message signs to advise motorists of accidents and alternate routes. In addition, the event organization and the government agency may both use their Internet Web sites to advise travelers, attendees, and residents of road closures during the event and preferred routes particular to the event.

PUBLIC AND MASS TRANSIT USE

Whenever possible, the professional event coordinator should incorporate and encourage the use of public transportation in the event transportation plan as well as the marketing plan. This not only alleviates traffic congestion, it also reduces the amount of parking space needed at the event site and the pollution associated with vehicle emissions. Public or mass transit may include buses, light rail, ferries, trolleys, and numerous other public conveyances. When coordinating an event that is open to the public, consult with the local transit authority about the available services such as direct routes to the event, special routes added for the event, special rates for event-goers, and the authority's ability to meet the special needs of disabled riders.

If the transit authority agrees to become part of the event's transportation plan, you must then confirm the schedules, transit routes, drop-off and pickup areas, and transit access to or next to the event site. The Australian *Traffic Management for Special Events* manual notes that once public transport has been determined, you should promote it as the preferred method of getting to and from the event, particularly by setting expectations as to the likely delays to be experienced in getting there and when the event concludes—comparing private with public transport (e.g., 90 minutes if you drive, 30 minutes if you ride). Include this public transportation in your event marketing strategies by posting and distributing public transit routes and schedules, advertising traffic arrangements, and highlighting this information in your public relations campaign. This is a public service you are offering, and it is also an excellent public relations tool for communicating the ecological benefits of mass transit and your commitment to a healthy environment. "Help the Environment—Ride the Metro" can improve the image of the event and the impact of the event.

CREATIVE OPPORTUNITIES

The professional event coordinator has numerous opportunities to be creative when it comes to moving a small (or large) group (see Figure 5-5). The conveyance equipment used can include a vast array of options, ranging from livestock to livery service (the use of luxury town cars instead of taxis or limousines). Particularly in coordinating a theme party, utilizing unusual transport will enhance the event experience. This is especially effective in offering shuttles from parking areas to the event entrance.

Parking

For every vehicle coming to an event, there must be a place to put it, even if that vehicle is staying for only a brief period of time, such as when dropping off guests or delivering supplies. You must think about staging vehicles (lining them up in the necessary order prior to arrival or departure), accommodating standing vehicles (those waiting, with or without the motor running, for loading, unloading, or while occupants are temporarily outside the vehicles), marshaling vehicles (providing an area where vehicles collect before they are staged or directed to parking

❑ Airplanes	❑ Double-Decker Buses	❑ Limousines	❑ Sleighs
❑ Army Trucks	❑ Ferries	❑ Minivans	❑ Stagecoaches
❑ Barges	❑ Floats	❑ Monorails	❑ Streetcars
❑ Bicycles	❑ Golf Carts	❑ Motor Coaches	❑ Subways
❑ Boats	❑ Gondolas	❑ Motorcycles	❑ Taxicabs
❑ Camels	❑ Helicopters	❑ Pedicabs	❑ Town Cars
❑ Canoes	❑ Horses	❑ Railway Cars	❑ Trains
❑ Carriages	❑ Jeeps	❑ Rental Cars	❑ Trams
❑ Catamarans	❑ Jitneys	❑ Rickshaws	❑ Trolley Cars
❑ Classic Cars	❑ Karaoke Party	❑ School Buses	❑ Wagons
❑ Dogsleds	Vans	❑ Shuttle Buses	❑ Yachts

Figure 5-5
Creative Conveyances Checklist

spaces), and parking vehicles in specific spaces. You must carefully consider all the parking needs, options, and issues in order to develop an efficient and effective parking plan based on the size, type, and scope of the event (see Figure 5-6). You must determine where all the different vehicles coming to the event site will be parked and how that parking will be allocated and controlled.

ANALYZE NEEDS, CAPACITY, AND CAPABILITIES

The professional event coordinator must consider the parking needs for the attendees or guests, exhibitors, participants or performers, staff and volunteers, suppliers and vendors, as well as the routes and parking for emergency vehicles and security services. Parking requirements may also include reserved parking for people with special needs, VIPs, sponsors, tour buses, or recreational vehicles staying overnight or over a week. The event coordinator may have to find parking for cars, limousines, motor coaches, trucks, delivery vans, a fleet of motorcycles, or even media satellite uplink trucks for network broadcast coverage.

It is important to analyze the expected numbers and types of vehicles likely to arrive, as well as evaluate the capacity and quality of space available for parking. You may be using a venue that has sufficient parking on the property, or you may need to identify remote, adjacent, or creative parking alternatives. You may be providing free parking or charging parking fees as a revenue stream. You might reserve public or private parking garages, lots, or covered car parks adjacent to the event site in advance, perhaps even prepaying all parking fees for your guests. You might even arrange to have parking meters bagged to reserve on-street

Parking Needs	Parking Options	Parking Issues
❑ Disabled Persons ❑ Emergency Vehicles ❑ Exhibitors ❑ Group Transfers ❑ Guests ❑ Limousines ❑ Participants ❑ Performers ❑ Recreational Vehicles ❑ Spectators ❑ Staff and Volunteers ❑ Staging/Marshaling ❑ Suppliers/Vendors ❑ VIPs	❑ Controlled-Access Lots/ Car Parks ❑ Covered ❑ Designated ❑ Garages ❑ On-property ❑ On-street—Controlled ❑ Open Lots/Car Parks ❑ Paid or Free ❑ Private Lots/Car Parks ❑ Reserved ❑ Satellite/Remote Lots ❑ Temporary Lots ❑ Valet Parking	❑ Access and Proximity ❑ Arrival/Departure Demand ❑ Capacity/Availability ❑ Communications ❑ Control ❑ Credentials/Passes ❑ Hours of Operation ❑ Insurance ❑ Loading Zones ❑ Motorist Assistance ❑ Parking Personnel ❑ Regulations/Permits ❑ Safety and Security ❑ Signage

Figure 5-6
Parking Checklist

parking for limousines or other vehicles. When reserving parking areas or specific spaces or floors of a parking garage or structure, you will need to place an attendant and post signs so others do not enter.

If your event is very large or you are creating a temporary parking area, it is wise to consult experts to determine the correct layout and site preparation. Open fields may have to be mowed and maintained, open spaces may have to be graded or evened out, and appropriate space allotment may have to be marked with chalk, pylons, paint, or stakes. The entire area may have to be temporarily fenced or designated with flags or signs. You must also analyze the arrival and departure patterns (i.e., trickle or dump) to determine peak demand periods and the routing and equipment needs, such as barricades or traffic cones.

DESIGNATE PARKING PLAN

The professional event coordinator will create (or cause to be created) a parking plan that encompasses the appropriate ingress and egress routes, access for equipment, deliveries, and emergency vehicles, as well as assigned parking areas for the various vehicles and personnel coming to the event site. The event coordinator works with public officials, municipal authorities, venue management, various stakeholders, and/or traffic and parking consultants to devise and verify the parking plan, then incorporates it into the overall event plan and budget, including identifying and communicating the roles and responsibilities of parking personnel.

Drop-off and pickup zones and routes should be established for shuttles, tour buses, taxicabs, limousines, and other vehicles delivering guests to the event. You might arrange for an entrance marquee or plan to have greeters with umbrellas should weather be a concern. You may also designate specific entrance gates or routes for different parking areas to mitigate traffic congestion. You might station personnel at points of entry to count vehicles as they arrive in order to estimate attendance at the event.

Distinct and segregated areas may be designated for different groups, such as VIP parking, staff and volunteer parking, exhibitor parking, motor coach or tour bus parking, and general public or spectator parking. The designation of these areas will most likely be based on the proximity requirements of the assigned group; exhibitors and suppliers will probably need close-in load-in/out access, and VIPs and sponsors will likely be accorded preferential parking. These designated parking areas must be clearly identified and the various groups granted special parking privileges or areas should be issued different parking passes that authorize entry accordingly.

Staging and marshaling areas may be required for larger vehicles such as trucks or motor coaches. A major trade show could have hundreds of trucks arriving, lining up at loading docks, and then needing parking spaces during the run of the show. An off-premise party for a convention group could have dozens of motor coaches to park while the guests are enjoying the event, which must then be lined up for the return to various hotels. Charity or entertainment events for which the audience uses taxicabs must establish an efficient staging strategy at the close of the event to ensure that the line of taxicabs does not impede other traffic or egress. Some tourism events establish parking areas specifically for visitors driving recreational vehicles or motor homes who wish to stay on or near the event site, which may provide a revenue source for the event. These areas may be developed with electrical, water, and sewage hookups, and spaces are often reserved many months prior to the event.

PARKING SERVICES AND CONTROLS

Depending on the type of event or attendance figures, the professional event coordinator may decide to (or be required to) provide parking personnel such as stewards or flaggers to maximize the efficiency of the traffic flow into and out of the parking areas. These parking personnel also improve the space usage by monitoring the number and positions of empty parking spaces and directing people to park their own vehicles in the available spaces. Parking stewards or flaggers should have distinctive safety clothing, such as orange vests with reflective strips, as well as paddles or flags and safety flashlights. There should be two-way communication between the stewards or flaggers and the supervisor or manager. These parking personnel might be members of an adult service organization (perhaps hired for the price of a donation to their organization), personnel of a contracted professional service, or off-duty uniformed policemen. If a service organization or contracted parking service provider is engaged, you must confirm who is responsible for liability insurance coverage (you or the organization) and secure a certificate of insurance from the organization or have this coverage added to your policy.

For upscale events such as charity functions or high-level government events, the professional event coordinator may arrange for valet parking services whereby parking attendants collect the car from the owner at the event entrance and drive it to a secure parking area until the guest is ready to depart. This service, however, does not negate the need for parking space arrangements. The parking area for valet-parked vehicles must be secured with the appropriate permissions or rental to prevent the towing of unauthorized or incorrectly parked vehicles. When contracting a valet parking service, it is also important to make certain that the attendants have been appropriately screened and trained in the proper operation of all makes of vehicles.

Other parking services include motorist assistance (e.g., jump starts for dead batteries or unlocking doors for those who locked their keys in a car), shuttle service to and from the event entrance and specific pickup points, and extended hours of operation for adjacent parking facilities so that guests will not be rushed at the close of the evening (or find themselves locked out and unable to claim their cars). Again, you may secure some of these services from service contractors or service organizations, and you must always consider liability and confirm that proper insurance coverage is in place.

PRIVATE PROPERTY AND PUBLIC SAFETY

No one can assume that he or she may park any type of vehicle anywhere there happens to be space. Private property is just that—private—not public. Special permits may be required for parking areas, particularly for controlled venues such as a college campus or stadium property, or for event vehicles parked on city streets. Parking may be restricted during certain times of the day. Event parking may be prohibited in residential areas, and a towing service may be required to remove illegally parked vehicles. You may require special permits to park a fleet of limousines or to park motor coaches waiting for boarding time.

The professional event coordinator must always consider the safety and security of those attending the event, whether guests or staff. Parking areas should have adequate lighting, signage, and security to prevent thefts, vandalism, or assault. You may wish to arrange for safety escorts for staff or participants leaving the venue in the wee hours of the morning (which is not unusual), or for security personnel to patrol the parking area in golf carts throughout the event. You must ensure that the parking plan complies with all municipal legislation, proper insurance coverage is in place, and the appropriate warnings or disclaimers (e.g., "Do not leave valuables in your car," "Lock your vehicle," "The management is not responsible for . . .") are clearly displayed on signs and on parking or valet tickets.

Waste Management and Recycling

A primary component of any community infrastructure is a suitable sanitation system including waste management, sewage services, and recycling initiatives. It is a matter of public health, whether the public is a general population or an event population. It is also a cosmetic matter; an event site that is littered with trash and debris will not be appealing to guests, nor to important stakeholders. Waste management consists of planning for the collection and disposal of all solid, semisolid, and liquid waste created at the event.

Depending on the event site, the professional event coordinator may simply confirm the presence of suitable capabilities at a facility or may subcontract services to utilize an undeveloped or underdeveloped site (see Figure 5-7). One might ask why you must consider all these factors

Typical Waste Types	Waste Collection	Waste Disposal
❑ Bottles, Cans, Containers ❑ Cleaning (Gray Water) ❑ Cooking/Food Waste ❑ Disposables ❑ Green (Yard) Waste ❑ Hazardous/Toxic ❑ Human (Black Water) ❑ Packing Materials ❑ Rubbish/Litter/Debris	❑ Bags ❑ Bins ❑ Cans/Receptacles ❑ Dumpsters ❑ Front-end Loaders ❑ Roll-off Containers ❑ Source Separation ❑ Stationary Compacters ❑ Wheeled Carts	❑ Compacting ❑ Composting ❑ Incineration ❑ Recycling ❑ Sanitary Landfill ❑ Shredding ❑ Waste-to-Energy Incineration

Figure 5-7
Waste Management Checklist

if you are using a purpose-built or standard venue—can't waste management and toilet facilities be taken for granted in these types of venues? You will not know whether the venue is capable of accommodating the specific types or volumes of waste unless you confirm its capacities and capabilities based on the specific characteristics of your event.

A festival held on purpose-built fairgrounds may exceed standard amounts of waste, requiring additional cleanup crews, receptacles, or scheduled collections. A hotel may have separate stationary compacters for wet garbage, dry trash that will be incinerated, and recyclables, requiring you to sort materials before disposal. Recycling of certain materials may be municipally mandated. The exhibitors may leave hundreds of pounds of leftover materials when they pack up their booths or stands. The confetti canons or balloon drop you used for an exciting finale may leave a layer of debris on the ballroom floor. These contingencies all have operational impacts and costs attached that must be factored into the event plan and budget.

You must assess and analyze the waste that will be generated by your event, then plan the strategies and secure the appropriate services and equipment for controlling, collecting, and disposing of that waste properly. There may be environmental impacts, and certainly budgetary impacts, that must be controlled. You should consult with local authorities and make certain your event is in compliance with all applicable legislation, as well as communicate your waste management policies and procedures to all personnel, participants, and providers.

ANALYZE THE TRASH

Different events generate different types of waste, based on the purpose, activities, audience, and duration of the event. Meetings or conferences may generate more paper waste than cooking waste, a food fair or cook-off may produce the reverse. Concessionaires at a sports event may be selling beverages in cans or plastic cups (preferably not bottles), and a health fair may have medical waste such as sharps (needles, syringes, etc.) used in a child immunization drive or diagnostic activities. A park beautification event may have green waste, and a car race may generate automotive product waste. You must also consider the odors associated with cooking, livestock, toilets, or other aspects of the event or the event site. The volume of waste should be calculated by reviewing previous or comparable events, as well as analyzing the event elements.

TOXIC AND CONTROLLED WASTE ISSUES

Toxic or hazardous waste must always be disposed of according to prescribed and required procedures. Medical and biohazard waste is strictly controlled, including sharps, human blood or blood products, and any infectious solid waste (discarded materials contaminated with blood, excretions, exudates, and secretions from humans or animals with certain communicable diseases). Although these regulations do not pertain to most events, some medical events such as training programs or meetings (or a health fair, as mentioned earlier) may require special attention.

Hazardous household materials, common products used around the home, are often used in the context of an event and must be disposed of properly—not put in the trash or poured down a drain. Nothing should ever be poured down storm drains, as they flow "untreated" into rivers, lakes, or oceans. A substance is considered hazardous if it ignites easily, reacts or explodes when mixed with other substances, and/or is corrosive or toxic. Check for labels that bear the words *caution, danger, poison, toxic,* and/or *warning.*

COLLECTION AND REMOVAL

Sufficient trash receptacles, efficient clearing and cleaning, and properly scheduled waste removal must be factored into the site plan and operations. The professional event coordinator must work with the venue management and local authorities to arrange for waste disposal and recycling containers suitable for the needs of the event. Containers may include bins or Dumpsters (named after those of the original developer, the Dempster Company, called Dempster Dumpsters), large wheeled carts/ Dumpsters, trash cans or other litter receptacles, or large roll-off containers (such as those seen at construction sites) for events requiring holding bins. Temporary food service stalls will probably require covered trash containers.

You must obtain the sufficient size and number of containers and place them in suitable locations so they do not block pedestrian traffic. They must be readily accessible at the points where trash is likely to be thrown away, and they must be clearly labeled (e.g., recyclable materials, paper only, or hazardous waste). You might have logo-imprinted trash receptacles created for your event. You may need to have a crew of volunteers or paid personnel strolling throughout the event grounds, picking up rubbish during the event. You may need to set aside a storage area for exhibitors' packing materials.

The appropriate schedules and routes for waste removal and recycling must be confirmed or arranged. If your event is likely to generate more waste than the regular trash collection schedule accommodates, you may need to pay for additional pickup during or directly following your event. Collection vehicles, particularly front-end loaders, can be large and loud, so you must make sure that they are routed and scheduled in such a way that they do not disturb the event or its neighbors and do not damage the event grounds. You may need to contractually specify trash removal responsibilities with your suppliers, such as requiring off-premise caterers remove gray water (wastewater other than sewage, such as sink or washing drainage, also known as sullage) rather than disposing of it on-site.

SANITATION AND SEWAGE

An event site must comply with all sanitation regulations, which govern everything from pest control to portable toilets. Toilet facilities, whether permanent or portable, must be considered for every event. Even if there are toilet facilities at the venue you are using, are they sufficient for the number of attendees or the event schedule? According to Richard A. Hildreth, author of *The Essentials of Meeting Management,* the statistical average amount of time to go to the toilet is five minutes for women and three minutes for men, with air hand-driers extending that time by 30 seconds. If everyone is heading for the lavatories during a short meeting break or program intermission, there may be long lines forming and many frustrated attendees.

For undeveloped or underdeveloped event sites, portable sanitation units may be brought in. These can include anything from single units housed in narrow plastic shells to deluxe portable toilet trailers with running water, flush toilets, exhaust fans for ventilation, trash receptacles, washbasins, liquid soap dispensers, mirrors, fluorescent lights, air-conditioning and heating, and even AM/FM stereo equipment to play background music. According to Portable Sanitation Association International, deluxe trailers requiring water or electrical hookups should be positioned within 100 ft (30.5 m) of the water/electrical lines, and individual units must be placed within 25 ft (7.6 m) of permanent hard-surface roadway for festivals or events where the units are to be serviced daily over several days. For big events with a large number of units, the service truck may remain on-site to provide continuous standby maintenance service (www.psai.org).

Depending on the event, you may also procure hand washing stations, shower facilities, baby changing stations, and/or wheelchair-accessible units. The average number of sanitation units required is illustrated in Figure 5-8, but you should check with local authorities to make certain you have sufficient and appropriate equipment based on the size and type of event as well as the local codes where your event is being held. The number of portable toilet units or stalls (those that contain both a seat and a urinal) required depends on the type, schedule, and duration of the event (there are typically four hours between individual uses), as well as the activities and the audience; serving alcohol increases the number needed, as well as the ratio of men to women and whether the units are single-sex designated. At a minimum, the ratio of single-sex units should be 2 to 1, women to men. (Even if individual

Event Duration (hours daily)

Attendance	1	2	3	4	5	6	7	8	9	10
0–100	2	2	2	2	2	3	3	3	3	3
250	3	3	3	3	4	4	4	4	6	6
500	4	4	6	6	6	8	8	8	10	10
1,000	5	6	6	7	7	8	10	10	12	12
2,500	8	10	12	14	16	18	20	20	22	24
5,000	12	16	18	20	22	24	28	30	34	36
7,500	22	26	32	36	40	42	46	48	50	54
10,000	30	36	42	50	54	58	60	68	72	72
125,000	36	38	47	63	78	94	109	125	141	156
150,000	36	38	56	75	94	113	131	150	169	188
200,000	40	50	75	100	125	150	175	200	225	250

Number of Toilet Units

Sources: Portable Sanitation Association International Industry (www.psai.org); Acme Toilet Rentals, Inc. (www.turdman.com/tips.htm); Ar-Jon Portable Toilets (www.ar-jon. com/home.htm); Stanford University Facilities Operations (www.stanford.edu/group/ eventservice/portable_toilet_chart.htm); Walters Company (www.walterscompany.com/ specialevents.html); J&J Chemical Company Portable Toilet Calculator (www.jjchem. com/ConversionChart.html).

Figure 5-8
Portable Toilet Calculator (Confirm with local authorities for jurisdictional codes and event type.)

units are single-sex designated, in the United States many women will now disregard this designation if waiting lines are disproportionate and will commandeer the units as needed.) Rental costs for single units average approximately $70 for a two-day event, and the executive-style trailers start at approximately $2000 per day.

If there is an elephant in the middle of the room, put a costume on it! People will need to use the toilet, so you may as well incorporate it into the overall event design. Portable toilets can be procured in various colors to coordinate with a theme, to specify single-sex usage, or to identify a particular zone of an event site. They may be dressed or concealed with décor such as latticework, fencing, or panels. They should be monitored regularly to make certain they are clean and well stocked with the appropriate supplies. You may also wish to segregate guest facilities from staff and crew facilities by positioning staff toilets out of sight or in a separate tent.

RECYCLING AND PRECYCLING

Conservation and recycling is becoming increasingly important throughout the world—and at events. Strategies for conserving water and other natural resources should be incorporated throughout the event operations, including recycling and precycling activities. Recycling activities are characterized by three strategies: reduce, reuse, and recycle (see Figure 5-9), which constitute the diversion or removal of materials destined for disposal for reprocessing, remanufacturing, and reuse. Recycling reduces disposal costs and may even provide modest revenues. Mandatory recycling programs require by law that consumers separate trash so that some or all recyclable materials are not burned or dumped into landfills (see Jennings and Sneed, 1996). Precycling is the conscious preplanning to reduce, reuse, and recycle materials.

WASTE CONTROL INCENTIVES

The professional event coordinator should review the entire event operation to identify recycling opportunities and mandated requirements, in order to create policies and procedures for implementing waste control and recycling initiatives. A review of each line item of an event budget can reveal possible ways to minimize waste, buy recycled and recyclable materials, and donate used and unused items. For instance, by giving out reusable canvas conference tote bags instead of plastic ones, limiting printed handouts or digitizing proceedings at a conference, restricting the use of Styrofoam drinking cups and selling reusable plastic commemorative drinking cups at a festival, or selecting venues or vendors that practice sound conservation practices, an event organization can control waste.

The professional event coordinator may also institute disincentives, such as financial penalties for exhibitors who leave their unused printed materials and leftover packing materials, or establish a waste management surcharge for food concessionaires who do not use recyclable serving materials. These policies, however, must be confirmed with the local authorities, the event's legal advisors, and stakeholders to ensure that they are in compliance with all health and safety regulations and that they are legal, practical, and culturally permissible.

Reduce	Reuse	Recycle
❏ Avoid disposables—cups, napkins, plates, utensils. ❏ Buy in bulk—less packaging, buy concentrates. ❏ Give out reusable mugs or or commemorative cups. ❏ Go electronic—e-mail, on-line registration, and evaluation forms instead of printed material. ❏ Plan large-scale sandwich buffets vs. box luncheons. ❏ Use paperless check-in, check-out, and billing. ❏ Use recyclable packing materials—paper and corrugated boxes vs. polystyrene and plastic wrap. ❏ Use recycled paper and soy-based ink.	❏ Containers. ❏ Donate centerpieces, leftover supplies, exhibitor giveaways, foam-core and vinyl drape to local shelters, hospitals, senior centers, or schools. ❏ Donate surplus food to food banks or shelters as appropriate. ❏ Paper—use back sides for drafts or scratch paper. ❏ Plastic bags. ❏ Plastic/vinyl badge holders. ❏ Polystyrene packing and peanuts. ❏ Signs. ❏ Use white boards instead of flip charts.	❏ Batteries. ❏ Computers—donation and recycling. ❏ Computer floppy disks. ❏ Disposable cameras—be sure to take to a developer that explicitly promises to recycle the remains. ❏ Glass. ❏ Metals—aluminum and tin cans, coat hangers. ❏ Paper*—including corrugated boxes, newspaper, stationery. ❏ Place recycling bins in meeting rooms and throughout event site. ❏ Plastics. ❏ Printer/toner cartridges.

*Paper that cannot be recycled includes food-contaminated paper, waxed paper, waxed cardboard milk and juice containers, oil-soaked paper, carbon paper, sanitary products or tissues, thermal fax paper, stickers and plastic-lamimated paper such as fast food wrappers, juice boxes, and pet food bags.

Sources: MPI, Green Meetings, *www.mpiweb.org/resources/GreenMeetings/; Jennifer Carless (1992)*, Taking Out the Trash *(Washington, DC: Island Press); The Internet Consumer Recycling Guide, www.obviously.com/recycle/.*

Figure 5-9
Recycling Checklist

Utilities

Virtually all events require sources for power, water, and other utilities. However, not all event sites have accessible connections to these sources and some have no utilities at all. The professional event coordinator must then procure portable or temporary sources. Even if the event site has plentiful and easy access to power, water, gas, and telecommunication lines, there may be a surcharge for their use, particularly in areas where consumption is strictly regulated or resources are scarce. The professional event coordinator must understand the electrical, water, and gas needs, including the volume, proximity, and distribution requirements and the installation, operation, and safety restrictions.

Depending on the event type, scope, site, and its elements, utility needs can range from simply the ability to plug in a few electrical appliances to creating the infrastructure for a completely self-contained temporary community (see Figure 5-10). The professional event coordinator must assess the capabilities of the event site and compare them with the needs of the various products and providers to determine the appropriate layout of the site and acquire the supplemental systems or equipment needed.

ELECTRICAL POWER

Elecitricity may be needed at an event simply for plugging in a caterer's coffeemaker, or for lighting an entire city block and powering a dozen television uplink trucks. Our reliance on electrical and electronic appliances makes a reliable power source virtually imperative; even the tools used to install the simplest item of décor may require electricity. Lighting is required throughout an event site and for its duration, including setup and breakdown. Self-contained high-intensity outdoor lighting fixtures may use generator power or even solar power battery packs. Other items of equipment to consider are the computers used at the registration area, inflatable games, audiovisual and entertainment equipment, and even the golf carts used to get around the event grounds.

Potential power fluctuations or outages may dictate that emergency or backup systems be in place, either provided by the facility or brought in by the professional event coordinator. Portable power generators in a broad range of sizes and styles may be rented to compensate for power inconsistencies or deficiencies. Newer equipment is sound attenuated

Electricity	Water	Gas
❑ Appliances ❑ AV Equipment ❑ Décor ❑ Entertainment ❑ HVAC Systems ❑ Lighting—Décor and Safety ❑ Sound Equipment	❑ Cleaning ❑ Cooling ❑ Cooking ❑ Décor ❑ Drinking ❑ Dust Abatement ❑ Safety and Sanitation	❑ Cooking ❑ Heating ❑ Generators ❑ Natural Gas ❑ Petrol ❑ Propane ❑ Specialty Gases

Figure 5-10
Utilities Checklist

and very quiet, but older equipment can be quite loud and may need to be placed a significant distance from the main action of the event, which will require installation of additional distribution equipment, such as cables and connectors, to span the distance. Portable generators are fuel-powered (diesel or gasoline), and the exhaust emissions may have to be regulated; their use should certainly be considered carefully in terms of proximity to people or animals. In other words, they can be noisy and smelly.

On-Site Insight

Daniel Mulhern, project manager for the Las Vegas, Nevada, office of Kohler Event Services, notes, "An event coordinator is not required to be a 'power expert.' However, having a basic understanding of power-generated equipment and technical terminology can be helpful. It's all about knowing the right questions to ask to make servicing your client simple and effective. Being acquainted with your power company, along with knowing the essential requirements needed, will assist in making your event a success." Key questions to ask yourself and your clients include the following:

- Who actually needs the power? Is it directly with one client? Or, are there numerous subclients (i.e., lighting, sound, catering companies, etc.—their needs can differ dramatically)? Service the entire event!
- How much power do they need? What are the numbers of amps required? What equipment will be running? And how long will the equipment be running? Is it stage lighting? A PA system? Or simply a 55-cup coffeemaker?
- Where is it going? How far will the end user be from the source? And what connections will need to be dropped in between? Keep all local event and fire codes in check! Verify any permitting requirements.

"As a final point, advance planning for power will increase the chances of a successful event. Have a site map and production schedule on hand. When last-minute changes come up, and you know they always do, you'll be ready to react knowing you have the most accurate information about your temporary power supply."

WATER

The water needs of an event can range from bottled water for 50 meeting attendees to cups of water on tables stationed along a route for thousands of marathon runners, or running water for sanitation accommodations to the cooling mechanisms for decorative laser light displays. For outdoor or temporary sites using food concessions or off-premise caterers, sufficient potable water must be available for food preparation, cleaning, sanitizing utensils and equipment, and hand washing. Potable water may be required for portable toilets and showers. It may be required for evaporative cooling mechanisms such as misters or sprinklers. You may need to have trucks spray nonpotable water on a dirt playing field or parking lot to reduce dust prior to the event each day. Standby water trucks may be required for fire protection.

Sufficient potable water must be available for drinking at all times; dehydration is a critical health issue at events, particularly outdoor events occurring in hot weather. Bottled Water Web (www. bottledwaterweb.com) states: "The human body contains over 75% water. Even mild dehydration will slow down one's metabolism as much as 3%. A mere 2% drop in body water can trigger fuzzy short-term memory." The professional event coordinator should identify the location and capabilities of water sources and connections. If suitable water connections are not available, potable water must be supplied by means of approved water-holding tanks, containers, or other equipment. This could include portable bottled water drinking fountains/coolers, 5-gal jugs, water tanks, or tanker trucks. It may be possible to tap into a water supply by means of an adjacent fire hydrant (with permission from the local fire department or other authorities).

As with other waste management applications, you must plan for the disposal of all wastewater, including drainage of groundwater. This is a health and a safety issue. Water connections and hoses must be suitable and sufficient for the intended uses and monitored for leakage and condition. Keep in mind that water and electricity do not mix. Their connections and lines must be safely segregated.

GAS

The gas needs of an event can range from diesel fuel for portable generators to propane for heaters or cooking equipment, or even a tank of helium to inflate decorative balloons. A hot air balloon uses propane to heat the air inside the balloon to keep it aloft. Many buildings use natural gas heating systems and kitchen equipment. A number of vehicles now use natural gas for fuel. Some events offer "oxygen bars," where guests can inhale to their hearts' content. Most gases, however, are toxic, and the professional event coordinator must make certain that the areas in which gas-powered equipment is used are well ventilated and that the containers for the gases are properly secured. A helium tank can become a lethal missile if the cap is dislodged. The event coordinator must work closely with the site management, vendors, and local authorities to make certain all gas utilities are installed to code and operated correctly.

ENVIRONMENTAL CONTROLS—HVAC

The ambient atmosphere of the event site will have an impact on the success of the event. If the event space is too hot, cold, humid, arid, breezy, or still, the event will suffer, as will the audience—those who attend and endure the conditions. Controlling the climatic atmosphere will raise enjoyment levels and increase productivity. The professional event coordinator should become familiar with a venue's heating, ventilation, and air-conditioning (HVAC) systems and their controls to be able to modify the atmosphere within a meeting or function room properly.

Ventilation systems circulate air. The air coming in should be fresh (from the outside), and the air extracted expelled outside so that the system is not simply recirculating stale air. This is especially important if there will be smoke from cigarettes, cigars, cooking, or special effects such as fog machines or indoor pyrotechnics. You may need to increase the ventilation or add special filters so as not to set off smoke alarms, and you should make certain that you do not block any vents with décor or equipment.

Controlling the atmosphere in a temporary structure or tent may require portable HVAC equipment such as heaters, air-conditioning units, evaporative coolers, and fans. The American Rental Association (www.ararental.org) advises that there are generally two types of tent heaters—direct-fired, such as the tall patio heaters with aluminum umbrellas that reflect heat downward, and indirect-fired units including heat exchangers that allow fumes to vent away from the heated area. Cooling options include air-conditioning units and evaporative cooling systems. Selecting the right heating or cooling system depends on the size and position of the tent or temporary structure, the time of day and time of year, and the atmospheric conditions outside.

TELECOMMUNICATIONS

Telephone and telecommunication lines may be available or accessible, depending on the facility in which the event is taking place. Some facilities have existing lines or connections you can plug into, and others have contractual agreements with specific service providers for temporary telecommunications equipment and access. The telecommunications needs of an event will vary according to the type of event and client needs. Public festivals may need a bank of public telephones on-site for visitor use. Conventions may require both wired and wireless means of communications. An out-of-town client may need a temporary combination cellular telephone and two-way radio while on-site. Certain expositions or media centers may require significant access to sophisticated technology such as ISDN or T1 lines and DSL connections.

- ISDN (integrated services digital network) lines permit the integration of computer data and video by allowing for faster transmission of data over telephone lines. An ISDN line is a dial-up line four times as large (faster) as a regular telephone line.
- T1 lines are leased dedicated telephone lines (no dial-up fees) that have 12 times the capacity of an ISDN line.
- DSL (digital subscriber line) is a service that offers a faster Internet connection than a standard dial-up connection, using a standard telephone line and a DSL router to provide continuous connection to the Internet and use of the telephone at the same time. DSL offers the speed of a T1 line without the cost of a T1 line.

CALCULATING YOUR NEEDS

The professional event coordinator should carefully calculate the power needs for each event to be able to work with the venue's electrical engineer or the power provider for an undeveloped or underdeveloped site, to coordinate the required load or pull—the amount of power each user will need. Each electrical or electronic device or piece of equipment will have specific power consumption specifications, expressed or measured in amps (amperes); amp is the unit of measurement for electrical current. Amps (the current) are calculated by dividing the number of watts (the quantity of electricity) by the volts (the pressure at which electric current is delivered). Voltage will vary in different parts of the world; the European standard voltage is 220 V, and the U.S. standard is 120 V. Some appliances are rated in kilowatts (1000 watts per kilowatt).

Prepare or collect electrical load sheets, one for each supplier, and forward copies to your power supplier or venue electrician to plot the power needs, distribution, and equipment. Each supplier should be able to provide you with the total number of amps required for the equipment to be used at the event. At the very least, providers should be able to identify the wattage rating for each piece of equipment. When additional power is required or use of a secondary power source is indicated, portable power generators can be procured. Kohler Event Services notes that generators and power distribution units are used to interface with or function independently from existing power supplies. Different sizes of tow-behind portable generators can accommodate 20 to 180 kW, and trailer-mounted generator packages are available up to 2000 kW, each with variable voltage selectors (www.kohlereventservices.com).

POWER DISTRIBUTION

Electrical power may be plentiful, but the loads must be distributed appropriately to prevent overloading a single source or circuit. A circuit is a complete electrical path from the electrical supply to the outlet (or *reverse*—the international term for an outlet). Electricity is carried and controlled through power distribution equipment, such as wires, cables, snakes, circuit breakers, fuses, distribution boxes, connectors, and switches (which are load-rated by their current-carrying capacity), that intakes electricity and routes it to an output device—where you plug in. Feeder cables or snakes are used to get the power outlets to where they are needed, which can involve miles of cables when the event is large and complex. Power lines may be laid on the floor or ground, rigged throughout a ceiling, or dropped from above to provide the connections you need. Cables, wires, cords, and connectors must be laid carefully and covered with ramps when on the floor or ground to ensure that they do not become a slip-and-trip hazard and that they are protected from damage.

COST CONTROLS

The use of utilities may be included in the rental fees for the venue, or you may be charged for the amounts used. It is not uncommon to have a surcharge on electricity usage, and the surcharge may be based on the total amount of electrical power used or the power used during certain times of the day. You may wish to compare the cost difference between the in-house power charges and bringing in a portable generator system, particularly during peak times of use. You may also decide that ordering redundant equipment is necessary to ensure an uninterrupted power source. Telephone charges are customary, particularly long distance charges, but you may be able to negotiate lower access fees or you might compare costs for procuring a service provider other than the one the facility uses (if permissible).

If there are usage fees, make certain you understand how that usage will be measured and monitor those measurements throughout the duration of the event. Make certain these charges are separated on the invoice or master bill so that you can address any discrepancies as well as develop a usage profile for future events. You should survey and brainstorm with your suppliers to determine conservation and efficiency strategies for cost savings in conjunction with utility usage.

INSTALLATION, OPERATION, AND SAFETY INSPECTIONS

The site selected for an event should be examined to determine the power and other utility capabilities, including the number and locations of outlets, the capacities, the distribution requirements, and the backup systems in case of a power failure. Depending on the event and its power needs, you may consult with the local power authorities, building maintenance personnel or engineer, or subcontracted service providers. You may wish to arrange for a standby electrician throughout the duration of your event. You may wish to specify that an on-site technician or technicians be included in the quote for temporary power services.

Undeveloped or underdeveloped sites may require official site inspections prior to use to determine the capabilities and equipment needed to produce the event as designed. Additional inspections may then be necessary once the utilities are installed, to ensure that the installation is up to code, the equipment is in proper working order, and the access or perimeters are properly restricted. Such inspection must be factored into the use of an unusual or onetime event site, particularly in regard to the budget, timeline, and site layout.

The installation, operation, and dismantling of utilities should always be left to professionals. Unless you are a licensed electrician, you do not want to be meddling with electrical power configurations and connections. In fact, some jurisdictions require a portable power provider to have an electrical contractor license, and many jurisdictions require permits for specific electrical supply uses (e.g., pulling power from an adjacent building). The same may apply in regard to installing or utilizing gas or water utilities.

In some jurisdictions, all the installation, operation, and dismantling of utilities, as well as other aspects of the event setup, require that specific labor unions do all the work. The professional event coordinator must understand these jurisdictional requirements in order to get the workers needed to bring the event environment to life.

Labor and Labor Unions

Labor refers to contracted workers who perform services, who may come from a union or specialized labor-for-hire agency. They may be skilled union craftspersons or they may be readymen (nonunion, temporary labor hired from a personnel agency). They may be secured through the venue, a supplier, the client or host, or a government employment bureau. You might be required to use union workers or venue-supplied workers exclusively and to abide by the specific employment practices of that union or venue (e.g., minimum hours, wages, overtime rates, and working conditions). Even if not mandated, union workers may be the best workers for the job because of their training and expertise. Union labor issues, in regard to events, most often relate to exposition events, but they can affect other special events and entertainment productions as well (see Figure 5-11).

A union is an organization of workers formed for mutual protection and for the purpose of dealing collectively with their employers on issues related to wages, working conditions, and other work rules pertaining to their employment. They were established to control fair labor practices and working conditions. Sometimes they are used to control how work will be performed, which has both good and bad effects. There are many stories about having to pay a union worker an exorbitant amount to plug in and turn on a lamp or string an extension cord, but from the previous discussion, you should realize that one cannot simply plug anything in just anywhere; laying an extension cord must be done according to safety specifications. Although excesses do occur, such as featherbedding (make-work practices requiring more workers than necessary or requiring unnecessary work), adherence to labor union requirements is a sound risk management practice.

Pricing Factors	Positions	Typical Jurisdictions	Union Issues
Dead Time	Apprentice	AV Technicians	Craft Union
Double Time	Business Agent	Carpenters	Featherbedding
Holidays	Craftsperson	Decorators	Hiring Hall
Minimums	Dispatcher	Drayage	Industrial/Vertical Union
Overtime	Floater	Electricians	Local
Premium Pay	Job Foreman	Maintenance	Open Shop
Reporting Pay	Journeyman	Musicians	Permit Card
Straight Time	Leadman	Plumbing	Rank and File
Supervisor Ratios	Readymen	Riggers	Right-to-Work States
Time-and-a-Half	Semiskilled Labor	Stagehands	Union Referral
Work Rules—	Shop Steward	Telephone Installation	Union Shop
wage rates and	Working Foreman	Transport	
working conditions			

Figure 5-11
Union Labor Considerations

UNION JURISDICTIONS

In some locations, using union labor is mandated and different unions may represent workers who perform different functions, known as jurisdictions. A union jurisdiction is the specific industry, craft, and/or geographical area for which a local union is chartered to organize or represent. You may be dealing with a craft union representing individuals possessing or working at a specific skill or trade such as carpentry or plumbing, or an industrial/vertical union whose membership includes all workers in a particular industry regardless of particular skills or occupation. You may deal with teamsters for the transport of materials to the event site; an expo union for the drayage (using forklifts and other heavy equipment to move materials from the dock to the event or exhibit space); stagehands or carpenters for assembling and installing the exhibit or décor; electricians for assembling and maintaining electrical fixtures and other heating, lighting, and power systems; plumbers to install water, gas, or water disposal systems; riggers, who use equipment to move, place, or attach machinery or displays; and porters or maintenance workers to sweep, clean, and dust.

You may be required to use union labor for only certain specific tasks or for all the work within a facility. The facility may be a union shop (all employees must belong to a union) or an open shop (union membership is not a condition of employment). Some locations in the United States are in right-to-work states, which have passed legislation mandating that joining a union may not be required as a condition of employment. There may be a jurisdictional dispute as to which union's members will perform a certain type of work, and you may not be dealing with the same union in different locations.

IDENTIFY LABOR NEEDS AND COSTS

The professional event coordinator should carefully estimate labor needs and schedules, and then incorporate this information into the applicable labor regulations. Some unions require a minimum of four hours' work. Some regulations specify how long a worker may work and when meals and breaks must be taken. Different types of union workers have different straight-time pay rates, the base wage. Overtime, time-and-a-half, and double-time wage rates may apply, particularly when workers are scheduled for long hours, after regular hours, or during holidays. It may be more cost-effective to hire the venue an extra day or two rather than pay the increased wage rates for premium pay conditions. An event coordinator certainly wants to avoid paying for dead time (when a laborer is on the job but unable to work or waiting because of factors beyond his or her control) or reporting pay (guaranteed payment when a worker reports for a job as specified but finds no work to be done).

Payment of wages may be made through the union or agency, or directly to the worker. At all times, however, you must comply with all the applicable labor laws, rules, and regulations regarding employment taxes, working conditions, and/or employee benefits. For temporary staffing or labor from a personnel agency or supplier, the hourly rate includes the costs of payroll bookkeeping, employment taxes, and other administrative necessities. It is wise to confirm the company's references and financial condition, as well as the training it provides, so that the event organization does not become liable for taxes through default of the supplier. It is also wise to check with the venue management during your site inspections to determine when union contracts are due to be renegotiated, as such timing may indicate the possibility of disputes or strikes that could affect your ability to install and produce the event.

UNION HIERARCHIES

Unions often have a specific hierarchy, including who supervises whom and particular conflict resolution protocols, which you must respect and follow. You may initially be dealing with the union's business agent, the official at the top of the hierarchy, to establish the labor requirements and work rules for the event, including the labor call—the number of laborers and skill level (e.g., journeyman, apprentice, or semiskilled), the ratio of supervisors or job foremen, floaters, dispatchers, leadman specifications, and the tasks to be completed. You may need journeymen (those who have successfully completed an apprenticeship in a skilled trade) or semiskilled labor (whose performance will not cause excessive damage to a product or equipment).

You may select workers via a hiring hall (the union and/or employer dispatching workers to a job as needed), or you may select the workers sent by a union referral whereby applicants are referred to the employer rather than selected by the union. On the job site, you will deal with the shop steward (or stewards) in charge of the rank and file—the union members. All grievances or dissatisfaction, either employer's or employee's, should be communicated through the union steward.

You should get written guidelines and work rules from the applicable union and plan to comply with them to the letter. Work with the venue, general services contractor, and/or local officials to determine the union requirements and your labor options. You may be able to subcontract your own union workers who hold permit cards from a separate or different union and still be in compliance with union jurisdictional requirements.

POSITIVE RELATIONSHIPS

The professional event coordinator must define and communicate the job expectations and provide the tools, training, and orientation necessary for each worker to do his or her job in an atmosphere of mutual respect and communal achievement. Whether hired or inherited, casual laborers or union workers, you must develop an effective, honest, and mutually beneficial relationship with these workers. Respect, communication, recognition, and reward are the cornerstones of good labor relations.

Bringing an event to life is hard work. Setting up an event can involve a handful of friends and family for a personal celebration or hundreds (or thousands) of hired workers for a large meeting or public festival, but these people are all working toward the successful implementation of the event vision. They must be motivated and engaged in the successful outcome of the event project. Whether paid or volunteer, part-time or full-time, each person should be treated as a valued participant in the project.

Target Competency Review

An event site is a microcosmic community requiring an infrastructure similar to that of any municipality to ensure the quality of life at the event. It must have an effective transportation system, sufficient facilities for parking and people, sanitary conditions, utilities, and ample labor resources. Transportation needs must be addressed for both getting to the event destination or locale and getting to and around the event site, which can involve public and private transport providers and the impact of such transportation on the surrounding community.

Comprehensive assessment and planning must be done to ensure that the facilities for people and vehicles are appropriate and in compliance with all local, regional, and national legislation. Parking plans and services must be sensitive to the needs of the event's neighbors as well as the event-goers and must reflect the nature and purpose of the event. Waste management and sanitation requirements must be meticulously addressed to ensure a healthy and safe environment. The essential utilities must be confirmed or imported to make the event site fully functional, and the appropriate labor force must be procured to bring the event to life.

There are numerous creative opportunities for providing this infrastructure. The professional event coordinator must make certain that these basic human services and human resources are in place. They are either invisible because they are coordinated so flawlessly, or they are integrated, when appropriate, into the design aspects of the event to provide a visible expression of the goals and objectives of the event and the event organization.

EXERCISES IN PROFESSIONAL EVENT COORDINATION

Outline and describe the infrastructure requirements and plans, including transportation, parking, waste management, utilities, and labor, for each of the following events.

1. Your community has decided to create a festival celebrating its cultural heritage in an effort to build tourism during its slowest season. It will take place over two weekends and include an opening day parade, daytime exhibits and activities, food concessions and a cook-off competition, and evening entertainment attractions. This first year you expect an attendance of 25,000 local people and 5,000 tourists.

2. You are coordinating a three-day regional Health and Wellness Exposition, sponsored by the three health maintenance organizations (HMOs) serving your region. Each HMO will have a large display area and will be offering free diagnostic and immunization clinics to the attendees. This gate show will also have 100 other exhibitors, ranging from health food restaurants giving out samples to spa dealers displaying hot tubs and Jacuzzis.

3. A local corporation has hired you to coordinate an employee appreciation party for 1,000 guests to be held this summer at the sports fields on a local school campus. It will start at 4:00 in the afternoon and end at midnight and will feature outdoor carnival and inflatable games until sunset and disco dancing in a tent after dark. A barbecue dinner will be served at 6:30 P.M., and snacks and beverages will be available throughout the event.

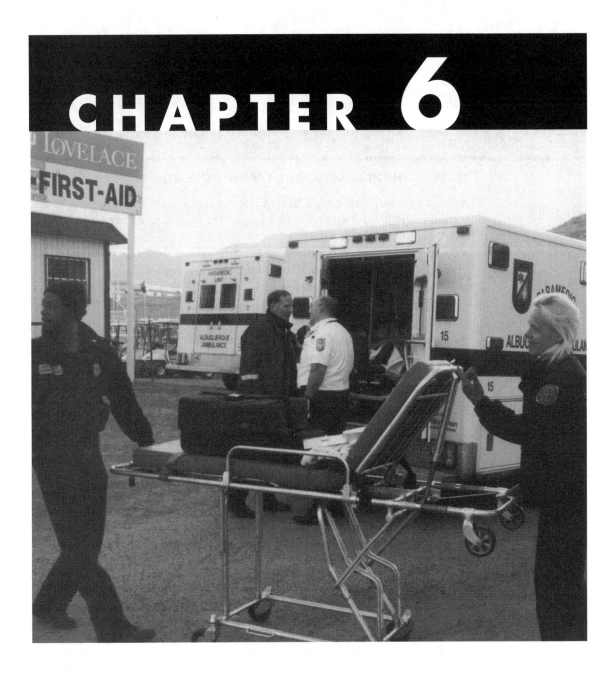

CHAPTER 6

Safe Operations

Early and provident fear is the mother of safety.

—EDMUND BURKE (1729–1797)

IN THIS CHAPTER YOU WILL LEARN HOW TO:

- Establish and implement the appropriate internal and external on-site communications systems and organizational procedures, including procurement of the proper equipment.
- Ensure that event operations provide a safe and healthy environment for all those in attendance and involved.
- Determine, procure, and deploy the appropriate security personnel and equipment to protect the people, property, and assets of and at the event.
- Coordinate medical and emergency services and procedures, including liaison with the proper authorities and provision of the appropriate level of on-site medical care and emergency response.

The event coordinator called together all the staff, volunteer department heads, and suppliers for a meeting the day before the start of a three-day summer concert series. Although they had come together many times before to discuss operations and risk management issues, the event coordinator wanted one more meeting to review all the plans and procedures for managing and controlling the risks they had identified. The whole team reviewed, point by point, the entire event plan and went over the protocols for each contingency and possible emergency. With the full commitment of the entire team to a zero-tolerance goal for all safety and security hazards, the event coordinator closed the meeting in the style of the police squad shift briefings from the television show *Hill Street Blues,* "Let's be careful out there . . . and let's save the surprises for the audience!"

Being careful and being prepared are not only sensible as event coordination guidelines, they are ever more important (and increasingly regulated into legislation and policy) for all events and event professionals. Paul Wertheimer of Chicago-based Crowd Management Strategies reported that of 275 events surveyed between 1992 and 2001, there were 212 crowd safety–related deaths and 62,520 injuries at concerts and festivals worldwide (www.crowdsafe.com). These facts, combined with statistics from the previous decade (including one terrifying loss of more than 1400 lives due to a crowd crush at a religious festival in 1990), show that safety must be at the forefront of all event planning and operations. Safety issues must be considered throughout the event coordination process and for all the facets, features, and elements of the event plan because there is potential risk associated with every aspect of an event.

The greatest threats to running a safe operation are habit, inertia, and ignorance. These are also the hardest practices to overcome, particularly within an established or long-standing organization. Unfortunately, until something bad happens, many people do not make a conscious or dedicated commitment to the safety and welfare of those involved in or attending an event. When something bad does happen, fingers are pointed, lawsuits are filed, reputations are ruined, and the emotional and financial consequences are devastating. Finally, policies and procedures are put in place—policies and procedures that should have been in place all along, including:

- Prevention plans
- Contingency plans
- Crisis plans

Whether we are considering threats posed by people's behavior or threats emanating from natural causes or disasters, plans must be made to ensure readiness to address the consequences. Some of these occurrences may be prevented, but many can only be anticipated so that the appropriate procedures and services are in place to handle such situations should they arise. The standard risk management procedure should be followed—assessment, analysis, planning, and control.

The professional event coordinator incorporates safety procedures throughout the planning and production of an event, as well as communicating to and securing from everyone involved a commitment to the highest standards of safety throughout the operations. This responsibility may be the responsibility of the professional event coordinator alone, or may rest with a safety committee, safety officer, risk manager, or head of security, yet it is the duty of the professional event coordinator to make certain this commitment is infused throughout the organizational structure of the event team. Safety is everyone's job, and everyone must accept it as such.

The scope of your prevention, contingency, and crisis plans will depend on the intent, extent, and content of the event being produced. As you examine the event elements and components, you must evaluate the potential health and safety hazards of each (see Figure 6-1). You must uncover and understand the vulnerabilities and implement the appropriate precautionary safeguards. Absolutely everything in the event plan and at the event site must be evaluated from a safety perspective.

As a professional, you have a legal, ethical, and financial responsibility to make certain that the event and its operations maintain the

Typical Health and Safety Hazards		Safeguards	Protection Priority

❑ Animals/Insects
❑ Activities
❑ Car Parks
❑ Communications
❑ Crowd Capacity
❑ Decorations
❑ Electricity
❑ Equipment
❑ Fire
❑ Food and Water
  Contamination
❑ Ingress/Egress
❑ Installation/
  Rigging
	❑ Noise Level
	❑ Pedestrians and
	  Vehicles
	❑ Power/Utility Lines
	❑ Slips and Trips
	❑ Special Effects
	❑ Temporary
	  Structures
	❑ Terrain/
	  Topography
	❑ Terrorism
	❑ Violence/Crime
	❑ Water/Drowning
	❑ Weather
		❑ Communication
		  Systems
		❑ Crowd Management
		❑ Emergency Services
		❑ Evacuation Plans
		❑ Incident Procedures
		❑ Safety Lighting
		❑ Sanitation Systems
		❑ Security Personnel
		❑ Transportation
		  Management
		❑ Venue and Site
		  Design
		❑ Waste Management
			1. **People**
			2. **Property**
			3. **Reputation**
			4. **Revenues**
			
			An event's assets
			are:
			
			People
			Equipment
			Finances

Figure 6-1
Event Safety Checklist

highest standards of safety possible, otherwise you or the event organization may be held negligently liable for any harm that occurs. Negligence is the failure to use, either by act or omission, the degree of care that an ordinary person of reasonable prudence would use under the given circumstances. Yet because you are a professional, you may be held to a higher standard of care than an ordinary person. You must not neglect these safeguards, because such neglect can indicate indifference to the probable consequences that should have been recognized by a professional.

Communications

Although there is a constant flow of information throughout the event coordination process, on-site communications are a separate challenge during the often-frenzied activity just prior to, during, and just after the event. The professional event coordinator must plan for this frenzy with the proper systems, hierarchy, equipment, and predetermined protocols to ensure that the necessary information is communicated in a timely manner to the appropriate internal and external constituencies (see Figure 6-2).

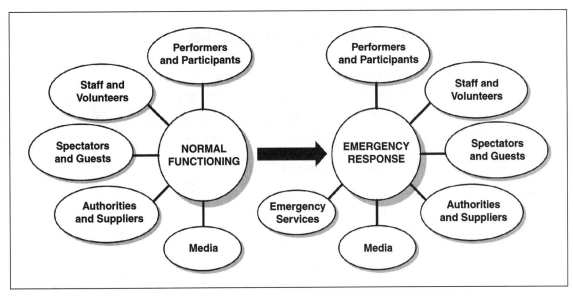

Figure 6-2
On-Site Event Communications

On-site communications will encompass the normal information exchange required during the run of the event, but must also be set up for a quick response to an emergency, should it occur. Particularly in an emergency, communication channels with the media must be anticipated and implemented in such as way as to control the damage that could occur as a result of speculation or misinformation. This is why it is so important to designate (and train) a spokesperson to respond to the media in times of crisis, and you might consider specific access controls to prevent damaging or distressful footage from being broadcast.

STRUCTURE THE COMMUNICATION CHANNELS

The channels of communication at an event will probably be similar to the channels established within the organizational chart for the event team. This organizational chart is segmented into various components or departments (see Figure 6-3), which are often used to provide the hierarchy of communications on-site at the event. When this chart is combined with the site or floor plan and the event running order or production schedule (all three should be posted on-site), the channels should be apparent and reinforced with a contact list, including the telephone numbers and frequencies of radios or other equipment assigned to each

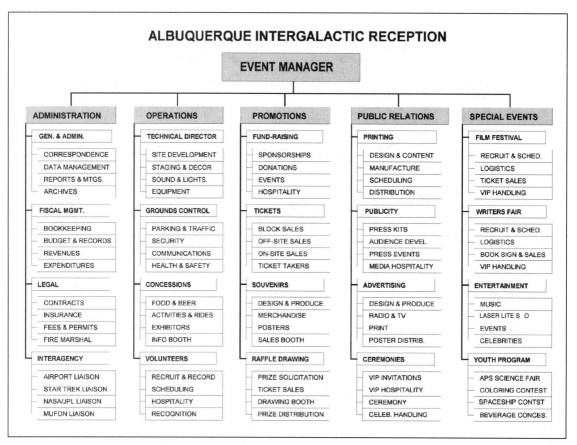

Figure 6-3
Organizational Chart Example

contact person. The organizational chart is used for assigning manageable packages of responsibility, the site plan is used for assigning manageable zones of responsibility, and the production schedule is used for assigning responsibility for manageable segments of activity.

The entire event team should be thoroughly briefed on this hierarchy of communications, and each person should be provided with a copy of the contact list. This includes the event staff, all suppliers and vendors on-site, as well as all the emergency personnel and authorities that will have jurisdiction over the event and be on-site at the event, either during or if responding to an emergency. It must be made absolutely clear, to everyone, who is authorized to implement contingency plans and crisis plans and who will respond to authorities or the media should an incident occur. The organizational chart may also be important in a legal dispute (i.e., illustrating assignment of liability, responsibility, and/or authority).

On-Site Insight

Technical producer Robert Estrin of California-based Creative Event Technology asserts that all the providers at an event should take responsibility for ensuring that the event is a safe environment. He recounts that he was involved in an 18-month-long lawsuit over injuries caused by another vendor's negligence, but, as is the standard practice in filing a lawsuit, the plaintiff's lawyer named anyone and everyone connected with the event, including all the subcontractors. After those 18 months of depositions and court appearances, of course his company was acquitted of any liability, but that did not prevent his being required to deal with the accusation. He notes that every vendor should be aware of every other vendor and speak to the event coordinator or planner if he or she sees something that is unsafe or likely to cause a safety hazard. "If ice is spilled on the dance floor, whoever sees it should speak up. Don't just leave it to the banquet captain because it's his job. It's everyone's job!"

Estrin also contends,

What many don't recognize is that security does not equal safety at events. Making sure that an event is secure does not automatically make it safe. Injuries to a worker at an event drive up workers' compensation costs, and they are often the result of an on-the-job injury caused by some sort of unsafe situation. While a security plan needs to be shared only with those directly involved with it, a safety plan needs to be shared with everyone working at the event. In addition, it needs to start when the first person arrives at the venue to start setup and continues until the last employee leaves after the event. Safety will always remain an issue for every event, regardless of size.

By making the communication channels obvious and accessible, and making it clear that safety is the top priority, everyone can "speak up" and speak to the right person when vulnerabilities, hazards, and emergencies-waiting-to-happen are uncovered or recognized. However, it is up to the professional event coordinator to give this permission and mandate to speak up, as well as providing the appropriate channels to eliminate potential conflicts or hard feelings between competitive rivals who may be working together as subcontractors at the same event.

BRIEFING AND DEBRIEFING MEETINGS

A primary component of the communication process, in the planning phase as well as during on-site implementation, is the face-to-face meeting. The on-site meetings include the pre-con (the pre-event briefing), the post-con (the post-event debriefing), daily briefings, and the all-important safety meeting. The pre-con includes all the primary stakeholders, including subcontractors, and is a review of all the event components, the production schedule, roles and responsibilities, and updates on all expectations and conditions—what is supposed to happen. The post-con is a review of what actually took place to resolve any complaints and document suggestions for future events. The daily briefings are for the purpose of monitoring and updating plans for all the functional aspects and emerging issues of the event.

The safety meeting, however, is for those involved in the actual setup to review the actions to take place and confirm the safety imperatives established for the event operations. Although risk management meetings often involve the department heads or management of the subcontracted suppliers, the safety meeting on-site should involve all their staff—the workers (and volunteers) who will be installing and operating the equipment for and during the event. These people are often excluded from the chain of communications; consequently, they do not get the important safety messages. Robert Estrin notes that having an on-site safety meeting with all subcontractors and their staffs can reduce accidents and help bring down insurance costs. You should always have a sign-in sheet for safety and risk management meetings so that you are able to monitor attendance and participation.

ESTABLISHING A COMMAND CENTER

The professional event coordinator should create a functional network of all assistance methods and personnel so that potential or emerging problems may be responded to before they become hazards or emergencies. Both special event risk management expert Alexander Berlonghi, author of *The Special Event Risk Management Manual,* and the Australian Emergency Manual, *Safe and Healthy Mass Gatherings,* published by Emergency Management Australia, specify that this is best achieved by centralizing your oversight personnel in a command center. For large events, this will probably be an office or a trailer strategically placed within the event grounds, and many purpose-built facilities have a room designated and equipped for just this function. For smaller events, such as a banquet or reception, the command center may simply be a table in or near the tech booth or at the back of the function room. Robert Estrin suggests that the sound booth or table is a logical location because, whereas other event suppliers install their equipment and leave, "the sound guys are there all evening and they can usually spot problems from their vantage point."

KEEPING CONNECTED THROUGH HIGH AND LOW TECHNOLOGY

The professional event coordinator uses a variety of communication methods and modalities to keep connected with the people and the pulse of the event operation (see Figure 6-4). This connection must be maintained not only within the confines of the event site; there must be a connection with external constituencies and conditions during the event production. The professional event coordinator needs to know what is going on outside the event that could affect what is going on inside the event, and vice versa. The means of maintaining this connection and communication can include high-tech and sophisticated systems, such as computer networks and closed-circuit television surveillance, and/or

❑ Alarm Bells
❑ Answering Machines and Voice Mail
❑ Cameras (Digital and Film)
❑ Clothing
❑ Computers
❑ Couriers
❑ Electronic Kiosks
❑ E-mail
❑ Facsimile (Fax) Machines
❑ Flags/Flashlights/Wands
❑ Hand Signals
❑ Intercom Systems
❑ Local Area Networks (LANs)

❑ Megaphones
❑ Message Boards
❑ Microphones/Sound Systems
❑ Observers/Rovers
❑ Pager and Beeper Systems
❑ PDAs
❑ Person-to-Person
❑ Projection Screens
❑ Public Address Systems
❑ Scoreboards
❑ Signal Lights
❑ Signs
❑ Sirens/Horns
❑ Tape Recorders

❑ Telephones—Public, Private, Cellular
❑ Television—Broadcast, Cable, Closed Circuit
❑ Two-Way Radios
❑ Variable Message Signs
❑ Video Monitors
❑ Video Recorders—Tape and Digital
❑ Wide Area Networks (WANs)
❑ Wireless Application Protocol (WAP)
❑ Word Processing

Figure 6-4
Communication Modes and Types of Equipment

low-tech methods, such as designated personnel roving through the event observing the audience and activities or the professional event coordinator stationed at the back of the function room. The level of connection will depend on the scope and needs of each particular event.

It is important to remember that communication can be audible or visual. Signs, message boards, video monitors, and projection screens may be used to visually augment any verbal announcements delivered to an audience. Hand signals may be used between staff members to quickly communicate standard instructions. Signal lights (lamp annunciators) can serve as a paging mechanism. Flags may be used to send a message, such as the checkered and yellow flags used in car races. Moreover, recording devices such as cameras and video recorders may be used to provide visual images that communicate a message (e.g., the arrival of an important dignitary or celebrity or the crowd density or waiting lines at an activity, entrance, or concession).

The most common event-related types of communication equipment include a public address (PA) system for communication to an audience and two-way radios (walkie-talkies) for communication between event personnel. All systems for oral communication between event staff and security personnel should have two-way functionality, should be multimodal, and should have their own backup power supplies. Two-way radios are battery-operated and will become useless unless charged properly and regularly. You may need to have extra radios so that you can always keep one set in its battery charger. When the event has loud activities or noisy areas, security, medical, and operations personnel should use headsets and/or earpieces.

COMMUNICATING WITH THE CROWD

The PA system is a vital link between the event and its audience. For many large events such as festivals, fairs, sports events, and expositions, such systems are used to deliver information about activities and promotional messages throughout the events in addition to important safety and/or emergency announcements. For some events, these announcements may be audio loops of prerecorded announcements, such as those at the 2002 Winter Olympic Games, which included welcome messages and advisories about the entrance procedures and security checks (called Mag & Bag—all patrons went through a magnetometer and had their bags physically searched). This constant "voice-over" connection with the crowd is an audible layer of the event experience, and the professional event coordinator must make certain that there is a distinct difference between these announcements and announcements related to the safety and welfare of those in attendance. Note: Fire officials advise that at any event with an attendance of 300 or more, even meetings of short duration, an announcement should be made indicating where the exits are.

Welfare announcements (e.g., lost child, lost and found, instructing people to meet their family at a certain location, etc.) and safety or emergency announcements (e.g., cancellations or closures, evacuation, egress routes, location of safe or secure zones, etc.) must be carefully planned and scripted to ensure that people listen to them and do not panic. You must determine in what style and languages these announcements must be broadcast. They must be delivered in a professional and calm tone of voice, at the correct volume, and must be worded so they are perceived as authentic and responded to appropriately. Alexander Berlonghi advises, "Various scripts must be prepared in advance. There should be a sequence of announcements depending on the immediacy and severity of the emergency situation. Each script should state the reason(s) for the emergency evacuation and provide clear directions for the public. Announcements should be repeated several times in the same tone and mood." Ensure that the tone and wording of emergency announcements are proper so as to avoid panic caused by unprofessional announcements (a source of legal action in some cases).

If you are planning to use the onstage sound system provided by an entertainment or audiovisual (AV) program to deliver safety announcements, you must confirm this with the entertainers and/or AV technicians. If using a house PA system instead of an onstage sound system, you must make certain you have a way to mute the onstage system in the event that an emergency announcement must be broadcast. If using the PA system as a primary communications method, you may wish to code certain messages to alert specific personnel instead of the entire audience.

- "Dr. Able, please meet your party at the beer garden"—to signify to the first aid team that there is a medical emergency at the beer garden
- "Will Mr. Baker please report to the information booth"—to signify to security personnel that a bomb threat has been received and they should report to the command center

The professional event coordinator must make certain that PA broadcasts reach all the required areas of the event site. Such areas may include inside and outside a building or buildings, within dressing rooms or meeting rooms, parking areas, and the corridors and stairwells leading into and out of the event venue. Other audible communications may include sirens and alarm bells to signify an emergency or evacuation, but these must be supplemented with calming and credible announcements.

Safety

The professional event coordinator is responsible for ensuring that the site and all elements of the event provide a safe and healthy environment for those who have been invited, either personally or promotionally, to the event experience. These elements include the venue and site design, fire safety, incident planning, communication, crowd management, transportation management, structures, barriers, electrical installations, lighting, food, drink, water, sanitation facilities, waste management, noise and sound vibration, special effects, and everything else pertaining to the event. Of paramount concern must be any life safety issues such as fire, electrocution, drowning, structural collapses, and anything that could cause a person's death. Absolutely everything in the event plans and at the event site must be evaluated from a safety perspective. As with all other aspects of professional event coordination, there should be no surprises.

DETERMINE THE HAZARDS

The hazards or dangers associated with an event can range from someone slipping on a wet floor to being assaulted in the parking lot, or tripping over a power cord to being crushed to death in the collapse of a building or grandstand. The event site or venue must be scrutinized both before and after the event has been set up. When conducting the site inspection, you should consider every potential structural and topographical hazard. This is especially important for outdoor venues. You should be looking at the use of the site or venue in the context in which it will be used for your event—from the moment the first staff member or worker arrives, to the time when the attendees or guests arrive, and until they have all safely departed.

- What could they trip over?
- What could they slip on?
- What could they fall from?
- What could fall on them?
- What could they fall into?
- What could they run into?
- What could run into them?
- What could they get sick from?
- What could stick or cut them?
- What could bite or sting them?

Consider what you are bringing into or onto the event site and the layout of the event site. The equipment and décor must be in good structural condition, not just cosmetically appealing. Tents and marquees must be made with suitable (fireproof/retardant) materials and installed properly. Any temporary structures, such as those listed in Figure 6-5, must be properly installed and suitable for the expected use and loads, and the bases must be protected from vehicular damage. Staging sections

❏ Archways	❏ Fencing	❏ Seating
❏ AV Screens/Stands	❏ Flooring	❏ Stages
❏ Balconies/Verandas	❏ Light Towers and Trusses	❏ Tents and Marquees
❏ Bleachers/Grandstands	❏ Overhead Signage	❏ Towers and Masts
❏ Dance Platforms	❏ Roofs and Ceiling Décor	❏ Viewing Platforms

Figure 6-5
Temporary Structure Hazard Checklist

and platform risers will have to be braced and/or clamped securely together and must have appropriate safety railings and steps. All décor items must be anchored properly to prevent their collapse or falling over. Anything suspended overhead must be rigged securely.

Check the ambient or house lighting to make sure it will be sufficient to illuminate the entire event space. The lack of lighting can make hazards invisible and antisocial activity anonymous. Consider also the decorative lighting and its installation and/or rigging (as well as sound system equipment). Lighting instruments and the battens on which they are hung can be very heavy—and deadly if they come crashing down. In addition, lighting and sound systems require electricity to operate, which involves cords and cables that must be secured and ramped (covered).

Consider the movement to and through the event space, including the distances, the terrain, the pedestrian surfaces, corridors, aisles, stairwells, tunnels, passageways, and flow barriers. Also think about the perimeters and access controls. Unfenced, unticketed, and oversold events often give rise to unsafe occupancy conditions, such as loads exceeding the limits, crowd density hazards, and audience members seeking sight lines by climbing on something or going where they should not. In addition, fences and barriers should be designed to flex under pressure to prevent crowd crush injury, yet should not collapse and thus cause crowd collapse injuries. A possible exception is the use of breakaway stage skirts to prevent crowd surge injuries for stages with an underneath clearance of 6½ ft (2 m).

Finally, consider the activities that will take place and how these will increase or affect the possible hazards at the event. The use of alcohol often impairs judgment, which can turn minor hazards into major perils (e.g., slip-and-trip hazards, rough terrain, unfamiliar layouts) and may instigate inappropriate behavior (e.g., throwing debris or bottles, climbing structures or standing on seats for better vantage points, or even using chairs as weapons). Loud music or noise (e.g., concerts or car races) may require hearing protection for staff members. Special effects such as pyrotechnics and smoke or fog effects may create hazardous situations or leave hazardous materials (the event site must always be searched for un-exploded fireworks when a pyrotechnics show is over).

SAFETY ON THE JOB SITE

As Robert Estrin notes, worker safety on the job site is just as important as the safety plans for the audience or guests. He recommends that professional event coordinators discuss safety practices with all subcontracted suppliers during the bid or proposal stage. "A significantly lower bid should be scrutinized for shortcuts that will compromise safety, such as fewer or less experienced workers, insufficient installation equipment, or older equipment that may need repair." Talk with your vendors and suppliers about their safety policies and procedures. Question them about safety requirements particular to their products or services. Become familiar with the rules, regulations, and precautions associated with on-the-job safety (see Figure 6-6). Make certain you have mandated job site safety with your staff as well; following safe lifting and carrying practices, never standing on a chair as a ladder, and using the right tools and equipment for the job.

Another factor that compromises safety is the time allotment for installation and dismantling. Robert Estrin declares, "When workers are rushing, particularly when they're carrying equipment, that's when people get hurt." Estrin contends that the breakdown and load-out should be choreographed as carefully (and the production schedule for these activ-

❑ Aerial Lifts—High Jacker, Scissor, Boom, Snorkel, Cherry Picker	❑ Grid Ceilings	❑ Pushing and Pulling
	❑ Handrails	❑ Respiratory Protection
	❑ Hand Tools	❑ Safety Chains
❑ Back Braces	❑ Hand Trucks/Carts	❑ Safety Rails
❑ Face Guards and Goggles	❑ Hard Hats	❑ Safety Straps
❑ Fall Protection	❑ Harnesses	❑ Scaffolds
❑ Fire Extinguishers	❑ Hearing Protection	❑ Spill Control
❑ Flammable and Combustible Materials	❑ Heavy Machinery	❑ Toe Guards
	❑ Hazardous/Corrosive Materials	❑ Vehicle-mounted Work Platforms
❑ Food Preparation Equipment	❑ Ladders	❑ Warning Signage
❑ Footwear	❑ Lifting and Carrying	❑ Work Clothes
❑ Forklifts—High and Low	❑ Power Tools	❑ Work Gloves

Figure 6-6
Job Site Safety Precaution Checklist

ities should be just as detailed) as the load-in and setup. In *Theatrical Hazards Cross Reference* (bruce.wybron.com/tsp/hazards.htm), Jerrold Gorrell of Theatre Safety Programs identified several nonregulatory work hazards associated with the entertainment industry for the Entertainment Services and Technology Association (ESTA). These on-the-job worker safety hazards are applicable to the event industry as well.

- Lack of rest/sleep
- Irregular hours/shifts
- Inadequate time to accomplish the task at hand
- Lack of sufficient personnel to accomplish the task at hand
- Lack of appreciation of safety requirements and procedures
- Coworkers working improperly

The National Institute for Occupation Safety and Health publication *Cumulative Trauma Disorders in the Workplace Bibliography* states, "Ergonomic principles can be applied to prevent both overt and cumulative traumas. Back problems are by far the most common cumulative trauma injuries" (www.cdc.gov/niosh). To save all our aching backs, and workers' compensation claims, careful attention must be paid to manual handling procedures such as proper lifting, loading, carrying, pushing, and pulling.

RISK MANAGEMENT WALK-THROUGH

A risk management walk-through should be conducted prior to the opening of an event, periodically during the event, and after the event has ended. A risk management walk-through is a walking tour and survey of an event site to observe and correct any safety hazards and should include the professional event coordinator, venue management, key suppliers, and safety officials such as the fire marshal, health officer, or police authority. At this point, the event coordinator looks at the event site as it will be used by the audience or attendees, searching for anything that needs attention prior to opening the event. If anything is found, it must be corrected, repaired, or removed before the event opens. The same holds true for the walk-through during and after the event.

Neatness does count. Fastidious attention to keeping goods and materials neatly stored, rubbish and debris cleared, and equipment maintained properly will help to reduce the possibility of accident or injury. The site must be clean, safe, and secure throughout the duration of the event operations. Safety concerns do not stop when the party starts, and what was safe yesterday may not be safe today. Do not assume anything (with the possible exception of assuming that one of the attendees will be a reckless, uncoordinated, and oblivious person whose brother-in-law is a ruthless personal injury lawyer).

DEVELOP EVACUATION PLANS TO AVOID PANIC

A crisis is a critical moment when a situation or condition can turn into a catastrophe, causing damage, losses, injuries, and/or fatalities. To protect life and limb in a situation of crisis, there must be a specific, reasonable, and agreed-to plan of response that can be implemented efficiently and calmly. Although emergencies requiring evacuation are much less likely to occur than crowd conflicts, they have the greatest potential for crowd panic and injury. Adequately training employees to respond to major emergencies requires, first and foremost, the existence of an evacuation plan.

An evacuation plan must include a hierarchy of decision makers, prearranged procedures, clear communication methods, and unobstructed routes. Many venues have evacuation plans specific to their facilities, with which the professional event coordinator should become familiar and incorporate into the event planning. For sites without such plans, the professional event coordinator will work with police, fire, venue, and other officials to develop the appropriate routes and protocols. Evacuation plans should be part of all staff briefings, and drills should be conducted if possible.

Alexander Berlonghi advises that there must be an agreed-to hierarchy of how, and by whom, an evacuation is decided upon. Once evacuation has been determined to be necessary, all event personnel should move to preassigned locations and all exits and gates should be opened. Security personnel and event staff should help to direct people at critical points along the evacuation route, and their demeanor will help to maintain a calm and orderly evacuation. Specific personnel may be assigned to aid in evacuating disabled and elderly persons. Traffic officials and parking personnel must be alerted as well, and they should also maintain a calm and authoritative demeanor.

All means of egress must be unobstructed, well lit, and clearly identified with the proper signage, including doorways, hallways, corridors, passageways, balconies, enclosures, lobbies, escalators, ramps, stairs and stairwells, tunnels, courts, and yards. Legislation in Europe regarding exit signs stipulated that the word "Exit" be removed from these signs and replaced by the graphic "Running Man" icon (known as the more politically correct "Person Moving Purposefully"). Elevators should not be used during an evacuation (except by emergency response personnel). All exits must be unlocked and capable of opening in the direction of escape, including exit doors equipped with panic hardware—latches that release upon the application of force in the direction of egress travel. In some cases, evacuees should be directed to predetermined gathering points at safe distances away from a building (Point of Safety) so it can be determined whether everyone has been evacuated from a structure.

Once an evacuation has started it should not be halted, even if the original threat has been eliminated, because the chaos of a reverse flow can cause an even greater hazard. No one should be allowed to reenter the venue *for any reason.*

PAY ATTENTION TO THE AUDIENCE

The larger the audience (and the more animated their anticipated behavior), the more safety and security controls must considered. Many of the most severe disasters have occurred at events with very large audiences, and most of the deaths resulted from panic or crowding so closely that the victims were suffocated (see Figure 6-7). This risk may be mitigated by the design and layout of the site, as well as the admissions controls established for the event. Obviously, a dignified audience at a classical concert will require fewer controls than a boisterous audience at a rock concert. However, emergencies requiring evacuation or mass movement of any crowd can become hazardous, no matter how dignified or sedate the event.

Crowd Collapse	A "falling domino" collapse of a crowd due to individuals at the front falling, causing those behind to sequentially lose their balance and fall on top
Crowd Craze	A critical crowd pressure caused by the competitive rush or push of a crowd in pursuit of or toward a desirable objective or individual
Crowd Crush	A critical crowd pressure caused by the compression of a crowd into a smaller and smaller area due to the absence of a portal or escape
Crowd Panic	The frenzied movement to escape a real or perceived danger, often including the trampling of those who have fallen in the way
Crowd Surge	A rapid compression movement in a particular direction caused by any of a variety of reasons

Figure 6-7
Hazardous Crowd Movements

The professional event coordinator must pay attention to the actions and mood of the audience. If things seem to be getting too unruly, or specific segments of the crowd are instigating inappropriate behavior, then things must be calmed down. How this is to be accomplished also depends on the audience. For some events, simply the visibility of security personnel or authorities may suppress the action. For others, specific spectators or attendees may have to be ejected from the event.

Crowd management practices must be applied throughout the duration of an event, from arrival (if queues extend past a certain point, you open another service counter) through departure (adjust traffic signals to accommodate a mass exodus of vehicles). The pamphlet *Managing Crowds Safely,* published by the U.K. Health and Safety Executive, advises that behavior is affected by the amount of information provided. "Poor communications can lead to people stopping, moving against the flow of the crowd, blocking passages or making frequent demands on staff for directions. Visitors without information, or given contradictory information, can become frustrated and aggressive." It also identifies the potential crowd hazards that must be identified and controlled, including reverse or cross flows in a dense crowd, flows obstructed by queues, crowds mixing with animals or traffic, and moving attractions within a crowd (www.hse.gov.uk/pubns/indg142.htm).

AUDIENCE WELFARE

Attending to problems such as lost companions, children, or parents, or lost possessions, and providing visitor guides and gathering places for parents while their preteens are inside at a concert (to eliminate the line-up of vehicles waiting to pick them up), are among the numerous ways the professional event coordinator can and should attend to the welfare of the audience. These guest services must be coordinated with as much attention to safety and security as any other part of the event. As visitors to an event may be in unfamiliar surroundings, they may benefit from gentle reminders about specific messages and cautions regarding site features and foibles delivered over the public address systems, as well as with signage and printed materials. Caution signs should always be placed at specific hazards, particularly temporary hazards (e.g., "Caution—Wet Floor").

Areas designated for children who have lost their parents should be segregated, comfortably furnished, and staffed with cheerful personnel who can alleviate the stress of both child and parent. Depending on the type, scope, and jurisdiction of the event, these staff members may need to have security checks performed before they are allowed to care for children, but, in most cases, "Mom-like" volunteers are the most appropriate for soothing a frightened child. The sheer relief on the faces of parent and child will probably indicate the reunion successful; however, turning a child over to a "found" parent may need specific precautions, perhaps requiring the completion of and signing an incident report and collecting proof of identification. Other precautions include not giving the waiting child any food or beverage other than water (because of potential allergies or dietary restrictions), keeping the child confined to the designated area, and supervising the child throughout his or her confinement. A few toys and coloring books will help pass the time.

Security

"Security" pertains to the protection of property from loss or damage, as differentiated from "safety"—the protection of people from harm, but it also pertains to the personnel used to perform both these functions. Security personnel are used, in part, for "checking delegates' credentials, searching hand luggage, protecting equipment, and patrolling congress and exhibition areas" (Goldblatt and Nelson, 2001). They are used to control admissions, crowds, and crime. (See Figure 6-8.) They also constitute a vital component linked with fire, first aid, and emergency personnel within any emergency response or crisis management plan.

IDENTIFY THE RISKS AND VULNERABILITIES

The professional event coordinator must determine the security plan and personnel needed, depending on the type, scope, and objectives of the event being produced. A corporate product launch will have different needs than a charity fund-raiser; a benefit concert will have different needs than a beach party. A large sports competition will have different needs than a large cultural festival, and a government meeting will have different needs than a conference or incentive final

❑ Admissions Control	❑ Detention/Ejection	❑ Observing/Patrolling
❑ Apprehension and Arrest*	❑ Emergency Response	❑ Prevention
❑ Credential Checking	❑ Evacuation	❑ Searches
❑ Crowd Control	❑ Guarding	❑ Stewarding

*In many jurisdictions, only the police have the authority to carry a weapon and make arrests.

Figure 6-8
Typical Security Personnel Functions

night gala. The event coordinator must identify and specify the risks and vulnerabilities that need protection.

Security plans must be specifically developed for each and every event, even if the event has occurred many times before. There will always be new elements, new features, or new conditions that require a fresh look at the security needs. The professional event coordinator may use a standard outline for developing a security plan, but each plan must be specific to the individual event. The security plan should be drafted using the site plan, organizational chart, program agenda, and contractual agreements to define what, where, when, why, and how people and property must be protected (see Figure 6-9).

In the United States there are two different types of law to consider in relation to security plans—criminal law, whereby offenders are arrested and may be incarcerated, and civil law (tort) whereby offenders may be sued for damages due to negligence but are not put in jail. A written security plan becomes a strong offense in the commitment to safe operations, by both the removal of negligent civil liability and the prevention of criminal activity, and a strong defense against claims of negligence. The security plan starts with sensible (documented) presecurity precautions such as limiting the number of keys or changing the locks to restricted areas or storage rooms, creating and positioning cautionary

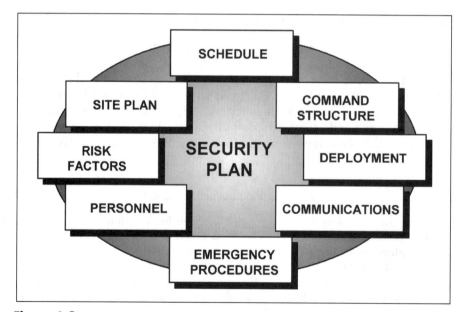

Figure 6-9
The Scope of a Security Plan (adapted from Berlonghi, 1990)

signage that is highly visible, and providing pre-event communications with the audience about safety precautions, such as not wearing one's conference badge outside the event (to prevent targeting by entrepreneurial criminals). The plan is then further developed in relation to the risk factors specifically identified, based on the risk assessment and the allocation of sufficient funds to acquire the people and equipment necessary to perform the security functions identified.

COMFORT VERSUS CONFRONTATION

The type and demeanor of the security presence will communicate a message—comfort or confrontation. The appropriate attitude and authority should be established for all event security personnel, whether peer, private, or professional. Whether security personnel are used to conduct searches for controlled substances prior to admission, to guard and protect valuables, or to assist with emergencies, they are part of the event team and the event experience. One might think of this as a "stewarding" (caretaker) rather than "security" function. The wrong attitude may provoke situations rather than prevent them.

Security personnel and equipment may be almost invisible, semivisible, or highly visible, depending on the needs of the event, the potential risks, and the likely behaviors of the audience. You may need one type of security presence at one location, such as uniformed guards at the ticket window where money is kept, and another type elsewhere, such as plainclothes personnel in the backstage areas. Security that is almost invisible, such as surveillance equipment or plainclothes personnel roving the event grounds, may be all that is needed at events where there are few risks. Semivisible security personnel, such as peer or volunteer security in "friendly" T-shirts ("Security—Please Feel Secure") and uniformed personnel at restricted area entrances, will likely be sufficient for many large events with uncontroversial activities and sedate audiences. Highly visible security may be required at events that have a reputation or potential for violence or criminal activity, such as the expectation of gang attendance or industrial espionage.

EMPLOY AND DEPLOY THE APPROPRIATE SECURITY

Security personnel and equipment must be employed and deployed in a manner that suits and serves the purpose, goals, and objectives of the event (see Figure 6-10). You want the right people, of the right level of authority, at the right places, at the right times. Your personnel options include plainclothes, uniformed (either in uniform or event-specific attire), and sworn (those with authority to carry a weapon and make arrests), or a combination (e.g., Secret Service personnel or bodyguards

Typical Security Types	Typical Security Deployment/Posts	
❑ Contractual ❑ "God Squads" (ministers and mothers) ❑ Law Enforcement ❑ Peer ❑ Personal ❑ Proprietary (in-house) ❑ Technological ❑ Volunteer	❑ Admission Points ❑ Alcohol Service Zones ❑ Cash Collection Points ❑ Command Center ❑ Equipment Installations ❑ Loading/Unloading Areas ❑ Parking Areas ❑ Perimeters	❑ Public Areas ❑ Registration ❑ Restricted Area Access Points ❑ Stage Areas—Front and Back ❑ Storage Areas ❑ VIP Protection

Figure 6-10
Typical Security Types and Deployment

may be both plainclothes and sworn; police are both uniformed and sworn).

When hiring security personnel from a private contractual company, you must be diligent about specifying the needs of the event and the training criteria for the personnel assigned to the event, as well as checking the references of the security company awarded the contract. Some security companies do not perform background checks on employees or provide appropriate training—they just provide people in uniform, some of whom are even convicted felons. As with all your suppliers, research complaints and reliability with better business organizations and colleagues, check the company's references, specify levels of expertise in your Request for Proposal (RFP), require a Certificate of Insurance and a copy of its license (if licensing is statutory), and use a written contract. Berlonghi also advises you ask to see the company's policies and procedures manual (including its hiring/screening policies), outlines of its training and briefing activities, and its sample deployment assignment sheets and job descriptions.

Incorporate the security chain of command into your communications plan, and centralize security supervision within your command center, including supervisory personnel from each type of security service included at the event (peer, private, personal, and law enforcement). It is vitally important to create a network of interagency cooperation, particularly in terms of emergency response, and to respect each entity's hierarchy. In addition, if hiring a private security company, you must limit your liability and maximize the company's accountability by leaving the management and supervision of its personnel to its supervisors.

USING TECHNOLOGY

There are a variety of technologies that the professional event coordinator may use within the context of security operations, ranging from golf carts for getting around the event site or bicycles for getting through the event site, to metal and motion detectors for screening entrants (see Figure 6-11). Communications are facilitated by using two-way radios, cellular phones, and, for noisy environments, headsets, earphones, and hand or collar microphones. Supervisory personnel should have multichannel radios with dedicated channels so that they can communicate with different command groups or with emergency personnel separately. All security personnel should be issued or have access to clipboards for taking notes, incident or accident forms to be filled out should something occur, and a camera to document a scene. Roving security personnel should have flashlights so they can check all areas of the event site, even under the grandstands.

Screening of individuals at admission points can include passive and active search methods. Passive search methods may include the use of handheld or walk-through metal detectors (magnetometers) and X-ray screening for packages or baggage. Security personnel involved in active search methods should be carefully trained in the appropriate pat-down or other personal search techniques and the correct procedures for searching handbags, backpacks, and other personal belongings. In conducting pat-down checks, there should be female security personnel available to search female entrants. Personnel searching belongings should always wear protective gloves.

Remote or passive security options include surveillance equipment such as closed-circuit television (CCTV), cameras, and motion detectors, plus the use of intrusion alarms to alert personnel of unauthorized entry. When using passive or covert surveillance equipment, you may be required to post warning signs. A camera can be a tool for social control,

---

- ❏ Cameras—Still and Video
- ❏ Cellular Phones
- ❏ Clipboards
- ❏ Closed-Circuit TV
- ❏ Earphones
- ❏ Flashlights
- ❏ Gloves
- ❏ Hand/Collar Microphones
- ❏ Handcuffs
- ❏ Incident/Accident Forms
- ❏ Intrusion Alarms
- ❏ Metal Detectors—Handheld and Walk-Through
- ❏ Motion Detectors
- ❏ Multichannel Two-Way Radios
- ❏ Vehicles—Golf Carts, Bicycles, Automobiles, Motorcycles, etc.
- ❏ X-Ray Screening

Figure 6-11
Security Equipment Checklist

but there are rules about where, when, and how you are allowed to use it. However, it can be a labor-saving device because it allows one or two people to observe and monitor multiple locations constantly and concurrently, and, combined with recording capabilities, can provide objective evidence.

Technology Tip

CCTV has gone wireless. Video surveillance equipment continues to get smaller and more affordable, as well as the matching wireless technologies as they emerge and improve. A wireless surveillance camera has a built-in transmitter that sends video signals to a receiver that can be connected to a TV, VCR, or other equipment, with a line of sight (LOS) range of 700 ft, and, with a long-range antenna, up to 10 miles. The signal penetrates most solid objects, including glass, plastic, wood, fiberglass, and some metals.

You are also now able to receive live video and audio feed from anywhere over the Internet with digital surveillance systems. Using Web cameras, you can simultaneously and remotely watch a video from most anywhere in the world via limited area networks (LANs), wide area networks (WANs), the Internet, or by direct dial via computer modem. Video may even be viewed via a handheld personal digital assistant (PDA)-type PC via wireless Internet access. Video surveillance camera options include black and white, color, or infrared (for seeing in extremely low light conditions) with constant, timed, and/or motion-detection-based recording. You can even mask the particular part or parts of the picture that you do not wish to be included in the motion detection process, thereby excluding those areas you are not allowed or do not need to have under surveillance.

BRIEFING AND TRAINING

With all security personnel, even law enforcement, it is important to conduct briefings to review the expectations surrounding the event. Particularly with peer or volunteer security personnel, you must convey the fact that they are there to prevent incidents or accidents, *not* to watch the event. You must also understand that you cannot expect these individuals to jeopardize their own safety. You must specify when, how, and why they must call law enforcement authorities. You must also specify the limits of their authority.

You should conduct security personnel briefings just prior to the event. Briefings can also include representatives of emergency response agencies and should address the following points.

- **Site and deployment**—Everyone needs to know the layout of the event and where he or she is to be deployed within that layout, including entrances, exits, first aid stations, and potential hazards. (If you are telling personnel to go to Door D17 to assist with an incident or emergency, they need to know which door is D17.) Individuals should be issued credentials and uniforms immediately prior to going on duty.
- **Schedule**—This item includes the opening and closing times for the event and specific areas or activities within the event (parking areas, admission gates, concessions, etc.), as well as anticipated major crowd movements (intermissions, breaks, entertainment attractions, etc.) and VIP or high-profile guest movements. It also includes the schedules for overnight or after-hours security (including specification of who is authorized to enter the site during these time periods).
- **Chain of command and communication**—This item includes instructions on to whom and how to report incidents or observations, identification of key security personnel (supervisors, zone captains, stewards, or other hierarchy) and other department heads, and issuance of communications and other equipment.
- **Scope of duties and authority**—This item includes deployment assignments, job responsibilities, and clear directions on the management of unacceptable behavior. If personnel have authority to detain or arrest, the procedures for these actions must be clearly specified. Excessive force and/or abuse of authority should not take place.
- **Specific risk factors**—Any unique risks or hazards pertaining to the particular event or site and any special instructions regarding specific risk factors must be reviewed.
- **Emergency procedures**—Personnel must be instructed as to protocols for raising alarms, requesting assistance, and evacuation, as well as the operation or deactivation of any equipment, mechanisms, machinery, or utilities necessary in an emergency.

The event organization may need to, or may be required to, provide training in addition to the instruction on the aforementioned briefing points, including the use of specific equipment, filling out incident/

accident forms, credential verification, observation techniques, how to conduct searches, and the procedures for handling disruptive or intoxicated individuals. This training and all security personnel briefings should be infused with customer service training, including social and communication skills, to ensure the appropriate attitude, demeanor, and conduct. In addition to the security personnel, all staff and volunteers should be briefed on the response procedures for incidents, accidents, fires, evacuations, and other situations of crisis.

LOCKUP, LOCKDOWN, AND LOST AND FOUND

There are often a variety of materials and equipment that should be secured in storage areas under lock and key, including electronics, personal computers, two-way radios, personal effects, and other valuables. The professional event coordinator should work with the security team to determine the appropriate storage locations, locking mechanisms, and protocols for checking these items out and back in to reduce the possibility of loss or damage. There are also a variety of equipment and/or décor items that must be secured in place with locking mechanisms, such as vehicles on display, trailer-mounted equipment, or computers used for registration. Locking covers, chains and padlocks, or standard bicycle locks may be used to secure items to unmovable or awkward-to-move objects.

When closing down the event overnight, the professional event coordinator should establish a walk-through checking procedure for all areas and access doors to make certain the site or facility is empty and securely locked down. For multiday events, he or she should also work with the security personnel to define the possible concerns regarding vulnerable areas and property, perhaps even changing their inspection routes and timing periodically. Overnight security personnel should be provided with a list of any people authorized to enter the site while it is closed, as well as a list of contact numbers for the professional event coordinator and/or those with authority to grant after-hours access.

The location and procedures for Lost and Found should be established and incorporated into the site and security plans, as well as communicated to the audience through the event's printed collateral materials and signage. The Lost and Found holding area can be as simple as a box under the registration or information counter, or found items may be placed in a secured storage area. It is not usually recommended that you make announcements when items are found, but if they are, you must make certain you do not give a too-detailed description in the announcement—leave out some unique descriptive information that the claimant must give to identify the item as his or her property. You may wish to have claimants fill out and sign a receipt when an item has been returned. You should also predetermine what will be done with items found that have not been claimed by the end of the event (e.g., donated to charity, turned over to the police, etc.).

Medical and Emergency Services

No matter how well designed, planned, and implemented the event program or event site, there is always the possibility of a crisis or emergency that can endanger the people attending, participating in, or working at an event. The professional event coordinator must always consider the possibility of a medical incident, fire, or disorderly (dangerous) conduct among the audience. These incidents may be precipitated by unsafe conditions or ill-advised or illegal activities. They may be caused by calculated rebellion or sheer exuberance. They may be the result of malicious behavior or caused by Mother Nature. The level of normal response required by the event organization will depend on the context of the event (the purpose, scope, site, and audience) and will have an impact on the event's site, budget, and operations. The level of emergency response will depend on the incident.

MEDICAL SERVICES

Given that many public events concentrate an audience population equal to or greater than that of a small municipality in a single location, it is reasonable to assume that there will be incidents of injury or illness (see Figure 6-12). The professional event coordinator must establish procedures and provisions for dealing with these incidents, large or small, and secure the on-site medical services appropriate for the type, scope, and audience demographics of the event. It is important to remember that no matter how minor or severe the injury or illness is medically, it can be extremely severe to the person experiencing it.

The professional event coordinator should liaison with venue officials, the sponsoring host or organization, and local health authorities or ambulance services early in the planning process to determine the protocols and procedures for dealing with medical incidents and emergencies that might occur at the event. This includes identifying the distance to the nearest 24-hour hospital, medical center, or trauma center that will be the receptive medical facility for major or mass casualties. The distances and directions from the event site to all area hospitals, as well as the response times to the event site for ambulances, should also be determined.

- ❑ Abrasions
- ❑ Alcohol Overuse
- ❑ Allergic Reactions (rashes, swelling, anaphylactic shock)
- ❑ Assault and Rape
- ❑ Biological Terrorism
- ❑ Burns and Sunburn
- ❑ Cardiac Arrest
- ❑ Chemical Spills
- ❑ Choking
- ❑ Contusions

- ❑ Cuts (often from broken glass or drink can pulls)
- ❑ Dehydration
- ❑ Electrical Shock
- ❑ Epileptic Seizures (brought on by strobe lighting)
- ❑ Fainting (hysteria, heat, alcohol)
- ❑ Fractures and Broken Bones
- ❑ Gastrointestinal Distress (food poisoning, overeating, eating too fast)

- ❑ Gunshot Wounds
- ❑ Heatstroke/Exhaustion
- ❑ Hypothermia
- ❑ Illicit Drug Overdose
- ❑ Lacerations
- ❑ Overexertion
- ❑ Puncture Wounds
- ❑ Respiratory Distress (asthma attacks, crowd crush)
- ❑ Sprains
- ❑ Stings and Bites

Figure 6-12
Potential Medical Incidents at Events

In some jurisdictions, only certain medical facilities are certified as trauma centers and all medical emergencies are transported to those facilities. In other jurisdictions, there may be overlapping medical emergency response services and facilities, and you may need to coordinate with these entities to define the jurisdiction for your event within the mutual aid plans of public safety agencies. For large or public events, you should notify the designated medical facility or facilities, in writing, of the event, giving all pertinent information (i.e., date(s), hours of operation, expected attendance, types of activities, etc.).

Pre-event communications with the event's audience and participants may include, depending on the event, advisories on weather conditions and environmental conditions (terrain, flora, and fauna), suggestions as to suitable clothing, promotions for responsible drinking, and/or information about the level of and procedures for on-site medical care. On-site communications should include the location(s) of facilities and advice on health care on signage and printed materials, as well as public announcement scripts advising people what to do and where to go for on-site medical attention. Sports events may need to collect specific medical information from team members or participants and provide specific medical personnel or facilities. International events may need to advise international visitors regarding the transport and/or refilling of prescription medications.

LEVEL OF SERVICES

The level of on-site and off-site medical care is determined by the size, demographics, and expected behaviors of the event population (including attendees, participants, staff, volunteers, and others), as well as the specific health risks associated with the event activities and event site (see Figure 6-13). Obviously, the riskier the activities or the terrain, the more likely it is that someone will experience an injury, and the older the event population, the more likely that someone will experience an illness.

The professional event coordinator should, first and foremost and for all events, check with staff and volunteers to determine who has training in first aid, cardiopulmonary resuscitation (CPR), and the Heimlich maneuver and make certain a fully stocked first aid kit is included in the event equipment. Information about communicable diseases and viruses should be included in the staff briefing or volunteer orientation, and first aid personnel should be required to notify the event coordinator if numerous similar cases of gastrointestinal distress are reported within a short time (indicating the possible contamination of food, air, or the water supply). Levels of on-site medical care beyond a first aid kit differ, depending on the event. The professional event coordinator is advised to consult with local public safety and/or health services for the requirements for the event, based on its unique characteristics.

An on-site first aid post, station, room, or tent should preferably be positioned so that it is accessible within five minutes from any location within the event site. It must be visible, well lit, with signage giving directions to it throughout the event site. It should be in as quiet a location as possible, sheltered from the elements, and designed or laid out to provide patient privacy and personal dignity. A first aid station should also have a place for a sick or injured person to lie down. The professional event coordinator must determine how help will be summoned by/for a sick or injured person and how the patient will be extricated and transported to the first aid station. First aiders may carry stretchers or a special golf cart may be equipped with a litter to move injured patrons to the first aid station, or it may be possible (or necessary) to treat or begin treatment for some cases on the spot. A four-wheel drive vehicle may be needed if the terrain is unsuitable for golf cart or ambulance access.

EMERGENCY RESPONSE

An emergency is any condition endangering, or thought to be endangering, life or property requiring urgent response (see Figure 6-14). The first 30 minutes of a situation are the most dangerous; therefore, it is critical that the appropriate emergency response agency is contacted and arrives at the scene to respond to the situation in a timely manner. A disaster—natural, technological, or human-made—can involve mass casualties and major losses. It is important for the professional event coordinator to prepare for this possibility by understanding both the external hazards and those specific to the activity or nature of the event itself.

Level of Care	Scope of Medical Care	Medical Personnel
First Aid Kit	Including antiseptics, bandages and sterile gauze, bee sting kits, cotton-tipped swabs, creams and lotions, handwipes, nail clippers, plastic gloves, scissors, slings, tapes, tongue depressors, and tweezers.	Staff—with CPR and Heimlich maneuver training. Trained first aiders—roving or posted.
Basic First Aid	Including equipment or devices for managing infection exposure, airways, spinal immobilization, fracture immobilization, shock, and bleeding control.	Trained first aiders—roving or posted. Registered nurse with a physician on call
Basic Life Support	Including Basic First Aid plus intravenous therapy and oxygen. May include on-site ambulance(s).	Registered nurse with a physician on call. Emergency medical technician (EMT)—a person trained to administer emergency medical treatment more advanced than Basic First Aid.
Advanced Life Support	Emergency medical treatment beyond Basic Life Support, including early management of severe trauma. May include on-site ambulance(s).	Paramedic—a medical technician who has received extensive training in advanced life support and emergency medicine. Such personnel are usually permitted to administer intravenous fluids and other drugs that can arrest a life-threatening physiological condition.
On-site or Mobile Hospital	A specialized, self-contained vehicle that can provide a clinical environment that enables a physician to provide definitive treatment, including full monitoring and ventilation.	Physician (Note: In many jurisdictions, only physicians are authorized to prescribe medicine, even aspirin).

Sources: Australian Emergency Manuals Series, Manual 2 (1999), Safe and Healthy Mass Gatherings: A Medical, Health and Safety Planning Manual for Public Events *(Commonwealth of Australia: Emergency Management Australia (www.health.sa.gov.au/pehs/PDF-files/ema-mass-gatherings-manual.pfd); Alexander Berlongi (1990),* The Special Event Risk Management Manual *(Dana Point, CA: Berlongi);* National Fire Protection Association Glossary of Terms *(www.nfpa.org).*

Figure 6-13
Levels of On-site Medical Care

Natural	Human-Made		Technological
❏ Earthquake ❏ Extreme Winds ❏ Flash Flood ❏ Landslide/Avalanche ❏ Lightning ❏ Rain Deluge ❏ Severe Weather ❏ Wildfires	❏ Biological Spill/ Release ❏ Bomb Threats/ Bombing ❏ Chemical Spill ❏ Civil or Military Disturbance ❏ Crowd Riot/Panic	❏ Fires (Arson) ❏ Gang/Crowd Violence ❏ Kidnapping/ Hostage Taking ❏ Mass Food Poisoning ❏ Sabotage ❏ Structural Failure	❏ Equipment Failure ❏ Fires (Electrical) ❏ Gas Leaks ❏ Mechanical Failure ❏ Power Outage ❏ Utility Failure— Other

Figure 6-14
Potential Emergencies and Disasters

Emergency response agencies provide law enforcement, rescue, fire suppression, emergency medical care, disaster assistance, special operations, and other forms of hazard control and mitigation. They may include public, governmental, private, for-profit and not-for-profit, industrial, or military organizations. Most communities have well-established emergency response plans dictating the specific actions to be performed by all personnel who are expected to respond during an emergency, including the use of communication systems, security of the scene, and traffic control. You must establish the protocols for the identification of an emergency and the notification of the appropriate or lead emergency response agencies. Prepare a list of agencies you are to contact or notify should an emergency or disaster occur, which may include the following:

- Police
- Ambulance service
- Fire department
- Hospital/medical facility

- Search and rescue service
- State emergency service
- Security personnel
- Transportation authority

You should also establish the charges and liability for charges for emergency response services (what they will cost and who is to pay).

EMERGENCY SITE ACCESS AND EGRESS

Of critical importance in a situation of emergency or disaster is access and egress for the responding services and their equipment, as well as the identification of the specific location of the emergency within the event site. Fire officials recommend the creation of a grid map of the site, including an overview of the vicinity with numbered and lettered squares superimposed on it to provide fixed reference points for all locations within the area. You may need to provide special areas of access within your site plan, including marshaling areas for emergency response vehicles and equipment, a staging area where they may be organized, a sheltered triage area for casualties, or even a helicopter pad or landing strip (an empty road) for aeromedical response.

On-Site Insight

Robert Sivek, CSEP, CERP, of The Meetinghouse Companies, Inc. noted that for one event for 50,000 he produced on an island with only one bridge as access, he arranged for a fleet of jet boats and a Medivac helicopter to be on-site so that should a medical emergency occur, they would be able to evacuate the injured despite the limited access route. There were no emergencies, but he said the organization got some great pictures of the event from the helicopter.

As event coordinator, you will work with law enforcement or fire officials to establish the emergency response site requirements for your event. These can include the access routes, designated or dedicated perimeter roads or streets, designated and dedicated parking areas, and segregated routes for responding services, audience evacuation, and casualty removal. You may be required to have certain emergency response personnel stationed on-site, such as fire personnel if pyrotechnics are included, or rescue divers if an underwater activity is conducted. All onsite emergency or medical response personnel must be provided with the access credentials that will allow them to get wherever they need to go.

PREPARE FOR THE WORST AND PRACTICE YOUR PLAN

People have been injured at the safest event sites. People have died at the smallest of celebrations. Think everything through to the worst possible conclusion so you will be prepared to deal with any situation that does occur. This preparation can arguably be the difference between an amateur event coordinator and a professional one. The consideration of and planning for the health, safety, and welfare of the people involved in an event under any and all circumstances is a cornerstone of professional event coordination.

You must seek out the officials and authorities that can provide the right direction, allocate the proper resources to secure the requisite equipment and services, make the plans, and provide the right tools, training, and practice so that your staff and volunteers will be able to respond in the appropriate manner should an incident occur. These plans provide the protocols and procedures for all contingencies so that decisions and actions will be effective. This training and practice allows your staff and volunteers to become desensitized to the panic of the moment and react correctly without hesitation.

Target Competency Review

Every event has vulnerabilities that must be considered and controlled in order to provide a safe, secure, and healthy environment for those creating, installing, operating, and attending the event. The type and scope of these hazards will vary according to the size and nature of the event, its site, its activities, and those in attendance. The professional event coordinator sets the tone for safe operations with a strong commitment to safety, which must be infused throughout the event team of staff and suppliers.

The appropriate communications protocols and technology support this safety mandate, as well as help to provide a quality experience within the context of any occurrence or incident that might take place at the event. Security personnel, whether peer or professional, are employed and deployed to protect people and property and may offer a sense of care and well-being for event-goers. There is a mandate for all security personnel, staff, and volunteers to be vigilant observers of the conditions and conduct that can lead to unsafe situations.

Illness or injuries are possible at any event, no matter the type or size or audience. Responding to medical incidents, whether minor or major, must be factored into planning the event site, budget, and operations to provide the appropriate level of care. Coordination and cooperation with emergency response agencies is critical in order to be prepared for the worst that could happen. Although disasters and mass casualties are not usual at events, they must be planned for nevertheless. Attention to these important facets of professional event coordination separates the amateurs from the experts.

EXERCISES IN PROFESSIONAL EVENT COORDINATION

Outline and describe the safety and security plans, including on-site communications and medical services, for each of the following events.

1. You are coordinating a training program for 800 regional sales managers of a high-tech corporation. The program will include proprietary information on the company's newest product lines

and the marketing strategies for the upcoming year, something its competitors would do anything to get a look at. The program presentations will include significant AV installations and the rigging of complex and heavy decorative displays throughout the meeting space, including in the ceiling.

2. The executive director of an association for which you coordinate the annual conference for 5000 attendees has just informed you that she has gotten an affirmative response to her invitation to your country's head of state. He or she will appear at the opening session of your upcoming conference to give a short but internationally significant speech, which means that there will be a small army of local, national, and international media to cover it.

3. You have been hired to coordinate a charity gala to benefit a children's hospital. The guest list of 300 includes celebrities from stage and screen, dignitaries from city and state government, and executives from the top corporations in the country. The site selected for this evening of dining, dancing, and a special appearance by a world-renowned musician is the rooftop of the hospital itself.

Facing Page

The event environment can be designed using creative configurations and unusual furnishings. *Photograph by RUDA Photography, courtesy of Steve Kemble Event Design.*

CHAPTER 7

Coordinating the Environment

The two most engaging powers are to make new things familiar and familiar things new.

—WILLIAM MAKEPEACE THACKERAY (1811–1863)

IN THIS CHAPTER YOU WILL LEARN HOW TO:

- Develop themes that support the event objectives and communicate the desired message.
- Coordinate the event environment, incorporating the theme with the use of décor items and illusions.
- Identify the staging and equipment needs to facilitate the functional requirements of the event environment.
- Incorporate visual communication tools to guide guests and enhance event objectives.

A convention and visitors bureau (CVB) had been awarded an excellence-in-service gold medal by a national magazine, and the local hospitality community decided to hold a luncheon to congratulate the CVB's staff. Although the staff knew they were attending a free luncheon sponsored by the convention center, they did not know that one of the local suppliers was decorating the room. The decorator hung 18-in.-diameter gold medals made of painted Styrofoam, suspended from red, white, and blue lengths of draping vinyl, over individual tables to resemble lanyard-style award medals. These inexpensive floating centerpieces filled the room with celebratory splashes of color from the tabletops up to the high ceiling. As the CVB staff arrived, they were astounded to find these colorful decorations when they had expected just another plain luncheon function in the unadorned convention center. A staff member approached the decorator, and with a slight mist in her eye, exclaimed in awe, *"You did this for us?"*

Even the simplest of decorations is an expression of care and appreciation. It creates an environment or atmosphere of celebration, motivation, commemoration, education, or congratulation. The event environment is a form of nonverbal communication, communicating on many levels, both conscious and subconscious. It is up to the professional event coordinator to work with the appropriate designers and suppliers to create an environment with a purpose, the desired message, and a legacy of memories. Using good taste, creativity, and ingenuity, the professional event coordinator must create an environment that facilitates the function, goals, and objectives of the event.

Frank M. Whiting, in his book *An Introduction to the Theatre,* stated, "A background or environment of some kind is inevitable. Is the environment appropriate or inappropriate, effective or ineffective, an asset or a source of distraction?" At any event, there is always some sort of inherent environment or atmosphere. It may be warm or cool, wet or dry, crowded or spacious, stimulating or relaxing, comfortable or unpleasant. There are lights, colors, sights, sounds, and smells. You must consider the inherent background or environment and procure the proper staging, décor, and equipment to create an appropriate and effective environment that becomes an asset to the event experience.

Theme Development

Themes are very popular devices for a broad variety of events, from fundraisers to festivals, and marketing events to meetings. The *American College Dictionary* defines a theme as a subject or topic. Theatrical scholars associate theme with the principle message of a play. In an article on meeting themes on The Writing Works Web site, John K. Mackenzie asserts that a theme is a "psycho-syntactic" device for compressing a big idea. A theme allows us to quickly communicate a broad range of ideas and images based on widely held cultural assumptions and associations.

Pine and Gilmore, authors of *The Experience Economy,* trace the word *theme* to the Greek *thema,* denoting "the place" or "something placed." They contend that "experiences occur in places, and the best of those places are themed." They propose that there are five principles for developing a theme.

1. It must alter a guest's sense of reality.
2. It must affect the experience of space, time, and matter.
3. It must integrate space, time, and matter into a cohesive realistic whole.
4. It is strengthened by creating multiple places within a place.
5. It must fit the character of the enterprise staging the experience.

They also assert, "The theme must drive all the design elements and staged events of the experience toward a unified storyline that wholly captivates the customer."

A theme establishes expectations by putting the experience in a recognizable context. A theme builds excitement, creates anticipation, and promotes involvement in the experience to come. Themes are used to reinforce a message, marketing goals, and/or desired behavior. Mackenzie asserts, however, "A theme, by itself, doesn't mean much. It gains value in three ways: 1. The experiences audience members invest to interpret it. 2. How convincingly you develop it. 3. How well it amplifies your core concepts."

CREATIVITY—INSPIRATION TO IDEA

There are libraries filled with books on creativity—how it works, how it is cultivated, how to be creative, and so on ad infinitum. The poet Robert Frost said, "An idea is a feat of association." Jenny Sullivan, profiling five creativity gurus in the August/September 2001 issue of *Navigator,* the in-flight magazine of Comair, states, "What we produce depends on what we ingest." Marian L. Davis, author of *Visual Design in Dress,* advises, "To increase one's originality and creativity, one should seek new ways of using old, familiar media and items plus practice 'cross-sensory interpretation' . . . sensitizing oneself to a wide range of experiences and translating them into other forms of expression." I am a strong proponent of Adopt and Adapt—taking an existing idea or image and reinterpreting it to meet the particular needs and conditions of an event.

The sources of and methods for sparking inspiration are as varied as individuals, but most rely on a broad variety of stimuli and the ability to translate such stimuli into new manifestations. Ideas can come from television, movies, theater, music, magazines, books, conversations, shopping, photographs, locations, politics, fashion, religious or cultural rituals, other industries, and surfing the Internet. Some people use brainstorming techniques, some use mind mapping, and others conduct in-depth research into a topic. All these methods rely on a well-stocked inventory of experiences, references, and information.

Theme development, like event coordination, starts with the purpose of the event and the client's expectations of the outcome. Deborah Borsum, CSEP, CMD (Certified Marketing Director), of The Meetinghouse Companies, Inc., in Elmhurst, Illinois, and former president of the International Special Events Society (ISES), emphatically believes that this begins with listening—listening to the client talk about why he or she is having the event and what the client wants to happen as a result of the event. Defining the end product and customer profile establishes the criteria to be met by the selection and development of the theme. The type of function, the date and time, or the location of the event may be the inspiration that guides the creative process. All of these will certainly shape the final design.

WORK FROM THE FAMILIAR

Many event designers advise that a theme should be based on something familiar to the audience, then expanded and interpreted in an unusual way. A joke is no good if you have to explain it, and a theme is not effective if you have to explain it. You want the audience to quickly understand the overall concept or circumstances so they are able to anticipate and participate in the experience. A theme based on a familiar topic, locale, or phrase provides clarity and connection.

Selection of a familiar theme of course, depends on the designer's understanding of what is familiar to each particular audience. A Wild West Rodeo theme will likely be familiar in the United States but may not be relative or familiar in South Africa. A theme also depends on the context. "Go for the Gold" may communicate achievement in the context of the Olympic Games, a historical reference to the nineteenth-century gold rush in the United States, or a hunt for buried pirate treasure. "Carnival" may conjure up images of clowns, cotton candy, and merry-go-rounds; it may evoke images of the bright, raucous parades in Rio de Janeiro; or it may bring to mind the elegant masks and costumes of Venice. The event designer must understand the audience's geographic culture, corporate culture, ethnic culture, and popular culture in order to find images and/or concepts that will be familiar.

USE CULTURAL ICONS

Using cultural icons, those images that are deeply ingrained or widely understood, communicate a theme quickly and effectively (see Figure 7-1). They provide a base from which the designer can expand and develop a theme environment. Cultural icons differ according to the geographic, socioeconomic, and educational backgrounds of the audience. John J. Daly Jr., CSEP, advises that the event designer must be sensitive to authenticity in developing a theme. "Guests are more sophisticated and sensitive to cultural authenticity. You can no longer simply do an 'Oriental' theme—it will need to be Korean or Cantonese or other specific Asian culture, even narrowed to a specific province within a country."

Movies are the single most commonly shared experience in modern culture and, in the United States particularly, television is probably second. Other entertainment domains such as theater, music, and sports vary according to current popularity within a demographic or ethnographic group. Historical icons may be real (e.g., from the eighteenth century) or imagined (e.g., futuristic or based on fantasy). Nostalgia is applicable to within one or two generations only (otherwise it becomes "history"), and very popular when segmented into an overview of a specific decade (e.g., the '50s, '60s, and '70s). Personal experiences may include common or shared events or leisure pursuits. Politics and current events are, indeed, current, and can be powerful because of their immediate relevance.

Indigenous icons may relate to a specific ethnic culture, corporate culture, or demographic. "The Big Five" can indicate the five animal species one would hope to see on an African safari, and "The Big Ten"

Entertainment Media	History	Location
Film Television Music Literature Theater Sports	Nostalgia Historical Eras and Events Real or Imagined Eras Current Events Personal Experiences Politics	Indigenous Rites and Rituals Indigenous Geography Indigenous Architecture Indigenous Attractions International Cities and Sites Folk Arts and Crafts
Occasions	**Conceptual**	**Fashion**
Personal/Life-cycle Events Religious Rites and Rituals Festivals Holidays Seasonal Events	Emotions and Values The Five Senses Philosophical Concepts Psychological Concepts Physical Concepts	Colors Clothing Interior Design Technology Fine Arts and Crafts

Figure 7-1
Cultural Icon Domains

refers to college sports in the United States. Architectural or geographic icons can create an immediate association with a location, such as the Sydney Opera House or Ayers Rock for Australia, the Eiffel Tower for Paris, or saguaro cactus for the U.S. Southwest.

Various personal and public occasions differ depending on the culture. Holidays vary from place to place, both in existence and importance. Festivals may be associated with a particular culture or location (the cornerstones of many tourism marketing plans), and seasons have different characteristics throughout the world (winter is not the same in a tropical zone as it is in an alpine zone). Conceptual icons may be virtually universal, such as the psychological concepts of happiness or achievement, or they may be culturally based and philosophical, such as heaven and hell, Americana, or "family values." The event designer may be given a word, phrase, or slogan to interpret, such as "We Are the World" or "Shine."

Many event designers pay close attention to current fashion when crafting a theme environment, incorporating the latest colors, images, and attitudes from clothing styles, interior design trends, and technological advances. Themes may also be gleaned from historical fine art contexts such as impressionism, cubism, or surrealism; fine art or fashion itself (e.g., "A Work of Art" or "Haute Couture"); or a single color such as red or blue.

INCORPORATE THE FIVE SENSES

A theme should incorporate all five senses throughout the event design, including sight, sound, taste, touch, and smell. The more senses affected by the environment, the more memorable the event will be. The sensory attributes of an event are forms of nonverbal communication and have the ability to touch both our conscious and subconscious minds and emotions. Sights and sounds are cerebral—processed in our minds, whereas taste, touch, and smell are physical—processed in our bodies. Many believe that smell is the most powerful of the senses and able to conjure up intense reactions based on memories of life experiences. The event designer can enhance positive sensory cues and qualities and should make every attempt to eliminate negative ones. The sensory cues in an event environment may include the following:

- **Sight**—setting, props, floral arrangements, color, fabrics, food presentation, lighting, attire
- **Sound**—ambient noise (good or bad), soundscaping, musical entertainment, dialogue, dining sounds (i.e., glasses clinking, crunchy foods, etc.)
- **Taste**—food, beverage, atmospheric and olfactory aftertaste
- **Touch**—surfaces, fabrics, furnishings, food texture, visual textures (that stimulate a tactile sensation)
- **Smell**—food aromas, flowers, fuels (cooking and power generation), scented candles/incense/oils, ambient aromas (natural scents and malodorous smells)

PACKAGE THE EXPERIENCE

A great title can communicate the vision of the event, but the name alone cannot express the theme without the support and reinforcement of multiple dimensions. With the theme clearly defined and the image distilled to its essence, the event designer uses that foundation for reinforcing the theme throughout the dimensions of the experience—anticipation, arrival, atmosphere, appetite, activity, and amenities. All of the elements are tied into the theme, inception to completion, to package an integrated experience that supports the event objectives and communicates the desired message.

Relating to the Pine and Gilmore principle, that a theme must alter reality, all these themed elements and details should put the guests "somewhere" they could not go themselves. The environment and experience should literally be out of the ordinary. There is, however, a caveat—

the presentation *must* be theater. The audience must be able to discern staged events from actual events. For example, a shoot-out by cowboys in costume during a Wild West theme party, or between men in space-suits with laser tag guns during a futuristic theme party, is easily recognizable as an entertainment activity, but a mock shoot-out between "gang members" or "terrorists" during an avant-garde or "urban extreme" theme party may not be recognizable as theater.

The Layers of Décor

Décor is a primary means of establishing a theme environment or enhancing the desired atmosphere. It can transform a venue into a new vista, direct pedestrian traffic flow, facilitate learning or interaction, express powerful emotions, and communicate important messages. Like theatrical stage design, event décor is an art form that literally "sets the stage" for the event experience. It can be as simple as highlighting the inherent setting or as complex as creating an alternate reality within a specific space.

Janet Landey, CSEP, of Party Design in Johannesburg, South Africa, contends that an event environment "should have layer upon layer upon layer of imagery and details." Interior designers approach the decoration of a living space or workspace with a multilevel or multilayered methodology. These layers begin with the inherent architecture and architectural features, followed by paint colors for the walls and ceiling, then the floor coverings. These are the largest design areas and those least likely to change over a period of time. They then select furniture, drapery and upholstery fabrics, accessories and accent fabrics, plants, and lighting fixtures—those items that may be changed more frequently depending on the mood or taste of the current occupant. The event designer may find this approach useful.

BACKGROUND

The background is the "inevitable environment." It includes the walls, ceiling, floor, and architectural features of the venue. Remember, there is a background even if there are no walls, ceiling, or floor (the great outdoors), or these elements may be temporary (a tent). The designer may approach the basic environment as a "blank canvas" onto which color, lines, shapes, and textures may be added, or the setting may already serve the needs of the overall design. The professional event coordinator must work closely with the designer to make certain that the appropriate installation time and equipment will be available and that all décor is safely installed and securely rigged.

- **Walls**—Walls and perimeters may be concealed or enhanced with digital murals, draping, façades, fiber-optic or Mylar curtains, foliage, painted scenic backdrops, panels, scenery, spandex shapes, and/or video landscapes. There are even mural backdrops that change scene when lit with ultraviolet light.
- **Ceilings**—Ceilings (and the space from the top of the head up to the ceiling) may be decorated with air-filled tubes, balloons, banners, chandeliers (functional or faux), fabric draping, dripping or draping twinkle lights, flags, floating latticework panels or picture frames, hanging gardens, suspended props, and/or lighting projections.
- **Floors**—Floors may be redecorated with custom carpets in the color of your choice (even decorated with an inlaid logo or event title), paint, sheet linoleum, or dance floors, which may be oak or teak wood parquet, black and white parquet, assorted marble colors, custom painted, or covered in special plastic coverings (which may also be customized with logos or images).
- **Architectural features**—Windows may be draped or masked with fabric or foliage. Structural columns (and tent poles) can be draped with fabrics, surrounded with foliage or faux fixtures, washed with dramatic lighting, wrapped with spiraling balloons, or dressed with fabrics or sculpted fiberglass to resemble a forest of giant trees with branches dripping in moss and flowers to create an enchanted forest.

Technology Tip

Scenic backgrounds can be digitally printed or projected, providing incredible photo-imaging capabilities. Photographs or illustrations can be reproduced via digital printing on backdrops, scrims, banners, signs, and wall coverings with practically no dimensional restrictions and seamless up to 16 ft (4.88 m) wide. Theatrical fabric and fabrication companies such as Rose Brand (www.rosebrand.com) can create "computer printed and painted images in large scale with a depth and clarity of color superior to photo enlargement processes." You can also create a digital vista by projecting a series of scenic images or picture segments on a series of projection screens, which can span the length of a ballroom or surround an audience, given sufficient screens and projectors. The screens may be placed touching

(Continued)

each other to provide a panorama that is practically seamless, with only a thin line like a window mullion segmenting the view. If controlled via a computerized presentation program such as PowerPoint, these images can fade and swipe into new landscapes or can be emblazoned with changing messages.

COLOR

Color is probably the most evocative element of décor available to the designer. Color is a primary component of design in everything from themes to promotional collateral materials. It can create strong emotions and induce physical reactions. It will be included within every layer of the décor, from the walls to the furnishings, from the floors to the flowers. Color is always present—even clear plastic draping, bubble wrap coverings, glass bricks, and Plexiglas lecterns reveal or reflect the surrounding colors and lights.

- **Palettes**—A palette or color scheme is a harmonious grouping of colors. It may consist of primary colors, complementary colors, analogous colors, monochromatic colors, earth tones, jewel tones, bold and bright, subdued and pale, or any number of color combinations. For information on color theory, visit the Pantone Web site at www.pantone.com.
- **Connotations**—Although market researchers study people's emotional responses to color, no color has an intrinsic meaning. Responses to color seem to be fairly universal within Western societies, but other cultures may endow specific colors with completely different symbolic meanings.

On-Site Insight

John J. Daly Jr., CSEP, of John Daly, Inc., International, based in Santa Barbara, California, recounts a story about decorating a hotel ballroom in Korea for an event celebrating the tenth anniversary of a hotel, which Buddhist monks were coming to bless. Knowing that this was a very joyous occasion, Daly had decorated the entire ballroom in yellow and white flowers and fabrics, believing that this was just the "happy" look appropriate for the celebration. Three hours before the ceremony was to start, the monks arrived to review the site and prepare for the blessing. Upon entering the ballroom, they were stunned and horrified. Daly had not done his research. The color scheme signified a death in this culture. He had to redo the entire room in less than three hours by adding many more colors to the décor to mitigate the predominance of yellow and white. He has never neglected his research since.

FOCAL POINTS

Focal points within the décor design are those areas and items that you want the audience to pay attention to and the décor elements that will be instrumental in defining the theme or style of the event. These will likely be the larger expenditures in your décor budget because they will make the largest statement in terms of your décor design, and they may be the best items on which to spend a small budget.

- **Entrances**—Entrances set the tone for the experience and provide the transition from the real world to the altered reality of the event inside. Entrances truly give the proverbial first impression. They may be decorated with scenic props, fabrics, façades, flowers, foliage, sculptures, carpet runners, balloons, scenic tableaux, costumed characters, live animals, searchlights, intelligent lights, lasers, giant puppets dancing in the air propelled by continuously blowing fans, banners, flags, two- or three-dimensional spandex shapes, fountains, gardens, colonnades, or canopies.
- **Stages**—Stages include entertainment stages, platforms for presenters, distinctive displays, and any other raised area that features activities or images important to the purpose of the event. They may be enclosed proscenium-style (bordered on three sides) or thrust-style with a background or presented in the round (open on all sides). They may have multiple levels, numerous entrances and exits, or projection screens and can include functional and decorative apparatus, equipment, and machinery. Stages may be stationary or movable. They can float out into the audience or roll from place to place like theatrical stage wagons.
- **Buffets and bars**—Food and beverage locations are sure to be focal points for guests, so the designer should use this behavioral proclivity as an opportunity to transmit a motifed message. Buffets can be a cornucopia of sensory effects as well as centers of theme interpretation. The buffet or bar itself can be a decorative (or entertainment) focus—it may be made of ice, neon, an aquarium filled with exotic fish, or industrial materials. It may be a tall column of spandex with shelves projecting from it (or with hands coming through to give the guest a drink or an hors d'oeuvre). It may have

props or people floating over it or emerging from it. It may be built onto a wagon or cart and pushed, pulled, or driven by remote control through the party.

- **Scenic props**—From façades to flats, statues to sculptural forms, or fountains to giant faux foliage or animals, scenic props are used to create the theatrical illusions that alter reality. Sources for scenic props (either in stock or custom-made) include decorating companies, theatrical companies (including schools and university theater departments), scenic prop studios, and the venue itself. Always check the condition of the props and the costs for rental and installation.

FABRICS

Fabrics are used throughout the décor of an event—ranging from the pipe and drape of exhibit booths or stands to the upholstery on the chairs, to the linens on the tables and scrunched up on the buffet. Fabrics offer an opportunity to add color, texture, and patterns to the décor. You must be sure, however, that the fabrics and fibers you use for decorating are flame retardant or flame resistant, either inherently or as a result of being treated with an additive.

- **Drapery**—Fabrics and fibers can be draped from ceiling to floor to create or cover walls. Deep swags of rich fabric can frame the edges of walls, windows, stages, or architectural obstructions. Tent poles or technical equipment such as light trees may be dressed with rich draping, topped with glorious poufs and puddled into sculptural shapes at the bottom. Suspended cylinders of draping can disguise light fixtures and sound equipment or simply fill an enormous ceiling void.
- **Linens and napery**—The most common form of fabric associated with events is the table linen and napkins (or serviettes). These are now available in an astounding variety of fabrics, colors, patterns, shapes, and sizes. Table coverings may be custom fitted to architecturally encase a table or designed in spandex to stretch over tables of practically any shape. Customizing and enhancing table fabrics is also possible via hand-painted, custom-printed, or iron-on transfers, or runners, weavings, or showers of ribbons from edge to floor.
- **Upholstery**—Chairs are being dressed for success as well. The standard chrome and upholstered hotel stacking chairs may be covered in sleek spandex, sheer chiffon, rich velvet or brocade, and countless other fabrics. Chair covers may be customized with iron-on transfers of a photo of the guest of honor or imprinted with a cor-

porate logo. Couches, benches, ottomans, and floor cushions upholstered in such fabrics as rich brocade, lush leather, or fake fur may be used to create intimate conversation areas or stylistic tableaux.

FURNISHINGS

Furniture and other functional or decorative furnishings are a stylistic statement at an event just as they are in our own homes. The way they are built and the materials from which they are fabricated are design elements that can reinforce a theme or atmosphere. An overabundance of furnishings may suggest an ornate historical era, be intimidating, or feel too crowded; a scarcity of furnishings may suggest frugality, ensure the brevity of a guest's stay, or allow traffic flow. From heavyweight antiques to sleek chrome sculptural shapes, furnishings communicate a lot about where you are, what to do, and what the host wants you to think (about him or her and about the event).

- **Tables**—Tables may be used for dining, writing, display, or pure decoration. They can be made of wood, metal, glass, plastic, fiberglass, Plexiglas, or stone. They can be dressed with draping, skirting, lighting, corrugated metal siding, sod, neon, spandex, tile, bamboo shades, plastic bubble wrap, flowers, leaves, or bedsheets. They can be stationary, rolled in and around, suspended and floating, or they can descend from the ceiling for a dramatic reveal.
- **Chairs**—Chairs come in many different shapes, styles, and materials, ranging from chrome to wood to wicker. In addition to chairs, places to sit include bales of hay, banquettes, beanbag chairs, benches, bleachers, boulders, boxes, couches, crates, cushions, overturned troughs, pews, pillows, platforms, stacked suitcases, stone steps, stools, thrones, or the backseat of a '56 Chevy.
- **Counters and displays**—Counters may be used for check-in and registration, distributing collateral materials, serving food and drink, and displaying products or floral arrangements. An étagère (a tall backless cabinet with open shelves) may be used as a bar back displaying specialty liquors, pedestals may be used to display platters of pastry or exhibit edible sculptures, and bookcases may be used to hold plates and utensils at the starting point of a buffet line, or conference materials in a meeting room.
- **Foliage**—All sorts of potted plants, trees, bushes, arrangements, and other vegetation (real or fake) may add a touch of nature to a design and give it extra "life." Foliage may be used to conceal unattractive equipment, soften edges, create pathways, and dress empty corners. Ficus trees, the workhorses of plant décor, can be

laced with twinkle lights to add a sparkling dimension to practically any setting.

LIGHTING

Lighting can illuminate and highlight, create focal points or dramatic shadows, and add color and dimension to all the different layers of décor. Lighting fixtures can include floor lamps, table lamps, wall sconces, chandeliers, faux street lamps, and a broad range of theatrical luminaires (discussed further in Chapter 8). The designer can use lighting balloons, searchlights, floodlights, tiki torches, showers of twinkle lights, or a ring of cars with their headlights on. The savvy event designer makes the lighting a deliberately integrated part of the overall design.

- **Natural**—The natural or ambient light may include sunlight streaming through a window or skylight, firelight from a bonfire on the beach or a roaring fire in a fireplace, or candles of all shapes, sizes, and colors. Natural lighting may or may not be sufficient to provide the appropriate illumination, either in brightness or coverage, so it may have to be enhanced with additional light sources and fixtures.
- **Functional**—Functional lighting provides the illumination to perform the tasks associated with the event activities. It may include the houselights in a function room, task lighting at specific activities, or spotlighting to highlight specific items or displays.
- **Decorative**—The options for decorative lighting are practically infinite. Neon can be used to make tables, trays, and glass brick bars glow in the dark with brilliant color. Projections can create pools of color or an underwater fantasy. Chaser lights can edge a sign or stage. Plain white spandex shapes can be saturated with colors that change throughout the event or pulse to the beat of the music. Even fire can be faked, either with fabric flames illuminated as they dance about propelled by a blower or with video projections shown on a screen.

DETAILING

Detailing is related to "merchandizing"—the addition and arrangement of lots of ornaments and amenities to create an appealing presentation. These details may be added to any part of the overall décor, from flowers clustered around the base of a lectern or along the front edge of a stage, to ribbons and bouquets tied on the sides of chairs or pews along the aisle at a wedding ceremony. These are the added touches that finish the picture and give it emotional texture. And they do not have to be expensive—a little creativity can change the ordinary into the extraordinary.

- **Tablescapes**—The source for a microenvironment within the overall macroenvironment of theme décor is the tablescape—a work of art (and a visual story) in and of itself. Tablescaping (like landscaping) entails adding layer upon layer of detail and interest to create an evocative table setting. This can be very effective at banquet events when the guests spend a significant portion of the time seated at their tables.

- **Place settings**—The options for rented dishes, crockery, glassware, and utensils have increased immeasurably. These items are available in a broad variety of patterns, colors, detailing, shapes, and styles such as elegant, traditional, abstract, or animalistic. Place settings may be marked with individual place mats or runners of virtually any material imaginable, including straw mats, custom imprinted fabric, slabs of stone or glass, burnished sheet metal, hand-carved wooden chargers, bamboo, a large banana leaf, bandannas, or unfolded road maps.

- **Centerpieces and floral arrangements**—Creative centerpieces may be fashioned with balloons, books, bricks, fabric, feathers, flowers (real, silk, or paper), foamcore, fruit, hardware store finds, hats, household goods, mannequins, masks, metal, neon, paper, props, rocks, toys, sculptures, sporting goods, stuffed animals, and virtually any other material. Centerpieces can be freestanding, suspended, or created by the guests themselves with craft materials that have been placed in the center of the table (and if butcher paper is used as an overlay, with crayons sprinkled around, the guests can illustrate their own tabletops with greetings, graphics, or graffiti).

- **Accessories**—Candles come in countless sizes, shapes, and colors and may be placed in candelabras, in glass hurricane shades, on ceramic pedestals, or in any number of innovative containers. (Always check the fire code for "open flame" regulations when using candles.) Containers for condiments and edibles can be in unique shapes, patterns, textures, and materials, such as shells, leaves, boxes, flower pots, or any other conceivable holder.

- **Amenities**—A broad assortment of gifts and other amenities may be integrated into the scene and theme, including menu cards, programs, table numbers, place cards, napkin holders, and gifts. Menu cards, table numbers, and place cards may be printed on or attached to numerous objects or materials. Napkins may be folded in dozens of ways and ornamented with mementos or thematic details.

Staging Considerations

Creating an event environment can include a vast array of products, services, equipment, and labor to provide the framework for the functional and decorative components of the design. The extent of the staging requirements will be determined based on the type of event, existing venue capabilities and constraints, functional requirements, time, budget, and humanpower. Although volunteers, family members, or untrained staff may be used to set up many of your event decorations, only experienced, well-trained, and, in some cases, licensed professionals should be employed to erect and install the staging equipment such as stages, scaffolding constructions (e.g., sound wing bays), tents, flooring systems, and any other temporary structures. These professional decorators or contractors should be selected early and included in the planning process.

STAGES

Stages and platforms may be needed and used for entertainment attractions, visibility of presentations, technical platforms, camera platforms, runways, bridging platforms, or to add multiple levels to a function room or turn a swimming pool into a dining or dancing area (there are even floating platforms on which a pianist and a grand piano drift around the pool). "Apart from the usual applications for concerts and events, Showtech Australia has put scaffold platforms and stages in some rather unusual places—over pools, fountains, in the ocean/bay, and even in a lake" (www.showtechaustralia.com.au).

Stages may be a permanent feature of a facility such as a theater or auditorium, constructed with scaffolding and decking specifically for an event, or they may be portable. Portable stages can be modular sections that roll in and fold out, or they can be self-contained trucks or trailers that are driven in and opened up, which are effective for undeveloped or temporary outdoor sites. Mobile trailer stages are sometimes attached together to provide a larger performance area.

Modular staging sections may be configured to create a stage of practically any size and geometric shape and are usually available in various sizes (3 × 4 ft, 3 × 6 ft, 3 × 8 ft, 4 × 4 ft, 4 × 6 ft, and 4 × 8 ft) with a selection of leg lengths (8, 16, 24, 32, and 40 in.). Other stage equipment includes guardrails and handrails, stairs and ramps, choral risers, bandstand or stage shells, stage-front barrier systems, roof trussing, and wheelchair lifts. Not all stages must be perpendicular to the audience (see Figure 7-2), and you are encouraged to cut out templates of standard staging sections and play around with them to design creative configurations.

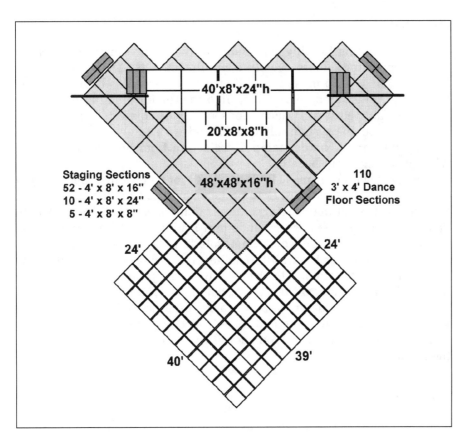

Figure 7-2
Diagonal Stage Layout with Dance Floor

Depending on what is to take place on the stage, the levelness of the stage may be an important factor. Uneven stages can cause problems for dancers and other performers, not to mention the possibility of heavy packing cases rolling off. Robert Estrin of Creative Event Technology recalls leveling a stage to precise specifications for a circus-style performer whose act was performed while he was on a unicycle. "A centimeter or two of slope or crown could have thrown off his performance." Estrin notes that uneven ridges in a stage surface can be and often are caused by a rubber cap missing from the bottom of a leg. These uneven ridges can become a trip hazard, which is not solved simply by taping over them. Estrin recommends that all modular stage sections be clamped together.

FLOORING

The most common flooring considered in the context of an event is the dance floor. Dance floors usually come in 3 × 3 ft (0.91 × 0.91 m) or 3 × 4 ft (0.91 × 1.22 m) sections. Dance floors may also be used for exhibits, VIP tents, food service area flooring, or for creating distinctive entryways and pathways. Dance floor sections are connected via a tongue-and-groove locking system, often stabilized with screws, and should be edged with a raked border ramp to transition from floor to dance floor without posing a trip hazard.

Temporary flooring may also be required for tents or marquees erected on uneven outdoor surfaces, or to protect a surface from the staging (and the construction of that staging). Arenas that change from ice hockey to motocross racing to exposition and sport stadiums with turf protect the primary surface with plywood, homosote (a compressed cardboard primarily used to cover ice rinks), or other material. Special flooring may be required for certain sports or may have to be protected in sports arenas. Professional dancers (e.g., tap, ballet, jazz, modern, lyrical, Irish dancing, clogging, flamenco, and others) often require special sprung wood or cushioned flooring and a controlled-slip floor covering to prevent accidents and injuries (you should get the exact specifications from the particular dance troupe).

TENTING

Tents and marquees come in an astounding variety of shapes and sizes, from pop-up canopies to pole tents, semipermanent clearspan tents to high-peaked circus tents, or tensile structures to two-story tents. They can be square, rectangular, circular, hexagonal, or oval; they can create a bandshell or look like a pagoda. They can have plain side walls, window walls, hard walls, clear walls, domes, and doors. Tents can be brightly striped, white, clear, or made of custom fabrics and may be customized with liners, draping, lighting, heating, cooling, flooring, carpeting, and chandeliers. Tent installations have been used to create covered walkways or to cover hundreds of thousands of square feet at air shows, trade shows, and festivals. Tents may be installed in the most seemingly inaccessible spots—the Maryland-based company Losberger U.S., LLC (www.losberger.com), once had to have a crane reach over a house to install a tent structure.

A tenting professional must survey a tent site so that the structure will be positioned and installed correctly (and without causing damage to surfaces or sprinkler systems). A tent must be anchored properly to ensure stability and wind tolerance, and the tent fabric or material must meet fire safety codes. The site preparation and installation must be included in the budget and the schedule. Depending on the size or type of tent structure and the location where it will be installed, this can be costly, but having a temporary ballroom on a bluff overlooking the ocean may well be worth the expense.

MAKING AND MASKING THE MAGIC

To sustain an illusion, a magician carefully disguises or hides the mechanics of the magic. Making event magic requires the same care. Staging equipment may be minimal or extensive, but should always be considered in terms of visibility and aesthetics. Professional event coordinators know it can take a small army outfitted with a vast amount of equipment and materials to create an event environment, but the audience does not necessarily need to see that. Stages should be designed to either incorporate or conceal technical equipment such as projection screens, loudspeakers, microphones, lights, wires, cables, and other mechanics. Backstage may look like a cacophony of paraphernalia (even though neatly arranged), but the front of the stage should look deliberate and clean.

Projection screens should be dressed with valances, skirts, and/or screen surrounds that complement the rest of the stage setting. Sound wings should be draped or decorated to look like an integrated part of the overall design. Monitors for musicians may be dressed with a few potted plants or floral arrangements in front. Electrical cords should be completely taped down, preferably along the edge of the stage. The hotel lectern (which usually bears an insignia of the hotel) may be dressed with the event's own banner or draping, with rich folds drawn taut. The stage and all risers should be skirted or faced with décor material. Pipe and drape draping panels should be clipped along the back seams with clothespins or clamps to ensure that they remain closed. This is not necessarily something that technical or AV providers automatically think about. You must manage the final visual image.

RIGGING AND INSTALLATION REQUIREMENTS

The professional event coordinator must become familiar with the rigging and installation requirements for all décor and equipment to be incorporated into the event design. These requirements will have an impact on the site selected, the budget, the production schedule, and the labor needs. For anything rigged overhead, there must be a rigging system sufficient to ensure the safety of both the installers and the audience beneath. This may include a grid system, beams and battens, steel cables, a truss system, and chain motor system. It is important to know the weight restrictions or load limits so that the system is not overloaded with too much or too heavy equipment or that too much stress is put on any one section or rigging point. These factors must be discussed with the technical providers, particularly if more than one supplier or subcontractor is used to provide various parts of the program (e.g., decorator, AV provider, lighting company, etc.). It is also important to consider any aerial effects or entertainment, such as cirque-style performers, that requires rigged apparatus (e.g., harness, trapeze, cradle, cloud swing, bungee rigging, or guy wires for flying).

Equipment and décor installed on the floor or on the ground also require attention. Light or sound trees must be installed and anchored so they do not tip over. All props, façades, and freestanding décor elements must be securely braced and weighted down. Sandbags work well for this purpose, but they are not what you would call "décor details." You must think of the entire picture, from floor to ceiling and wall to wall. When using a chain motor system to create a descending dessert table or buffet, make certain to test it thoroughly or you may have dust and debris descending on the food while the table is descending to the floor (you may need a decorative cover for the food presentation during the descent).

An overhead rigging system may be suspended or rigged from two bracing trees or ground supports, which may have telescopic legs that extend out to provide the necessary balance. This may look like a small dot on your floor plan for the tree; its effect can be somewhat greater, as those extended legs can become a tripping hazard (not to mention their cosmetic appearance, or lack thereof). You will need to mask these as well. You must also have the right installation equipment (i.e., lifts, ladders, scaffolding) and sufficient time to do the job. Safety is paramount. Rigging and installation of staging equipment is a complicated and possibly hazardous job, with potentially catastrophic consequences if it is not done correctly, and riggers are often licensed for this reason. You must use professionals.

EQUIPMENT RENTALS

Almost anything you may need to develop and decorate an event environment can be rented from a rental company or equipment-for-hire dealer. If you need portable picket fencing to create a charming walkway or to edge a concession area, wrought-iron arches and kneeling benches for the perfect wedding ceremony, or partitions to segment a large space, rental equipment is available to meet the needs of the event (see Figure 7-3). Installation equipment such as ladders and lifts are available as well. However, this seemingly unexciting installation equipment need not be relegated to its primary function only. Scaffolding may be used to create an interesting urban jungle entryway, hydraulic lifts can be used to raise a person to light a cauldron at an Olympic-style sports opening

❏ Air-Conditioning	❏ Fencing and Barricades	❏ Office Furniture
❏ Arches	❏ Foggers	❏ Partitions and Trellises
❏ Audiovisual Equipment	❏ Food Service Equipment	❏ Pedestals, Urns, Balusters
❏ Banners	❏ Forklifts	❏ Plants (Live and Faux)
❏ Bleachers	❏ Fountains	❏ Portable Bars
❏ Bubble Machines	❏ Fun Food Machines	❏ Portable Flooring
❏ Bunting	❏ Garment Racks	❏ Portable Toilets
❏ Candles and Candelabras	❏ Gazebos	❏ Props
❏ Carpeting	❏ Generators	❏ Rope and Stanchions
❏ Casino Equipment	❏ Golf Carts	❏ Scaffolding
❏ Chairs	❏ Heaters	❏ Stages, Risers, and
❏ China	❏ Lecterns	Platforms
❏ Cranes	❏ Lifts: Aerial, Hydraulic,	❏ Stage Skirting
❏ Crystal	Platform, Scissor, Boom	❏ Steps and Ramps
❏ Dance Floors	❏ Lighting	❏ Street Lamps
❏ Draping	❏ Linens and Table Skirting	❏ Tables
❏ Fans	❏ Market Umbrellas	❏ Tents/Marquees and Liners

Source: American Rental Association (www.rentalhq.com/).

Figure 7-3
Equipment for Hire

ceremony, or a pair of lifts can be used to dramatically raise a giant flag at a patriotic rally. Work with your rental dealer to select the equipment and supplies that will meet the needs of your event at the prices you can afford, carefully checking the terms and charges for delivery or self-pickup, installation, and returning items after the event.

Signs and Signals

Almost every type of event requires some sort of signage or symbolic signal system to help the audience and/or other "users" understand and experience the event environment in a positive manner. Signs facilitate getting from "here" to "there," provide reassurance, create a welcoming environment, manage traffic flow (pedestrian and vehicular), and answer questions before they need to be asked (see Figure 7-4). Signage should be visible, plentiful, positioned properly, and appropriate in content and style.

The communication principles of signage are grounded in the science of semiotics, originated by Charles Sanders Pierce and Ferdinand de Saussure in the nineteenth century, relating to the study of signs and

Signage Functions	Sign Options	Signal Aspects
❑ Branding ❑ Identification ❑ Information ❑ Instructions ❑ Navigation ❑ Orientation ❑ Restrictions ❑ Safety	❑ Balloons and Inflatables ❑ Banners ❑ Billboards ❑ Electronic Message Boards ❑ "Human Arrows" ❑ Kiosks ❑ Landmarks ❑ Placards on Easels ❑ Posters ❑ Projections ❑ Signposts ❑ Television Monitors	❑ Audible ❑ Color ❑ Graphics ❑ Numerical ❑ Shape ❑ Symbols and Icons ❑ Tactile ❑ Verbal ❑ Visual ❑ Written

Figure 7-4
Signage Functions, Options, and Aspects

their alphabets, meanings, connections, and attitudes expressed, and the science of *wayfinding,* a term coined in 1960 by architect Kevin Lynch, relating to environmental communication and the science of "organizing and defining a field of messages to make an area as self-navigatable as possible" (www.uande.com.au/wayfinding.html). The science of semiotics is based on the premise that "communication is an act of information exchange by means of sign systems" (www.solki.jyu.fi/semiotics/glossary.htm).

PROVIDING CUES AND INFORMATION

Event signage, like any other signage, uses verbal and nonverbal cues to communicate essential and interesting information to event-goers and others. Signs work only if there is an agreement about the appropriate uses of and responses to a sign. This is sometimes related to cultural biases, but the Laboratory of Nonverbal Semiotics contends, "We have a nonverbal comprehension system almost as coherent and consistent as language itself" (www.is.tohoku.ac.jp/lab/nonver/main-e.html). Providing cues and information at events often incorporates the full range of signal aspects, from words and numbers to color and shape, as well as symbols and icons such as the international pictographs illustrated in Figure 7-5 for male and female, elevators, stairs, toilets, and so forth. (The icon for female is depicted wearing a skirt; however, this is not a

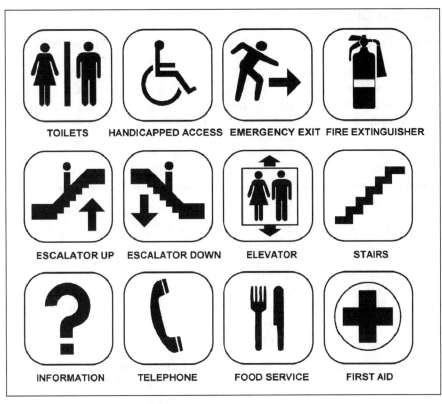

Figure 7-5
International Pictographic Icons

universal clothing distinction, illustrating the fact that icons and symbols must be mutually agreed upon.)

Information and instructions using both words and icons (including illustrations and photographs) may be placed on a sign positioned so that an individual may operate a mechanism, perform an action, or learn more about a topic or exhibit. Audible signals can include "human arrows" (uniformed or costumed individuals positioned in stationary locations to provide directional assistance to attendees), public address announcements, or heraldic music indicating the start of a ceremony or the entrance of a significant individual. Braille and audio signs may be required to comply with the requirements of the Americans, with Disabilities Act (ADA). How a sign is designed affects how effective the communication will be; using high-contrast colors makes a sign more visible and legible, and adding simple graphics improves comprehension.

NAVIGATIONAL AIDS

One of the primary purposes for signs and other signals at an event is to provide directional, navigational, and orientation assistance. The science of wayfinding, according to wayfinding consultants Carpman Grant Associates, encompasses the study of "knowing where you are, knowing your destination, following the best route, recognizing your destination, and finding your way back out. When people cannot do any or all of these things, outside or inside complex facilities, we say they are *disoriented*" (www.wayfinding.com/). In his thesis *Designing Navigable Information Spaces,* Mark A. Foltz identifies eight design principles for wayfinding (www.infoarch.ai.mit.edu/publications/mfoltz-thesis/node8.html).

1. Create a unique identity for each location.
2. Use landmarks for orientation cues.
3. Create well-structured paths.
4. Create regions of differing visual character.
5. Don't give too many navigation choices.
6. Provide a vista or map.
7. Provide signs at decision points.
8. Sight lines should show what is ahead.

Although public festivals, large conventions, and other complex or comprehensive event sites should pay particular attention to wayfinding principles, any event of any size can benefit from employing these tenets. Location identity and landmarks can be achieved with themes, activities, props, inflatable sculptures, or different colored balloon arches. Paths must be directional and should have an obvious beginning, middle, and end, which can be achieved with story line or "Now Serving Number ____" signage, entertainment, neon traffic cones lining the route, or brightly colored inflated tubes, along fences or suspended from the ceiling, that change colors progressively along the path. Regions may be established by theme, function, or entertainment, such as a "Heaven and Hell" theme décor, food courts at expositions, conversation (quiet) zones at networking receptions, or a Country and Western stage and a Salsa stage at a Southwestern celebration.

Signs providing navigation choices, overview maps, and decision-point placements enhance the ability of the attendee to get in and around the event site in a manner that meets the objectives of the attendee and delivers the progressive event experience as designed. Common examples of these types of signs include "You Are Here" site maps, enlarged seating charts or shuttle bus routes (and schedules), and aisle banners. An overview site map allows the individual to establish his or her own orientation within the macroenvironment of the event site, as well as to determine the hierarchy of features and areas of interest. A person's ability to make the correct (or preferable) navigational choices may be enhanced by creating "visual magnets" or sneak previews of areas or activities ahead. This may be accomplished by including storytelling on signage, using distinctive landmarks, or laying out the space so that inviting sight lines are established. For education sessions at a conference, for example, a slide or data projector could be projecting a colorful title, opening, or "welcome" slide on the screen that may be seen from the door to the meeting room.

INCORPORATING THE THEME AND IMAGE

Signs should be a part of the décor and ambiance, but they must also be distinctive from it. They should always be of good quality (quickly hand-drawn signs rarely look professional), and they should be integrated into the theme image. This is a branding issue. The event logo or theme icons should be on each sign, and although the wording or graphics may be influenced by semiotic principles (simple, declarative words or phrases and unambiguous icons), there is wide latitude for creative presentation methods and designs. Graphical branding will be particularly important if there are numerous events taking place concurrently or contiguously. Branding objectives will also be critically important to civic, corporate, and/or commercial sponsors of an event. Banners on light posts or spanning city streets, for example, announce a festival, welcome conventioneers, and contribute to community pride.

SIGNAGE TECHNICALITIES

The professional event coordinator must also consider the installation requirements and restrictions of the signage selected. Most venues prohibit attaching signs to walls or doors with tape or tacks. In lieu of attaching signs, easels may be used, but these must be positioned so they do not become a tripping hazard. Many venues have discreet wall-mounted sign holders next to meeting rooms that must be used for session placards. Others restrict signage altogether or limit it to specific dimensions that fit within custom-built easels. Using décor elements as nonverbal cues may overcome these restrictions and extend the theme imaging (e.g., balloon arches, inflatables, theatrical lighting, etc.). Special rigging may be required for hanging banners, and outdoor banners must have wind cuts so that they will not be damaged or cause damage to the rigging support. Special lift equipment may also be necessary—aerial lifts indoors and bucket trucks or cherry pickers outdoors.

Directional, informational, decorative, and safety signage is placed to facilitate the event attendee's comfort, enjoyment, and welfare. Signs must be visible, easy to read and understand, and must communicate the right information at the right time. They may direct or control traffic flow, identify important facilities or features, and/or impart educational content. They should be carefully considered in developing the site plan and theme concept so that they will constitute an integrated component of the overall event experience.

Target Competency Review

That there is a setting for every event is inevitable, whether it is inherent or imposed. A theme is often used as a device to compress the overall concept or message into an image that is quickly understood and anticipated, and, when used, should be integrated throughout the entire event experience. A vast array of décor options may be used to create a thematic or ambient atmosphere that serves the purpose and objectives of the event and meets the needs and expectations of the audience. The professional event coordinator has the opportunity to enhance the event environment and event experience through careful attention to every facet and feature of the event facility, top to bottom and wall to wall, using décor items and illusions.

Creating an effective and expressive environment requires equipment, which must be procured, delivered, and installed properly. Staging equipment of all types and sizes may be rented to meet the functional requirements of the event as designed, and may be arranged in hundreds of creative configurations. It must, however, always be anchored and/or rigged correctly, to ensure the safety of workers and guests, and dressed so as to mask the mechanics of the magic of the event.

The professional event coordinator must make certain that the event environment is user-friendly for those in attendance, providing multisensory cues and tools that will allow guests or visitors to get to, around, and through the site in a manner that meets their needs and objectives while communicating the messages required and desired by the event host. Signage and other visual communication tools should not be an afterthought—they should be fully integrated into the theme and/or image of the décor.

EXERCISES IN PROFESSIONAL EVENT COORDINATION

Outline and describe the décor, staging, and signage you would design for the following events. Tell how you determined the theme and why you selected the décor elements you did.

1. You have just won the contract to design a ten-city product launch and sales event for a new series of dolls and action figures based on popular cartoon characters. The theme must be designed to at-

tract children and adults. The event is to be a two-day festival-like entertainment and activity spectacle staged in parking lots, which will travel to a shopping mall in a different city every other weekend and is expected to attract 15,000 people at each site.

2. You have been hired to design a one-day in-plant employee training and motivational event for a telemarketing company selling cellular telephone calling plans. The employees are 98 percent male, between 21 and 25 years old, and extremely competitive. The company needs to deliver five key training messages about new rules and restrictions imposed by government regulatory agencies, but management wants the event to have a theme and to be fun for the employees so that they will participate.

3. You have been asked to design and coordinate a theme party for a dual celebration of a father's 50th birthday and his daughter's bat mitzvah. The theme needs to reflect father and daughter equally, yet they have no particular hobbies or interests in common. They want the party to take place in a tent in their expansive backyard, and it is to include dinner, dancing for both adults and youngsters, and other activities to keep their guests entertained for the entire evening.

Facing Page
Equipment such as this sound console illustrates the complexity of technical production. *Photograph courtesy of Mike Rudahl.*

CHAPTER 8

Fundamentals of
the Production

What's a sun dial in the shade?

—BENJAMIN FRANKLIN (1706–1790)

IN THIS CHAPTER YOU WILL LEARN HOW TO:

- Secure, implement, and monitor technical programming and services to support the communication goals and objectives of an event.
- Select the designs, equipment, and providers for the illumination and decorative lighting needs of an event.
- Determine and procure the appropriate sound and presentation services and equipment for an event.
- Coordinate multimedia production services when required to meet the needs of an event.
- Determine the need and most appropriate applications for special effects necessary within the event program and select the necessary equipment and professional providers for the effects desired.

The event coordinator was reviewing her proposal for an annual meeting's gala dinner with the potential client, discussing all the elements included and the costs for investment in each. The client was enthralled with all the creative ideas proposed for the theme décor, food and beverages, and entertainment, which included special props, elaborate buffet displays, nationally known speakers, specialty acts, and an interactive dance band. As they reached the technical category on the investment page (we don't have price lists, we show the required investment), the client started to question the event coordinator about the necessity of all the sound and lighting equipment included in the proposal. The event coordinator simply asked, "You want your guests to be able to see and hear, and experience and appreciate what you've paid for, don't you?"

Modern events have a plethora of production tools available to enhance, enchant, excite, and enthrall guests and audiences. Lighting, sound, and other audiovisual technology, plus special effects, are the production values that support the theatrical dimensions of an event experience—the show. This technology allows the event designer and professional event coordinator to highlight and/or hide parts of the event environment and the event program in order to communicate the message of the event in the most effective manner, at the appropriate or most effective time during the event. It may be used to reveal production elements or products, transform spaces or create illusions, direct and redirect focus and movement, and choreograph the progression of the event experience from an entrancing entrance to a thrilling finale.

Crafting the Production

In his book *Advance Coordination Manual,* Jan Moxley defines a production as "an entire event, including the producing; load-in and set-up; staging and performance of the event, film, show or TV program; and load-out. [The term *production* is] often used to refer to just the show or performance." (Load-in and load-out are also known as bump-in and bump-out in many locations outside the United States). The professional event coordinator must look at an event as an entire production, similar to a theatrical, film, or television production. Whether it is self-directed (e.g., a festival) or carefully controlled (e.g., an awards gala), an event experience is a show or performance, one that is carefully crafted to deliver a message and a meaning.

SPECIFY GOALS, OBJECTIVES, AND PRIORITIES

With all the high-tech and high-touch tools available to the production or event designer, it is critically important to determine which tools will meet the needs, purpose, and budget of an event. Decorative lighting, sound, projection, video, and numerous special effects may be added to any event, but they are not requisite for all events. They must be incorporated into the event design only if they will enhance the achievement of the goals and objectives of the event. However, virtually any event can benefit from the inclusion of production technology to create or enhance the atmosphere, the environment, interaction, and effective message communication. In fact, because of the prevalence of television, film, video, and other theatrical productions in their day-to-day lives, audiences and attendees expect sophisticated production values similar to those they see in other entertainment media. Many conferences and meetings, for example, no longer use an overhead projector for visuals but have turned to computer data projection, such as PowerPoint, as the standard.

Production technology is changing and improving every day, and the tools we are familiar with now may become outdated in a short time. This is not to say that older technology is no longer useful. All audiovisual technology, old and new, has potential for creative and effective applications in an event production. It is up to the professional event coordinator to work with the client and other stakeholders to determine which technologies will deliver the event experience desired and required, within the confines of the event budget, site, schedule, and program, and which will be the most effective for delivering the message of the event in a manner that meets the needs of its audience.

On-Site Insight

Cal Kennedy, CSEP, of Luminon Productions in Randburg, South Africa, shares this experience in production priorities:

We produced an event involving a two-week video editing process that included a lot of graphics for the video presentation to accompany the Managing Director's speech. At the rehearsal on the day of the event, he stopped us at one point and said that the graphic in one particular area was too short and we needed to lengthen it. Well, as most video professionals know, graphics don't just get "lengthened" at will, so I naively replied, "Sorry, with two hours to go to the function, 22 miles from the production house, we can't change the graphic." His reply was, "Spell can't."

I don't often get stuck for words, but to tell the truth, this had me tongue-tied. I had to admit that I didn't know exactly what he meant, and he gave me the answer that I should have known for the last 20 years. He said, "Can't is spelled M-O-N-E-Y! Now get on your bicycle and turn Can't into Money into Can, and do it now!"

Guess what, he was right . . . we could, we did, and boy, did we charge for the privilege of adding three seconds of graphics. I think it is important to realize with whom you are dealing. We charged premium and he paid with a smile because he got what he asked for.

INTEGRATE THE TECHNOLOGY

Technology should support the event production, not become the focus (unless the purpose of the event itself is to highlight such technology). Lighting should illuminate rather than overpower the environment. Sound systems should make communication possible rather than painful. Projected visuals should communicate rather than distract. Computer data presentations and videos should be used to enhance a speaker's presentation rather than overwhelm it. You use production technology because you should, not because you can.

The professional event coordinator should integrate the technology selected into the event site design, the program design, and the overall production. Each type of equipment will have spatial and installation requirements that must be plotted into the floor or site plan as well as the production schedule. Each type of technology will have design capabilities and qualities that must be utilized cost-effectively. And each type of technology will have conditions and constraints that must be understood in order to get the most out of it.

USE THE RIGHT EFFECTS FOR THE JOB

You must determine what it is you want and need to achieve in order to select the right effects and equipment for the job, based on the resources (time, money, space) available. For example, rear projection requires more space than front projection, but it gives a cleaner look to the event space because the projection equipment is hidden. However, front projection is often brighter than rear projection, and the equipment may be suspended from the ceiling to open up the floor space.

Live video for image magnification can involve camera operators moving in and around the stage and audience, or robotic cameras may be moved through the space on booms and tracks by remote operators. Intelligent lighting systems are more expensive, but they are more versatile and may replace the need for numerous other lighting instruments. (Most lighting professionals refer to these lights as automated or moving lights, with an *intelligent operator* controlling them.) Slide projectors may be suitable for projecting corporate logos or theme images on surfaces instead of gobos in ellipsoidal lighting instruments.

TECHNICAL DIFFICULTIES—PLEASE STAND BY

As with any technology, lighting, sound, and multimedia technology is subject to breakdowns, failures, and other problems that may interfere with a seamless production. The more technology you are using (and relying on), the more safeguards you should consider to prevent such problems from destroying your carefully crafted production. For any important aspect of an event production, securing redundant equipment must be seriously considered. Ralph Traxler, CSEP, senior designer for RTx inc., based in Atlanta, Georgia, and the 2002 Event Solutions Technical Producer of the Year, advises, "There should be redundant lighting, audio and special effect controllers, computers, video monitors, and projectors whenever possible."

Your first safeguard is making sure that the technical providers have sufficient time to prepare, install, and test their equipment properly. You must incorporate technical rehearsals into your schedule so that the entire production may be tested, and in the manner in which it should be tested. For example, in order to test the lighting the houselights must be extinguished, meaning that others working in the space will not have the illumination they may need to do their jobs properly. Sound checks must be done, which can be loud and disjointed and may interfere with a meeting or other function taking place next door. Data and video projection must be well rehearsed, and transitions between various technologies (e.g., live and recorded sound or video) must be practiced. All such testing requires time.

If, despite these measures, there is a technical failure, be prepared to carry on. This is when a calm and quick-thinking professional event coordinator will find a creative solution. You might bring out the a cappella choir early, turn on the houselights and have the guests or attendees discuss topics in a roundtable-style session, or send in the dessert while you wait for the problem to be fixed. The audience will know (or should be told) that you are having difficulties—"Please stand by." A good emcee, speaker, or entertainer will be able to incorporate such an incident into his or her presentation with humor and grace, preventing uncertainty (or panic) within the audience.

BUY THE BEST YOU CAN AFFORD

Based on the prioritized goals and objectives for the event, you should always buy the best production values you can afford. Selecting equipment and providers based on price alone is a recipe for disappointment and difficulties. When the budget is limited, focus your expenditures on those features that will communicate the message most effectively, and then supplement them with the creative use of less expensive options sparingly. Find ways to utilize the technology you do invest in to its fullest potential, perhaps redesigning the program or the use of the site so that one type of technology or equipment can serve numerous parts of the event.

Also purchase the best service you can afford. Make certain that on-site technicians are included in the bid. Check the costs of power usage. Closely compare the bids from providers who own their equipment and those who must rent or hire it from other sources. Those who own their own equipment often have lower prices, but they may be using older equipment. Those who subcontract equipment may have higher costs, but they may be securing better or more up-to-date equipment. As always, you must be a savvy buyer. Become familiar with the production technologies discussed throughout this chapter so that you are able to work with the designers and production providers to create the environment you want and communicate the messages you need to communicate in the most cost-efficient and effective manner possible.

Lighting

In *An Introduction to the Theatre,* author Frank M. Whiting states, "Some of the most successful excursions into expressionism on the stage have relied heavily on lighting, which can give a fluid projection of color and form that is dynamic and moving, patterns that can change to fit varying rhythms of dance and drama just as music does." Drew Campbell, author of *Technical Theater for Nontechnical People,* asserts, "Lighting can affect our mood, determine time of day or season, and move the play forward by separating the scenes and telling us when the show has begun and ended. Lighting also discriminates between where the show is happening and where it is not. Lighting is the opposite of masking. It says, 'Look here. This is the show.' Of course, the most important job that lighting does is to provide *illumination.*" The aesthetic functions of lighting, according to Norman C. Boulanger and Warren C. Lounsbury, in *Theatre Lighting from A to Z,* are as follows:

- Selective visibility, controlling audience attention, from spotlights to subtle changes in intensity in given areas
- Showing form, modeling, emphasizing structure, accentuating three-dimensional effects with key lighting, side or fill lighting, and backlighting
- Establishing mood and ambiance through color, intensity, focus, and/or angle
- Illusion of nature, establishing realism in a theatrical setting (or an altered reality)
- Composition, complementing the design with projections of patterns, shadows, and/or images with gobos or effects projectors

It is no accident that these illustrations are from books on theatrical production. This is the milieu from which many event professionals draw for creative lighting applications. Studying production techniques for plays, dance performances, operas, musicals, concerts, ice shows, and other presentations gives the professional event coordinator a strong understanding of the options suitable for events of all types.

ILLUMINATE THE SPACE AND THE INVESTMENT

The first consideration in a lighting design is to illuminate the event space in such a way that it is safe and draws the guest or attendee's focus to where it should be. As noted in the opening of this chapter, you want the audience to be able to see what you have paid for (and what they have paid for). Lighting may, indeed, become your primary source of décor, used to establish a mood or theme or to illuminate and accentuate the inherent features of the event venue. The manipulation of color, intensity, and texture through lighting allows you to create the alternate reality of a themed environment, direct attention to key messages or images, and move people where you want them to go.

The professional event coordinator should make sure that the primary areas of activity are literally "attractive"—attracting people and attention to them. Areas of activity must also be lit suitably for the function to be carried out—providing sufficient illumination for taking notes at an educational session or seeing the keynote speaker at a conference or the food at a banquet. In an indoor venue, this may sometimes be accomplished simply with the houselights, but not always. We have all been in seminars where the lights were dimmed at the front of the room so that the screen images were visible, yet the speaker was in the dark and, often, so were we. This problem may be overcome with a simple spotlight focused on the speaker and lectern.

THE LIGHTING TOOLBOX

The professional event coordinator most often works with a lighting provider, and sometimes an audiovisual provider, to procure the appropriate design and equipment for the specific event, based on its type and purpose. These professionals should be brought into the event design process in the early planning stages so they understand the scope of the lighting needs in conjunction with the overall event. There are several terms with which the professional event coordinator must be familiar, as shown in Figure 8-1. The tools and luminaires available vary in cost, installation requirements, and capabilities (see Figure 8-2). Armed with an understanding of these tools, the event coordinator will be able to assist the lighting providers in achieving the look desired, at an affordable price (see Figure 8-3).

THE DIMENSIONS OF LIGHT

The use of shadows and sculptural lighting requires special consideration. Frank M. Whiting quotes scenic designer Lee Simonson, "Diffused light produces blank visibility, in which we recognize objects without emotion. But the light that is blocked by an object and casts shadows has a sculpturesque quality that by the vehemence of its definition, by the balance of light and shade, can carve an object before our eyes." The standard setup for lighting an object or individual is "key, back, and fill," (see definitions in Figure 8-3) so the shadows created by each light po-

Beam	The illumination emitting from a single lamp or luminaire.	**Lens**	A curved or shaped piece of glass used to refract light rays to control and focus a light beam.
Flood	A wide or large beam.	**Luminaire**	The international term for any type of lighting instrument.
Focus	The aiming of a beam in the desired direction.	**Pan**	Movement of a beam laterally from side to side.
Gel	A thin color filter (gelatin, polyester, polycarbonate) placed in a luminaire to change the color of the beam (the term is derived from the term *gelatin*— animal or grain jelly and dye, originally used for color filters).	**Reflector**	The part of a luminaire or lamp that reflects and amplifies the light emitted from a bulb.
Gobo Derived from "go-between"	A cut or etched metal stencil placed between the lamp and the lens in a focusable spotlight. New technology allows glass gobos with as many as four colors, with the ability to reproduce almost any color graphic image or photograph.	**Shutter**	A device that varies the size of a beam with rectangular flaps (external shutters with independent flaps on a luminaire are called barn doors).
Intensity	The wattage or brilliance of a beam.	**Spot**	A narrow or focused beam.
Iris	A circular device that varies the size of a beam by expanding and contracting.	**Throw**	The distance between the luminaire and the area/object/ person being lit.
Lamp	The light source—an encased filament (bulb); sometimes the reflector is part of the lamp rather than the luminaire.	**Tilt**	Movement of a beam vertically up and down.

Figure 8-1
Lighting Terms

Equipment	Capabilities	Typical Uses and Effects
Aircraft Landing Light (ACL)	Aircraft headlight—extremely high-intensity lamp providing a bright narrow beam.	Used primarily for special effects in concerts and theatrical performances. May be used to create a spray of aerial beams similar to those of lasers or arc spotlights.
Arc Spotlight	A spotlight with a very long throw and a lamp that can be 2500 to 10,000 W.	Used as a spotlight in arenas or other large venues or as an aerial beam.
Automated/Movable Lights (Intelligent Lights)	Computer-controlled luminaire whose beam can spot or flood, vary in intensity, pan or tilt, spin, strobe, change color, and project gobos, changing very rapidly and precisely.	Often used for light shows, concerts, discos, and when numerous changes are required within a lighting design or program.
Chaser and Rope Lights *Caution:* Because stroboscopic lights, including some chaser effects, may affect those with epilepsy or other disabilities, a warning sign must always be posted prominently notifying the audience that this effect will be used.	Miniature lamps connected together on an electrical cord and/or encased in plastic tubing (known as rope lights) that may be controlled to go on and off (chase) in various patterns, such as forward, reverse, alternating, or random blinking.	Often used to outline or edge an item such as an arch, bar, sign, stage, steps, or scenic prop.
Color Changer	A device for changing color filters. Color Wheel: revolving motorized disk fitted with a sequence of color filters. Color Box (semaphore): various color filters may be used individually or in combination by sliding one or more into position. Color Scroller: a continuous color filter scroll with up to 32 colors that may be automatically located via the control board.	Used to create changing color patterns or to quickly change colored gels of an individual luminaire.

Figure 8-2
Luminaire Capabilities and Applications

Equipment	Capabilities	Typical Uses and Effects
Dimmer	An electronic device used to control light intensity by regulating the current.	Used to fade beams in and out during a production.
Ellipsoidal (Leko)	A spotlight with shutters and lenses that may be focused in a narrow or wide hard-edged beam; allows for the use of a gobo to project images.	Used as a spotlight and to project gobos.
Fiber-optic Curtain or Drop	Thousands of microthin fibers carry light from a central source to points throughout the curtain and may change colors or create chaser effects.	Often used to replicate a starry night sky or outer space, but may also be programmed to reveal image outlines or patterns.
Floodlight	A luminaire, with simply a lamp and a reflector (often with a linear bulb), that aims an unfocused wide beam in one direction.	Used to provide general illumination or to evenly light a cyclorama.
Follow Spot	A focusable spotlight mounted on a stand, often fitted with an iris, which can be swiveled in a pan, tilt, or ballyhoo motion (sweeping in a figure-eight pattern throughout a room) by an operator.	Often used to follow the movement of a performer, an object, or an audience member going up onto the stage.
Fresnel Spotlight (Pronounced "fra-nell," named for its lamp inventor Augustin-Jean Fresnel, originally designed for use in lighthouses.)	A luminaire with a Fresnel lens (or pebble-convex lens) that gives an even field of directional light with diffused, soft edges. The spacing between the lamp and the lens may be adjusted to alter the beam spread from spot to flood.	Often used for area lighting because the soft edges allow color or light blending of individual beams. The most commonly used lighting fixture in TV production.
Helicopter	A luminaire with a rotating head containing four to twelve sealed, spinning colored beam lights.	Often used by disc jockeys for special-effect lighting in a disco setting.
Laser Light (*l*ight *a*mplification by *s*timulated *e*mission of *r*adiation)	A device that produces a narrow intense ray of deeply colored bright light that is parallel, pure, and razor sharp.	Often used to create a horizontal fan of beams waving over an audience, a vertical cone of beams to

Figure 8-2
(Continued)

Equipment	Capabilities	Typical Uses and Effects
Caution: Prolonged exposure to even low-power lasers can cause eye damage; should be operated only by licensed professionals.		surround a person or object, or an animated image.
Lighting Balloon	A helium-filled fabric balloon with a lamp inside. The lighting balloon floats above an area or space and provides diffused illumination	Often used to provide general area lighting or a special effect; can be imprinted with a sponsor logo.
Miniature Lights	Tiny lamps connected on an electrical cord, often referred to as fairy or twinkle lights.	May be used to create canopies, ceiling designs, and mobiles and to decorate such items as trees, bushes, windows, etc. These are often used to add a sparkling effect to décor items and settings.
Mirror Ball	A motor-driven globe covered with small mirror squares that reflect lights.	Often used for disco settings and dances.
PARcan (*parabolic aluminized reflector*)	A high-intensity, low-wattage lamp (like a car headlight) mounted in a round frame resembling a can. The lamp combines a fixed-focus lens, light source, and reflector and does not require an external lens. Provides an intense, fixed parallel beam capable of projecting deep colors.	Often used for uplighting and downlighting and creating light curtains; an inexpensive substitute for a spotlight.
Pin Spot	A small luminaire that provides a narrow, low-wattage beam.	Most often used to highlight table centerpieces, mirror balls, or small banners or signs.
Scene Machine (PANI projector, among others)	An effects projector used to project static or moving images from special glass slides, disks, or filmstrips.	Often used to project a series of artistic images, flames of a fire, rain, or images of international flags moving across a wall or on the side of a building.

Figure 8-2
(Continued)

Equipment	Capabilities	Typical Uses and Effects
Scoop Light	An aluminum parabolic or ellipsoidal reflector luminaire with no outside housing.	Often used as a floodlight for lighting a cyclorama.
Searchlight	A large apparatus, often capable of pan or rotating movement, for projecting a strong beam up into the night sky. Space Cannons, created by Lasertainment Productions International, are 7000-W searchlights capable of color changing, high-speed strobing, and dimming.	Most often used outside at a movie premier or other promotion, and may be used to provide intense static beams for lighting buildings.
Strip Light	A long, narrow luminaire with a row of segregated individual lamps, often with reflectors and color filters.	Most often used for colored uplighting of an expanse of wall or for blended wash illumination on a stage.
Strobe Light _Caution:_ Because stroboscopic lights may affect those with epilepsy or other disabilities, a warning sign must always be posted prominently notifying the audience that this effect will be used.	A luminaire capable of producing a rapid series of bright flashes of light of varying intensity and speed.	May be used to simulate slow motion or lightning, create a starlight or fireworks effect, or reinforce the beat of a musical performance.
Ultraviolet (UV) or Black Light	Ultraviolet lamp that specifically illuminates white surfaces and fluorescent paints, often giving them a neonlike appearance.	In an otherwise completely darkened environment, this theatrical effect can make items covered in fluorescent paint seem to magically move or float, because they are the only things illuminated.

Figure 8-2
(Continued)

Lighting Effect	Technique	Typical Uses
Area Lighting	Areas may simply be flooded with light so they are identified or well lit, or they may be carefully lit with different colors and intensities for a more dramatic or dynamic setting.	General illumination of a specific area or broad space.
Accent Lighting (Specials)	Specific illumination of architectural, decorative, or functional features or elements of an event or event site.	Items so lit may include décor items, floral arrangements, buffets, ice sculptures, and other event elements.
Backlighting	Illuminating a person or object with a lighting instrument from above and/or behind.	Gives the person or object "clearer dimensions and greater definition" within its sphere of space. Used alone, it creates a silhouette of an object or person.
Color Changes	Using a color changer to vary the color of spot or ambient lighting in a programmed progression.	Often used to suggest a change in time or mood, such as progressing from amber to blue for summer to winter, or to signal changes in the event program.
Direct Lighting	Aiming of a luminaire directly at an object, individual, or area to be illuminated.	Without the inclusion of additional luminaires at different angles, this will provide a general wash of light but will not provide a dimensional effect.
Downlighting (The "God" Light)	Use of a luminaire above an item, individual, or area to shine a beam downward onto the object, person, or area below.	Often used to provide saturated pools colored light and in conjunction with uplighting to illuminate the tops and bottoms of an item (such as an architectural column), either in the same or different colors, giving the item emphasis and dimension.
Fill Light	Side or supporting source of illumination on a person or object, used to "fill" gaps and reduce shadows.	Used to provide a more three-dimensional or luminous visual effect.

Figure 8-3
Lighting Effects & Techniques

Lighting Effect	Technique	Typical Uses
Gobo Projection/ Animation	The projection of images, logos, words, or designs through a template inserted in a focusable spotlight. Animation may be achieved by using a series of gobo projections in a chased illumination.	Three images may be projected on walls, curtains, screens, floors, and other surfaces to create textures, pictures, messages and provide sponsor recognition.
Indirect Lighting	The aiming of a luminaire in a different direction, allowing the light to "bounce" into the area to be illuminated.	The reflection of a light aimed at a white ceiling illuminates the area below.
Key Lighting	The principal source of illumination on a person or object, preferably a spotlight, best delivered from 45 degrees.	A single source of light focused from directly in front often produces a "flat" or two-dimensional image.
Light Curtain	A series of closely spaced luminaires with intense and parallel beams, usually PARcans, aimed downward, creating a curtain of colored light.	Atmospheric dust diffuses the light, and smoke provides a very dense curtain capable of obscuring anything behind. Often used for backlighting stage or concert performers.
Light Shapes	Luminaires are placed within three-dimensional forms created of opaque material (e.g., spandex). The colored light is captured by the shape and not projected elsewhere (similar to the surface of a rear projection screen).	The illuminated shape can change color during the event with a color changer or may simply be a luminous form as part of the décor. The addition of a rotating gobo will add an organic morphology to the shape.
Light Show	Automated movable luminaires are preprogrammed to go on and off, pulse, pan, tilt, spin, and change color.	Often used to create an energized entertainment effect; may be used to control the lighting for an entire show.
Mood Lighting	Using luminaires for illumination that creates a mood or atmosphere, such as colored ambient light throughout an event space.	Often includes uplighting of walls or perimeter, or washes of colored light, and/or gobo projections on a dance floor, walls, or other surfaces.

Figure 8-3
(Continued)

Lighting Effect	Technique	Typical Uses
Scrim Lighting	Luminaires are focused on a thin gauze curtain. The gauze curtain or panel is opaque, translucent, or transparent, depending on the position of the luminaire.	Lit from the front, the scrim is opaque, allowing a reveal of what is behind. Adding light on the surface or object behind renders the scrim translucent. Lighting only the object or area behind renders the scrim transparent.
Uplighting	The use of luminaires at the base of an item or area to shine a beam upward onto the object or wash a vertical area with color.	Often used for color washes on walls or to highlight scenic props or architectural features.

Figure 8-3
(Continued)

sition will be dimensional rather than distorted or dramatic (unless dramatic is what you are going for).

Drew Campbell notes that lighting angles are divided into five categories: front, side, back, down, and up. Both Campbell and *Stage Lighting Step-by-Step* author Graham Walters also discuss the degrees of angles in the horizontal and vertical planes (see Figure 8-4). Two lights aimed 45 degrees downward, from 45 degrees side front, onto a person is the most flattering lighting (and does not blind the person). Dancers (and speakers) are best lit from the sides at four positions, called head, mid, crotch, and shin buster. Interesting dimensions are achieved when different colors are projected on different sides of an object or person, creating sculptural shadows and effects. The lighting designer should take this into consideration when lighting people, props, and architectural features.

CREATING A COLORFUL ATMOSPHERE

Color, as in other aspects of the event design, can have a significant physical, psychological, and emotional impact on the effect of lighting. Yellows and straws soften, reds warm, and blues isolate. Pinks and ambers are very flattering for food, but white lights should also be used to provide a true impression of a food's actual color (and appetizing freshness). Early in my event career, a lighting designer advised me to always incorporate at least one item of white into the décor and to make certain it

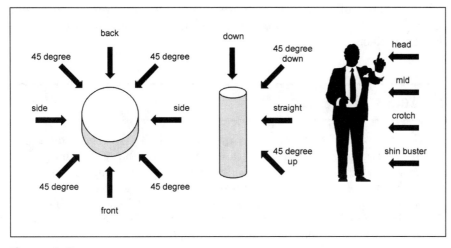

Figure 8-4
Lighting Angles

was illuminated with pure white light so that the human eye could discern the saturation of the other hues. Just as a television camera needs to be "told" what color is white in order to calibrate all other colors, our eyes needs the same cue.

Regarding the effect of colored light on people, Boulanger and Lounsbury advise, "Colors suitable for area lighting include tints of pink, amber, straw, blue, lavender, gray, and chocolate. Darker shades of straw and amber tend to turn skin pigments yellow, giving a sickly appearance. As every fading actor and actress knows, the most flattering and youthful colors include pink, lavender, and light blue. Certain colors should be avoided for certain skin tones: blues for black skin, lemons for yellow skin, greens for white skin."

LIGHT SHOWS—BUILDINGS, BALLROOMS, AND BACKGROUNDS

Lighting professionals know how to craft a light show that will be decorative and truly entertaining. These productions are very popular as an integral part of an entertainment element, pulsing and moving with the beat of the music of a dance band or disc jockey. Moving and flashing lights and images swirling around guests capture, retain, and enhance interest (and excitement) in the event experience. With today's technology, these light shows may be produced indoors and outdoors, on walls, floors, ceilings, scenic shapes, and the sides of buildings. Many event productions use automated luminaires (intelligent lighting) to add intense and moving color and shapes to the event environment. These computer-controlled instruments are able to change position, direction, gobo projection, and color quickly and accurately, allowing you to create exciting effects.

Technology Tip

The movement of automated (intelligent) lights is programmed into a computer within a control console, and many systems allow the designer to create the lighting plan in a virtual three-dimensional setting. These computer-aided design (CAD) programs allow the designer to create light plans, floor plans, elevations, digital set models, and photorealistically rendered animations and simulations with lighting visualization software. Once the finished design is programmed into the computer and the luminaires are positioned, the show progresses at the touch of a button. Within each cue, every parameter of each luminaire has its own fade and delay times, split times, and cross-fade paths. Multiple cues may be run simultaneously and triggered manually or automatically.

The Ecodome weather-resistant modular outdoor housing system is often used to hold automated lighting systems for interior, exterior, or architectural light shows in any weather. It rolls into place like the *Star Wars* character R2D2 and may be secured in place with bolts to prevent theft. For a glossary of lighting terms and information about automated lighting systems, visit the Intelligent Lighting Systems, Inc., Web site at www.intelligentlighting.com.

EQUIPMENT NEEDS AND RIGGING REQUIREMENTS

With the exception of the rolling R2D2-style Ecodome automated lighting system, all luminaires must be mounted on the floor, hung, or flown from a rigging system overhead. Luminaires may be hung on battens, booms, ladders (not the climbing type), towers, trees, tripod stands, or trusses. The luminaires must then be connected to the power source and the control console. Because much of this equipment must be mounted overhead, care must be taken to ensure that it is installed and rigged properly. Flown (suspended) luminaires must be clamped and secured properly, often with a safety chain in addition to a clamp for extra security. This is a job for professionals only, and one that should not be rushed. Some venues have built-in rigging points with overhead catwalks; others do not. A lighting professional should be involved in a site inspection to determine the installation, rigging, and equipment requirements for the lighting plan.

The professional event coordinator must liaise with the lighting professional to ensure that this equipment will be integrated into the overall décor and floor or site plan. Truss modules now come in a circular configuration and are often dressed with opaque material that becomes part of the overall décor, serving as a light shape. All installation equipment not flown should be dressed or masked appropriately to blend into or become part of the décor. Luminaires positioned on the floor for uplighting can be masked with potted foliage, which will provide additional texture and dimension, as the spill light will illuminate the greenery. Lighting trees and tripods may be dressed with fabrics to resemble richly draped columns. The lighting equipment must also be integrated with all sound and audiovisual equipment because these items will likely be sharing some of the same rigging and mounting systems.

Sound and Audiovisual

As with other production technology, the products and equipment used for sound and audiovisual (AV) support are evolving and emerging at a fast pace, and as each new technology enters the entertainment industry it is quickly adopted by the event industry. The type and scope of technology the professional event coordinator will use depends on the needs it will be used to meet (see Figure 8-5). This equipment can range from a simple in-house PA system, with a single microphone on a lectern for a seminar or a cassette player hidden in the buffet display producing sound effects, to a full-fledged concert setup with stacks and stacks of loudspeakers, stage monitors, amplifiers, image magnification video, and a control console the size of a pickup truck with six or seven headphoned technicians poised like aerospace engineers over it. But the purpose will be the same—to provide the audio and visual reinforcement needed to create the desired event experience.

AUDIO BASICS

An understanding of the basics of sound amplification and how we hear can assist in determining the best equipment and effects for the job at hand, as well as pique the imagination for creative applications. Sound has two qualities—volume (decibels) and pitch. Decibels (dBA) range from zero (the average least perceptible sound) to about 120 dBA (the average pain level). According to the League for the Hard of Hearing (LHH)

- ❏ Audience Response System
- ❏ Audio Amplifiers
- ❏ Audio Delay System
- ❏ Audio Distribution
- ❏ Audio Effects Equipment
- ❏ Audio Mixers
- ❏ Audio Playback Equipment
- ❏ Boom Arm Attachment
- ❏ Boombox (Cassette and CD Player with Loudspeakers)
- ❏ Cables—Power and Connector
- ❏ Carts, Stands, and Racks
- ❏ Carpeted Podium
- ❏ Cassette/DAT Duplicator
- ❏ Cassette Player/Recorder
- ❏ CD Player
- ❏ Communication Systems—Two-Way Radios, Two-Channel Base Station, Single Muff Headset, Belt Pack
- ❏ Computer Equipment—PC/Mac Laptop, PC/Mac Zip Drive, Printers, Computer/TV Converter, Wireless Mouse, Laser Advance, Joysticks
- ❏ Digital Camera/Camcorders
- ❏ DVD Player
- ❏ Electronic Whiteboard
- ❏ Equalizer

- ❏ Flip Chart, Paper, and Easel
- ❏ Interactive Touchscreens
- ❏ Image Magnification
- ❏ Laser Disk Player
- ❏ LCD Monitor
- ❏ Lectern
- ❏ Loudspeakers
- ❏ Microphones—Wired (Vocal, Lavaliere, Handheld, Headset), Wireless (Lavaliere, Handheld, Headset, Body with Belt Pack), Lectern (Gooseneck), PZM, Shotgun, Condenser, Sound Grabber
- ❏ Microphone Accessories—Windscreen Covers, Microphone Mixer, Snake Cables, Stands (Floor and Tabletop), Press Box Mults
- ❏ Monitors—Computer Display, Sound (Stage or Ear), Video
- ❏ Portable PA Systems
- ❏ Projectors—16 mm Film, 35 mm Slide, Data/Video, LCD, Opaque, Overhead, Video, Scenic (PANI, PIGI, Martin, Firefly, Highend, XENON Hardware), Large Format (JumboTron, Diamond Vision, LED)

- ❏ Projector Accessories—Slide Dissolve Unit, Long-Throw Lenses, Slide Viewer, Slide Tray, Power Strip, Wall and Ceiling Mounts, Wireless Zoom Remote, Electronic or Laser Pointer
- ❏ Record Player (Mono or Stereo)
- ❏ Reel-to-Reel Tape Recorder
- ❏ Screens—Front, Rear, Tripod, Fast-Fold, Plasma, Dress Kits, Screen Stands and Mounts
- ❏ Sound Console or Rack
- ❏ Speaker Timer
- ❏ Speaker Cue Light
- ❏ Teleconferencing Equipment
- ❏ Teleprompters
- ❏ TVs (Various sizes, incl. Large Screen)
- ❏ Videocassette Player (NTSC, PAL, SECAM)
- ❏ Videocassette Recorder (VHS, Betacam, Digital)
- ❏ Video Scalers and Switchers
- ❏ Video Wall Equipment
- ❏ Videoconferencing and Satellite Uplink/Downlink
- ❏ Whiteboards

Sources include Ralph Traxler, CSEP, and Robert Estrin. For glossaries of AV terms, visit these Web sites: sharpsav. com, www.ita.com/avglossary.htm, and www.inlandav.com/terms.html.

Figure 8-5
Audiovisual Equipment Checklist

(www.lhh.org), "Experts agree that continued exposure to noise above 85 dBA will eventually harm your hearing. Noise levels above 140 dBA can cause damage to hearing after just one exposure." The LHH points out that the National Institute for Occupational Safety and Health advises that the maximum exposure time at 85 dBA (approximately the level of a city street or a noisy restaurant) is eight hours, and at 110 dBA (a car horn or busy video arcade), the maximum exposure time is 1 minute and 29 seconds. The LHH reports that sound levels at live music concerts can be measured at 120 dBA and beyond, and sound levels at a sporting event can be measured up to 127 dBA. (Contrary to what many bands or disc jockeys would have you believe, you can focus the sound and decibel level to stay within the stage and dance floor area and leave other areas of a function room suitable for reasonable conversation.)

Pitch has a range between two tonal levels—bass (low frequency) and treble (high frequency). Treble or higher notes are directional and stop when they hit a surface. Bass or lower notes are omnidirectional, travel farther, and can seep through walls, which is why you can hear the thump, thump, thump of a stereo system being played next door. This is also why, when dressing or masking loudspeakers, you must use gauze or other open-weave material so that it will not distort the treble balance of the sound.

Sound amplification is the process of converting the sound waves of a voice or acoustic musical instrument into electrical impulses (the signal) through a microphone(s) or connecting an electronic musical instrument or record, CD, or cassette player(s) to a mixer, which modulates quality and volume levels (with an equalizer) and routes the signal into an amplifier to increase the strength of the signal, which sends it to the loudspeaker, which changes the electrical impulses back into acoustical energy and transmits the amplified audible sound (see Figure 8-6). (*Note:* The high, annoying squeal of feedback is caused when a microphone is receiving the sound waves projected from the loudspeaker, creating an ever-increasing loop of amplification.)

A broad variety of microphones are available, which should be selected based on the type of event, use, user, and sound amplification requirements. Microphones (referred to as mikes) are omnidirectional (picking up sound in all directions) or unidirectional (picking up sound from one direction, referred to as cartioid) and may be wired or wireless. A wired microphone is wired directly into the sound mixer, and a wireless microphone sends the sound via a radio signal to a receiver connected to the mixer and may be handheld, clipped to an individual's clothing or a sound source, or used as a body mike incorporated into a headset. Wearers of wireless lavaliere or body mikes must be advised to turn them off when not performing to prevent the amplification of "ambient noise," such as produced when whispering to a colleague or going to the toilet.

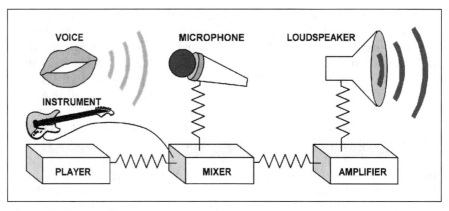

Figure 8-6
Sound Amplification

PLACEMENT OF SOUND EQUIPMENT

Depending on the size of the event space and the effects desired, the type, quantity, and positioning of sound equipment will vary. Simple PA systems may include only a microphone connected to a combination amplifier/loudspeaker. Amplifying sound for a large space may involve several loudspeakers stacked on top of each other to provide the volume required to hear at the back of the room, or sound distribution systems wherein loudspeakers are placed at various points along the sides and back of the room. Very large spaces may require sound delay systems whereby, according to Cal Kennedy, CSEP, "Sound is delayed by using second (or more) loudspeaker stacks so that the listener perceives to hear the same signal at the same time, no matter where one is within the venue. This is done to prevent an echo or reverberation effect and help balance the overall audio perception on the ears." The sound is delayed so that it is transmitted out of the distributed loudspeakers at the same time as the sound waves from the other loudspeakers on the stage would reach that part of an audience (also allowing for lower decibel levels).

Loudspeakers project sound directionally, using woofers to produce the bass tones and tweeters to produce treble tones. Neil Fraser, author of *Lighting and Sound,* notes, "Because our ears are on either side of our heads the brain is good at analyzing sound on the horizontal axis but not the vertical." This has significant implications for the placement of loudspeakers for amplified sound and explains why loudspeaker stacks are often positioned at head level or a little higher and angled down when suspended from the ceiling—the sound designer needs to create overlapping pools of sound waves, just as the lighting designer creates overlapping pools of light beams.

The loudspeakers are connected to the amplifiers and controlled by the mixer in a sound console. The console includes inputs and channels for all the various sound sources, uses an equalizer to manipulate the treble, bass, and volume (and other effects), and sends the signal to the appropriate output(s) (including stage or ear monitors so performers are able to hear themselves). The sound console may also include a recorder, CD or cassette player, headphones, and effects equipment.

SOUNDSCAPING

Soundscaping, or sound sculpting, is a composition of recorded and/or amplified audio that creates a particular mood and equipment is positioned in various and specific areas within an event site. According to soundscape pioneer Robert Estrin, "Soundscaping came about because it is easier to trick the eye into believing what it is seeing if it is backed up by another sense. A few simple sounds at a moderate level reinforce a visual to create the illusion that the designer wants. However, some people have taken soundscapes to an extreme and then it is just annoying noise." Drew Campbell describes sound as an "audible atmosphere." Sounds alone can conjure up anything in our imagination, from a steamy jungle to a stadium of roaring fans. Soundscaping may also be used to establish ambient noise suitable for a theme, such as running water, leaves rustling in a breeze, the snapping of twigs for a magical forest setting, or beeps, bleeps, and other electronic sounds for a spaceship interior.

VISUALLY SUPPORTING THE PROGRAM AND PRESENTERS

The other half of the audiovisual component is the visual support of the event, including anything from the humble flip chart to an extravagant multimedia spectacle including live and recorded video, photos, film, computer data, and much more. There are countless functional and artistic applications for the projection equipment and services available (with new technology introduced continually), limited only by your creativity and the budget. Images from slides, overhead cells, computers, and video may be projected from the front onto opaque or glass-beaded screens, from the rear onto translucent screens, or through a closed-circuit television or data projection system into television or data monitors of practically any size, including video walls and large-scale video display equipment such as the Diamond Vision or JumboTron systems and the newest outdoor video 8 mil light emitting diode (LED) screens, or high-definition plasma screens (which may be placed at specific points throughout an event space to ensure that the entire audience is able to see clearly), or even on large, clear TelePrompTer screens. There are inflatable screens, smoke screens, slotted screens through which a person may walk, and water screens that can be unlimited in height and width—

flat, semicircular, cylindrical, fan-shaped, or with customized contours. You can project onto scrims, spandex shapes, a curtain of ribbons, balloons, balloon walls, ceilings, walls, floors, and even people (especially those in fantastic costumes designed with expansive opaque extensions).

Live video image magnification (I-Mag) may be used to project the current or concurrent action and should be used particularly for groups of 200 or more so that the audience may see the faces of those speaking and the action onstage. Cameras used to capture this action may be stationary, handheld, or boom operated. In using I-Mag, screens should be placed on either side of the stage when using two screens (see Figure 8-7), or if using only one screen, to the right of the speaker to capitalize on the natural reading movement from left to right. Screens placed center stage must be positioned high enough so that a "feedback image" is not projected if the speaker walks in front of the screen. Note, however, that a person's likeness is proprietary and you must secure permission to use that likeness in any product you will publish or offer for sale to the public after the event (or, in some cases, publish via a Web site), so you may wish to include such a permission agreement in your registration form and speaker or entertainer contracts.

Figure 8-7
Typical I-Mag Screen Setup

On-Site Insight

An expert in I-Mag video production for live presentations, Bob Johnson, of California-based VideoBob Robotic Systems, notes that some of the benefits of using fluid motion robotic cameras are the reduction of humanpower requirements and the elimination of line-of-sight distractions to an audience by a camera crew at a live performance. "Whereas a traditional camera setup would include a platform within the audience that could require an area equal to 12 seats or an entire table at a banquet, a robotic system uses a telescopic pole that takes up only one seat and there is no operator diverting the attention of the surrounding audience—and audiences *are* distracted by the camera operator moving about. I've even known of camera operators who have fallen asleep during a presentation and fallen off the platform. Now that's distracting." Johnson also notes that a robotic system allows you to place cameras where a camera operator cannot go. For a Microsoft company meeting, Johnson placed a robotic camera in the ceiling above the stage so he could focus on the computer keyboard Bill Gates was operating during the presentation (www.videobob.com).

Projection Specifications and Placement

If projection is included in an event production, the professional event coordinator must make certain that the proper equipment is used and sufficient space is allotted. Projectors for front screen projection may be placed on an adjustable or purpose-built stand or rolling AV cart (which often includes a power strip) within the audience or at the back of the room, or on a platform hung from the ceiling. Some venues have a projection booth for this purpose. Rear screen projection requires sufficient unobstructed space behind the screen to accommodate the throw required for the screen size. All carts, stands, and mounted platforms must be suitable for the size and weight of the equipment to be placed on it, and carts or stands within the audience area should be skirted for a more professional look (and, of course, all wires and cables must be taped and/or covered to guard against tripping hazards).

If the projector is not on a perpendicular plane with the screen (e.g., ceiling-mounted), you may have a keystone effect whereby the image becomes distorted in a trapezoidal manner; some projectors are able to adjust this internally, or the screen can be tilted slightly to compensate. You must always remember that the projector is throwing a beam of light and anything or anyone entering that beam will cast a shadow on the screen, so the projector and/or screen may have to be positioned above head height. This placement will have an impact on the room setup for front screen projection and the backstage area for rear screen projection (a parade of waitstaff or technicians in black silhouette is probably not the image you plan to project). The larger the image, the longer the throw required, and the longer the throw required, the more powerful the projection beam must be (your AV provider or producer will work with you to select the appropriate type of projection system).

MULTIMEDIA CONSIDERATIONS

Multimedia presentations using numerous live and recorded video images, computer graphics, sound, lights, special effects, and live action are exciting, motivating, and entertaining. They are, in fact, full-fledged theatrical productions and must be treated as such. The producer serves as the professional coordinator for this portion of the overall event and must be included as a primary event team member throughout the design, planning, implementation, and evaluation phases of the event. The producer will work with the lighting, sound, audiovisual, set, and entertainment designers and providers to incorporate all their technical requirements into a seamless, integrated production.

When using projection screens as the output for a variety of inputs (computer graphics, prerecorded video, slides, film, and numerous cameras for live image magnification), a single person must be the one to direct when, where, and what camera feed is to be projected. Much of this is often predetermined within the script, but the person calling the show must have an excellent command of the desired order and impact in order to adjust directions according to what is actually happening. It is also important to remember that the more complex the production, the more complex the equipment will be, including numerous switchers, interfaces, projection devices, and mixers (audio and visual), which is why such a console looks as though it belongs in an aerospace command center just prior to a rocket launch.

Special Effects

Used in a variety of settings, ranging from haunted houses to product launches to sporting spectacles, special effects can direct attention, create emphasis, captivate, marvel, amuse, and add an element of surprise to an event. With the use of air, fire, water, paper, chemicals, and other earthly substances, you can create a fantastic array of out-of-this-world effects (see Figure 8-8). These attention getters and adrenaline triggers provide an emotional payoff that can leave an audience awestruck. They may be used to alter reality and establish identity or proclaim a message and express celebration. They are the punctuation marks in your event vocabulary.

TIMING YOUR EMPHASIS AND EXCITEMENT

Special effects can add the emphasis needed to alert an audience to the important messages of an event production and contribute significantly to the excitement level. There may be a tendency to "overproduce" because you are enthralled by the possibilities, but unless you are trying to achieve a sensory overload, these effects must be used judiciously. Special effects should remain just that—special. They must be incorporated into the production in just the right place and at just the right moment to achieve the goals and objectives of the event. Timing is everything. A butterfly release should take place when all the wedding guests are outside. Fog blasts in an entryway or onstage should startle the guests, not become expected. Pyrotechnic shows should build to an exciting climax, not go on and on with just more of the same. Confetti cannons should mark a high point, but not spew bits of paper onto everyone's dinner. And you must not release the doves just before your aerial fireworks display (unless you are going for a falling roast dove effect).

❏ Aerial Reader Board
❏ Air/Mist/Steam Bursts
❏ Animation
❏ Aromatics
❏ Atmospheric Haze and Fog
❏ Balloons—Drops, Explosions, Releases, Reveals
❏ Bubbles
❏ Butterfly Releases
❏ Card Tricks
❏ Colored Smoke
❏ Confetti and Streamers— Cannons, Geysers, Tubes, Drops
❏ Digital Avatars
❏ Electronic and Mechanical Props
❏ Fans and Wind Machines
❏ Fire and Flames
❏ Flash Pots
❏ Flying and Floating Objects
❏ Flying Performers
❏ Holograms
❏ Inflatables
❏ Launchers
❏ Motion and Proximity Sensors
❏ Pneumatic Devices
❏ Pyrotechnics—Outdoor and Indoor, Aerial Displays, Close Proximity, Synchronized, Lateral, Tabletop, Handheld
❏ Rain and Snow
❏ Sparks and Explosions
❏ Thunder and Lightning
❏ Water Blasts

Figure 8-8
Special Effects Checklist

PYRO—THE SKY'S THE LIMIT

There is nothing that says "celebration" more than fireworks. Their light, sound, smell, and tangible excitement have added an emotional impact to celebrations since the Chinese first discovered gunpowder and Marco Polo brought their fireworks recipes from the East to Italy in the thirteenth century. They have been popular climaxes for large outdoor civic events since the 1730s, when the first scheduled fireworks shows began in London's pleasure gardens (similar to today's theme parks). Pyrotechnics are an art and a science, as well as a potentially dangerous, even deadly, enterprise, yet it is partially that danger that makes them so exciting.

Pyrotechnics may be included in events of all sizes in practically any location. Outdoor displays can range from simple set pieces to create a flaming logo or emblem, to a major computer-controlled orchestrated display, synchronized to live and/or recorded music, that shoots thousands of shells hundreds of feet into the sky at 300 miles per hour. Outdoor displays can cost $500 to $2000 for burning logos, $2500 to $5000 for a small aerial display (a few minutes long), or $1000 to $3000 or more per minute for a choreographed spectacular. Aerial and outdoor displays have been used as finales for events ranging from civic festivals to wedding celebrations, to herald a new home run record at a baseball stadium, create a waterfall the entire length of a bridge to celebrate its centennial, and to mark the demolition of a high-rise hotel casino, as well as a spectacular entertainment feature at theme parks, resort properties, marketing events, and opening or closing ceremonies at sports events.

Increasingly popular now are "indoor" or close-proximity pyrotechnics that use the same science of fire, combustion, and explosion with refinements that limit or eliminate the smoke and may be as close as 15 ft (4.5 m) to the audience for such effects as fountains, curtains, gerbs, line rockets, fireballs (dragon's cough), flame projections, concussions (salutes), flash pots, stage mines, and sparkle pots.

Modern pyrotechnicians are constantly developing new and exciting devices and applications that bring dazzling dimensions to corporate, cause-related, and conference events: line rockets that whistle along cables from the back of the house to the stage to pinpoint an explosive reveal, or walls of fire that ignite upon the entrance of a star performer. Costs can range from $1000 to $4000, for simpler effects, up to hundreds of thousands of dollars for custom-made shows. The costs for both indoor and outdoor pyrotechnics include design, materials and equipment, generating the necessary paperwork, creating required floor plans, obtaining local permits, obtaining or verifying insurance, working with the event's stage designer and its setup, cleanup, and on-site crews.

On-Site Insight

David L. Spear, CSEP, president of Classic Effects in New Orleans, Louisiana, and 2002–2003 president of the International Special Events Society, advises: "The things the pyro company should be asking you are, (1) What are the demographics of the audience? (We can do loud, in-your-face effects or graceful, low-smoke effects.) (2) Describe the room and the dimensions, including ceiling height and so forth. (3) What other elements do we interact with, such as sound, lasers, lighting, and so on. (4) When and at what time(s) does the pyro happen within the program?" He also advises that you should never discuss indoor pyrotechnics in terms of duration; they are meant to accent and complement a program. "The professional event coordinator should ask himself, 'What is the moment I want the audience to be moved to a higher emotional level?' If I can take the people who are waiting to cheer when their team comes running onto the field, and with some quick gerbs, some concussion mortars, and mines in the team's colors, and bring it up one notch higher for that audience, then I've done my job."

Spear, whose company has designed and produced the pyrotechnics for six Super Bowls, three Republican National Conventions, World Cup Soccer, and numerous national beauty pageants, also suggests that using pyrotechnics "with some flash and sparkle, some glitter and a whistle" is an excellent way to open a show—to make sure the audience focuses its attention on the start of a program, because just turning down the lights or making an announcement ("the voice of God") may not be sufficient. "Pyro may also be used during a speech wherein the speaker goes from one side of the stage and makes a point—flash—then to the other side of the stage for another point—flash—and it looks as though the speaker is setting off the pyro."

LAUNCHING INSTANT FUN

Confetti and streamers can be an alternative to close-proximity pyrotechnics, providing the same explosive sparkle without the fire. Using compressed air, air cannons can shoot out a burst of multicolored streamers up to 100 ft (30 m) and large colorful paper confetti or sparkling Mylar glitter in as much as a 40-ft (12-m) diameter, showering the audience with instant fun. (Traditional glitter should not be used because of its material composition, very small size, and difficulty with removal during cleanup.) Confetti comes in a variety of shapes and colors and may be die-cut in custom shapes (the larger the piece, the longer it will float in the air—so bigger is better). Streamers may be cut to length and customized with a company logo or a text message. There are also flame-treated streamers that may safely be mixed with pyrotechnic effects. Air cannons may be mounted onstage, on a truss, and/or hidden within the perimeter décor and may be detonated via remote control.

Confetti blasters or geysers are also available, which propel a continuous flow of color and motion like a fountain or fire hose; some may be handheld so that the direction can be controlled and adjusted physically by a technician. Handheld confetti sticks can be handed out or placed on tables so that guests can generate their own confetti shower. Air cannons may also be used to launch gifts into the air, such as T-shirts or coupons. You must be careful, however, about shooting (or throwing) anything into a group of people. Seminar speakers have been known to cause injuries and costly mishaps (e.g., broken glasses, splashed coffee, etc.) when they threw wrapped hard candy out into the audience in an attempt to add a bit of excitement to their presentations.

CREATING ATMOSPHERES

Special effects can replicate the forces of nature, including wind, rain, smoke, fire, fog, haze, snow, steam, thunder, and lightning. These atmospheric or environmental effects may be used to establish a theme locale and/or mood, or they may be used to help "tell the story" of the event production. In a trends report by Ted Uram in the June 1999 issue of *Event Solutions* magazine, Jeff Redner of Entertainment Lighting Services, based in North Hollywood, California, described how he re-created thunder and lightning for a movie premiere, which had a truly visceral effect. "The rooftop behind the press bleachers housed a specialized type of outdoor strobe light known as a lightning strike and flashed sporadic blasts of 250,000-watt strikes. Four enormous subwoofer cabinets mounted below the bleachers bellowed out synchronized sound blasts of thunder."

Wind is created with fans of varying sizes. Small fans may be used to make a flag flutter patriotically in the breeze behind a speaker at the lectern or to deliver scented breezes (scent-scaping) in a broad range of fragrances, from coconut to roasted coffee and numerous aromatherapy blends. Air darts and air cannons may be used to deliver an eerie invisible puff at audience members' feet in a haunted house, a slight mist of water synchronized with a video of sailing down the rapids, or a blast of heat from an erupting volcano. Air mortars can blast gallons of water 90 ft (27.5 m) in the air for a water explosion.

Fog and haze are used to create a mysterious atmosphere, a surface on which laser and other lighting can be seen, or fog/smoke screens for projections. Haze machines use a glycol- or mineral-oil-based fluid to create a misty smoke that fills the air, and fog machines use dry ice (frozen carbon dioxide) or liquid nitrogen to produce thick white clouds for ground cover, cascading vertical walls of flowing fog for projection, and blasts of freezing fog in any direction for a variety of exclamation points in an event program. These effects must be used with care, as extended or repetitious exposure may have harmful effects on performers or guests. Oil-based hazes send particulates into the air, and liquid nitrogen and dry ice deplete the oxygen in the air (which, if excessive, can cause suffocation).

Decorative smoke and fire may be used to signify a magical reveal of a product or person (e.g., speaker or entertainer), bring a volcano or dragon to life, or simply line a walkway with gas-fired tiki torches. Colored flames and colored smoke are possible and may be used in many of the ways a lighting designer might use automated lights. Flame-projector devices can shoot a flame up to 16 ft high (nearly 5 m) or shoot a fireball through the air, and when combined with smoke effects, they are suitable for simulating volcanoes, fumaroles, fire-breathing dragons, landing or launching spaceships, explosions, and other stage effects.

PNEUMATICS, ROBOTICS, ANIMATION, AND AVATARS

Adding robotic or animated movement to the décor and production (in addition to live entertainers) may offer just the interactive special effects to take an event from the expected to the extraordinary. From three-dimensional animation in the form of holograms (created with lasers), to interactive digital avatars, or hydraulic platforms and shaker tables that provide choreographed yet unexpected movement, to robotic movement controlled by remote operators and/or motion detectors—these surprising effects are sure to engage and entertain your guests.

Digital avatars are interactive animated characters created within a computer and manipulated via electrodes attached to points on an individual's face or body joints (fingers, elbows, shoulders, knees, etc.), which then transfer those movements to the animated image. This allows for preprogrammed or real-time movement. Digital avatars can be designed to replicate human or abstract characters, ranging from clowns to emblems. Combined with a talented actor on microphone, the character can interact with a speaker, answer questions, and ad lib comments while projected on a large screen during a program or on a video monitor within a trade show booth.

A less high-tech form of interactive character is a robot, which can move around an event space, turn its head, and move its arms via remote control, operated by an individual (with a small device within a shoulder bag) acting as just another guest, or from a remote location if the robot is fitted with a small video camera. The robot and operator each have a microphone and transmitter that allows the operator to hear and speak with the guests the robot encounters. Other robotics include jointed extensions on props or mannequins, which turn, extend, or literally jump out when triggered by an infrared or other motion-detector device; these are particularly effective when the objective is to scare or startle the guest.

Flying or floating performers, signs, and objects are aerial effects that can fill the space above the audience's heads with as much entertainment value as that onstage. Aerial reader boards may be flown over an event site to deliver changing messages and graphics. Helium-filled balloons and spaceships with tiny motorized fans may be flown by remote control above the crowd, seeming to float magically in well-choreographed directions, and, as demonstrated at the closing ceremonies of the 2002 Winter Olympics, the balloons may be illuminated from within and support aerial gymnasts (which were scheduled for the opening ceremony, but the wind was too strong). In addition, people, props, and products may be flown via a rigging system similar to that used in theatrical productions to make Peter Pan fly.

INVESTING WISELY

Many of the special effects discussed so far can be moderately or extremely expensive and should be invested in only when their effect is worth the cost. However, there are less expensive options for creating a magical "Wow" effect, including the humble bubble and balloon. Bubble machines release a constant stream of bubbles into the air, which can become tiny reflectors of light showered onto a dance floor, or from a giant clamshell and mermaid display at an entrance or buffet station (confirm that the bubble fluid is nontoxic and, if near a buffet, food grade in quality and content—you do not want soapy shrimp).

Colorful balloons may serve not only as décor, but also as a special effect. Balloon drops can signal the grand finale as they are released from nets in the ceiling to fall in a floating shower over the audience. A bag or net covering helium-filled balloons might be opened for a balloon release. However, because of environmental concerns, this practice may be strictly controlled outdoors (and Mylar balloons are usually not permitted because they can interfere with power lines), but may be achieved by securing long balloon strings to the ground so the balloons will float up but not escape. A balloon wall or large cylindrical column can serve as a colorful display until time for a reveal, then exploded to expose the product, person, or image behind it. Giant balloons filled with smaller balloons and confetti (or even coupons) may be rigged into the ceiling and detonated on cue via squibs to explode and release their shower of fun.

MAKING MAGIC IS SERIOUS BUSINESS

The magic of special effects carries with it serious responsibilities. First and foremost, *everyone in the show needs to know*. All the performers, technicians, installers, and operators must have a complete understanding of what effects will be used, exactly where they will be, exactly when they are to be executed, and how those effects are achieved. Those who need to know include any speakers and/or audience members who will be onstage while an effect is taking place, as well as the venue management (who may be called upon to adjust the smoke detection equipment in a function room so that the magical haze effect does not set off the sprinkler system). The professional event coordinator (as well as all others involved in the production) must also understand that the professional operating the effect has complete authority to cancel or postpone it if conditions will compromise safety.

For any effect used, make certain that a Material Safety Data Sheet (MSDS) is available for reference. Appropriate hearing protection for noise must be provided for technicians operating or near explosive devices or loudspeakers. If black light is used, you must ensure that it is low in harmful ultraviolet radiation. Signs must be posted, advising the use of strobe effects. All projected substances must be nontoxic, and preferably biodegradable. Written procedures should be provided to all performers and workers for all flying effects. Make certain that a comfortable temperature is maintained for the venue and that there is an adequate intake of clean outside air. And make certain that the appropriate fireproof curtains, props, sets, and costumes are used. Review the risk management procedures in Chapters 2 and 6. No special effect is worth a trip to the hospital (or worse).

Selecting Technical Providers

An event production, whether simple or complex, requires special equipment and knowledgeable operators. The size of the technical production will depend on the scope and prioritized objectives for the event, but the professional event coordinator must always ensure that the budget spent is a sound investment by selecting the right professionals for the job. There are strategies for minimizing costs, such as selecting local providers (to reduce travel expenses) and event-friendly venues (those with sufficient power and rigging points, accessible loading docks, and generous dimensions), but the event coordinator may not have control over these choices. The venue may have been selected with other objectives in mind, or there may not be local providers for a particular service. Some venues have exclusive contracts with technical providers or have their own in-house companies that must be used, and some organizations use and bring the same production company with them wherever their events are being held.

ALWAYS USE PROFESSIONALS

Many of the technical services and special effects that have been discussed are potentially hazardous (involving fire, electricity, and heavy equipment), so, as a professional event coordinator, you should always use professionals for their installation and operation. Robert Estrin of Creative Event Technology contends that experience should be a key criterion for selection. "There are safe short cuts you can take, but you know them only through experience. One-off, new, or annual—every event is a unique situation that requires the knowledge and eye of an experienced professional." Be certain to check a provider's qualifications and ask for and check references. Check providers' credentials and look at their previous work, particularly examples of productions similar to the production you require. Ask for evidence of any state, federal, local, or other requisite licenses or permits they must have to do business, as well as the appropriate insurance coverage (the insurance company should always be confirmed as a reputable insurance provider by your insurance company).

For pyrotechnics in particular, David L. Spear, CSEP, suggests you ask the company for the MSDS forms for those effects you are considering. He also notes, "Some cities and states are more sophisticated than others regarding licenses; some rely on national licensing processes and codes, while in others, you only work with the local fire department. Anywhere you go, and particularly in other countries, you should always contact the local authority having jurisdiction (AHJ), as specified in the National Fire Protection Association (NFPA) codes." Depending on the event, this can be one authority or can include the fire department, parks department, police department (state and local), transit authority, coast guard, and numerous other agencies. Spear suggests that this contact should be the responsibility of the provider, not the purchaser, and should be included in its scope of services provided.

You might also wish to look for membership in such associations as the International Special Events Society (www.ises.com), Entertainment Services and Technology Association (www.esta.org), Audio Engineering Society (www.aes.org), International Communication Industry Association (www.infocomm.org), Communications Media Management Association (www.cmma.net), the American Pyrotechnics Association (www.americanpyro.com), or other applicable professional organizations.

CONSOLIDATE, DESIGNATE, AND COMMUNICATE

Depending on the type, style, scope, and location of your event and its production, you may be working with numerous providers for each individual product and/or service, or you may wish to procure the services of a technical production company to handle this portion of your event. Robert Estrin advises that you either hire or designate a technical director to oversee the integration of all the various production elements and their respective needs. The more complex the production, the more complicated this integration of equipment, staff, installation requirements, and operations will be, and a technical director will be able to choreograph, navigate, and negotiate this effort more efficiently and safely. Ralph Traxler, CSEP, notes, "A technical director or technical producer is a valuable asset for any event planner. The preconceived notion that the addition of another manager to the team will cost the planner a portion of the profit is now no longer valid. The knowledge of technology and the venues will *increase* the profit. There are so many ways to create a smooth-running event and save money that it is becoming mandatory to bring in a technical producer for any important event."

Just as everyone involved needs to be knowledgeable about any special effects that are used, so all involved with the show need to know the extent and the content of the show, the lighting angles, the audio positions, the video screens, the special effects, the sight lines, the rigging points, the table layout, the food service, and the entertainment. Estrin notes, "There is nothing so special that it can't be told to all the vendors or providers. There is no reason to withhold information." You may need to secure confidentiality agreements from all participating providers, but they must all be included in the production planning process.

SITE CONSIDERATIONS

Technical productions take space, often lots of space, to accommodate the equipment, the effects, and the technicians and operators of that equipment and those effects. The professional event coordinator and/or the producer/technical director must work together to incorporate the requisite spatial and proximity needs of each type of equipment and operator into the overall layout of the floor or site plan. Both aerial and close-proximity pyrotechnics will require specific easements according to the effects produced. Lighting angles and plot designs will be based on the lighting effects and illumination required within the space and production program. Power will have to be distributed properly so that all involved have the electricity they need without overloading the capabilities of the power sources. The tech booth, platforms, and/or trailer must be positioned for optimal operational effectiveness.

TIME—SCHEDULING THE LOGISTICS

Technical productions also take time, which increases exponentially as the production increases in complexity. Limited hours for setup and difficult (or blocked) loading dock access are the factors that cause most problems—and the potential for cost overruns. In addition, inexperienced producers or individual vendors can cause costly delays. Sufficient and appropriately scheduled time for installation, equipment testing, and rehearsals must be included in the production schedule. Although some vendors are able to complete a certain amount of equipment preparation, such as prerigging some light bars or prehanging drapes on pipes, there is only so much that can be done prior to installation; some things simply must wait for on-site installation. Equipment must be rigged and checked, entertainers must be allowed to check their performance areas and apparatus, special effects must be tested and secured, and the actions and agenda must be rehearsed. And, as in the theater, everyone needs a little quiet time prior to the show itself to mentally prepare for the performance to come, because once the production begins, everyone must be completely focused on what he or she needs to do to make it the best show possible. There is only one chance to get it right.

Target Competency Review

The professional event coordinator has an astounding number of theatrical and technical options available to bring sophisticated and exciting production values to any event of any size in virtually any location. Similar to those created for and found in other entertainment media, these theatrical tricks, tools, and techniques may be used to enhance the communication and celebration objectives of an event, but should be employed only when it suits the purpose of the event, not just because they are possible. Like any other element of an event, these elements should be invested in only to further the goals and objectives of the event.

Lighting and sound augmentation and productions, which provide the illumination and amplification that allow the audience to see and hear the elements of the event, enhance the event environment as well. They may also be used to move the event experience along its carefully crafted progression. Audiovisual technology and multimedia productions allow the professional event coordinator to communicate the purpose and important messages intended by presenting them via diverse learning dimensions, as required by modern audiences. Special effects—ranging from the humble balloon drop, to the explosive power of pyrotechnics or the instant abandon of dancing inflatables and showers of confetti, to the imitations of thunder and lightning—accentuate and punctuate the message and purpose of an event at just the right time and place to move the audience to an emotionally satisfying moment.

Although the professional event coordinator is not expected to be an expert production designer, producer, or technician, he or she is expected to be familiar enough with these technologies to be an expert buyer. This requires bringing the right people and providers onto the event team so that these potentially hazardous elements are integrated seamlessly and safely into the overall event planning and production. Clear communication is paramount, so that *everyone in the show will know* exactly what is expected and how to deliver the best show possible.

EXERCISES IN PROFESSIONAL EVENT COORDINATION

Outline and describe the lighting, sound, multimedia, and special effects you would employ for the following events. Explain how these will enhance the fulfillment of the event's goals and objectives.

1. A regional shopping mall has been undergoing extensive renovations, which are now complete, and the owners have hired you to coordinate an exciting entertainment extravaganza to celebrate their grand reopening in conjunction with a special "Midnight Madness Sale" promotion. They want to highlight the new improvements and décor; they need an exciting way to introduce the 20 new upscale retail tenants, as well as promote their old tenants, and they want to dazzle both the media and the thousands of shoppers at this late-night event.

2. You have been contracted by a large software company to coordinate its reception at an annual computer electronics trade show at which the company will be unveiling and explaining its latest voice recognition software. It needs to make sure that the guests, composed of trade media and buyers from major retailers, understand the complexities of this product and its broad range of applications, from the consumer market (home and small business user) to the interactive entertainment industry.

3. Your city has been selected to be the site for a national beauty pageant, with the final judging event to be televised on a major network, and you have been selected to coordinate the two-night production. There will be 50 contestants included in a talent and a swimsuit competition before a live audience on the first night, highlights of which will be replayed on the second night while the judges are conferring. The final judging on the second night will

consist of a ball gown competition to select five finalists. The five finalists will then be judged based on their responses during on-stage interviews, and the winner will be announced and crowned in a grand finale. The sponsors want this to be an emotional and entertaining experience for both the live audience and the television viewers.

Facing Page
Walk-around entertainers such as this pirate add an entertaining dimension to the event experience. *Photograph by RUDA Photography, courtesy of Steve Kemble Event Design.*

CHAPTER 9

Staging the Entertainment Experience

If you would rule the world quietly, you must keep it amused.

—RALPH WALDO EMERSON (1803–1882)

IN THIS CHAPTER YOU WILL LEARN HOW TO:

- Develop the structure of an effective and progressive event experience.
- Organize the components of an entertainment experience to achieve the purpose, goals and objectives for an event.
- Determine the options for entertainment and attractions for an event experience and ensure their suitability for the event specifications and audience.
- Identify and procure the entertainment products, performers, and services to enhance the purpose and theme of an event experience within the budgetary resources for the event.
- Coordinate entertainers' needs, integrate the logistics into the event plan, monitor the performance delivery, and evaluate the effectiveness of the entertainment elements of the event experience.

In outlining the type and scope of entertainment activities for a large company party, the event coordinator had strongly recommended the inclusion of three caricaturists instead of the one the committee had planned. Her reasoning was that this would be a very popular activity, providing a memento many of the attendees would wish to have, and that one caricaturist would simply not be able to handle the volume of guests expected during the function. This advice was not taken and, as predicted, at the party the caricaturist had such a long line of people waiting that those in the queue started to get frustrated and angry. The mood became so antagonistic that the event coordinator had to close the caricaturist's booth and have security escort him out of the event. When asked by the head of the party committee why she had removed the caricaturist, the event coordinator explained that the situation had changed from an amusing activity to an unsafe condition, adding, "You wanted him to entertain your guests, not inflame them."

Entertainment is that which commands and holds attention, pleasantly diverts, or amuses. Entertainment in some form is included in virtually all events, primarily to enhance the event experience. Even the most solemn of occasions often utilize music and ritual performances to reinforce the significance of the event. Entertainment and entertainers may be used to reinforce a theme or mood, link event program components, enhance the environment, direct traffic flow, encourage interaction, deliver a message, capture attention, and increase attendance. Entertainment can amuse, arouse, and educate us. It can help us to celebrate or commemorate important points of our life, enjoy the world around us, or allow us to escape our everyday life. It supports our rituals and ceremonies, energizes our gatherings, and fills our leisure pursuits with fun and frolic.

Although frivolity may be the objective, selecting and procuring the right entertainment and entertainers for an event must not be frivolous. The entertainment provided must be suitable for the event and the event audience. It must be chosen with care to enhance the event's purpose and adhere to its budget, and it must be incorporated into the site and agenda to facilitate the proceedings. This involves structure and discipline—not simply picking the entertainment you happen to like.

Event Choreography

An event experience must be choreographed and blocked out as carefully as any dance or play. The professional event coordinator crafts a plan that takes the attendee or guest through a structured progression of various sights, sounds, tastes, textures, smells, highs, lows, climaxes, diversions, and discoveries that delivers the intended impact and message of the event. Nigel Collin of Absurd Entertainment, based in Sydney, Australia, noted in his seminar at The Special Event 2002 on the Effective Use of Entertainment, "Entertainment should not only be fun, but useful—enhancing the flow of an event by leading guests on a journey, hitting the highlights of the experience, and linking the various components of the agenda or program."

CONSTRUCTING THE EXPERIENCE—FINALE TO OPENING

Constructing or engineering an event experience is similar to writing a play. You start with the premise and plot (the purpose), determine the climax, assemble the components, define the characters and their motives, and arrange the action so that it takes the individual (viewer or visitor) to an emotionally satisfying conclusion. *The Experience Economy* authors Pine and Gilmore note, "Many times, experience stagers develop a list of impressions they wish guests to take away and then think creatively about different themes and story lines that will bring the impressions together in one cohesive narrative." Alfred Brenner, author of *The*

T.V. Scriptwriter's Handbook, also advises that you think about the ending, the defined goal, first. "The climax is of fundamental importance in the architecture of any drama and is causally connected to the opening. The first scene is determined by what takes place in the climax." Brenner also notes, "All drama appeals to the emotions, not the intellect," therefore the event experience must be saturated with sensation and passion in order to attain a satisfying finale.

Although you are not writing a play, the dynamics are the same, and the three acts are the same: (1) Premise, (2) Development, (3) Climax. This progression applies to everything from a multimedia stage production to a simple speech. Joyce Kupsh and Pat R. Graves, authors of *How to Create High Impact Business Presentations,* advise, "The introduction should be designed to set the stage and tone and gain the attention of the audience. The body provides the 'meat' of your message. A conclusion may recap or summarize your main ideas. Your ending words should be chosen to make a lasting impression on the audience. Therefore, plan a strong ending." Most event designers plan an event to end on a high note and recommend that you begin building excitement about 30 minutes prior to the close so that the party does not simply die out—it ends with a crescendo.

The progression from opening to climax is composed of scenes, and each scene must move the story forward. You can use various entertainment options to create or accompany each scene. For a festival in which the experience is self-directed, you might use different entertainment styles in different areas to draw visitors to a variety of locations. For a choreographed program, such as a theme party or awards ceremony, entertainment should be scheduled to move the "show" along at the appropriate pace and progression, perhaps by having costumed greeters at the entrance, acoustic music during the cocktail hour while guests are mingling and talking, a cirque-style gymnastic performance or the awards presentation during dinner, and an interactive band for after-dinner dancing, closing with a final production number incorporating an indoor pyrotechnical display.

DIMENSION, DIVERSITY, AND DIVERSION

The inclusion of entertainment gives added dimension to the event experience, including diversity and depth, as well as diversions that make the experience more meaningful and enriching. Various forms of entertainment may help to develop the "characters of the play" (components of the event program) and the subplots that add a deeper meaning to the climax. For example, using performance artists, such as a painter to paint the portrait of the recipient on a giant canvas to announce an award winner, or ice sculptors with chain saws to sculpt the martini bar before the guests' eyes, can turn the practical aspects of the event into memorable experiences. Offering temporary henna tattoos may allow the guests at a Polynesian incentive event or theme party to ornament themselves in keeping with the theme while learning about the history and meanings of the symbols used. Heraldic horns or Japanese taiko drummers might imbue an opening with cultural significance, and a Native American Friendship Circle Dance may conclude a program with deep communal significance.

Strolling and static performers (from operatic singers to juggling jesters, or cowboy fiddlers to gypsy violinists) can enhance the theme environment, and marching or moving groups (marching bands, drum corps, mariachis, or gospel choirs) might lead guests from one area to another. Celebrities and nationally known headliner acts can add value to attending an event, and celebrity look-alikes can add depth to a theme. Indigenous entertainment may provide the authentic experience visitors seek, and interactive games may provide the energy release attendees require. The professional event coordinator should consider entertainment options for every dimension of the event experience and every aspect of the event environment.

On-Site Insight

When no ordinary groundbreaking would do, Mary Tribble, CSEP, and Tribble Creative Group of Charlotte, North Carolina, created an earth-shattering event. After a VIP breakfast reception, guests walked across the street to a tent surrounded with colorful tubular balloons. Behind the tent, six earthmovers stood at attention, two holding up a welcome banner. Inside the tent, in front of a festive backdrop, a mound of dirt held several ceremonial shovels awaiting what the guests believed to be a traditional groundbreaking.

After the appropriate speeches, the dignitaries approached the shovels for the final ceremony. The action was stopped, however, by an actor playing a construction worker, saying, "You all have to get out of here! We're about to blow this place!" He unveiled an oversized TNT plunger and then encouraged the company's VIPs to gather around. When they plunged the handle, it cued a large explosion of confetti canons, which signaled the beginning of the theme song "I Feel the Earth Move," by Carol King.

(Continued)

Guests turned around as they heard the rumble of the heavy equipment, which was driven to either side of the tent. The operators (rehearsed by the management company the day before) began a series of highly choreographed moves, including whirling and twirling by the smaller skid-steers and synchronized "Motown" moves by the dozers and excavators. At the end of their "dance," the bulldozers returned to the starting points and "bowed" to a cheering audience, showing their appreciation for a most unique use of rental equipment.

Scripting the Program

Just as the professional event coordinator constructs an event experience as a playwright structures a play, the event should also be scripted like a play. The professional event coordinator should write a script or detailed description for the event, including the activities, timing, setting, and, if necessary, even the dialogue. Like the scenes in a play, the event program elements are put in their proper sequence to build to the appropriate climax, paced according to the type and scope of the event and the needs of the event audience, and staged according to sound dramatic principles including builds, respites, focus, and flow. Such a script allows the event coordinator to envision the event experience from start to finish to ensure that it meets the goals and objectives (the desired outcomes) in an effective and entertaining manner.

ARRANGE THE AGENDA

With the desired outcomes established and the program elements identified, you must put the scenes in their proper order to achieve a strong opening, eloquent body, and meaningful climax. This order, like all facets of professional event coordination, is based on the logical and necessary progression from one item to the next. Religious ceremonies may have a specific order of ritual action. Civic or government events may have a specific protocol that must be followed. Product launches may have specific units of information to be dispersed in between entertainment acts. Festivals and fairs may have a historic precedence for scheduling certain elements. Training programs may have a requisite progression of content modules based on learning dynamics. Fashion shows may have segments based on seasonal collections or a hierarchy of celebrity models.

The professional event coordinator takes the outline of entertainment elements or agenda items and, in collaboration with the appropriate stakeholders, puts them in a sequential linear order. This is when he or she should consider—and question—the sequence. Would a different order better meet the needs of the event? Perhaps it would be better to hold the wedding reception first and conclude with the ceremony at midnight. Maybe a further measure of pomp and pageantry should be added at certain points during a government event. Does the product launch agenda offer the right opportunities for media coverage? Is it possible that the historic schedule of events at the festival has become stale? Will adding energy breaks to the training agenda improve performance? Does the fashion show lineup allot sufficient time for quick changes? And does the event build to an emotionally satisfying finale?

CONTROL THE CONTENT

In the film genre, editing is the key to success—taking the scenes and action filmed, selecting those scenes that are most important to the story, and putting them in the best order to tell the story in the most effective and economic manner. Brenner states, "Everything in a good script is related. Everything fits together like the mechanism of a fine watch. All nonessentials have been discarded." You must select the most important elements, eliminate those that do not support the program or production, and condense the action and activity into a tight and effective presentation that delivers a "cohesive narrative," the desired event experience.

Such editing may involve some hard choices and assertive directions. You may need to cut the children's choir performance from two songs to one. You may need to move the instructional video from within the program to a looped presentation displayed as an exhibit. You may need to edit ten content points down to three. You may have to restrict a speech to three minutes instead of the ten minutes the speaker wanted. You may decide to use a videotaped message instead of a live speech. You may have to instruct the orchestra to simply start playing during an acceptance speech that is going on too long. This is why it is so important to create the script early enough that you are able to make these decisions before presenters, performers, and others have been promised something that should not (and ultimately will not) be included in the final production.

When specific rites, rituals, and other protocols are required, it is imperative to consult with the appropriate religious and/or organizational officials to determine your options. When specific learning objectives are expected, you must consult those resources that provide expert advice on adult learning dynamics. And when specific marketing and/or branding objectives must be met, you must consult with the marketing experts to define and refine your options. The overall objective is to put on a good "show," an entertaining experience that meets and exceeds expectations.

PACING THE PROGRAM

Good dramatic structure demands excellent timing. Punch lines should not be delivered too early. Critical information must not be delivered too late. Openings should not be soft, and climaxes should not be anticlimactic. Reveals and discoveries should have an element of surprise. The audience should always be hungry for the answers, and those answers must be satisfying. This may all be controlled with pacing—controlling the speed and complexity with which the experience is delivered. There must be a balance of stimuli and rest, content and cogitation, and emotional highs and reprieves. The program must be designed to flow toward the climax with builds, highlights, respites, focal points, and, as with the printed page or lighting design, some "white space" that allows the audience to pace their intake. As with special effects, you want the body of the show to flow beautifully, highlighted with effective punctuation marks.

A master of ceremonies (MC, or emcee) is often employed to provide an audience with an anchor personality and keep the action moving at the appropriate pace. A script may have to be written for an emcee so he or she is able to recognize important people in the audience and announce important information. Any notes or scripts prepared by or for an emcee should be scanned to ensure that they do not include any "in jokes" that may not be understood by portions of the audience, nor any introductory or biographical comments (or ad libs) that would be inappropriate or embarrassing to the person being introduced. The master of ceremonies originated in the eighteenth century with the position of toastmaster. The toastmaster's ceremonial clothes included the red tailcoat, the costume still worn by the ringmaster at circuses around the world (signifying the individual who announces the acts and "controls the circus").

IT'S SHOW TIME

Once you have the script developed, review it with your production team to ensure that it is technically feasible and review it with all the necessary performers and stakeholders to make certain it is understood and agreed to. Again, *everyone in the show needs to know,* from the production technicians and performers to the photographer, makeup artists, media personnel, and others. The performers need to know so they will be mentally and physically prepared to enter on cue and deliver outstanding performances. The event photographer or videographer needs to know so he or she can get the best shots and those that will be most important to the client or host. The costume, hair, and makeup professionals need to know so they can be prepared for touch-ups and quick changes. Members of the media need to know so they will get the story they need and provide the coverage you want. For example, if an address by a dignitary is to be presented via videotape instead of live, you might arrange for the media to receive copies of the videotape that they can incorporate into their broadcasts instead of reporting that your event was not important enough to merit an in-person appearance by that dignitary.

Your final script may be prepared in various formats, depending on the type and scope of the production. You may want a simple agenda for participants and media and a complete script, including the full text of the speeches, for the technicians, stage managers, and particularly those calling the cues for the show. You may need a separate script including just the text for those speeches to be displayed on TelePrompTers or monitors. You may have stage assistants who need a script to ensure that certain presenters make their way from their dinner tables to their places backstage in time for their entrances. You might need one for the caterer so that the dessert parade scheduled to occur between two segments of the awards presentation happens right on time. *Everyone in the show needs to know.*

Selecting and Booking Entertainment

Entertainment may be passive, interactive, decorative, instructional, interpretive, inspirational, musical, verbal, visual, ritual, and/or culturally indigenous. To select and book the best entertainment for an event, you must define the specific goals and objectives for the inclusion of entertainment and the conditions and restrictions for booking entertainment and attractions. Although your options are virtually endless, as illustrated in the Activity Elements Checklist in Chapter 1 (Figure 1-7) and the entertainment listed in Figure 9-1 (which is by no means complete), the budget rarely is. In addition, your local or regional sources for providers or performers may be limited. The event space and/or the time line may also be limited. The acts or performers you want may not be available. You must make the best choices, based on the resources available, and execute the proper contracts with the entertainers you have selected. You must then make certain that all the contractual specifications, including the entertainers' contract riders, are incorporated into your event plan. Finally, you must monitor and assess the value and effectiveness of the entertainment elements for the event.

ASSESS THE NEEDS AND RESOURCES

Entertainment must support the purpose and objectives of the event. This may include adding excitement, enhancing the flow and pacing of the event experience, expressing appreciation to the audience or guests,

A Cappella Groups	Go-Carts	Pianists/Organists
Accordion Player	Gunfighters	Pickpocket Artists
Animal Races	Gymnastic Performers	Plate Spinning
Arcade Games (Pinball/Video)	Harmonica Groups	Precision Riding
Astrologist	Harpists	Psychics
Auctioneers	Hat Making	Puppeteers
Bagpipers	Headliner Acts	Reenactors (Historical/Battle)
Balancing Act	Hostesses	Remote-Controlled Racing
Ballet Dancers	Hula/Polynesian Dancers	Ribbon Dancers
Ballet Folklorico	Hypnotists	Roller Skates Act
Balloon Sculpturing	Impersonators	Russian Ballet
Banjo Players	Impostor Speakers	Showgirls
Bavarian/Octoberfest Bands	Impressionists	Singing Telegrams
Bell Ringers	Jazzercise Group	Singing Waiters
Belly Dancers	Jesters	Skateboard Exhibitions
Brass Groups	Jousting	Skydivers
Break Dancers	Jugglers	Snake Charmer
Calligrapher	Jukebox Rental	Sport Simulators
Cancan Dancers	Junkanoo Dancers	Square Dancers
Cartoonists	Knife Throwing	Staging Show Productions
Chair Massages	Korean Acrobats	Steel Drum Band
Cheerleaders	Laser Shoot-outs/Tag	Stilt Walkers
Chinese Acrobats	Lie Detector Testing	String Quartet
Chinese Lion Dancers	Limbo Dancers	Strolling Troubadour
Cigar Rollers	Living Statues	Strong Man/Woman Act
Close-Up Magicians	Mandolin Players	Stuntmen
Clowns	Mannequins and Models	Stunt Sports Teams
Color Guards	Marimba Bands	Talking Buffet Heads
Country Cloggers	Martial Artists	Tap Dancers
Cowboy Trick Roping/Riding	Mascots	Tarot Card Readings
Dance Instructors	Melodrama	Tightrope Walkers
Dixieland Bands	Mimes	Town Crier
Drum and Bugle Corps	Minstrels	Trapeze/Aerial Acts
Escape Artists	Motorcycle Trick Act	Tribute Acts
Ethnic Cultural Shows	Murder Mysteries	Trick Riders/Ropers
Exotic Bird Shows	Native American Dancers	Unicyclists
Face/Body Painting	One-man Band	Vaudevillians
Female Impersonators	Oompah Band	Victorian Carolers
Fire Eaters	Organ Grinder	Video DJ
Fortune Tellers	Paint Ball	Vocalists
Full-Size Carnival Midways	Palm Readers	Wax Hand Casting
Game Shows	Petting Zoos	Woodwind Groups

Figure 9-1
Entertainment and Entertainer Sample Resources

focusing attention on important images and messages, and/or invigorating and motivating the attendees. You may wish to facilitate interaction, create a mood, or simply encourage play. Dan Nelson, CSEP, CMP, of Dan Nelson Productions in Las Vegas, Nevada, notes that many special events "can benefit from entertainment vignettes to liven up long programs, cleansing the palette, so to speak, between informational programming" (www.dannelsonproductions.com). Performers, performances, and attractions should be incorporated where and when they will effectively enhance the achievement of the desired event experience and deliver a return on the investment made.

Do not buy more—or less—than you need. If all you need is chaser or background music, using recorded music may be perfectly sufficient, but if investing in a headliner act will help you meet your attendance objectives, that is where you put your money. If what you need is an evening's entertainment for a conference or business meeting, you might simply purchase a block of tickets to a local concert, theatrical performance, fair, or sports event (perhaps with a special lounge area), rather than mounting your own event production. Establish your criteria and seek out the best value for your budget.

In their seminar, entitled "Ensure Successful Events: How to Get the Most Out of Your Entertainment Dollars," presented at the 1998 CMAA World Conference on Club Management, Kathy Nelson, CSEP, CMP, and Nancy Matheny, CSEP, advised, "Choose entertainment that fits the demographics and projects the appropriate image, never buy your personal taste, and . . . remember when you purchase entertainment, it is the entertainment value you are buying, not the number of bodies onstage" (www.club-mgmt.com/dining/9805/events.html). You must also consider the duration of the performance within the duration of the program. You may wish to hire a small band or DJ to fill in the gaps between acts or sets for a larger act. (A set—the length of time a musical group plays—is usually 45 minutes long with 15 minutes off for a break.)

Your entertainment options may include professional entertainers, semiprofessionals, and amateurs, categories that do not necessarily indicate performance quality (but often reflect the cost), and will be affected by the providers available where and when your event is to take place. To locate these resources, you might contact local or national entertainment agencies, speakers bureaus, local performing arts and fine arts groups, community groups, schools, and local visitor bureaus and chambers of commerce. Consult directories, check with performing arts guilds, and search the Internet. And, as fresh new entertainers and entertainment concepts are developed continuously, you should also review trade publications and periodicals, attend industry conferences and showcases, and network with other professional event coordinators.

PREVIEW BEFORE CONTRACTING

As event coordinator, you should preview entertainment acts and performers before booking them (if possible). You need to know what you are purchasing. You might arrange to visit another event where the group or entertainer is performing (with permission from that event's organizer or host), view videotaped examples, listen to a demo audiotape or CD, or preview the text of a speech or PowerPoint slide show by a speaker. You may need to rely on another person who has seen the performance and makes a strong recommendation. Such recommendations may come from someone within your organization, a professional talent consultant, or the references you have been given. You may decide to hold auditions for certain performers and participants. Professional performers expect this and will be prepared to provide you with the access or preview materials you need to make a decision. Disc jockey companies advise that you confirm that the specific DJ you have seen is the one who will be performing at your event, as many companies have numerous DJs, who vary in quality and style.

THE OFFER AND THE AGENT

Professional entertainers often work with entertainment agents or agencies that manage their bookings, negotiations, and contracts (see Figure 9-2). In regard to booking entertainment, Mark Sonder, CSEP, of Mark Sonder Productions, based in Chantilly, Virginia, and ViewPoint International DMCs, advises, "Three words, forms, forms, forms! If it is not written down, it didn't happen. I can tell you that headliners are not managers or agents. They do their thing and hopefully they do it well, but they may not be thinking about the specifics of your event, as that does not impact their art, their work, their creativity, their love, their performance."

The booking process often starts with an Artist Offer Letter, authorized by the purchaser (the client or host organization), extended to the performer from the professional event coordinator through the booking company and/or artist's agent. This letter outlines the terms of the engagement, including the performance date(s), venue, show time(s) or length of engagement, contract price (fees to be paid), and other contract costs (rider specifications) and/or conditions. The artist (entertainer) then decides whether he or she will accept the offer (usually based on availability). Once the artist accepts the offer, an engagement agreement or contract is issued. It is important to understand that within this process, the Artist Offer Letter is a legally binding contract if accepted and signed by the artist.

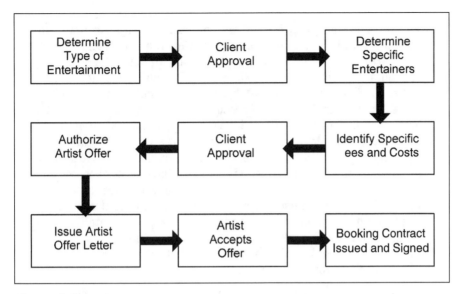

Figure 9-2
Entertainment Booking Process

On-Site Insight

Connie Riley, CSEP, is the vice president of event operations for T. Skorman Productions, Inc., in Orlando, Florida, a talent booking agency as well as a production firm. The organization develops custom shows and musical groups, based on emerging popular trends in the entertainment industry, such as retro acts, rhythmic groups, and other headliner types of shows. She explains that the benefits of booking talent through an entertainment agency include matching the right entertainment with the event objectives and audience. Because the agency knows the talent—good and bad, stylistic differences, and entertainer requirements—and, through its networks, knows artists' agents all over the country and the world, it can find the best entertainment and entertainment value wherever an event is to take place, providing qualified talent to meet the needs of the event and the expectations of the buyer.

(Continued)

The entertainment agency also offers protection for both the purchaser and the talent. "You don't want the act feeling abused and performing badly, and you don't want the client feeling abused and taking it out on the act on-site. Our job is to be the buffer to make certain everyone's needs are met." For example, an association insisted on two acts on one stage, an opener act and a headliner act to follow immediately. When the opening act accidentally damaged a cable that sent a power surge through the headliner act's personal equipment and destroyed it, the on-site entertainment agency representative was the one who delivered the bad news to the headliner act, negotiated with its members to use different equipment and still perform, even though, by contract, they were not legally obligated to, and arranged for the substitute equipment so that the concert, although delayed a bit, went on and thrilled the audience.

Riley went on to explain:

If people don't deal with entertainers, they don't understand the egos, the personalities, or the sensitivities. Most clients don't understand how performers prepare themselves for a performance, and the last thing you want before you go onstage is someone telling you something that is going to break your concentration. In one instance, the client had booked a stand-up comedian with a well-known reputation for slightly "raw" material, and right before he walked onstage the client caught him, as he was walking up the steps, and said, "Please be careful. Don't say anything too explicit." You just don't tell someone to curb his routine right as he walks onstage. Of course this distracted the comedian, he lost his focus, and he had a bad show. And then the clients don't understand when they don't get the show they thought they were getting."

THE RIDER—REQUIREMENTS AND HIDDEN COSTS

A contract rider is a list, specific to each entertainer or entertainment act, of what the performer requires in order to perform or make an appearance. It "rides," or is attached to, the contract (hence the term *rider*) and includes everything from transportation to technical requirements to the type of food and beverages required (see Figure 9-3). It is a legally binding part of the contract or engagement agreement between the artist and the purchaser, but some of the points within it may be negotiated prior to the contract. This is when it is advantageous to secure entertainment

- Accommodations—number and type of rooms (suite, king, nonsmoking, etc.)
- Advertising content and context
- Approval of announcers (MCs) and other performers
- Artist's billing—placement of name in ads and signage
- Broadcast rights and performance reproduction
- Control over all technical and performance aspects
- Credentials and passes—types and distribution
- Dressing rooms—size, proximity, amenities
- Equipment—use sharing restrictions/prohibitions
- Entourage—artist's table, comp tickets, hospitality
- Food and beverage—types, schedule, placement
- Insurance requirements
- International travel—procurement of visas, work permits, customs, carnets (customs documents), entrance/exit fees, per diem, etc.
- Interviews and special appearances
- Load-in/out—schedule and priority, personnel requirements
- Merchandising—sales and concessions
- Musicians—additional and separately contracted
- Percentage of ticket sales
- Performance—sets, timing, duration
- Prohibition of cameras, filming, video recording in audience
- Security requirements and deployment (stage and venue)
- Sound check—time, duration, authorized personnel, rehearsals
- Sponsor recognition restrictions
- Storage requirements
- Technical rider requirements—specifications on types and placement of staging, power, equipment, sound, lighting, backline (technical or instrumentation) equipment, etc.
- Transportation—flights (class, schedule approval), ground transfers, types of vehicles, shore power for tour bus/van, etc.

Figure 9-3
Rider Requirements Checklist

through a talent buyer or booking agent who knows the entertainment group and which items are negotiable.

The technical portion of the rider, which includes all the equipment and staging requirements, may also include a detailed description of the stage plot, including a diagram showing the layout of the stage, the artist's position, and where all the equipment, microphones, props, and so forth, are to be positioned. This portion can be accompanied by an entire production list including lighting plots, audio equipment specifications, power distribution requirements, and the provision and number of stagehands, riggers, and costume assistants. The larger the act, the more complicated the rider will probably be; some headliner acts' riders comprise 50 to 100 pages or more. And some riders are considered proprietary information, because they show exactly how a certain performer achieves certain special effects and are therefore not issued until after the acceptance of the offer. This is another reason to work with a talent buyer or entertainment agency—so you are able to calculate the true costs of an appearance before you issue an offer.

INCORPORATE THE LOGISTICS

Whether you are engaging a headliner act or a simple community choir, you must incorporate the entertainer's technical and performance needs and logistics into your event plan and production schedule. If they require dressing rooms with showers (perhaps to wash off the body makeup they use), you may need to secure an executive-style portable toilet or a motor home with a shower to be parked next to the facility or stage. If an act is arriving in its own tour bus and requires shore power (a power source connection to the building's power), you may need to designate parking areas differently. If a group specifies a certain artist's billing, this must be factored into your printing schedule and layout. If it stipulates the prohibition of cameras in the audience, you may need to add security personnel at the entrance to the event to check people's belongings and a storage desk where any cameras found will be tagged and stored for pickup after the performance.

It is no less important to consider all these ramifications for a small or amateur entertainment group. Whether the group has a rider or not, you should determine what its specific needs will be. A community choir may need parking spaces and passes for all its members. A children's group may require sufficient dressing room or lounge space to accommodate all the children's parents. And you may have to control those family members who want to see their children performing. (I have had to have aunts and uncles removed by security personnel, and then threaten to never use the group again if they didn't cease their protests asserting their rights to see their nieces or nephews perform.)

EVALUATE THE VALUE

The professional event coordinator must always evaluate the return on investment for the entertainment included in an event as well as the entertainers used. Did you provide enough entertainment? Was it scheduled effectively? Were there gaps in the program? Did the investment in the headliner act meet your expectations? Robert Jackson, author of *Making Special Events Fit in the 21st Century,* advises, "Watch the audience or spectators—*not* the show. No matter what the stage action may be, if this show is not for this crowd, for any reason, their actions will speak a lot louder than whatever applause they may offer out of politeness. Shuffling in seats; whispering or talking; yawns; reading something; nail-cleaning, -filing or -biting—all are the only 'reviews' you need to let you know that you have a problem." You must learn from each event you co-ordinate, and you should help the entertainers you use learn by letting them know what went right and what went wrong (and perhaps exploring the reasons so you may both benefit from the experience).

You can add value to an entertainer's appearance by determining early in the booking process where, when, and how that performer can contribute to the success of the event experience. Many entertainers have appeared at a broad variety of events and have valuable suggestions as to how they can improve or enhance their appearance within the context of your event, *if* you share with them the purpose, objectives, theme, and overall schedule, *and* you ask them. Mark Sonder, CSEP, advises,

> *Communicate to the performers who the client is and what the expectations are. If the event is a birthday party, the performers will want to introduce the birthday boy or girl and be ready with a rendition, in the style of music they perform, of "Happy Birthday." On the other hand, in a corporate setting, the performers may "need" to mention the corporate message or new product line from the stage. The meeting or event producer must communicate these objectives to the leader of the performers or a nonperformer staff person charged with the responsibility to deal with the performers. That person, in turn, will communicate this to all the performers.*

Managing Personalities and Performers

The performing artist, whether celebrity or amateur, speaker or musician, soloist or part of a group, is concerned primarily with one thing—giving the best performance possible. In order to do that, he or she must feel comfortable with the environment and the emotional atmosphere surrounding the performance. No matter how long the artist has been a performer, or how blasé the artist seems to appear, anyone going "onstage" has deep concerns about the response he or she will receive, both onstage and off. Even the most famous celebrities and experienced performers admit to experiencing severe nervousness or "butterflies" before going onstage. The professional event coordinator can do a number of things to ensure a stellar performance, such as demonstrating respect, communicating expectations in a timely manner, and providing what the performer needs to do his or her job.

PERFORMER AND PERFORMANCE EXPECTATIONS

The performing artist expects to be treated with care and regard. The artist needs to feel appreciated both onstage and off. The artist also needs to feel protected—from unsafe and/or substandard conditions that may jeopardize the performance, as well as from performing before the "wrong" audience. Nothing enhances a performance more than an enthusiastic audience, and nothing destroys a performance more quickly than an unreceptive one. Although entertainers may seem demanding or needy, you must recognize that, quite often, behind the self-centered façade is a very fragile ego. The artist's value should be recognized in word, deed, and compensation, which includes expressing your appreciation for the performer's contribution, providing the arrangements and amenities requested, and making prompt payments.

You must communicate the needs of the event and expectations for all performances early, clearly, and in writing. You must also communicate any changes or adjustments in a timely manner. If the start of the performance is to be delayed for some reason or a problem has arisen, you must tell the entertainers as soon as you know and tell them why. They may be able to assist you. When members of a dance group did not show up for an event I was producing (they got lost), the jazz singer offered to do another set to fill the gap in the program. When a speaker cancelled at the last minute for a conference at which I was speaking, I agreed to give the presentation because that speaker's topic was in my repertoire.

ESTABLISH PERFORMER GUIDELINES

As in any employment situation, the professional event coordinator must establish an atmosphere of mutual respect and supportive of optimal performance with the entertainment artists for an event. And, like the actual employees of an event organization, all performers should be provided with the rules and guidelines established to achieve the optimal working atmosphere. Most entertainment agencies have a set of performer guidelines they require their artists to adhere to, and these should be reviewed to ensure that they are sufficient and appropriate for the needs of the event. Connie Riley, CSEP, explains that these guidelines have been developed to address the "hot buttons that disturb the clients expecting a certain level of professionalism, . . . many entertainers don't understand the protocols or ethics because they've just never been told. They don't know the client is being charged for the food and beverage on a per-head basis. They don't know that the end client may be several levels away from the person or agency that booked them."

You should also generate your own set of performer guidelines to make available to performers you book directly, including local, semi-professional, or amateur entertainment artists or groups (do not submit them to headliner acts—these are professionals and such guidelines will be covered in their riders). The following guidelines, which protect and serve both the artist and your organization, should answer questions before they need to be asked and ensure a mutually profitable and professional experience for everyone.

- **Alcohol and euphoric substances**—Prohibit on-site consumption, even if the client or a guest offers. Stipulate that inebriation of any type will not be tolerated.
- **Artist report and ready time**—Specify when the artist is to arrive on-site and check in (e.g., 30 minutes prior to performance) and when the artist is to be ready to perform.
- **Attire**—Specify the appropriate attire for both artist (e.g., formal, costume, etc.) and supporting crew (e.g., black shirts and pants). Crew members may have to be prohibited from wearing logo wear (even the artist's) and may be provided with logo wear of the event or the event company.
- **Behavior problems**—Advise artists that they are not expected to tolerate abusive behavior of any kind, nor will abusive behavior by them be tolerated. Explain how such situations are to be handled. Abusive behavior includes offensive language, sexual advances/harassment, and physical contact.
- **Book-back policies**—Most entertainment agencies require a commission from the artist or purchaser should the artist be rebooked by the purchaser within a specific time period (e.g., 12 to 18 months).
- **Business cards**—Specify that the artist is to refrain from distributing his or her own business cards at the function and that you will supply the artist with yours (if appropriate). Also specify that the artist is to refrain from selling CDs or promoting his or her Web site (unless preapproved).
- **Dressing rooms, break areas, and amenities**—Specify the locations of dressing room(s) and/or break areas and the amenities to be provided (e.g., food, beverage, etc.). Also specify where the support crew is to take breaks or wait during the performance, including parents or guardians.
- **Eating and drinking**—Specify that the artist is prohibited from eating or drinking from the guest food service, even if offered (by client or guest).
- **Entourage guests**—Unless stipulated within the rider, specify that the artist must not bring personal guests (without prior permission).

- **Gratuities**—Specify how gratuities, if offered, are to be handled.
- **Handling requests and problems**—Specify how the artist is to handle special music requests by a client and/or guest. Stipulate that all problems or inquiries regarding the performance specifications or fees are to be referred by the artist (or supporting crew) to the on-site coordinator or representative.
- **Independent contractors**—Specify that the artist will be considered an independent contractor and will not be entitled to workers' or unemployment compensation, but will be responsible for the payment of all applicable income or employment taxes.
- **Load-In/load-out**—Specify the load-in time assigned, the loading area or dock, responsibility for loading equipment (e.g., hand trucks, trolleys, etc.), and the load-out time for the artist's equipment.
- **Location and directions**—Specify the exact location (i.e., building, room, etc.) of the performance and provide directions to the site. Stipulate that the artist is responsible for transportation to and from the venue (or meeting area for shuttle to the site) and for knowing how to get there.
- **Mingling with guests**—Specify whether the artist is encouraged or allowed to mingle with guests before, during breaks, or after performance.
- **On-site contact**—Specify with whom the artist is to check in upon arrival, and provide a contact number for the artist to call should he or she be running late or have an emergency. Also secure contact numbers for the artist, preferably for a cell or mobile telephone, so the coordinator may reach the artist while en route.
- **Overtime policies**—Specify how overtime requests are to be handled, including the fees to be charged per time increment (i.e., per hour, half hour, etc.), the change order form to be filled out and signed and by whom, and reporting overtime after the performance (e.g., submitting the form to the coordinator, notifying the booking agency, etc.).
- **Parking areas and fees/passes**—Specify the artist's responsibility for parking, including designated parking areas, reimbursement (if any) of fees, validation, and/or parking passes. Stipulate that the artist must not request parking validation, fee reimbursement, or passes from the client or venue.
- **Payment procedures**—Specify how and when the artist will receive payment for the performance. Stipulate that the artist must not discuss with or request payment from the client.
- **Smoking**—Specify smoking policies. Many entertainment agencies prohibit smoking anywhere onstage or within function rooms, and many venues prohibit smoking anywhere on the premises.
- **Storage areas**—Specify storage areas for the artist's equipment, packing cases, and personal effects, including security measures or

personnel to be (or not to be) provided and artist's responsibility for materials stored.

ORIENTATIONS AND REHEARSALS

A singer who has performed the same songs for 20 or 30 years will still want and need a rehearsal before a performance. A dance group that has performed all over the world will still want and need to rehearse their dance on a particular stage. Even the cast that has performed the same play on the same stage for weeks or months on end will still have pickup rehearsals to refine and refresh their performance. It is no wonder, then, that one-time events require orientations and rehearsals prior to their start. Not only does the technical equipment and timing need to be checked, the performers need to practice their movements and voicing within the environment specific to the particular venue.

Every event venue has a "feel" of its own, and every performer needs to get a feel for that space. Speakers need to prepare their materials at the lectern and/or walk through the audience area. Singers need to vocalize, and musicians need to play their instruments under performance conditions to ensure that the sounds are accurate. Dancers need to accustom themselves to the size and surface of the stage. Gymnastic or aerial performers need to test their apparatus and actions. Connie Riley, CSEP, advises that you schedule a minimum of eight hours prior to the start of an event (after all other staging, décor, and electrical components are in place) for headliner acts to move in, set up their equipment, and rehearse, and a minimum of three hours for a standard band.

PURCHASER OBLIGATIONS

The professional event coordinator must ensure that the performance of music (including the ubiquitous "Happy Birthday") complies with music licensing regulations and that the appropriate fees are paid to the applicable performance rights organizations (see Figure 9-4). Performance rights organizations collect royalties for nondramatic performances of intellectual property, which are, in turn, paid to the various publishers and authors associated with a particular recording or performance. There are exemptions from music licensing fees for certain private life-cycle events, but the event coordinator must become familiar with these regulations and plan to comply. The fees are based on the context in which the performance takes place, the manner in which the music is performed (live, track act—live performance to taped music, or recorded), and the size of the audience. It is technically the responsibility of the host or sponsoring organization to pay these fees, but the professional event coordinator

APRA	Australasian Performing Right Association Limited	www.apra.com.au
ASCAP	American Society of Composers, Authors and Publishers	www.ascap.com
BMI	Broadcast Music, Inc.	www.bmi.com
CAL	Copyright Agency Limited (Australia)	www.copyright.com.au
CISAC	International Confederation of Authors and Composers Societies (France)	www.cisac.org
GEMA	German Authors' Rights Society	www.gema.de
IMRO	Irish Music Rights Organization	www.imro.ie
ISA	International Songwriters Association (United Kingdom)	www.songwriter.co.uk
MCPS	The Mechanical Copyright Protection Society (United Kingdom)	www.mcps.co.uk
PRS	Performing Right Society (United Kingdom)	www.prs.co.uk
SACEM	Society of Authors, Composers and Editors of Music (France)	www.sacem.fr
SESAC	Society of European Stage Authors and Composers	www.sesac.com
SOCAN	Society of Composers, Authors and Music Publishers of Canada	www.socan.ca
TONO	Norwegian Performing Rights Society	www.tono.no

Figure 9-4
Performance Rights Organizations

should apprise the client of this requirement, or he or she may be subject to vicarious liability for unauthorized use.

Target Competency Review

An entertaining experience must be engineered, structured, and choreographed so that it delivers a strong opening, a satisfying core, and a meaningful climax. The structure and components must be designed to meet the needs and expectations of both the host and guest, delivering the event experience they desire. The professional event coordinator uses the tools and techniques of the dramatist to create a progressive and rewarding experience, which include dimension, diversity, builds, respites, focus, balance, contrast, and rhythm. Entertainment elements may be added at numerous times and in numerous places to facilitate a well-crafted experience, provide entertaining solutions to challenges, and enhance occasions of all types.

The professional event coordinator should script the program, arranging the event elements and entertainment components in the proper sequence to deliver the event experience as designed. This sequence is often dictated by necessity, ritual, and/or protocol, but controls are often necessary to ensure a cohesive presentation with the proper pacing and content. The final script, which may be generated in a variety of formats depending on the uses and users, must have the consensus of all those involved in the event production and must be distributed appropriately.

Selecting and booking entertainment is a detailed process. The professional event coordinator determines the most appropriate entertainment and/or attractions, based on the goals and objectives of the event, the event's character and its audience, and the resources available. Entertainers and performers may be amateur, semiprofessional, or professional; local or regional; headliner or name acts. They may be booked directly by the professional event coordinator, but often are booked through a talent buyer or entertainment agency, which manages the many negotiations, contractual obligations, and logistical specifications associated with professional artists. The professional event coordinator must understand the personality traits and needs specific to performing artists and then provide the necessary information and guidelines to ensure a good performance and good relationship based on mutual respect. All music licensing regulations and union requirements must be met.

EXERCISES IN PROFESSIONAL EVENT COORDINATION

Outline and describe the entertainment components you would employ for the following events, including why you have selected them and how they support the structure of the event experience. Explain the logistical requirements associated with each act or component and how these will be incorporated into your overall event plan.

1. You have been contracted to coordinate the groundbreaking for a new casino, and the owners want something new and exciting (they have already seen the dancing bulldozers) to ensure that this ceremony gets media coverage and impresses their stockholders.

2. Your local convention center has decided to produce a New Year's Eve celebration with dancing and dining to raise ticket revenue and show off the center to its local market. You have been asked to design and coordinate the party. There are five large function areas to highlight, and the center wants to attract attendees from all markets in your area.

3. A sporting goods gate show (an exposition open to the public with an admission charge) has asked you to coordinate entertainment and activities to attract new exhibitors and increase attendance at its annual exposition. In particular, it is important to attract new and younger customers to revitalize the reputation of this show, which has come to be seen as just a camping and fisherman's show.

CHAPTER 10

Food and Beverage Operations

The discovery of a new dish does more for human happiness than the discovery of a new star.

—Jean-Anthelme Brillat-Savarin (1755–1826)

IN THIS CHAPTER YOU WILL LEARN HOW TO:

- Identify the food and beverage needs of the audience, participants, staff, and other stakeholders at an event.
- Determine and procure the appropriate purveyors, products, and service providers for the catering needs of the event.
- Select nutritional menus that meet the budgetary requirements of the event and incorporate the necessary dietary restrictions, cultural preferences, and thematic considerations.
- Coordinate the food and beverage service style, sites, and schedule in accordance with the needs of the event and applicable licensing, health, and safety regulations.

The event coordinator had been working with the chairperson of a fund-raising committee to design an elegant gala event to attract new sponsors and donors for a charity organization. The chairperson was adamant about using a new restaurant, at which she had dined, to do the catering because it was "the talk of the town." The restaurant, however, had never catered an off-premise event before. Despite the event coordinator's advice to secure proposals from numerous caterers, the committee acquiesced to the chairperson. Later, the event coordinator overheard two guests discussing the dinner. "Oh well, the average person has more than 40,000 meals in a lifetime. I can live without this one, and I can live without supporting this organization as well."

Food and beverages may be an integral or tangential component of an event, but they are the primary focus of many events. They can make or break an event, or, as illustrated earlier, if not selected properly, can fail to fulfill the aspirations of an event. The professional event coordinator must understand the function of food and beverage within the purpose of the event in order to meet and exceed expectations while fulfilling the nutritional needs and preferences of those being served. From a chocolate extravaganza as a fund-raising event, to candied apples at a harvest festival, gourmet box lunches for a sightseeing tour, or a seven-course banquet honoring a visiting head of state, the right food service can facilitate the achievement of an event's goals and objectives.

Margaret Visser, author of *The Rituals of Dinner,* states, "We play with food, show off with it, revere and disdain it. The main rules about eating are simple: If you do not eat you die; and no matter how large your dinner, you will soon be hungry again. Precisely because we must both eat and keep on eating, human beings have poured enormous effort into making food more than itself, so that it bears manifold meanings beyond its primary purpose of physical nutrition." Eating and drinking are necessary and should be pleasurable for people, whether they are grabbing a snack or dining in style. The professional event coordinator must determine the functional needs of food service:

- Who must be fed—attendee/stakeholder groups, how many, demographics
- Why they must be fed—sustenance, energy, attentiveness, hydration, refreshment
- What they must be fed—meal type, special diets, variety, nutrition, budget
- When they must be fed—time, position within program, speed of food service, trickle/dump arrival
- Where they must be fed—on/off-premise, meeting room, tent, backstage, break area, sit-down, standing, strolling

The professional event coordinator must then determine the creative options available to fulfill these needs and the catering operations to provide the food and beverages in an attractive, efficient, and cost-effective manner. It is critical to ensure that the food and beverage service is sufficient, sanitary, and safe and that it complies with all applicable regulations.

Catering Operations

The role and scope of catering at an event will be based on the type, purpose, scope, and objectives of the event. The professional event coordinator may be selecting a variety of menus for a multiday conference in a convention center or hotel, a dinner for a wedding celebration held on a private estate, food vendors for a festival, participants in a cook-off competition, refreshments for a hospitality reception, breakfast for participants after a charity fun run, or a picnic for a reunion. The type of caterer or catering operation used may be an in-house department at the venue or an independent provider at an off-premise location, and there may be policies and procedures specific to each type. The professional event coordinator must research the options and select the caterer that is best able to offer the menus, prices, and experience to meet the specific needs of the event.

DETERMINE FUNCTION OF FOOD SERVICE

Food service, as form, follows function. The types of food and beverage served will be determined by the functions they are to fulfill (see Figure 10-1), and the way in which food and beverages are served can facilitate the function the event is meant to serve. Meals such as breakfast, lunch, and dinner are meant to satisfy hunger, but not all events require a sit-down meal. For example, at a conference, you might have a stand-up continental-style breakfast with bite-size pastries, tiny cups with a sundae of granola and yogurt adorned with a plastic spoon, fruit kebobs, and miniature quiches that allow attendees to graze while mingling before the first session. Lunch at a car show may consist of gourmet wrap sandwiches and pizza sold at food concessions, which may increase attendance during the midday hours of the exhibit. Dinner might be served at different venues during a multivenue progressive feast. Between-meal refreshments are often added to ensure that energy levels are maintained and that attendees remain on-site.

It is important to ascertain which internal and external groups (or customers) require food service (see Figure 10-2) and when. Some of these groups may not have complimentary food and beverages provided by the event; rather, food and beverage service may have to be identified or procured, from which these individuals may purchase meals and

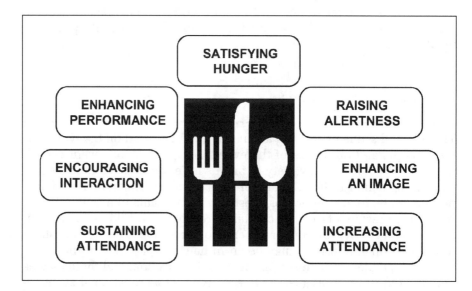

Figure 10-1
The Functions of Food Service

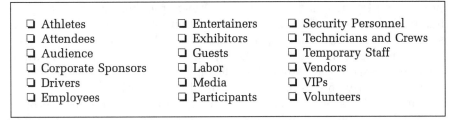

❏ Athletes	❏ Entertainers	❏ Security Personnel
❏ Attendees	❏ Exhibitors	❏ Technicians and Crews
❏ Audience	❏ Guests	❏ Temporary Staff
❏ Corporate Sponsors	❏ Labor	❏ Vendors
❏ Drivers	❏ Media	❏ VIPs
❏ Employees	❏ Participants	❏ Volunteers

Figure 10-2
Typical Stakeholders Requiring Food Service

snacks. Whether the event is providing food service or not, the same attention to quality, quantity, and cost should be considered. If you are arranging purchasable meals for staff, crews, and participants, the food service provider's access to the event site must be factored into the event plan. Catering specifications in entertainers' riders must be incorporated into the requests for proposals. Separate and less costly meals may have to be ordered for personnel such as the drivers who have transported your guests to an off-premise event. Separate and more extravagant menus may be required for VIP or corporate hospitality areas. Volunteers and the media always appreciate refreshments.

Specify the meals and other refreshments to be provided, including breakfasts, lunches, dinners, breaks, snacks, and/or beverage service (including water stations), and the time when each should be provided. Determine if and which food services are to be profit centers for the event. Identify any special dietary needs of various internal or external groups, including specific nutritional requirements, special food types or brand stipulations, rider specifications, foods to avoid, hydration needs, and price points. Estimate the number of participants or individuals to be served for each type of food service. Establish your budget parameters. Then research and select the best catering operation to meet each group's needs.

TYPES AND SCOPE OF CATERING OPERATIONS

Food preparation and food service are two distinct activities, and where these activities take place determines the type of catering operation. In-house (or on-premise) catering operations have on-site kitchens that service the facility in which they are housed. Off-premise caterers have a commissary (kitchen facility) where the food is prepared, which is then transported to where the food service will take place, and where finish cooking may also occur. Take-out (or take-away) caterers have a food preparation kitchen, and either the customers pick up the prepared platters or dishes or the caterer will deliver them and leave. There is considerable competition among these types of catering operations for the various markets, including events, but the professional event coordinator must determine whether the catering operation seeking the event's business is truly able to meet the needs of the specific event.

Off-premise events, those held at a site or venue that does not have an in-house catering department, require a different food service approach because of the nature of temporary or limited food preparation facilities. Independent caterers and mobile caterers (those with preparation and serving equipment in a self-contained vehicle) are able to provide food service in almost any location imaginable, and some independent catering operations also hold the contracts for canteens and cafeterias in various venues. Concessionaires often offer preprepared, specialty, or limited food services from the side or back of a truck, such as those found at construction sites or food stands and outlets at fairs and festivals or within arenas. The professional event coordinator must confirm that any catering operation seeking to service an off-premise event understands the operational difficulties and differences between on- and off-premise food service—there is a big difference between carrying dinners across a hall and transporting them across town, and between serving 500 gourmet meals over the course of an evening and serving them all at the same time.

On-Site Insight

Both Ginger Kramer of Classic World Events, Inc., in San Jose, California, and Steve Kemble of Steve Kemble Event Design in Dallas, Texas, strongly recommend visiting a caterer's operation prior to contracting. Kramer advocates looking at the toilet facilities. "If they are sparkling clean, the operation as a whole is likely to be well run; if they are messy, you should have doubts about the quality of the company's practices and products. If the toilet facilities are filthy, get out of there immediately!"

Kemble advises you to prequalify a caterer through a telephone interview, then visit with the caterer at his or her shop, review the portfolio, and tour the kitchens. He also likes to, if at all possible, visit the caterer while on-site setting up for an actual event. "You can get a good idea of their organizational skills and a feel for how well their staff works."

SELECTING AND CONTRACTING CATERERS

As the professional event coordinator for an event, you must select the caterer that is able to handle the particular specifications for the event to be held. With approximately 53,000 caterers, excluding hotels, listed in the U.S. Yellow Pages (www.catersource.com), your options should be plentiful. You will consider the available menus, the specialized menus offered for your event, the caterer's experience with events similar to yours, its personnel, and the prices, including gratuities, service charges, and taxes. You must also get references and check them thoroughly. Steve Kemble notes that although a caterer may not be right for a particular job, you should keep its name as a resource to consider for other events. "Not every caterer is right for every single event. One may do very well with a cocktail reception of 1000 people but absolutely cannot do a seated dinner for 300." You may also wish to schedule a tasting to sample the dishes proposed for your event to confirm the presentation and flavor.

The professional event coordinator should be familiar with the standard catering contract policies in order to negotiate and execute the proper agreement. Information from the contract will be transferred to the Banquet Event Order (BEO), an internal document used by the catering staff listing the menu, setup, and other details for the function. A catering contract includes the following components.

- **Day(s) and date(s) of the event**—Including both the day and the date will clarify any mistakes regarding when the event is to take place, and the day of the week may influence the pricing based on supply and demand.
- **Starting, ending, and serving times**—The caterer needs to know exactly how food service fits into the overall event program in order to calculate setup, clearing, and other costs.
- **Location of the event**—The specific site, including the room or space, may have an impact on the setup, preparation, and cleanup costs, particularly for off-premise venues with limited or difficult access.
- **Number of guests**—Used to calculate pricing and quantities to be ordered. Pricing is based on the cost of the foodstuffs, labor, overhead, and profit. There are certain per person economies of scale that are calculated into the final costing and pricing, which may fluctuate if attendance increases or decreases. The caterer and the client should agree on how the final head count (the number actually served) will be determined (e.g., tickets, counter, number of rolled napkins with flatware used, etc.).

- **Date for final guarantee**—Usually 48 to 72 hours before the event; specifies the number of meals the caterer agrees to prepare and the client agrees to pay for whether served or not. Guarantees are estimates, often calculated according to such factors as the history of the event, registration or reply counts, or comparable events.
- **Minimum number of guests**—Because of volume pricing, this number represents the fewest meals the caterer will provide at the prices quoted. If the final guarantee goes below this number (usually 5 to 7 percent), the caterer may reserve the right to increase the per-person price.
- **Charges for additional guests**—The per-person price can be increased if more than the final guaranteed number of meals is required. Most caterers prepare for 3 to 5 percent over the final guarantee, but increases beyond that will likely incur charges for special foodstuff orders and increased labor costs.
- **Food and beverages selected**—An itemized menu specifying the quantities, quality, and brand-name products if stipulated. If certain food items or products are subject to a price change because of increased costs (due to availability, seasonality, or span of time between the contract and the event), the caterer will stipulate the probable limits of a percentage increase in price. The caterer should also stipulate how substitutions in product or venue will be handled.
- **Staffing levels**—Certain styles of service require more waitstaff than others, and certain clients desire more waitstaff than the minimum levels. In addition, many independent or off-premise caterers specify the number of staff and their hours, both front of house (FOH) and back of house (BOH), as a separate line item to differentiate between the costs for the food and the costs for the labor. This item may also include the uniform or attire the waitstaff is to wear.
- **List of charges**—All charges the client is expected to pay (which must be included in the analysis the professional event coordinator will make to determine the selection of a caterer and will factor into the event budget) should be clearly itemized.
  - **Food and beverages**—The itemized quantities, quality, and per-person or per-item prices.
  - **Taxes**—Including local, state, federal, and/or luxury taxes on certain items.
  - **Gratuities/service charges**—The obligatory charges for service personnel.
  - **Tipping**—The optional amount paid to service personnel based on extra or exceptional service. Some caterers have a policy

that tips are to be paid to the caterer, who will then distribute the amount evenly among the FOH and BOH staff.

- **Equipment charges**—An itemized list of equipment to be provided by the caterer (e.g., tables, chairs, linens, etc.) that is not included in the menu pricing, particularly for off-premise catered events. This list will also include the assignment of responsibility for lost or damaged equipment.
- **Setup charges**—The fee for labor to set up the function room if not included in the menu pricing, often incurred for off-premise events or events requiring additional labor for a fast turnover of a room.
- **Room rental rates**—Many hotels charge room rental if the catered event is not linked with sleeping room nights, and some event facilities charge room rental as a separate line item from the in-house catering fees.
- **Site commissions**—Some venues charge a per-person commission on catering conducted at their facilities, and this may be reflected in the caterer's price quote as a differential rate "Pending Site Selected" or as a separate line item.
- **Overtime/other staff rates**—The per hour overtime charges for staff if the event extends beyond the times specified, and the per-staff person charges for additional or outsourced staffing such as action station chefs, bartenders, cashiers, security, and the like.

- **Deposit policies and dates**—The amounts and dates when deposits will be required. Most caterers require a deposit to book the date, often based on the length of time between booking and the actual function.
- **Refund and cancellation policies**—These policies stipulate the rates, dates, and conditions under which payments are to be made by the caterer (refunds) and the client (cancellation). These are usually based on the costs incurred and the ability to rebook the date.
- **Alcohol service policy**—This policy states the pertinent liquor laws and stipulates that they must be in full force during the catered event. If the caterer is not providing the alcoholic beverage service, the policy will verify the party that will be providing this service (client or liquor caterer).
- **Leftover and brought-in food policies**—Such policies specify what is to be done with leftover food (e.g., donated to a shelter or food bank). Because of product liability concerns, most caterers typically do not allow leftovers to be taken by the client. Outside food brought in by the client or guests, unless agreed to by the caterer because he or she does not provide a particular item (such as a wedding cake), is not allowed, also because of product liability

issues as well as prohibitions imposed by health permits and licenses.

- **Indemnification, insurance, licenses, and permits**—These standard contract items cover liability issues and assign the appropriate responsibilities to the appropriate parties.

SANITATION, SAFETY, AND LEGALITIES

All food service and catering operations must comply meticulously with all health and food safety regulations, as well as the sanitation standards specific to the preparation and serving of food and beverages to the public (see Figure 10-3). Many catering organizations also adopt the Hazard Analysis Critical Control Points (HACCP) system of food safety management to identify, monitor, and control contamination risks and hazards associated with food-borne illness. The hazards include the biological, chemical, and physical properties that may cause contamination, and the critical control points are those points, steps, or procedures during which a food safety hazard can be prevented, eliminated, or reduced.

The professional event coordinator must always confirm that the catering operation complies with the legal regulations associated with food service operations and has the requisite health permits and appropriate business and occupational licenses. Of particular note, the professional event coordinator should confirm that the caterer's commissary has the proper zoning permit. Many zoning laws prohibit catering operations in residential neighborhoods, which would subsequently disqualify any caterer preparing foods in his or her home. Remember, anyone can have business cards printed. The event coordinator must do the necessary due diligence to ensure that the caterer selected is qualified *and* authorized to prepare and serve food to the public.

Sanitation and Handling	Safety	Legalities
Cooling and Reheating Employee Hygiene Holding and Displaying Pest Control Preparation/Cooking Storage Transporting	Broken Glass Burns Cuts Falls Fire Fumes	Employment Legalities Health Permits Licensing Zoning

Figure 10-3
Food Service Safety Issues

Menu Design

Selecting the menus for the various food functions at an event will be co-ordinated between the client, the chef or catering executive, and the professional event coordinator. Menus must meet the nutritional needs of those consuming the food and beverages, as well as meet the goals, objectives, and purpose of the event. The menus selected will have both an emotional impact and a physical effect on the attendees. Certain foods can improve an attendee's perception of the event (and host) and affect the attendee's performance at the event (see Figure 10-4).

IDENTIFY MEAL FUNCTIONS

The time, place, positioning, and purpose of a meal may help in determining what should be served at that meal (see Figure 10-5). Serving chicken dishes at both lunch and dinner will likely cause negative comment.) The professional event coordinator must have a complete overview of the food service, even if not responsible for more than one meal within that schedule, in order to serve a balanced menu of the right foods at the right times. The overall menu should have a pleasing balance of flavors, textures, and colors. Food is, after all, an art form to a talented chef and a form of nurturing to the hungry guest.

DIETARY RESTRICTIONS AND SPECIAL NEEDS

Dietary restrictions and special dietary needs—medical, religious, philosophical, political, or ethical—must also be considered. Physical or medical concerns may include food allergies, gluten or lactose intolerance, digestive problems, or low-sodium restrictions, as well as access to water or a refrigerator for medicines. The American College of Allergy,

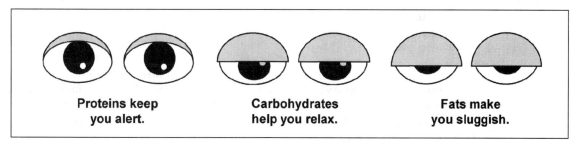

Proteins keep you alert. Carbohydrates help you relax. Fats make you sluggish.

Figure 10-4
The Effects of Food

Meal Function	Meal Considerations	Menu Recommendations
Breakfast	Provide energy and fuel the brain for morning activities; limit fats and sugars that provide temporary lift and sluggish aftereffects.	Proteins, whole grains (cereals and breads), dairy, fresh fruits.
A.M./P.M. Breaks and Refreshments	Refresh, motivate, and relieve boredom; include hot and cold beverages for hydration, handheld portions, chewy foods (chewing has been proven to be a destressing and relaxing action).	Whole fruits, muffins, energy bars, nuts, dried fruits, cookies, raw vegetables with dip.
Luncheon	Refueling and reenergizing for afternoon activities; avoid heavy meals that will make people drowsy or sluggish.	Proteins followed by complex carbohydrates; hearty salads with protein are popular.
Reception	Circulation of guests preceding or replacing dinner, usually with alcohol service; avoid too many salty foods that would increase alcohol consumption; foods should be bite-sized.	Predinner functions offering appetizers and receptions meant to replace dinner must have sufficient quantities and varieties of food.
Dinner	More elaborate meal with fewer time constraints, often including several courses including a rich dessert; broad latitude with theme and style.	Often includes soup and/or salad course, meat/fish, starch, vegetable, bread, cheese and/or dessert course, coffee/tea.
Concessions	Refueling and refreshments as a profit center.	Snack or comfort foods, sandwiches, beverages.

Figure 10-5
Meal Function Considerations

Asthma and Immunology advises, "Eggs, cows milk, peanuts, soy, wheat, tree nuts, fish and shellfish are the most common foods causing allergic reactions, but almost any food has the potential to trigger an allergy. Foods most likely to cause anaphylaxis are peanuts, tree nuts and shellfish" (allergy.mcg.edu/Advice/foods.html).

Jewish (kosher), Muslim (halal), caste-specific Hindu, and other religious dietary laws may require the exclusion of certain foods and restrict food preparation methods. Those with philosophical dietary convictions include vegan vegetarians, lacto vegetarians, ovo-lacto vegetarians, and fruitarians. Those with political or ethical convictions include animal rights activists and environmentalists, prohibiting certain foods (such as veal) or requiring specific food items or ingredients (such as dolphin-free tuna). Corporate or association affiliations, such as a beef council or a beverage company, may require the inclusion of their products within the menu. Recovering alcoholics do not consume any alcohol, even that used in the cooking process, which may be a difficult dietary restriction to identify as those involved in recovery programs such as Alcoholics Anonymous typically insist on anonymity (some will simply say they are allergic).

It is the responsibility of the guest to let you know of any dietary needs or restrictions, but it is your responsibility to provide the mechanism for letting you know. You may provide forms for special meal requests or ask for dietary needs when requesting notice of special needs in your registration forms. You should include signs on buffet displays or prepare descriptive menu cards listing the ingredients in certain dishes. You should also be prepared with vegetarian options or meals at a banquet or other food function. Many caterers and clients are including vegan stations as a matter of course, finding that these accommodate many dietary restrictions as well as attract health-conscious diners. *The Convention Industry Council Manual,* edited by Susan Krug, notes that many catering organizations "will often prepare the usual 3–5 percent overset (meals above guarantee) as vegetarian meals." You may wish to specify this practice when negotiating your catering contract.

CONSIDER COST AND QUALITY

The cost and market availability of the actual foodstuffs may drive your menu planning. Instead of a large steak, you might consider the protein as an ingredient rather than the main item, perhaps serving a smaller portion of beef, but sliced and beautifully displayed. The caterer may be able to "dress up" a less expensive cut of meat with a special sauce or presentation. There may be seasonal restrictions or shortages that affect pricing as well as the freshness of ingredients.

You must also confirm your food terminology, quality, and quantities. For example, to you a chicken salad may mean a bed of leafy greens with a grilled chicken breast sliced and splayed over the top, and to the caterer it may mean chopped chicken mixed with celery and mayonnaise next to a wedge of iceberg lettuce. And in the U.S. Southwest the actual ingredients in a bowl of chili varies from state to state (and is the subject of many prickly disputes). You must confirm portion sizes, ingredients, quality grades, brand names (if applicable), preparation methods, and presentation with your caterer so there will be no surprises when the guests sit down at the meal.

Food Service Styles

The style of service selected for a meal function at an event will affect the cost, timing, spatial requirements, and guests' impressions. The selection of the appropriate style of service will be based on the timing of and the time allotment for the meal function, the menu selected, the staffing capabilities, the budget, the venue, and safety and sanitation considerations. Certain styles require more serving staff, and others require more food per guest. Certain styles require highly trained waitstaff, and others require specialized equipment. Certain styles facilitate circulation, whereas others communicate formality and elegance. The professional event coordinator works with the caterer to determine the service style best suited to the purpose of the event, the budgetary requirements, the time restrictions of the food function, and the capabilities of the catering organization (see Figure 10-6).

No service style is better than another—the appropriate style for a particular event depends on the purpose, goals, and objectives of the event and the needs of those being served. Service styles requiring more or highly trained staff may cost more than self-service styles because of labor costs. Self-service styles, however, require more food per person, because it is not known who will eat how much of which food items, and therefore may not offer much in the way of cost savings. Certain foods are not suitable for preset or plated buffet service because they will cool off, warm up, or melt while waiting for guests to enter the event or serve themselves. The professional event coordinator must confirm the caterer's capabilities, and caterers should agree to provide only those service styles with which they are experienced.

SERVICE PLANNING FOR ON- AND OFF-PREMISE OPERATIONS

The catering operation must plan its preparation setup for the type and scope of the food service it is to provide for your event, based on the menu, quantities, presentation, and location. It must schedule sufficient FOH and BOH personnel, purchase and store the foodstuffs in a safe and timely manner, organize the prepreparations and cooking of foods, ensure sufficient tableware and serving equipment, choreograph the plating of perhaps hundreds or thousands of dishes, and design the path and traffic pattern from kitchen to guest or buffet so that the food is delivered efficiently and safely. The logistics of this precision operation are increased exponentially when the event is held at an off-premise location.

Service Style	Description	Typical Use
Action Station (Exhibition Cooking)	Chefs prepare foods to order and serve them to the guests at a separate station within a buffet setup.	Popular for added entertainment at hospitality functions
Buffet Service	A self-served food presentation offered on a table in trays, chafing dishes, and other similar equipment, often with a server or carving station at the end of the line to help with the more expensive items.	Popular at hospitality functions, social gatherings, and less formal events
Butler Table Service	Platters of foods are arranged BOH, servers present platters to each guest in succession, and guests serve themselves with utensils from platters.	Used at upscale elegant dinners.
Butler Hors d'Oeuvres	Trays of hors d'oeuvres are arranged BOH, servers pass among guests, and guests serve themselves.	Typical for upscale prefunction receptions; useful for controlling consumption
Cafeteria Service	Similar to buffet service, except guests are served by counter attendants and may utilize trays to carry all selections.	Often used for participant or employee meal service
Family-Style Service (English Service)	Platters and bowls of foods are arranged BOH, servers place them in the middle of dining tables, and guests serve themselves, passing the containers to one another.	Popular for casual events and "rustic" themed events
Food Stations	Similar to buffets, but with a different type of food or part of the menu at each station, and with stations located in different places within the event space.	Used to increase circulation and draw guests to different areas within the event; also often used for dessert or coffee stations
French Banquet Service	Platters of food are arranged BOH, guests select foods, and server then portions and serves each food item selected to individual plates with two large utensils manipulated as tongs.	Often used at formal banquet events
French Cart Service (Often confused with Russian Service)	Foods are prepared and/or cooked on a portable cooking stove (rechaud) that is on a tableside cart with wheels (gueridon). Foods are plated by server and served to guests.	Not often used for banquets, but may be used for preparing traditional Caesar Salads or flaming desserts

Figure 10-6
Service Style Gallery

Service Style	Description	Typical Use
Hand Service (White Glove Service, Military Service, or Dome Service)	For each course, food is preplated BOH, one server (wearing white gloves) is assigned for every two guests; when signal is given, all servers set plates before all guests at precisely the same time. Sometimes plates have dome covers, which are all lifted at the same time.	Used at very formal or elegant ceremonial events
Plated Buffet	A selection of preplated foods or individual meals are set on trays and placed on a buffet table or rolling cart and moved into function room at a predetermined time.	Often used for meetings when the participants will work and dine in the same function room
Plated Service (American Service)	Foods are portioned and arranged on individual plates BOH and then served to the seated guests.	Very efficient and economical, popular for large banquet events
Preset Service	Preplated foods are placed on dining tables prior to admitting and seating guests; suitable only for foods that can maintain culinary and sanitary quality when sitting out for an extended period of time.	Often used for meal functions when time is an issue
Reception Service	Foods in small portions are served buffet-style or placed on trays BOH and passed by servers; guests serve themselves and eat while standing.	Popular for refreshment breaks and stand-up receptions
Russian Service (Silver Service)	Foods are cooked tableside on a rechaud on a gueridon and put on platters. The server presents platters to the guests tableside, and the guests serve themselves from the platters.	Used at upscale or very formal events

Figure 10-6
(Continued)

Kitchen or preparation (prep) tents, even entire catering compounds, may be required to create and accommodate the catering operations at a temporary or underdeveloped site. The catering tents may need to be connected to the event space with covered walkways with nonslip flooring. The catering compound may have to be enclosed with screening or netting to ensure that it is free of insects. These temporary kitchens require sufficient power to operate equipment and provide work lighting, as well as fuels to operate cook stoves and/or grills, which must be in well-ventilated areas. There must be sufficient space for staff to conduct preparation, cooking, and plating operations, as well as take breaks. The kitchen or prep areas should not be visible to the guests and may be masked with pipe and draping or screens if it is necessary to have certain BOH areas within the function space. You may need to accommodate ovens, refrigerators, hot boxes, ice machines, outdoor barbecue grills, or a mobile kitchen truck the size of a mobile home. You must work closely with the catering organization to ensure that the site plan for an off-premise event meets its needs.

ADDITIONAL EQUIPMENT CONSIDERATIONS

All catering operations, both in-house and off-premise, supply the standard service ware, flatware, dishes, cups, glasses, tables, chairs, and plain linens needed for the catered event (off-premise or independent catering organizations may itemize these separately in the quote), but you must confirm this when contracting for any catering services. Depending on the type and style of the event, you may specify upgraded versions of these items, such as decorative china and other tableware for a more formal event (to be rented from a rental dealer) or disposables for a more casual event, which may alter the price of the food service. Particularly for off-premise events, you must allot sufficient time and site access for the delivery, setup, and removal of all food service equipment. If your event requires an entire temporary kitchen compound, it may require several days for setup and several more for tear-down and move-out, as well as special access roads for delivery and mobile catering trucks.

Technology Tip

Talented culinary and ice sculpture artisans may create beautiful ice sculptures to complement your event. These intriguing sculptures may also be created by pouring plain or colored water into standard molds and freezing them. Molds are available in various sizes and shapes, suitable for buffet displays or table centerpieces, and you can suspend decorative objects or flowers inside so that they appear to be frozen in time inside the ice sculpture. (Helpful Web sites include www.foodservicedirect. com/diningroom.cfm, www.icesculptures.ltd.uk, and www. icecraft.com.au, among others.)

(Continued)

There are even reusable "ice cubes" that light up. *Litecubes* are 1-in. plastic blocks with battery-operated lights inside that turn on and off with a tap on the side. A gel inside the cubes freezes to help keep drinks cold, and the cubes can be custom imprinted with a logo (www.nexus-promotions.com).

Alcohol Management

Alcohol consumption is a part of a great many events, and although it may be accompanied by numerous risks that must be managed, it is an activity that the professional event coordinator must be prepared to co-ordinate and manage appropriately and effectively. Local and/or state statutes often regulate alcohol service and must be diligently adhered to. The professional event coordinator must determine and comply with all legislation regarding the sales, service, and public health regulations per-taining to beverage service (whether alcohol or nonalcoholic beverages) and carefully consider the event's context and crowd to control the in-herent risks.

SPECIFY THE PURPOSE AND PROCEDURE

In today's world there are varied attitudes and opinions about alcohol consumption, ranging from total acceptance to total intolerance. You must not only confirm the sponsoring host's goals and objectives for serv-ing alcohol, you must also confirm its appropriateness within the context of the event location. For example, if the event is a corporate hos-pitality event held at a sports event, serving beer may be suitable at a public ballpark that sells beer to its regular patrons, but it may not be al-lowed on the grounds of a stadium on public school property. You must also confirm whether beverages will be sold or complimentary, how they will be dispensed (by ticket, cash bar, hosted bar, etc.), and how they will be controlled (by ticket, pricing, wristband credentials, etc.). You must arrange for the appropriate staff and equipment to serve the beverages, as well as the appropriate purveyors to provide the beverage products. Note that nonalcoholic beverage options must *always* be available at any event serving alcohol.

ALCOHOL AWARENESS AND SERVICE TRAINING

Most communities and governments, particularly in the United States, strictly regulate the sale and serving of alcoholic beverages through an Al-cohol Beverage Commission (ABC) or agency responsible for administering the state's liquor laws. Many have adopted a voluntary or government-mandated Responsible Beverage Service Program, designed to change the drinking context or environment by changing the behavior of those selling and serving alcohol. Such training programs deal with identification, prevention, intervention, and the legal responsibilities associated with local liquor codes. They address the alcohol server's legal and professional responsibility to control and limit the consumption of alcohol to prevent drinking to intoxication, to prevent minors from drinking alcohol, and to prevent an intoxicated person from driving, as well as educate the server about the effects of alcohol on the body.

Alcohol is a drug, and it is very important to understand how this drug works on and in the human body. Intoxication is measured by the blood alcohol concentration (BAC), the amount of alcohol in the bloodstream, which is affected by the size, weight, and gender of the consumer, as well as other factors. These include the type of alcohol (distilled alcohol enters the bloodstream faster than beer and wine), food consumption (alcohol reaches the brain in a few minutes on an empty stomach and takes up to six hours on a full stomach), style of beverage (carbonation accelerates absorption, and warm beverages enter the bloodstream faster than cold ones), and combination with other drugs (i.e., prescription, over-the-counter, and illegal). The brain responds to alcohol in stages corresponding to an increase in BAC (see Figure 10-7). Alcohol is removed from the bloodstream by the liver at a rate of approximately one drink per hour; otherwise it continues to build concentration in the bloodstream.

RISK MANAGEMENT STRATEGIES FOR ALCOHOL SERVICE

There are a number of strategies the professional event coordinator may employ to reduce the risks associated with serving alcohol.

- Use only licensed liquor providers and trained bartenders.
- Always provide food with alcohol service, avoiding salty snacks (high-protein, high-fat foods are best).
- Do not place bars near the door, but do place food stations near the door so that guests will begin eating before drinking.
- Use a portion-control system (jiggers or Posi-Pour dispensers) rather than free pouring.
- Limit portions to 1 oz of distilled spirits per mixed drink, 5 oz of wine, and 12 oz of beer.
- Do not allow doubles or shots.
- *Never* allow self-service.
- Close bars 30 minutes to one hour before the scheduled end of an event, offering coffee or other nonalcoholic beverage service for the remainder of the event.

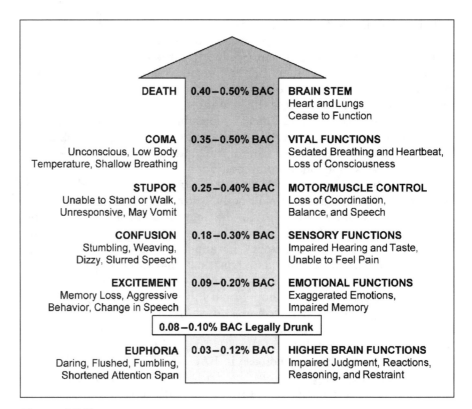

Figure 10-7
Stages of Blood Alcohol Concentration Effect on the Brain (*Adapted from* How Alcohol Works *by Craig C. Freudenrich, www.howstuffworks.com/alcohol.htm, and Hospitality Industry Education Advisory Committee,* Server Program Manual, *www.hieac.com/training/server/.)*

- Do not announce a "last call."
- Feature attractive alcohol-free drinks.
- Implement a designated driver program (perhaps offering free non-alcoholic beverages to drivers).
- Arrange for a subsidized taxi or other transportation service to drive guests home.
- Purchase liquor liability insurance for the hosting organization.
- Monitor entrance to the event and issue credentials.
- Arrange for security personnel.
- Provide "family" or "dry" (alcohol-free) seating areas at sporting or festival venues.

COST MANAGEMENT STRATEGIES

When negotiating contracts with the venue or liquor provider for a beverage function, you should specify how the pricing and consumption are to be calculated. For cash bar service (the guest pays for individual drinks), identify the prices to be charged for drinks and the fee for the bartender if a minimum of sales is not reached. For hosted bar service (the host pays), determine pricing based on consumption (per drink or per bottle) and conduct a bar reading before and at the conclusion of the event (counting the bottles opened and empties), and for per-person/per-hour prices, specify how the number of guests will be determined. If providing your own alcohol (either purchased or donated), determine the corkage fees and drink setup charges for the venue to serve the beverages.

Cost-saving measures include having servers pour wine rather than placing opened bottles on tables, providing drink tickets or coupons for two drinks only at hosted bars having guests pay for additional drinks, shortening the length of the beverage function, serving only beer and wine, serving frozen drinks (because patrons are less able to determine the amount of alcohol in the drink, you can use less alcohol), insisting on 1-oz jiggers, and using smaller glasses for beer and wine to make smaller portions look larger.

PUBLIC VERSUS PRIVATE EVENTS

There are usually significant differences between public and private events as related to alcohol service. Public events are often subject to stricter standards of care regarding the sale and serving of alcoholic beverages than private social events. They also often attract a different type of attendee, which must be carefully considered in determining whether to include alcohol in the event at all (particularly at sports events attracting rowdy fans). Additional attention must be paid to the use of licensed purveyors, attendance and credentialing control, and the segregation of serving areas, as well as securing the appropriate permissions from governmental agencies.

Private events, however, are not exempt from your duty of care. With respect to third-party liability, social host laws in the United States specify that the host of a party or function that provides alcohol to its guests can be held responsible for the actions of the guests if alcohol has been served improperly. Whenever possible, you are advised to always arrange for a licensed liquor caterer or purveyor to provide and serve alcoholic beverages at any function. You should also be wary of serving alcohol at any private functions where the attendees are participating in physical or sports activities, because people are more prone to accidents when they have been drinking.

Nutraceuticals	Use of food for self-medication and disease prevention linked to cancer, immune system, aging, heart disease, osteoporosis, diabetes, and high blood pressure; increased intake of calcium-rich, added-fiber, high-protein, and organic foods (genetically engineered foods are controversial); selecting health-promoting ingredients; increased use of probiotics to improve intestinal health and manage digestive problems; use of fresh herbs for medicinal benefits
Comfort Food	"Mom" food—basic, hearty, and familiar foods; authenticity and simplicity over innovation, ("enough of zoo food": ostrich, bison, etc.); quality, fresh ingredients; root vegetables; healthy snacks
Positive Eating	Selection of foods that contain desirable ingredients, do not contain undesirable ingredients, and are fortified with specific vitamins and minerals; limited fat, sugar, salt, and caffeine intake; increased intake of nutrient-dense foods such as grains, legumes, "good" oils, and soy products; shift from animal-based to plant-derived products (vegetarian-based menus)
Performance Eating	Consumption of food and beverages to improve mental performance, provide physical and emotional energy, and relieve depression; eating more minimeals rather than three full meals; consuming fat burners, sports drinks, and weight-loss products (the World Health Organization reported in 1999 that there are now more people overweight than underweight worldwide); selecting foods customized to gender, age, sports, etc.
Global Eating	Growing global and regional ethnic influence on what we eat; seeking variety and selecting new ethnic ingredients and exotic flavors; stimulating the senses with new and different foods available through global imports; incorporating ingredient palettes, spices, and sauces from all over the world
Agri-Tourism	Tasting the local cuisine when traveling; selecting locally grown produce and herbs; authentic and indigenous ingredients; fresh seasonal ingredients; increased awareness of where foods come from, how they are raised, and how they get to market

Sources: Elizabeth A. Sloan (2002), "The Top 10 Functional Food Trends: The Next Generation," Food Technology 56(4):32–56; Restaurants and Institutions (www.ring.com); NACE, The Professional (www.nace.net/procaterer/feb.02/theplate.html); Virginia Cattle Industry Board (www.vabeef.org/rffoodtrends.htm); Food Trends for 2000 (www.everything2000.com/news/news2000/foodtrends2000.asp); Johanna Burkhard, Top Ten Food Trends (www.mochasofa. ca/food/program/articles/02220103.asp); Institute of Food Technologists, Top Ten Food Trends (www.oznet.ksu.edu/ext_F&N/_Timely/topten.htm); Pat Kendall, (2000), "A Look at Food Trends in 2000 and Beyond," ColoradoState University Cooperative Extension (www.ext.colostate.edu/pubs/columnnn/nn000126.html); www.foodtv.com/cooking101/qandafoodnetworkkitchen2002trends/0,6988,,00.html; www.foodchannel.com; www.opta-food.com/ trends/2trends.html.

Figure 10-8
Food Trends for the Twenty-first Century

Twenty-first-century Food Trends

The professional event coordinator should be familiar with current and emerging food trends in order to select the catering organizations that offer the food products expected by clients and guests (see Figure 10-8). New flavors and new foods come into fashion at different times and in different places. Food fashions may come and go, but healthy eating, high-quality ingredients, authenticity, freshness, variety, and flavor remain top on any list of food trends. To keep current on the very latest, many experts advise that the event coordinator scan the menus of five-star restaurants in his or her area (or the area in which the event is to take place) and review the culinary industry's periodicals for the most popular food items and developments. The University of Nevada, Las Vegas, maintains a large collection of food links for caterers, chefs, and hospitality management students at www.unlv.edu/Tourism/catres.html.

Target Competency Review

Food and beverages are a significant aspect of most events, and the right selection of menu and service can enhance an event experience. The professional event coordinator must determine the functional needs of the food service to be provided and the preferential needs and desires of the host and guest. To select the best catering operation to meet these needs, wants, and desires, the professional event coordinator must be familiar with the types of catering operations available at or for the event location, type, size, scope, and purpose. The professional event coordinator must also understand how a catering organization conducts its operations in order to integrate those operations into the event site and other plans.

The professional event coordinator must be cognizant of the nutritional, physical, and emotional aspects of the foods we eat in order to select the menus that will fulfill the needs and desires of the attendees, participants, or staff to be fed, as well as the goals and objectives of the sponsoring host. Menu planning is based on the type of meal function, when the meal function is to take place, and the dietary preferences and restrictions of those being fed. The price of the food and beverage service selected will depend on the quantities and qualities of food required, the type of service requested, and the production costs involved. The menu planned must meet the hospitality objectives of the event as well as the budgetary restrictions. The menus selected should include foods and beverages that are healthy, fresh, full of flavor and variety, and suitable for the event agenda and the desired event experience.

The professional event coordinator must ensure that the catering operations are in complete compliance with all health and safety regulations and that providers have the appropriate licenses and insurance coverage required. This is particularly important when including alcohol service in an event, because of the potential risks and health implications associated with alcohol consumption. The professional event coordinator must be familiar with the effects of alcohol and the strategies to reduce and control risks, based on the context of an event and its crowd.

EXERCISES IN PROFESSIONAL EVENT COORDINATION

Outline and describe the food and beverage services you would employ for the following events, including the menu(s) and the service style selected. Explain the logistical requirements associated with the food and beverage service and how these will be incorporated into your overall event plan.

1. You have been contracted to coordinate the catering for an all-day golf outing for an incentive program, including an upscale luncheon inside a tent at the ninth hole. The 72 participants are the top salespeople for a pharmaceutical company known for its vitamin products, who expect to be wined and dined extravagantly.

2. You are coordinating a four-day international conference for 500 health care administrators to be held completely on-property at a remote seaside resort. You expect at least one-third of the attendees to have special dietary requests.

3. A new department store in a very upscale area of town has contracted you to coordinate a retail event with refreshments, to draw customers in to tour its various departments. The store's biggest concerns, however, are keeping costs down and making sure the food and beverage service does not soil or cause damage to its merchandise.

Facing Page

Many events gain important revenues by selling official souvenirs and commemorative items. *Photograph courtesy of Mike Rudahl.*

CHAPTER 11

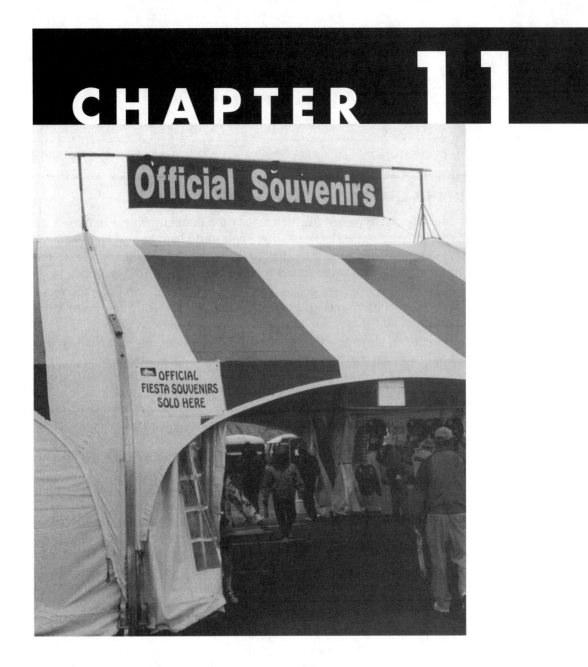

Making Event Memories

It is just the little touches after the average man would quit that make a master's fame.

—Orison Swett Marden, founder of Success Magazine

IN THIS CHAPTER YOU WILL LEARN HOW TO:

- Identify the types of and resources for mementos and materials required to enhance the marketing goals and objectives of an event.
- Organize award programs that provide the proper tangible and ceremonial recognition for award recipients.
- Select the appropriate prizes, gifts, and amenities to express the requisite appreciation, recognition, and commemoration to the event attendees and stakeholders.
- Conduct fair and equitable contests and competitions that comply with applicable legislative regulations.
- Identify and procure souvenirs and promotional merchandise appropriate for the direct sales marketing strategy of the event.

The event coordinator was meeting with the chief executive of a company to discuss the annual employee picnic. They had decided to hold a series of silly games as one of the entertainment activities. The chief executive wanted to award blue ribbons for the winners of each competition, but the event coordinator suggested creating enough blue ribbons for all the employees in totally unrelated award categories for such things as Most Creative Suntan and Best Use of Condiments. When asked why, the event coordinator replied, "Everyone needs to feel like a winner."

Making event memories relies on the ability to create a legacy by connecting personally with the people who have participated in the event experience. Human beings want and need attention and recognition. They need to be part of a group, excel in activities, learn new things (about the world, themselves, and others), share an experience, and treasure the moments in their lives. Many of these needs are met in the context of an event when people are gathered together to celebrate successes, express appreciation, share information, show off, confer, compete, and commemorate the special moments in their lives.

The professional event coordinator has an opportunity to recognize and celebrate achievements, contributions, accomplishments, and attendance with tangible tokens that make an event more meaningful and

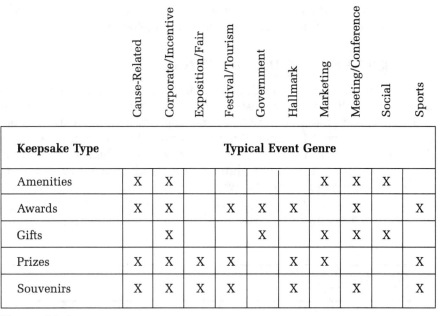

Keepsake Type	Cause-Related	Corporate/Incentive	Exposition/Fair	Festival/Tourism	Government	Hallmark	Marketing	Meeting/Conference	Social	Sports
Typical Event Genre										
Amenities	X	X					X	X	X	
Awards	X	X		X	X	X		X		X
Gifts		X			X		X	X	X	
Prizes	X	X	X	X		X	X			X
Souvenirs	X	X	X	X		X		X		X

Figure 11-1
Typical Events Using Keepsakes

memorable, thus increasing the value of the event. Awards, prizes, gifts, souvenirs, and other amenities are used to increase awareness, encourage performance, reward actions, enhance objectives, sculpt behavior, express appreciation, and retain volunteers, employees, sponsors, and customers. These are *keepsakes*—items kept for the sake of remembering the event experience. They can be incorporated into an event, based on the type and purpose of the event (see Figure 11-1).

Creating a Legacy

Mementos are physical reminders of an event experience, creating a legacy for the event as these keepsakes are displayed, used, and shared with or shown to others after the event. Both souvenirs collected and gifts given at an event keep the memories of the event alive for an individual. Functional items recall the event experience each time they are used. Decorative items remind the viewer of the occasion. Some items become more valuable over time as collectables; others become more meaningful as the owner collects a progression of keepsakes at subsequent events. A well-chosen memento helps to make an event unforgettable.

SUPPORTING MARKETING OBJECTIVES

The professional event coordinator should consider promotional products and advertising specialties for each dimension or facet of the event experience, from the invitation to a departing gift, with the marketing objectives of the event in mind. Such items must be selected to reinforce the message and purpose of the event, as well as enhance its meaning to the recipient. These items should be created or selected based on the event's image or imprinted with the logo of the event to support branding objectives. They should also be considered part of the image-building process and integrated into the overall marketing plan.

On-Site Insight

Brenda Schwerin, CSEP, of SYNAXIS Meetings & Events, Inc., in West Hollywood, California, uses toys, trinkets, and other promotional products to spice up her meetings.

Innovative and creative promotional products can excite people and create a "buzz" or anticipation prior to an event. Trinkets help "break the ice" between people, helping to start a conversation and making guests feel comfortable. A trinket is not only a memento of the event but a way to market your client's name or sponsor's company name. Along with providing a keepsake and marketing your company, it brings out the childlike nature in guests and serves as a tool for interactive fun at events. In a meeting, an educational toy can assist those who have trouble paying attention because handling toys can actually help a person retain the verbal and visual information presented. Trinkets can assist in softening up the sometimes-sterile environment that can loom in a meeting.

Shannon's meetings have been found to be very effective as the participants are provided with an abundance of toys and trinkets that foster creativity and camaraderie.

The Promotional Products Association International (PPAI) suggests that the promotional objectives these products may help to achieve include building an image, commemorating or recognizing, developing trade show traffic, educating or motivating employees or customers, encouraging attendance/involvement, stimulating sales, introducing new products or services, and promoting safety or other programs (www.ppai.org). Edward A. Chapman Jr., author of *Exhibit Marketing,* advises, "Premiums, incentives, advertising specialties, or giveaways are sometimes called 'trash and trinkets' by exhibit managers. Clearly defined goals must be developed. If a memory is to be created, the item should reinforce your sales message."

There are opportunities for meeting an attendee's needs with functional promotional items or mementos at any point when the attendee needs or wants to do something at an event. When such items are presented, whether they are mouse pads given out at a trade show or gift bags filled with indigenous edibles given to guests attending a destination wedding, an impression is made and a message is sent. Promotional messages or logos may be imprinted on hundreds of thousands of items, ranging from coffee mugs to chocolates, yarmulkes to yo-yos. The professional event coordinator must consider the event location and theme, consumer trends and audience profile, quality and quantity required, budgetary constraints, and customization capabilities.

On-Site Insight

Dana Zita, CSEP of a N d Logistix, Inc., in Toronto, Canada, an event management company specializing in corporate incentive trips and conferences, says she is always making time to listen to suppliers and sourcing new items and ideas for promotional products for her clients. She and her staff brainstorm tag lines and store gimmicky items for later use, often sending out examples with her company logo on them to communicate the message, "We can do this for your event." Zita also notes that the type and quality of the item must match the level of the event. "For incentive programs, the invitation has to be as nice as the items they will get while on the trip—even the ticket wallets and agendas must be special." And if the budget has been cut, Zita reports that the attendees will notice and comment on the difference. "What happened to the room gift?"

PUTTING LEGS ON THE EVENT

Physical tokens "put legs on an event," meaning that they extend the length of time the message of the event is communicated. This suggests that the more functional or desirable the item, the longer the message will be communicated. A customized calendar almost guarantees 12 to 18 months of visibility. Logo watches or clocks can provide an hourly reminder. (I still use a travel alarm clock I received as a speaker gift years ago.) Clothing items with an event emblem may be worn during the event, then for months or years afterward. Logo-imprinted computer peripherals rest on desks, and customized trophies, certificates, plaques, and framed photographs are proudly displayed on or in "memory" walls or cabinets in homes and offices. The professional event coordinator must consider the marketing function the amenity is to fill as well as the functionality of the item after the event and its potential branding legacy.

The legs or legacy of an event and its image will be particularly important to commercial sponsors of an event held in conjunction with their own branding objectives. Not only do these mementos provide the event organization with opportunities for recognizing sponsors, they are also prime packages for securing underwriting by sponsors. Leonard H. Hoyle Jr., CAE, CMP, author of *Event Marketing: How to Successfully Promote Events, Festivals, Conventions, and Expositions,* notes, "At your event itself, many opportunities exist for the marketing of the event and its sponsoring organization, creating not just a helpful item but also a memento of the event for the attendee to enjoy far beyond the final gavel . . . an effective cross-promotion, which is granted not just for an advertising fee but also to cover the cost of producing the [item]." The cobranding on such items benefits both event and commercial sponsor, but must be specifically agreed upon and contractually controlled.

On-Site Insight

When coordinating a regional educational conference in 2001 for the International Special Events Society, Kathy Nelson, CSEP, CMP, professor in the Tourism and Convention Administration Department of the University of Nevada, Las Vegas (UNLV), arranged for a special sponsorship of the conference bags for attendees. Aimee V. Brizuela, one of Nelson's former event management students at UNLV, had recently lost her parents, and when approached by Nelson in regard to supporting the event in some way, responded in the affirmative as a memorial to them because they had been so proud of her accomplishments in the field.

"The conference sponsorship was the first event that I undertook after I lost both of my parents. It was the beginning of the 'healing process' for me. My parents loved special events dearly and were always supportive of my passion for the spe-

> cial event industry. It was a way for me to 'include' them in my passion for event design. Naming the sponsorship in their honor was a simple way of remembering their love and respect for the professional event industry." Brizuela decided on high-quality messenger sling bags in blue and pink neon colors with an engraved insert—"Donated in Loving Memory of Victoria and Hugo Bennett Brizuela." These conference bags brought added value to the conference for the attendees and created a legacy commemorating a daughter's love.

Memorabilia and commemorative items are not only mementos of a single event; they may attain collectable status independent of the event and/or increase in value (either monetary or emotional) when obtained in succession. This is why such items must be branded and dated. Commemorative posters often appreciate in value when part of a series—something many annual festivals capitalize on for important revenue streams. Lapel pins signifying the number of years in service to a company or contributions made to an organization are often differentiated in design or material used, such as different gemstones for different levels of service or financial contribution. You might consider such items as a potential revenue stream for your event or as a way in which you can foster a sense of community and camaraderie within various stakeholder groups.

Awards and Award Ceremonies

Everyone loves to feel like a winner—to be recognized and honored for his or her achievements, accomplishments, contributions, expertise, beauty, talent, or just plain tenacity. Events of all types include or are staged to provide tangible and ceremonial recognition for anything from a particular act to a lifetime of good works. The tangible expression is the actual award presented, and the ceremonial recognition is the way in which that award is presented, both of which must be selected and coordinated in a manner that has value to the recipient and meets the goals and objectives of the presenting organization.

DETERMINE PURPOSE AND SCOPE

The professional event coordinator must determine the purpose for conducting an awards program and the scope of that program in order to select the appropriate awards and integrate the program into the overall event plan. The professional coordinator must identify the why, who, what, where, when, and how of the awards program. Every awards program has a purpose or motive for existing (see Figure 11-2) and should have specific and measurable objectives. The objectives may be based on sculpting desired behavior, motivating specific actions, increasing productivity, promoting certain agendas, attaching importance to accomplishments, and/or providing important revenues to the sponsoring organization.

The award recipients may be selected via competition, level of contribution, nomination, or consensus. They may be citizens, competitors, employees, entrants, members, officials, participants, patrons, supporters, or volunteers. Their motives for participating in an awards program may include recognition for personal achievements and/or expertise, professional promotion, esteem, power, and prestige. The common theme, however, is recognition of the recipient, which must be factored into the event's overall marketing and promotional strategy. You may need to solicit entrants, recognize nominees, promote participation, coordinate me-

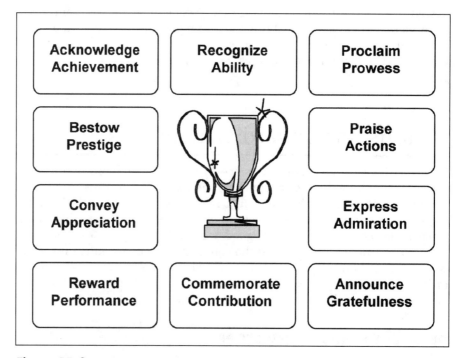

Figure 11-2
Purposes of Awards

dia coverage, and/or create special events within an event to celebrate the recipients.

IDENTIFY THE PROGRAM LOGISTICS

The professional event coordinator must identify the program logistics from selection to presentation. He or she must identify the type, quality, and supplier of the awards to be presented and determine the costs associated with procurement and presentation, which must be factored into the budget. The *where* must be integrated into the site plan, the *when* into the timeline, and the *how* into the operational plan of the event. Protocol requirements must be identified, procedures must be established, propriety must be confirmed, and the presentation production must be determined.

The awards ceremony may be part of an overall event program or the very purpose of the event. It may be a stand-alone ceremony, be incorporated into a meal function with different awards presented before or during different courses, precede or follow a meal function or other event component, be part of a meeting agenda, directly follow a competition, or be the focus of closing ceremonies. Darcy Campion Devney, author of *Organizing Special Events and Conferences,* suggests that presentations must be scheduled when they are assured attendance, avoiding the very first and last activities of a day or agenda. Whenever the awards presentation and/or ceremony is to take place, it must be given the same attention as if it were an event unto itself.

On-Site Insight

Steve Kemble of Steve Kemble Event Design in Dallas, Texas, advises that the type of ceremony depends on the personality of the group. He reports that his corporate groups prefer to have a separate awards ceremony (about 45 minutes long) in a separate auditorium or ballroom that is exciting and stimulating for the audience, yet with a clean, straightforward presentation, and then to move on into the dinner and party in a different room. "We all love award ceremonies, but in so many situations we have to remember that half the audience couldn't care less about that portion of the program. They didn't submit entries; they're not receiving an award; they didn't participate; they're just there for the party! The burden is then on us as

(Continued)

event designers to develop ways to make the entire program more interesting (and, we hope, to entice them to participate or enter next year)."

Kemble also notes that awards programs are "very big deals" to companies and associations and that his clients want "a serious and sophisticated ceremony that is well organized, tight in its presentation, that moves along at a great pace, and gives the opportunity for recipients to come up and say a few brief words, and BOOM, you're on to the next one. They are getting away from too much flash on stage. All that song and dance takes the focus off the award itself and the ability to showcase the person receiving it. We're there to show respect for those who are being honored. Don't diminish the value of the award by surrounding it with a lot of fluff."

The award recipient or recipients may be predetermined prior to the ceremony or selected on-site at the event. If recipients are be predetermined via judging, but the announcement of the winner is an on-site surprise, you don't want to ruin the moment by calling to confirm attendance. You do, however, want to ensure that the winners are present whenever possible. Steve Kemble suggests, "People want to see the winners. It is incumbent on the planner to do some due diligence and make sure they are there, perhaps calling an assistant, friend, or relative." It may also be appropriate to contact a family member or friend of an individual who is to be honored with a special award, but does not know about it beforehand, to ensure that those close to the recipient are present to share in the celebration while maintaining the secrecy and surprise. If the winners or recipients are to remain secret, you must ensure the security of that secret information within your operational practices and with the involved stakeholders.

SELECTION CRITERIA AND JUDGING

The crucial part of any awards program is the establishment of equitable selection criteria and judging procedures. Entry procedures must be clear and concise, and the judging process must be impeccably fair. The professional event coordinator may or may not be involved in the selection of recipients, but he or she must know how recipients are selected in order to integrate the program into the event timeline and agenda. Steve Kemble notes, "A successful awards program starts with the guidelines and rules for entering. If you make those easy to read and attainable, then people feel as though they can enter and win. The way they are written is a big indicator as to whether this is going to be a legitimate and fair competition and not just a popularity contest." Kemble advises that you have the rules reviewed by a committee and the entry guidelines reviewed by a broad spectrum of potential entrants to ensure that they are understandable and reasonable.

The selection criteria should be identified for all award categories, specifying the levels of performance required to qualify or the measurements the judges will be instructed to employ when reviewing entries or participants. The entry forms or guidelines should answer the question "How do I do this so I can win?" You must specify what materials in what format are to be included in an entry, what documentation will be required to qualify, where the submission should be sent or delivered, the deadlines for submission or qualification, and the date and manner in which nominees, winners, or qualifiers (and those not nominated, winning, or qualifying) will be notified.

If the awards program is a competition, the jury or judging committee should be selected carefully to ensure that they are qualified to evaluate the submissions entered, preferably a panel of industry or professional peers, and that they are recognized as reputable and ethical individuals. In *The Arts Festival Work Kit,* authors Pam Korza and Dian Magie suggest that jurors should be chosen to create a balanced panel representing expertise, involvement (practitioners, educators, etc.), male and female, ethnic diversity, and geographic equitability. Judges should be provided with a copy of the entry instructions as well as the evaluation criteria they are to use when reviewing submissions. Judges may be asked to interview entrants, view examples of the entrants' work, or evaluate the entry documentation.

The winner or qualifier may be selected based on a voting system (by simply counting the number of nominations or votes) or on the basis of a score received, or may be selected after a consensus has been reached among the judges or members of a selection committee. Many people believe that a "blind" or anonymous judging process is the most equitable, wherein each entry is identified by an entry number rather than the entrant's name (and the name is not visible anywhere within the entry) and the judging is based on a private scoring mechanism rather than consensus (preventing one strong personality from influencing or dominating the outcome).

SELECTING AND CUSTOMIZING THE AWARD

Awards may take the form of trophies, loving cups, framed certificates, plaques, statuettes, bowls, sculptures, medals, ribbons, paperweights, clocks, or artworks. They may be small, medium-sized, or tall, multi-tiered trophies as large as the recipient (often popular for sports events and children's beauty pageants—with the trophy towering above the toddler winning it). They may be made of plain or precious metal, crystal, glass, Plexiglas, ceramics, wood, or other materials. They may be purchased from a supplier of recognition merchandise or commissioned from an artist or craftsperson and may be relatively inexpensive or extremely costly. You may need to have security to protect such articles against theft (and for secrecy of the winner's identity) before and at the event.

Awards should be inscribed with the logo of the event or organization (branding), the name of the award and/or category, the recipient's name, and the date of the presentation. Engraving or customizing takes time and should be done prior to the ceremony if the recipient is known beforehand, or the name may be added after the event if the winner is not determined until the ceremony takes place. The professional event coordinator must make *absolutely certain* that all names and titles are spelled correctly. It is possible to have a mock award available for presentation and photographs at the event and then have the actual award engraved and sent to the recipient later. It may also be a good idea to arrange for a shipping service to ship awards home for recipients when the ceremony takes place in a city or country different from the recipient's place of residence. (I recently came home from an international conference with four awards that added 20 pounds to my already overstuffed and overweight luggage.)

AWARD PRESENTATION DYNAMICS

The logistical dynamics of an award presentation must be integrated into the production design and schedule, and you must have a script. How will the awards be displayed, if at all, prior to the presentation? Who will present the award itself? How will you get the award from the display area to the presenter? Will you have "trophy boys or girls" to run on and off the stage to hand over statuettes? Will the presenter need to have an introduction prepared? Will you need to have a description of the nominee's entry read and/or visuals projected prior to announcing the winner? How will you secure those visuals? Do you need to videotape interviews prior to the event, to be played at the event, or will you allow recipients to express their feelings live? Will the recipients come out of the audience to accept the award, or will they make an entrance from backstage? Will you have a follow spot to shine on a recipient as he or she goes from the audience to the stage? The entire procedure must be envisioned, and every detail must be prepared.

It is important to remember that this is, after all, a ceremony, and the appropriate pomp and circumstance must be incorporated into the program. You must choreograph all entrances and exits for presenters, recipients, assistants, and the emcee. You may wish to include a parade of all the nominees at the beginning of the ceremony to communicate the high honor of their being nominated. To ensure that the ceremony moves at the appropriate pace, you may wish to include walk-up and fanfare music, and you may need to advise all recipients or nominees of a time limit for acceptance speeches. Presenters should be rehearsed and should be prepared and instructed on how to "accept this award on behalf of . . ." should the winner not be present. These winning moments should always be captured on film, but not necessarily onstage. Most award ceremonies now set up a photo area offstage where the official documentation (and souvenir) photographs are taken.

Prizes, Gifts, and Amenities

Many types of events incorporate prizes, gifts, and amenities to increase excitement and create memorable moments within the event. These items enhance the celebratory aspects of an event and provide take-away value for the participants. The professional event coordinator must determine how and when these items will be incorporated into the event and how they will be presented (individually or collectively, privately or publicly). The costs of purchasing them must be factored into the budget, and the logistics of presentation must be incorporated into the event's operational plans.

UNDERSTAND THE MOTIVES

The professional event coordinator must understand the motives of the sponsor or host, as well as those of the winner or recipient. Contests are often conducted to increase participation and promotional coverage, and they are entered in order to acquire something important to the winner. Raffles are often held to raise important funds for the organization, and participants wish to support the cause while also having a chance to win a valuable prize for a small investment. Door prize drawings are often conducted to generate qualified mailing lists for an organization and give registrants an opportunity to walk away with valuable gifts. Gifts and commemorative tokens are given to recognize status or express appreciation. Incentives are given and incentive programs are conducted to reinforce and reward desired behavior or performance. Mementos are presented to create added value and enhance the experience. There is always a reason for investing in these items, both for the giver and the receiver, which will help determine what should be given and when. The more valuable the object or recognition is to the recipient, the more likely he or she will participate and the more likely the host's objectives will be met.

AUTHORIZE PROPRIETY AND APPROPRIATE CHOICES

Although most people love getting any type of prize or gift at any time, the professional event coordinator must always investigate the propriety of giving prizes or gifts and the propriety of the prizes or gifts to be given. Some attendees may be contractually prohibited from accepting gifts of a certain type or value, and others may be ethically prohibited from accepting any gifts at all because a gift may be perceived as an unfair inducement or bribe. Some dignitaries should not be given gifts of a certain type or value for cultural, political, or protocol reasons, and some government officials (or employees) are prohibited from accepting gifts of any value whatsoever. Some people may have religious, cultural, or physical restrictions that prohibit accepting (or using) certain types of gifts, such as wine or other alcohol. The event coordinator must examine the protocols and determine the restrictions on gift giving in order to select appropriate gifts that will achieve the objectives for giving and will not offend the receiver or be left behind in the hotel room for the housekeeping staff to clear away. When budgeting for amenities, it is important not to waste money on inappropriate gifts.

AMENITIES ADD MEANING—AT A PRICE

Gifts and amenities are gestures of appreciation that show how much the event host or sponsor cares about the attendee or guest. Every aspect of such a gift, from selection to presentation, will have costs attached that must be incorporated into the event budget, particularly if those costs are to be packaged into the price of a sponsorship of an item. This includes not only the gift or amenity itself; it also includes the procurement, customization (printing or imprinting), the packaging, and the delivery. There may be shipping costs, personnel costs to prepare or parcel out the items, the cost of the boxes or bags to package the gift, and hotel charges for the room drop (hotel staff delivering items) to individual guest rooms or to store and deliver items to the event office. Preparing gift bags or registration kits for 2000 attendees may take a small army of personnel and incur rental charges for the room in which it takes place. Asking the caterer to place table gifts while laying the dinner tables may incur additional labor fees. There may be a charge for the housekeeping staff to add special soaps or other products to toilet facilities or reception areas.

WELCOME, SPEAKER, AND PILLOW GIFTS

Welcome gifts are often placed in guests' rooms prior to arrival or given upon arrival. Speakers and dignitaries are often presented with commemorative tokens at the close of their appearance as a gesture of appreciation by the hosting organization. Incentive groups often receive gifts each night of their trip, placed in their rooms on their pillows (hence the term *pillow gifts*), which are designed to remind them of the day they just experienced or to promote the next day's activities. These gifts should always be considered from the recipients' point of view. Where are the recipients coming from? How long will they be at the event? What will they be doing while at the event? When and where are they going after the event? How are they getting there?

These gifts should be functional as well as gestural. A welcome basket should consist of items capable of being consumed during the person's stay or something that will facilitate participation in the event to come. Thank-you or speaker gifts should be selected with regard to their physical size and weight (must the item be packed for the flight home?) as well as their suitability for the event's objectives and the recipient's preferences. Although a person may not refuse the gift, it may be left behind unused or passed along to someone else, which is not the intent in budgeting for these gifts. Note that in regard to giving alcohol as gifts, a fine wine may seem to be both consumable and an elegant gesture; however, you must carefully consider its appropriateness. Giving alcoholic beverages as gifts may carry the same liabilities as serving alcohol, and alcohol may not be a suitable gift for an individual who does not imbibe. (Or you could have an inebriated or hungover speaker standing at the lectern the next day.)

Pillow gifts offer the professional event coordinator an opportunity to facilitate a progressive experience. Customized apparel can provide the personal costuming or sportswear needed for the next day's special events, such as a tournament, team activity, or theme party. Indigenous arts and crafts can provide a unique memento of a destination to be visited. Novels by local authors can provide a literary insight into sights seen, and picture books or photographs can commemorate places visited. When selecting gifts for a progressive presentation, the professional event coordinator should allocate the budget for gifts so that the final gift is the most impressive and memorable.

FUN AND FAIR CONTESTS

Contests are often incorporated into an event's promotional strategy to increase awareness and/or revenues and are included in the event's activities to encourage participation. Prizes are given to recognize a particular talent or proficiency, specific characteristics or effort, or by the luck of the draw, and the prizes awarded can include anything from a door prize to a grand prize to a booby prize. You might be conducting a drawing, raffle, beauty or talent contest (for people, pets, or photos), endurance or proficiency contests, games of skill, games of chance, or sport competitions. You might be awarding certificates, coupons, crowns, food, medals, merchandise, money, ribbons, scholarships, services, travel, trinkets, or trophies. Door prize drawings are very popular for increasing traffic and building databases. Raffles are very popular as fund-raising mechanisms. For boosting income at fund-raising events, Harry A. Freedman and Karen Feldman, authors of *The Business of Special Events,* suggest selling chances for prizes by selling numbered rubber ducks in a duck pond, keys to a treasure chest, grab bags, and selling guesses (e.g., the number of jelly beans in a jar).

Contests and games are fun, but they must be carefully planned to ensure that they are impeccably fair, particularly as the prizes increase in value. All aspects of a contest, from the methods for entry to the prizes to be awarded, must be meticulously planned before the contest is to commence. A time frame must be established specifying when the contest will begin and end, when entry forms will be available, the entry deadlines, and when winners will be selected and notified. A budget must be established to cover all the administration, marketing, equipment, prizes, and other costs associated with the contest. Then all the components of the contest must be integrated into the overall event plan and timeline.

- **Entry rules**—Specify who is eligible to enter; the fees for entering, what qualifications must be met and/or what materials must be submitted (e.g., puzzle solution, proof of purchase, etc.); how many times an individual may enter; how the winners will be selected (method and criteria); and whether an individual must be present to win.
- **Entry procedures**—Determine the distribution and collection system for entry forms (or raffle tickets/keys) and specify where, when, and how to enter; specify ownership of the entry materials.
- **Entry form**—Collect the required information (name, address, telephone number, etc.); clearly specify contents or limits of prize(s); include rules and regulations (the entry form can be considered a contract).
- **Prize system**—Determine the hierarchy of graduated value, size, names, color, etc.; purchase or solicit prizes from sponsors and donors; display prizes.
- **Selection procedures**—Specify criteria to be used to evaluate contestants and select judges; specify the method for drawing a winner (e.g., first come first draw, or one working key to a prize or prize container) and the entry form container; and specify how ties will be broken.

- **Prize presentation**—Determine the date and time and method for announcing winner(s); engage celebrities or dignitaries to present prizes; determine how a prize will be delivered if not on-site or if the winner is not present (shipped or picked up); determine how unclaimed prizes will be handled.
- **Publicity plan**—Publish and publicize contest rules and regulations, promote the contest, and publicize the results.
- **Security plan**—Determine the security system required for distribution, collection, and protection of entry forms; protection of prizes; and protection of entry fees.

LEGAL AND ETHICAL CONSIDERATIONS

When conducting a contest, first and foremost the professional event coordinator must confirm the propriety and legality of the contest, including any licenses, waivers, limitations, or specific wording of the rules required by the laws of the jurisdiction in which the contest is to be held (statements such as "Void Where Prohibited by Law," "All Decisions Are Final," etc. may have to be included). Some types of contests, particularly games of chance or raffles, may be strictly regulated by ordinances governing gaming or gambling, which could affect something as simple as a door prize drawing or coupon-entry contest. Fund-raising activities are often rigorously regulated and may require securing special permits, filing various tax forms, and preparing specific documentation.

The more valuable the prize, the more stringent the rules must be and the more the rules must be meticulously upheld. According to Ron Kaatz, author of *Advertising and Marketing Checklists,* "Whether you are conducting a large national sweepstakes or a small local contest, its success (and often the reputation and financial well-being of your company) can depend upon how clearly the rules are spelled out." Try to anticipate any way in which someone could abuse the entry procedure; then develop clear, fair, and unambiguous rules and regulations to prevent such loopholes. You must ensure that all contests are nondiscriminatory in terms of entry qualifications and access. You must also make certain that there is no actual or perceived conflict of interest with any of the event organizers or stakeholders. There must be no question as to the veracity of the outcome and how it was reached.

Souvenir Mementos and Merchandise

Many events, particularly those open to the public, incorporate the direct sale of merchandise into their marketing plan to provide souvenir mementos for the attendees and important revenues to the event organization. Whether planning to sell or give away such tokens of the event experience, the professional event coordinator must make certain that these souvenirs represent the event and the event organization appropriately and will have value for the buyer or recipient. The event coordinator may be selling commemorative collectibles, distributing souvenir programs, choosing concessionaires, licensing manufacturers, or creating the event's own logo merchandise. Providing a variety of souvenirs and for-sale merchandise allows the event attendee to select his or her own mementos, based on specific needs, desires, and the event experience he or she had, as well as the mementos to be shared with others who receive them as gifts after the event.

DEVELOP THE RETAIL MERCHANDISING PLAN

With respect to souvenir merchandise that will be sold to the event attendees, you must understand that these are *products*. These take-home memories must be selected, manufactured, promoted, and merchandised as any other product in the marketplace is, relying on sound marketing principles to shape the merchandising plan. However, as with any plan, you must determine the purpose of the merchandising plan and its position within the overall marketing plan. Are you selling souvenirs to increase revenues? To increase event visibility? To increase the legacy of the event? To meet customer demand? To enhance the event experience? To provide cross-promotional opportunities to sponsors? All of the above?

Merchandising should not be undertaken without a clear understanding of why and how it is important to the event and event organization's goals and objectives, as well as the impact it will have on the event and the safeguards required to implement a retail merchandising plan.

Donald Getz, author of *Event Management and Event Tourism*, suggests that the goals of a merchandising strategy are to "sell merchandise that benefits the event in terms of revenue, positive image, and long-term growth; partner with appropriate wholesalers and retailers in ways that maximize benefits to the event; license goods where the arrangement extends the reach of the event and secures revenue that could not otherwise be obtained; and regulate all merchandizing on and off the site to assure quality and proper image protection." If you do decide to invest in a merchandising program, you must approach it as any other retailer would. The four P's of an event merchandize marketing mix—Product, Price, Place, and Promotion—should be examined carefully in terms of how they will be integrated into the retail merchandising plan as well as the overall event operations plan. In *Event Marketing: How to Successfully Promote Events, Festivals, Conventions, and Expositions,* author Leonard Hoyle identifies a fifth "P"—Positioning—for target market segmentation, which is not addressed in this discussion because it will be inherent in the target audience identified for the event.

Product

You must determine whether there is a demand for souvenir merchandise and which products will meet the needs and desires of the event's buying public. The products you select will be determined based on the event type, date, location, and theme, as well as the target market represented by and representative of the audience, consumer trends, the quantity required, the quality and availability of items, the cost of production, and the lead time for ordering and reordering. You might be selling apparel, jewelry, pins and buttons, commemorative items, indigenous or event-themed crafts, functional items, decorative items, toys, posters and other printed items, and/or imprinted promotional products. Experts advise that you conduct market research in order to identify the items, and the features of those items, that will appeal to your audience. You must analyze the audience demographics and psychographics, review the history of souvenir sales at your event and at comparable events, and test market the items under consideration before investing in the merchandise.

Price

When determining which products you will offer, the retail price must match the perceived value of the item to the buyer. Some inexpensive products can be priced to include a significant profit margin because they are in great demand, whereas other products may command prices that include only a narrow profit margin. The prices that your audience will pay depend on the desirability of the particular item, the disposable income of the purchaser, and the competition for that purchase revenue. Many event organizers advise that you select a variety of products at low, medium, and higher price points in order to serve the variety of consumer budgets at your event. However, if you have an exclusive event with attendees just itching to spend serious amounts of money, by all means select high-end products with high-end prices.

Place

Place refers to distribution methods and where the products will be sold—how, when, and where the customer can make a purchase. The objective should be to make it convenient for the buyer to purchase your product at the time and place the buyer wishes to buy. You might have on-site sales kiosks, booths or stands, or walk-around vendors. You might also offer your merchandise via mail order through catalogs or an event Web site (see the following Technology Tip), through off-site retail outlets, on consignment or commission through community or affinity groups, and/or wholesaled through distributors. Products may be sold before, during, and after the event itself. Each type of distribution/sales method will require inventory management systems (ordering, maintaining, and controlling inventory), financial management systems (payment schedules to manufacturer and collecting and disbursing revenues or royalties), and distribution systems (shipping, retrieving unsold merchandise, and contingency plans for late arrival of merchandise).

On-site retail outlets should be positioned in high-traffic areas, including entrances and pathways to popular event features, as well as on the pathways to more functional features such as food service areas and toilet facilities. Analyze the traffic flow through the event site, and position permanent and temporary outlets based on the density of traffic as well as the type of traffic (you might have souvenirs targeted at different demographic groups that travel through the event site in different patterns). Also analyze the timing of the traffic flow so that you can ensure sufficient sales personnel and inventory for the peak sales times, often concentrated at the beginning or ending of the event or at specific attractions within the event. These on-site outlets must also be positioned where they are easily accessible for purposes of restocking inventory.

Promotion

If you are selling products, you must promote those products. Your merchandising strategy should include plans for advertising, promotions, cross-promotions, publicity, and the design of the retail outlet(s). You might use advertisements in your event program, signage throughout the event site, announcements over the public address system, and attractive and eye-catching displays at the points of sale. You should also identify potential promotional partners that can increase your coverage through cooperative advertising, including the distributors, manufacturers, media, sponsors, suppliers, and other stakeholder groups. Your merchandising promotion campaign must be integrated into your overall marketing plan and timed to coincide with your distribution and inventory management systems.

Technology Tip

Many events extend the marketability of their souvenir merchandise through e-commerce by offering it for sale on their Web sites, using a shopping cart system that generates an online catalog and allows customers to order and pay for products over the Internet. These systems allow you to create an on-line catalog with a searchable index by category and/or keyword that features photos (or thumbnail images the shopper may click on to see a full-size picture of an item), product descriptions and prices, and color and/or size options. On-line customers simply point and click their way through the catalog, adding their purchases to a shopping cart that maintains a running total on a scrolling receipt in a side frame, visible at all times, until the customer checks out and pays with a credit card via a secure server to your merchant account with a credit card processing gateway.

These systems also allow you to build a customer membership program wherein customers may register and the system will remember their billing and/or shipping addresses, shipping method, and payment preferences in a database, as well as allow customers to view a complete history of their orders. They also include a "Forgot Your Password" utility that can automatically e-mail the member his or her password to the registered e-mail address. This database may also be integrated into a blast e-mail program that allows you to e-mail newsletters, special offers, or promotions, or to issue coupons to your customers.

(SOURCES: www.smartcart.com/ and www.ecommerce-shopping-cart.biz/. Use the key words "shopping cart system" on any search engine for more resources.)

LOGO MERCHANDISE

Many public and repeat events, as well as event organizations and associations holding annual events, have recognizable logos or images that are emblazoned on a broad variety of merchandise items that are sold during an event and often year-round. This merchandise allows the purchaser to proclaim an affiliation with the event or organization as well as collect mementos of a specific event. From apparel items to zippered bags, logo merchandise can add significant revenues to an event's coffers, particularly if the items are of high quality and functional. Membership organizations should select items that are pertinent to the lifestyles and vocational activities of their members, promoting these goods not only as items members should collect but also as gifts for colleagues. Consecutive or annual events should consider the sequential collectability of progressive images and specific dates merged with the traditional branding or organizational logos.

PROTECTING YOUR IMAGE

Whether you are creating your own logo merchandise, granting a license to allow a manufacturer to put your logo on its products, or allowing vendors or concessionaires to sell products at your event, you are selling space, selling rights, and selling your image. You must always protect the image of the event and the event organization by carefully considering the partnerships you are entering into. Such protection can entail anything from establishing exclusive territories to product liability insurance or protection from counterfeit merchandise.

Donald Getz states, "Licensing is the legal tool used to obtain royalties, and protect the event's rights, when distributors and retailers are granted permission to sell event-related goods. In order to license products the event must have protection for its name, logo, or designs in the form of copyrights, trademarks, or other legal devices." This is a complex legal arrangement that must be handled by competent legal counsel to ensure that the licensing contracts protect and benefit the event organization as well as the licensee. Pick your partners carefully, and control the relationship with clear, comprehensive, and written agreements that specify all the operational details and image-protection conditions. Many event organizations contract out the entire merchandizing operation to professional retailers who have the experience and expertise to provide a profitable experience for both parties.

MERCHANDISING

The term *merchandising* also refers to how merchandise is displayed for sale. When setting up on-site sales outlets for event products, the professional event coordinator should adopt and adapt standard retailing methods to meet the needs and constraints of the event site and budget. You may be selling your merchandise from carts, kiosks, booths, stands, or tents. The sales area must be laid out to facilitate profitable traffic flow, including sufficient access to displays and products and sufficient aisle space (Paco Underhill, author of *Why We Buy: The Science of Shopping,* refers to this as the "butt-brush factor"—if aisles are so tight that shoppers are touched from behind, they become irritated and move on). The sales area should be brightly decorated so it is visible and recognizable as your souvenir outlet from a distance, and the interior should be designed to highlight your products and motivate shoppers to buy.

Completing the purchase should be efficient and easy. Your checkout counter(s) must have the appropriate equipment (cash registers, credit card terminals, etc.) and supplies (wrapping, bags, etc.) to complete the necessary transactions, and they must be staffed with efficient, friendly sales personnel. Your sales force must be properly trained to ensure that they are knowledgeable about the products, your inventory is maintained appropriately, and your cash-handling procedures are followed correctly.

The sale of merchandise at an event can be a profitable addition to your revenues, but it must be carefully planned and implemented to achieve the results you are seeking. If it is an afterthought, it will likely fall short of your revenue goals and objectives. The entire operation, from the accounting system to security at the retail outlet, must be integrated into your event site, budget, timeline, marketing, operations, and personnel plans to achieve success.

Target Competency Review

Tangible tokens help to create memories and achieve the marketing goals of an event and an event organization. The professional event coordinator must select the amenities, awards, gifts, prizes, and souvenirs to be presented by and available at the event so that they meet the objectives and expectations of the presenter and the recipient. Mementos, as reminders of the event experience, must support the marketing objectives of the event and must project the desired message and image, as well as extend the legacy of the event to provide a return on the investment made in them. These items may be functional or decorative and should be customized, branded, and dated to ensure they commemorate the event experience. Many of these keepsakes offer opportunities for sponsor recognition and sponsorship revenues.

Awards programs must be designed to provide the appropriate tangible and ceremonial recognition for the recipients, as well as encourage participation to achieve the underlying objectives for the program. The logistics of an awards program must be meticulously planned from selection to presentation, and all competitions and contests must be impeccably fair. All award, prize, and gift programs must conform to all legal restrictions and protocol requirements, and the professional event coordinator must confirm that the items presented are appropriate for the event context and culture.

The sale of souvenir mementos and merchandise provides important revenues for many events. When employing a retail merchandising plan, the professional event coordinator must apply sound marketing principles to the design, selection, promotion, and display of the products to be sold. By carefully considering the marketing mix of product, price, place, and promotion, the professional event coordinator will be able to secure and implement the direct sales of souvenir items that project and protect the image of the event and have value to the consumer. The giving and selling of tangible event keepsakes must be budgeted appropriately and integrated into the event's overall administrative, operational, and marketing plans to ensure a meaningful and profitable outcome.

EXERCISES IN PROFESSIONAL EVENT COORDINATION

Identify and describe the prizes, gifts, awards, souvenirs, and other mementos you would select and present at the following events. Explain the logistical requirements associated with these programs and how they will be incorporated into your overall event plan and budget.

1. The mayor of your city has appointed you to develop and coordinate a civic celebration that is to include recognition of ten citizens who have made significant contributions to the community in the past year. (You must determine the categories and selection process.)
2. You have been contracted to coordinate a five-day incentive reward trip whose winners are traveling to your destination. The itinerary consists of sports activities and sightseeing trips indigenous to your area, culminating in a final gala dinner at which the top performers in the incentive program will be recognized.
3. You are coordinating an annual four-day music festival including numerous music stages, each featuring a different popular music style, and numerous other exhibits and activities. The highlight is a "battle of the bands" with various local bands vying for prizes and promotional recognition. Your audience consists primarily of families and music fans. Your board of directors has charged you with creating new revenue streams through a retail merchandising program.

Facing Page
Special tours and excursions add an enriching dimension to many events. *Photograph by Mike Rudahl, courtesy of Expo Events, Inc.*

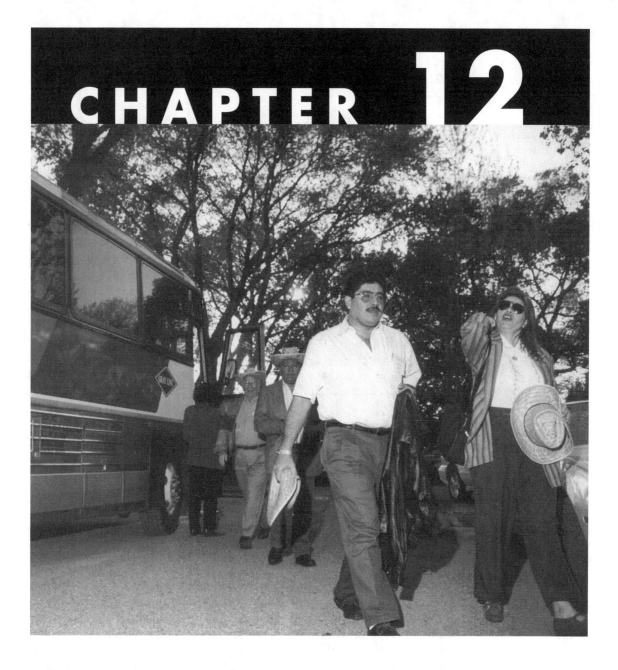

CHAPTER 12

Ancillary Programs

Simple pleasures . . . the last refuge of the complex.

—Oscar Wilde (1854–1900)

IN THIS CHAPTER YOU WILL LEARN HOW TO:

- Determine the need and purpose for ancillary programs in conjunction with the main event program.
- Develop companion programs and activities to occupy and entertain accompanying persons at an event.
- Identify and arrange for optional and integral side trips and tours that add value to the event experience.
- Coordinate special exhibits and activities that build interest, inform, and enhance an event.
- Organize sport and recreational activities to achieve the goals and objectives of an event.

The event coordinator was preparing her schedule for an international conference she was coordinating in a foreign country and set aside a week's vacation directly following the event before returning home. When her staff asked why she was staying on after the conference, she answered, "I've seen the inside of some of the finest hotels in the world. It's time I went outside."

Ancillary programs and events are those outside, "on the side," or in conjunction with the main event that the professional event coordinator includes to add value to the event and meet the needs of the event attendees. These activities and programs are added to an event to give further dimension to the overall event experience and attend to the needs and desires of the guest and the guest's guest. They can include companion or guest programs, tours before, during, and after the event, sports and recreational activities, and a broad variety of mini-events within an event. They are meant to entertain, inform, amuse, and enrich the participants, and they must be managed as carefully and conscientiously as any other part of the event experience.

Whether such programs are considered ancillary, auxiliary, subordinate, subsidiary, or supplementary is often a matter of degree or emphasis within the event context. A trade show may be ancillary to an educational conference, or educational sessions may be ancillary to a trade show. Tours may be an optional activity or an integral part of the event agenda. Tournaments may be the purpose of the event or may be added to build a team spirit or satisfy the desire for leisure pursuits. Ancillary events must be integrated into the main event with the same understanding of—and attention to—the goals and objectives, site requirements, budgetary implications, timeline influences, logistical concerns, and marketing endeavors (see Figure 12-1).

Companion Programs

Companion programs are special programs and events created and coordinated to entertain and occupy accompanying persons while the main event takes place. These programs have variously been referred to as spouse programs, family programs, leisure programs, partner programs, companion programs, and accompanying person programs. They are most often employed for meetings and convention events, but may be suitable for other events in which the attendee brings family or friends along for the trip, such as corporate meetings and incentives or trade show expositions.

Companion programs may be a selection of sightseeing tours highlighting the destination or a series of presentations paralleling the programming provided for the main delegate. They may include special or optional tours, entertainment attractions, recreational activities, self-improvement classes, shopping excursions, or special services (see Figure 12-2). They must be selected based on sound market research, meeting the needs and desires of the main delegate and the accompanying persons as well as adding value to the event experience, and then promoted aggressively to their intended markets.

CREATE A CUSTOMER PROFILE

When considering and selecting companion programs, the professional event coordinator must understand, first and foremost, that not all companions or spouses are women. Sandra L. Morrow, author of *The Art of the Show,* advises, "Today a spouse/partner may refer to a husband, significant other, friends, gay lovers. Rather than typecasting potential tagalong attendees as partners or spouses, consider the generic term Guest." This semantic shift will allow the selection of options and offerings that are gender-neutral.

The professional event coordinator should examine the history of companion programs for the particular event and analyze the demographics of the potential program participants (usually parallel to the

Ancillary Event	Primary Objectives	Cause-Related	Corporate/Incentive	Exposition/Fair	Festival/Tourism	Government	Hallmark	Marketing	Meeting/Conference	Social	Sports
		Typical Event Genre									
Children/Youth Activities	Occupy and Entertain Accompanying Persons			X	X		X		X	X	X
Companion Programs	Occupy and Entertain Accompanying Persons		X	X					X		
Hospitality Areas	Provide Gathering Place		X		X	X	X	X	X		X
Indulgent Services	Reward and Pamper		X				X		X	X	
Learning Journeys	Explore and Inform		X			X			X		
Optional Tours	Add Value and Explore Destination		X		X	X			X		
Parades	Promotion and Participation			X	X	X	X				X
Projects	Provide Meaningful Activity	X			X				X		
Recreational Activities	Entertain and Provide Relaxation		X						X	X	X
Special Exhibits	Inform and Add Value	X		X	X	X	X	X	X		
Special Occasions	Private Celebrations		X			X			X	X	
Sports Tournaments	Recreation and Participation	X	X						X		
Teambuilding	Enhance Camaraderie and Cooperation		X						X		

Figure 12-1
Typical Ancillary Events

❏ Aerobics Class	❏ Gallery Walks and Talks	❏ Personal Growth
❏ Antique Market Talks and Tours	❏ Gardening and Landscaping	❏ Recreational Activities
❏ Area Attractions	❏ Golf/Tennis Lessons	❏ Relationship Enrichment Class
❏ Arts and Crafts Workshops	❏ Handwriting Analysis	
❏ Character Portrayals	❏ Health and Nutrition Talks	❏ Retirement Planning Advice
❏ Children's Programs	❏ Heritage Talks	❏ Scavenger Hunt
❏ Communication Skills	❏ Historian Lectures	❏ Self-Defense Class
❏ CPR Certification	❏ Humorists	❏ Shopping Excursions
❏ Demonstrations	❏ Image and Self-Esteem Talks	❏ Sightseeing Excursions
❏ Destination Orientation		❏ Spa Services
❏ Educational Lectures	❏ Indigenous Architecture	❏ Stress Reduction Techniques
❏ Ethnic/Indigenous Cooking	❏ Indigenous Culture	
	❏ Local Authors	❏ Time Management
❏ Fashion Shows	❏ Luncheon with Speaker	❏ Volunteerism Talks
❏ Feng Shui Class	❏ Museum Tours/Lectures	❏ Walking Tours
❏ Financial Planning Talks	❏ Motivational Speakers	❏ Wine Tasting/Matching
	❏ Organizational Skills	

Figure 12-2
Typical Companion Programs Options

demographics of the delegates or attendees at the main event—age, economic and geographic status, etc.). The event coordinator might also survey the attendees and/or convene a focus group of past companion program participants to determine the preferred types and frequency of offerings. It is also important to survey the potential companion program market to determine what influences a companion's decision to accompany a delegate. Is it the destination? Is it the time of year? Is it a matter of time poverty dictating the need for them to spend time together? The answers to these and other questions will help shape the components and scheduling of a companion program.

SCHEDULING CONSIDERATIONS

A companion program should be scheduled to be concurrent with the main event, yet should not conflict with the delegate's schedule of "free time" or detract from the delegate's participation in the main event. If the delegate is to be engaged for the entire day, then the companion program should provide offerings, either half-day or full-day options, that end at the same time the delegate's program ends. If the delegate is to be engaged in the main event only until midafternoon, the companion program should offer only half-day and luncheon options, then perhaps a late afternoon option that the delegate and companion may enjoy together. If an attendee will be traveling through numerous time zones (such as overseas) to attend the main event, you should not schedule important or intensive activities on the first day. You might wish to include an entertaining orientation program on the host country's culture for both delegate and companion on the first day.

On-Site Insight

A Welcome or Orientation Program may make an optional tour or companion program more successful. It can include presentations by area experts and representatives of the major attractions, a question-and-answer session to discuss important information about the area attractions, how to get around, the city's nightlife, and even a "Tacky Tourist" character to present amusing anecdotes and insider tips. You may include a "goody bag" filled with brochures of area attractions, maps, souvenir gifts, tickets, and/or coupons for shopping attractions. You may also arrange for special prizes, donated by area attractions or other sponsors, to be given out randomly during the presentation.

When packaging a companion program, the professional event coordinator should merge the ancillary event with the main event, offering the accompanying person(s) the opportunity—at a price if necessary—to attend all appropriate meal functions and receptions along with the delegate. If there are "must see" attractions at a destination, they may be offered as pre- or postevent tours or incorporated into the main event's programming, with the companions offered a pass or ticket to attend that part of the program. If the delegates are going to participate in a golf or other tournament, transportation might be offered for the companions wishing to attend and observe, and/or parallel sport activities might be developed at the same site. The professional event coordinator should always remember that the accompanying person has accompanied the delegate so that they can spend time together.

PRICING AND MARKETING FACTORS

If not included as a budget expenditure, the pricing of the companion program offerings should cover the actual costs, the administrative costs, and a modest profit (if necessary). The offerings selected should be in a price range reflecting the economic price points of the main event—if the main event is targeted at a lower-price market, the companion program offerings should also be in a lower price range, particularly if they are optional. You may lose delegate participation in certain main event components (such as dinners and/or receptions) if the companion must pay an unusually or unreasonably high price for a ticket to accompany the delegate. People are very price conscious and will compare cost-benefit factors closely. You may also wish to explore sponsorships to underwrite program costs.

Once you have decided to offer a companion program, it must be incorporated into the overall marketing strategy and promoted from the very beginning to ensure participation. Unless the program is optional and being handled completely independently by a destination management company (DMC) or professional congress organizer (PCO), the companion program options should be included in the main event's registration materials and delegates should be able to include payment with all other registration fees and options. Even if the registration and fees are being handled by a DMC or PCO, the event should promote the program in all its materials, from invitation to Web site, to ensure that it contributes to the purchase decision to attend the main event. Including a companion program adds value to the main event by attracting those seeking opportunities to travel together and offering meaningful experiences for both delegates and accompanying persons.

ENRICHMENT PROGRAMS AND ACTIVITIES

People are looking for entertaining yet enriching experiences. Many participants in companion programs are looking for value through authenticity, adventure, inspiration, and education. Simply offering sightseeing tours and tea parties may not attract as many participants as providing a program rich with culture and adventure. Although shopping remains an extremely popular activity, participants are looking for exclusive access to shopping venues, shopping focused on indigenous and unusual items, and information on their manufacture, important product attributes, and special bargains particular to a destination.

Offering special lectures, hands-on workshops, seminars, and classes can provide added value. These may be on a broad variety of life and business skills. Many delegates and accompanying persons are from dual-career households, and the offering made available to the accompanying person may have to focus on the same lifelong learning objectives as the delegate's. Companion program components may even be qualified for continuing education units (CEU) if structured and registered correctly with an academic institution or certification body.

SHOWCASING THE DESTINATION

The companion program, as well as other ancillary events, should take advantage of the attractions and features of the main event's destination. These should be carefully considered in light of the companion program when conducting your site selection and inspection procedures. Showcase the destination with program offerings that include its historic, cultural, and commercial attractions, facilities, sites, and events. Take advantage of the concurrent events and opportunities that will occur while the main event takes place by checking the calendar of events available through the destination's convention and visitors bureau or chamber of commerce.

Perhaps you can reserve a block of tickets to a theatrical production or dinner theater attraction. You may be able to arrange special talks or tours in conjunction with an exhibit that will be on display at a local museum. If one of the destination's highlights is a body of water such as a lake, bay, or river, you should probably arrange for an excursion on a passenger or sailing vessel. If the venue is nestled in the mountains, you might wish to arrange for a nature walk. You might offer four-wheel-drive or jeep excursions in a desert setting or a photo safari in a jungle. Celebrate the indigenous culture and environment for which the destination is famous. For example, when in New York City, you might highlight the theater, in Washington. D.C., the national monuments, in Los Angeles the film industry, in Paris the Eiffel Tower, in London the royals, in Venice the canals, in Japan the tea ceremony, and so forth.

CHILDREN'S PROGRAMS

An increasing number of children are accompanying delegates and attendees to events as the pressure of dual-career or single-parent households shrinks the amount of quality time the family has to spend together. Events, ranging from conferences to festivals, are incorporating children's and youth activities into their programs to attract the family market segment and provide a safe and entertaining component that adds value to the overall event experience. Sandra L. Morrow advises, "The first step is to ensure that you are able to actually host such a program. Some state and municipal jurisdictions, facility policies, and/or insurance requirements may prohibit you from providing basic child care services."

A children's program should match the hours and major events or sessions of the main adult event, including sufficient time before and after main event elements for parents to drop off and pick up the children. Any children's program should include the following elements:

- **Admission and discharge procedures**—Establish a complete registration process, including a signed general release from parent or guardian; require parent or guardian to check in and check out a child via identity checks and signatures; provide waivers and/or permission forms for physical activities and off-site excursions.

- **Activity plans**—Activity plans should be age-appropriate, include socially interactive and self-directed activities, and focus on entertainment and fun.
- **Discipline policy**—Define the rules and the manner in which discipline will be dispensed (physical punishment, shaming, verbal abuse, or withholding food is considered inappropriate discipline); define the terms and conditions that would result in expelling a child from the program.
- **Appropriate personnel**—Require certified, trained, and/or bonded child care providers and supervisors, licensed or accredited by the proper authorities, sometimes including completion of a Child Abuse Record Information background check.
- **Proper insurance coverage**

INDULGENCES AND SPECIAL SERVICES

The professional event coordinator may arrange for a variety of salon and spa options to allow participants to indulge themselves in luxurious and sensual treatments and services. These amenities can range from manicures, pedicures, skin, hair, and other beauty treatments, to therapeutic massages and relaxation therapies, and may be of interest to both the delegate and the accompanying person. These services may already be available on-site, particularly at resort properties, for which appointments can be reserved. Alternately, special appointments can be made at local salons. Hair stylists and makeup artists may be reserved for guests attending a gala function or brought in for the members of a wedding party. A tuxedo rental service might be arranged for gentlemen attending a formal conference event, with an order form included in the conference registration materials. Perhaps a separate registration desk for these services can be set up adjacent to the main registration area for the event so that attendees can make appointments upon arrival.

VARIETY, BALANCE, AND SAFETY

A companion program should provide sufficient variety to attract a broad spectrum of participation, including a balance of active, passive, and adventurous options that will appeal to those of all ages, genders, and physical abilities. The professional event coordinator may be required to coordinate these programs as part of an overall program, such as an incentive trip, or may elect to coordinate them as options in conjunction with a main event, such as a conference or exposition, to increase attendance. The professional event coordinator must ensure that only reputable providers, meeting all safety, regulatory, and licensing requirements, are selected to supply these services. Special waivers may be required from participants, and special riders to the hosting organization's insurance policy may be necessary.

Optional Tours and Trips

Optional tours and trips may be offered in conjunction with a main event to enhance, enrich, or extend the event experience (see Figure 12-3). These activities are most often made available when the majority of attendees are traveling to the event from other parts of the country or the world, to create added value and provide them with an opportunity to take advantage of a tourism objective or perspective at the destination. Sightseeing tours primarily focus on the indigenous culture, environment, and attractions. Adventure tours and themed excursions offer an opportunity to participate in unique activities that people are not usually able to engage in on their own. Other types of tours, such as industrial/facility tours or learning journeys, may be included in an event agenda to address an educational or promotional objective.

CREATE A MENU OF TOUR OPTIONS

The professional event coordinator may arrange for a menu of options to be offered to event attendees and accompanying persons, for purchase prior to arrival through a preregistration mechanism or upon arrival at a tour desk adjacent to the main registration area. The purchase decision will be based on the following factors, which the professional event coordinator must take into consideration when selecting the tour offerings.

- **Price**—The price must provide value for money and must be within a range suitable for the economic demographics of the audience. Prices for sightseeing tours should be inclusive of all entrance fees for attractions and meals or refreshments on the tour. Prices for over-the-road tours (multiday tours, staying overnight at a hotel/motel) should include the accommodations, entrance fees for attractions, porterage, and the meals specified in the itinerary description. Prices may vary depending on whether the tour is given during a low, shoulder, or peak season.
- **Itinerary**—The itinerary should include a balance of attractions packaged in an interesting progression. It must clearly, concisely, and correctly identify the attractions, accommodations, mode of travel, and meals included in the tour, as well as whether the tour

❏ Adventure Tours	❏ Facility Tours	❏ Monuments and Memorials
❏ Agricultural Tours	❏ Factory Tours	❏ Movie Studio Tours
❏ Amphibious Tours	❏ Farm/Ranch Tours	❏ Museums
❏ Amusement Parks	❏ Folklore Tours	❏ National Parks
❏ Aquarium Tours	❏ Gallery Tours	❏ Nightclub Excursions
❏ Archaeological Tours	❏ Game/Nature Preserves	❏ Outlet Mall Tours
❏ Architectural Tours	❏ Garden Tours	❏ Photo Safaris
❏ Artist Studios	❏ Ghost Town Tours	❏ Planetarium Tours
❏ Athletic Activities	❏ Hall of Fame Tours	❏ Plantation Tours
❏ Avian (Bird Watching) Tours	❏ Haunted Houses Tours	❏ Pub Tours/Crawls
❏ Back-of-House Tours	❏ Helicopter Tours	❏ Railway Tours
❏ Backstage Tours	❏ Heritage Tours	❏ Recreational Activities
❏ Beach Excursions	❏ Historic Church Tours	❏ Restaurant Tours
❏ Bicycle Tours	❏ Historic Home Tours	❏ Scenery Tours
❏ Botanical Park Tours	❏ Historic Landmarks	❏ Scenic Attraction Tours
❏ Brewery Tours	❏ Historic Neighborhood Tours	❏ Scientific Tours
❏ Campus Tours	❏ Hobby-Specific Tours	❏ Shopping Shuttles
❏ Casino Shuttles	❏ Horticultural Tours	❏ Special Interest Tours
❏ Castle Tours	❏ Hot Air Balloon Rides	❏ Sports Tours
❏ Celebrity Home Tours	❏ IMAX or OMNI Performances	❏ Swamp Tours
❏ City Tours	❏ Indigenous Culture Tours	❏ Theater Tours
❏ Countryside Tours	❏ Industrial Tours	❏ Theme Tours
❏ Cultural Tours	❏ Jeep Excursions	❏ Walking Tours
❏ Dinner Cruises	❏ Learning Journeys	❏ Whale-watching
❏ Ecological Tours	❏ Living History Attractions	❏ Wildlife Tours
❏ Educational Tours	❏ Mansions	❏ Wineries/Wine Tasting Tours
❏ Ethnic Neighborhood Tours	❏ Marine Life Tours	❏ Zoological/Biological Parks

Figure 12-3
Typical Tours and Trip Options

will have an escort or step-on guide or the driver will be providing the topical commentary on the sights, history, and attractions. Marilyn J. Reis, author of *The Receptive Operator,* advises, "There is a world of difference between 'visit,' 'stop,' 'see,' and 'drive past.'" The language of the itinerary description must be precise because it may serve as a binding agreement, which, according to Reis, is subject to stringent consumer protection laws that favor the consumer (particularly in countries other than the United States, a fact that international travelers are well aware of). Reis notes, "Whatever a U.S.-based supplier puts in a brochure or on its Web site, whatever is promised, and whatever is said regarding delivery become the basis for the overseas clients' expectations."

- **Pace**—The volume and scheduling of activities, as defined in the *International Dictionary of Event Management,* edited by Goldblatt and Nelson, should allow for a realistic operation and provide a "balance of travel time, sightseeing, social events, free time, and rest." The pace of the itinerary may be fast or slower, depending on the attributes of the attractions visited and the special interests of the group, as well as the demographics and size of the group.
- **Schedule Harmony**—The full- and half-day tour options, as well as pre- and postevent trips, must begin and end in concurrence with the schedule of the main event. When offering a variety of sightseeing tours throughout a multiday event for a large group, you may wish to repeat the most popular ones on several days so that guests are not faced with an "either/or" choice but can package the experience they prefer. Evening options such as a dinner and/or entertainment attraction should be offered only if and when the main event does not have something scheduled. Tours should return in time for participants to dress for evening events or to participate in other events in the main event such as receptions, exhibits, or meal functions.

For those groups requiring something extra or out of the ordinary, the professional event coordinator may need to work with a tour operator to create new and/or exclusive itineraries that include attractions not usually available to the individual tourist. Custom tours may also be created to take advantage of concurrent events such as festivals, entertainment attractions, or sports events. Because many tour operators serve both the individual and group markets with the same menu, it may be necessary to guarantee a certain number of participants to warrant a separate motor coach, otherwise your guests may be mingled with individual travelers or other groups on the same tour. It may be helpful to find out when tours arrive and depart certain popular attractions or restaurants so that guests are not delayed or underserved during high-traffic peak times.

EXTENDING THE EXPERIENCE

The professional event coordinator should consider offering pre- and postevent tours and package trips for groups traveling to a destination to allow guests to extend the event experience. Group or FIT (For Independent Traveler) travel packages may be arranged through a tour operator or coordinated by the professional event coordinator. These tours or packages can provide those interested in an additional vacation or extended stay with an opportunity to visit attractions that are outside the usual radius of travel time allowed for half- or full-day tours (usually a maximum of 60 to 100 miles for a full-day tour) or experience more attractions available at a destination (particularly at popular resort destinations). The pricing and coordination of these offerings will depend on the destination, size of group, time of year, and the attractions, services, and amenities included in the package. If presented in conjunction with the overall event program, these offerings must be marketed early and aggressively so that potential participants can make plans accordingly.

Technology Tip

The Web site of an event can become the portal to a plethora of information about the event site's features and attractions by providing hyperlinks to the destination's convention and visitors bureau's Web site and/or the Web sites of area attractions featured in the companion programs or optional tours menu. Adding a hyperlink to a calendar of events allows your guests to view and select concurrent or close-in events to attend in conjunction with your event. You might also wish to search out and include hyperlinks to Web sites that provide historical or cultural information related to the destination, so as to allow those interested to prepare for a deeper and more enriching experience.

ACCESS TO RECREATION AND RELAXATION

Many tour operators offer packages that primarily provide transportation and admissions to popular attractions such as theme parks, water parks, or nature parks and recreational activities such as horseback riding, golf, fishing, or skiing. Although the individual visitor can certainly make these arrangements independently, by offering these packages the professional event coordinator facilitates participation for those who may not have their own transportation and/or may not feel comfortable navigating a new environment. This can be particularly important if the group speaks a different language(s) than that of the destination, and if this is the case, it will be necessary to ensure that the tour operator has special or multilanguage capabilities specific to that group.

Often, the simple provision of shuttle services will be a welcome amenity for event participants and accompanying persons. Such services may be used to provide scheduled transportation to and from shopping areas, casinos, and historic districts. You should investigate these areas and outlets to determine whether they have existing shuttle services or would be willing to provide this service for your group. Particularly if your group is large, these outlets may see the value of providing complimentary transportation to their properties, and all you may need to do is work with them to develop the schedule and pickup points. Individual activity providers, such as operators of hot air balloon rides, may be interested in packaging special deals just for your group and will customize their standard offerings, as well as their brochures, just for your event.

You may find that there are recreational activities that do not necessarily require transportation—just access to an appropriate space and place—such as a bridge or chess tournament, and that you can coordinate the requisite area and equipment to accommodate these activities. You may also wish to purchase or reserve a block of tickets to entertainment attractions and/or performances (and arrange transfer transportation) to ensure that your attendees will have access on the day or time that best fits into the overall event schedule. Any of these special arrangements must be highlighted in your event promotional materials to ensure participation, as well as to illustrate your attention to the details that will add value to their event experience.

EXCURSIONS AND ADVENTURES

The athletic will likely want active options such as hiking, white-water river rafting, jet boat rides, scuba diving, bicycle tours, bungee jumping, and other vigorous activities. The adventurous will likely take advantage of options such as jeep or four-wheel-drive expeditions, wildlife excursions, and helicopter tours to remote environments. Those seeking authenticity may prefer excursions to living history attractions or archeological sites or digs, visits to artists' studios, bird watching or whale watching tours, ecological tours, and other programs that provide an in-depth or hands-on exploration of the culture or environment.

Depending on the results of the market research, the professional event coordinator may wish to organize special excursions to attractions relevant to a common hobby or special interest, such as agricultural or horticultural facilities, aviaries, apiaries, technical institutes, and other points of specialized interest. Perhaps an expert on a specific topic can be engaged to give a demonstration or presentation in conjunction with the tour to provide a more enriching or educational dimension to the excursion.

LEARNING JOURNEYS

A learning journey or educational field trip may be a component of the main event for attendees and may also be of interest to accompanying persons. Such tours and activities are often conducted to acquaint participants with the physical plant, operations, and/or capabilities of a commercial or industrial facility or entity. These may include factory tours, back-of-the-house tours, backstage tours, tours of government facilities, sports facilities, or any other facility pertinent to the purpose of the main event. The professional event coordinator should work with the host facility to design an itinerary that is safe, efficient, and educational. The host facility should provide a knowledgeable and engaging escort who is able to provide expert commentary and answer questions.

These excursions should be designed to be entertaining as well as educational. You may conduct a Chef's Table event in the kitchen to introduce a group to a restaurant operation, conduct a scavenger hunt to acquaint the group with the physical plant of an industrial facility, or conduct a hands-on demonstration to allow the group to experience the mechanics of a manufacturing operation. You must remember the principles of adult learning, particularly that adults prefer interactive learning environments and approach learning from a problem-solving point of view.

SELECT A PROFESSIONAL PROVIDER

The professional event coordinator should maximize his or her time investment in coordinating optional tours by selecting a professional tour operator to provide such services. It may be possible to secure these services through a DMC or PCO, and it may be advantageous to use the same company providing the ground transportation needed for the event itself. It is important to make certain that the provider has the experience, equipment, and capacity to deliver a quality product for a group; the event coordinator may even take the tour him- or herself to make an appraisal.

Many tour operators also offer commissionable rates for group bookings, often 5 to 10 percent of the retail tour price, which could offset certain administrative costs. You must confirm the minimums required, booking deadlines, and cancellation policies and procedures for undersubscribed tours. You must also confirm that any tour provider selected has all the appropriate licenses and insurance coverage. Although any recreational event has elements of risk, some are riskier than others. You must always investigate any liability issues regarding an activity offered or endorsed by the event organization, as well as confirm the reliability of the provider, ensure that appropriate safety measures are employed, and secure the appropriate waivers of indemnification from participants.

Mini-Events

Mini-events are those events held in conjunction with a main event that could be considered stand-alone events in another context. These include certain hospitality functions, exhibits, energizers, icebreakers, charitable projects, fund-raising programs, parades, and promotional events. They may be optional activities or integral parts of the overall event experience. The professional event coordinator may be called upon to organize special events for special occasions such as a birthday or anniversary celebration for a CEO or a particular attendee, a private reception for certain dignitaries, or even a wedding ceremony at a sports event. Each mini-event requires the same comprehensive approach to research, design, planning, coordination, and evaluation as the main event and must be fully integrated into the logistical and budgetary operations of the main event.

HOSPITALITY FUNCTIONS

Hospitality functions are held in conjunction with a main event to promote interaction and facilitate special recognition. The professional event coordinator may have to organize or accommodate a variety of hospitality events, desks, lounges, and/or suites that provide gathering places for special interest groups within the main event's audience. A special event or area may be developed to recognize and entertain international delegates to a conference, individuals who have achieved a specific certification, members of a fraternal or affinity organization, or sponsors and dignitaries associated with the main event. Dine Around events may be organized to allow attendees to sample the local cuisine while meeting and getting to know other attendees in a social setting. Dine Around events involve making reservations at area restaurants, using a registration mechanism to randomly create parties of eight to ten guests for each restaurant, and organizing transportation to and from the restaurants (e.g., shuttle service route or taxi service).

SPECIAL EXHIBITS AND EXHIBITIONS

Special exhibits at an event can include anything from tabletop displays in a common area to tablescapes created for a design competition. Exhibitions may include anything from a juried art show to an exposition, defined by Sandra L. Morrow as "a temporary, time-sensitive marketplace organized by an individual or corporation, where buyer and seller interact for the express purpose of purchasing displayed goods or services, either at the time of presentation or at a future date." Morrow reports that, according to the Center for Exhibition Industry Research (CEIR), the functions of an exposition include "buying, selling, new product introduction, media coverage, gaining competitive intelligence, updating industry developments and trends, and networking and problem solving."

These exhibits and expositions add an informative and interactive dimension to a main event, perhaps displaying the history of an organization, the newest technological advances, indigenous attractions and attributes of a destination, or the entries in an awards competition. You may need to coordinate a poster session wherein the papers or reports on a topic are displayed and their authors and/or researchers are present to discuss the contents with interested persons. You may wish to set up a small crafts market featuring demonstrations by local or ethnic artists and craftspersons adjacent to your main event so that the audience can interact, learn, and shop without leaving your event site. The spatial and equipment needs for these special displays must be incorporated into your site plan so that they are effectively accessible and enhance rather than impede the traffic patterns and flow.

CHARITABLE PROJECTS

Many events incorporate a charitable component into the overall program to add a meaningful dimension to the purpose of the event and to communicate a message of care and goodwill by the event's hosting organization. Sometimes an event conducts a fund-raising drive during its operation or undertakes a charitable project as a component of the event itself. Visiting sports teams, delegates, or dignitaries might be involved in a one-day project to build a playground, refurbish a community center, or clean up a city park. A local festival might collect coats for kids, or a marketing event might collect canned goods for a food drive. This philanthropic affiliation may be a long-standing relationship between organizations or adopted based on the needs of the community in which the event takes place. The professional event coordinator can check with local agencies such as the United Way to determine projects suitable for a specific event.

CREATIVE ENERGIZERS

Many events may benefit from strategies to energize the proceedings and promote interaction. A broad variety of devices can be employed to enhance the event theme and increase participation, from themed refreshment breaks to daily puzzle-solving contests. Numerous board games and other games such as bingo, Monopoly, and Trivial Pursuit may be used or adapted to create fun icebreakers and energizers. Icebreakers offer an audience of attendees who are not familiar with each other an entertaining activity that facilitates introductions and interaction, and they may be designed to incorporate the theme of the main event. For a Wild West or Las Vegas theme, you might play Human Poker, giving each guest a playing card with instructions to find four other people with cards that will create a winning poker hand; for a Hollywood or film festival theme, you might hand out buttons with movie stars' photos on them and have people find the casts of famous movies. For additional icebreaker and energizer ideas, visit www.nwlink.com/~donclark/leader/icebreak.html, www.smp.org/icebreaker.cfm, adulted.about.com/cs/icebreakers/index. htm, and topten.org/content/tt.AU20.htm, or check out books such as *The Big Book of Icebreakers: Quick, Fun Activities for Energizing Meetings and Workshops* and *201 Icebreakers,* by Edie West.

PROMOTIONAL EVENTS AND PARADES

Promotional events are incorporated into many marketing plans for events. These usually take place prior to the main event to boost ticket sales and increase attendance, but they may also be conducted during an event to promote specific event elements. You might have a cook-off, a contest, a stunt, a book signing, a bonfire, or a celebrity appearance. These events must be conducted in a timely manner to achieve their marketing objectives and require special attention to any risk management issues. After all, an accident or disaster is not the marketing message you mean to send.

Parades are events that promote a main event, communicate a message, and encourage participation. From pet parades to protest marches, or a parade of athletes to a parade of fantastic floats, these movable and moving displays have traditionally been used to promote everything from the circus coming to town (originally taking advantage of the mechanism for moving the animals and equipment from the railway station or town entrance to the event grounds) to demonstrating a country's military might. They are now also used to rally affinity or celebrate diversity, as well as bring audience and event together in an entertaining manner.

The professional event coordinator may have responsibility for organizing these ancillary mini-events or may need to work with committees or independent producers to integrate them into the overall event plans. It is important to be very careful about controlling ad hoc or impromptu mini-events that take place in conjunction with a main event, because they will be connected with that event in the minds of the audience and can affect the ability of the event coordinator to efficiently and effectively coordinate the main event.

The Sporting Life

The professional event coordinator may be required to arrange or incorporate sports activities into an event as an entertainment option, to facilitate interaction and relationship building, to promote healthy competition, or to accommodate the desire to participate in recreational activities as part of a healthy lifestyle. The professional event coordinator may be selecting spectator or participatory activities, organizing tournaments and competitions, coordinating teambuilding programs, or identifying recreational sports activities and facilities (such as exercise gymnasiums) available at the destination (see Figure 12-4).

These activities must be selected based on the interests, age, and fitness levels of the audience and integrated into the event schedule so they do not exhaust the attendees before an important component of the main event program. You must make certain that the venue is appropriate and well maintained, has the necessary facilities such as changing or locker rooms (including showers, towels, etc., if appropriate), includes access to or rents the necessary equipment, and that the appropriate supervision or facilitation of the activity is provided.

SPECTATOR AND PARTICIPATORY EVENTS

Spectator sports activities may include an exhibition game of stunt/display teams or athletes, admissions to local or concurrent competitions, or play-offs featuring division or department heads and the CEO and other upper management members. The professional event coordinator should also consider incorporating a spectator component into a participatory sports activity or tournament so that those not participating may watch and cheer the action from the grandstands.

❑ Badminton	❑ Horseback Riding	❑ Shooting (Actual/Simulated)
❑ Baseball	❑ In-line Skating	❑ Snorkeling
❑ Biathlon	❑ Kayaking	❑ Snowmobiling
❑ Bicycle Races	❑ Obstacle Courses	❑ Soccer
❑ Bowling	❑ Orienteering	❑ Softball
❑ Challenge Courses	❑ Paintball Wars	❑ Sports Clinics
❑ Climbing	❑ Pentathlon	❑ Squash
❑ Canoeing	❑ Polo	❑ Surfing
❑ Cricket	❑ Races	❑ Swimming
❑ Darts	❑ Racquetball	❑ Table Tennis
❑ Exercise Gymnasium	❑ Road Rally	❑ Tennis
❑ Flag Football	❑ Rodeo (Simulated)	❑ Track and Field Games
❑ Frisbee Challenge	❑ Rope Courses	❑ Triathlon
❑ Fun Runs	❑ Rugby	❑ Volleyball
❑ Golf	❑ Sailing	❑ Water Polo
❑ Handball	❑ Scuba Diving	❑ White Water Rafting

Figure 12-4
Typical Sports Activities

Participatory athletic activities can include any sport imaginable organized for pure recreation or serious competition. You might arrange for a miniature golf course to be laid out in an exposition hall or along the passageways between meeting rooms at a convention. You might set up billiard tables in a hospitality lounge or schedule races on motorized beer kegs. You may wish to include a fun run for joggers or a laser skeet-shooting competition for marksmen. Softball and volleyball are popular at picnics, skiing and snowmobiling can be popular at snowbound destinations, rugby and football games may be more popular during the professional sports' seasons, and "extreme sports" such as stunt skateboarding and in-line skating are popular with younger attendees. Sports clinics of all types can offer participants a chance to improve their games or offer novices a chance to try a sport they have never tried before.

TOURNAMENTS AND COMPETITIONS

The two most often produced tournaments in the context of a conference or corporate event are golf and tennis (most incentive events include golf as a primary component), but the professional event coordinator may be called upon to organize tournaments and competitions for any number of sporting activities, from road rallies to tricycle races. This effort can include securing the proper venue, judges and/or referees, the appropriate equipment, transportation, registration and player matching, refreshments, and prizes ranging from ribbons, medals, trophies, or perpetual trophies (those that stay with the winning team until the next competition) to souvenir merchandise and sport-specific gifts.

The type of tournament offered will depend on the sport, the time allotted for play, the facilities available for play, and the number of players participating. The type of tournament may also depend on the seriousness of the competition and/or the value of the prize to be won (which may require specific entry policies, scoring regulations, and tie-breaking procedures). John Byl, author of *Organizing Successful Tournaments,* identifies the standard tournament types as follows:

- Single Elimination—Losers are eliminated and winners advance to the next round.
- Multilevel—Losers move successively to second or third brackets, playing concurrently to determine winners in different classes.
- Round Robin—All entrants play each other, and the cumulative scores determine winners.
- Extended—Entrants challenge players ranked above them to make their way to the top level (may include such types as Ladder, Pyramid, Crown, Spiderweb, and Level Rotation tournaments).

You may also need to consider different divisions, such as men's singles, women's singles, doubles, mixed doubles, junior/senior players, and player caliber categories such as novice, intermediate, and advanced.

Even if the professional event coordinator knows how to play a specific sport, that does not mean he or she is qualified (or will have the time) to organize a tournament or competition. Many sports venues such as resort properties, clubs, courts, and courses have experienced in-house professionals who can coordinate a fair and evenly matched competition, as well as secure the proper scoring/referee officials and appropriate equipment. Another possibility is to contact athletic programs at local schools, universities, or recreational departments for assistance. There are also commercial ventures offering recreational and team-building programs such as sailing regattas, zany games, and even motorcycle road rallies.

MATCHING SKILLS AND ENTERTAINMENT

Sports activities and programs should be entertaining as well as challenging. For a game to be fun, it must be fair and the skill levels of the players should be comparable. Sandra L. Morrow advises that when you are conducting activities or tournaments in which individuals or teams will play against one another, you should ask for information on years played, handicap levels, average scores, tournaments won, and so on, to ensure that the levels of competency match. The structure of the sports activity or program should allow for all levels of ability in order to be accessible and inclusive. You may wish to include entertainment options, such as a putting green obstacle course at a golf tournament or sport-specific/themed inflatable games for the nonaficionado or nonplaying attendees or accompanying persons.

Prepare participants by including a full description of the activities offered and the equipment options available (bring-your-own or rental specifics) and recommending the appropriate attire. If teams are to be formed, you may need to order uniforms or colored team T-shirts for participants. You may have to send out a survey to gather ranking information or advise potential participants to bring specific certification or documentation of capabilities (e.g., scuba diving certifications). You may need to send out the tournament rules, tie-breaking procedures, and playing schedule. You may need to specify certain equipment regulations or send out preregistration forms and participant waivers of indemnity. You must specify the conditions that would cause changes in or cancellation of a particular activity, because someone may decide to attend the main event just because it includes this golf course or that recreational option, and if it is not available, could dispute the "contractual agreement" stipulated by the event brochure.

TEAMBUILDING DYNAMICS

Teambuilding activities are often incorporated into corporate and other events and used to move from breaking the ice to bonding, bringing diverse individuals together to achieve a common goal and overcome challenges that require cooperative efforts. They may include sports-based activities, adventure-based activities, simulated physical challenges, problem-solving missions, simulated situations, or team projects. You might have a road rally or scavenger hunt, a rope course or paintball war, an indoor or outdoor rock- or tower-climbing challenge; you might have teams build a raft out of recycled materials or develop a video documentary, strand team members (metaphorically) on a deserted island or on another planet, convene an espionage academy or stage a murder mystery, or challenge teams to design a working robot.

Although teambuilding events are often designed to result in recognizing a winner, they are not simply competitions. They must be designed to fulfill a purpose and address specific objectives (see Figure 12-5). In Jon Michaels's article "Building the Better Team" in the October 2002 issue of *Event Solutions,* David Peters, owner of Absolute Amusements, based in Orlando, Florida, describes his company's approach to teambuilding as finding effective goals and accomplishing those goals. "We try to look at a company's needs and solve a problem in a certain area, whether it's motivation, trust, communication or a number of other areas. Most times, there is more than one area a teambuilding event needs to solve." Peters also notes, "Fun definitely increases retention."

❑ Accepting New Ideas	❑ Fun	❑ Relationship Building
❑ Adaptability	❑ Goal Setting	❑ Releasing Stress
❑ Collaboration	❑ Group Cohesion	❑ Removing Barriers
❑ Commitment	❑ Improved Listening Skills	❑ Resource Utilization
❑ Communication	❑ Innovation	❑ Respect
❑ Confidence	❑ Introductions and Interaction	❑ Risk Tolerance
❑ Conflict Resolution	❑ Leadership Development	❑ Spontaneity
❑ Constructive Feedback	❑ Morale Boosting	❑ Strategic Planning
❑ Creativity	❑ Negotiation Skills	❑ Testing Perceived Limits
❑ Decision Making	❑ Pride	❑ Time Management
❑ Delegation	❑ Prioritization	❑ Trust
❑ Dependability	❑ Problem Solving	❑ Valuing Diversity

Figure 12-5
Typical Teambuilding Objectives

Teambuilding events should be customized to the corporate culture and incorporate the corporation's branding within the theme, activities, and setting. They require a strong facilitator, an emotionally and physically safe environment, the proper selection and sequence of activities, and a way for everyone to participate and contribute (not everyone will be physically or emotionally able to do everything, because of personal limitations—i.e., disabilities, back problems, pregnancy, phobias, etc.). A teambuilding event should include a debriefing session focusing on the skills and techniques used during the event as well as a follow-up application or transfer to the workplace, such as setting goals, implementing objectives, monitoring progress, and management's reinforcement of the teambuilding experience after the event.

SAFETY AND LIABILITY CONSIDERATIONS

As with all recreational activities, but particularly in regard to sports activities, you must consider the risk management issues and liabilities associated with such event-related programs. You must make certain that the appropriate insurance coverage is in place for both the event organization and the entity producing the sports activity. You must arrange for the appropriate level of first aid and/or on-site medical facilities (it is advised that for any strenuous activity you have an emergency medical technician (EMT) on-site). You must make certain that the playing site is safe and the appropriate protective measures are in place (e.g., padded poles and/or flooring, chalk or talc field marking instead of lime, etc.). You must ensure that the equipment is in good condition and appropriate (e.g., regulation balls, regulation heights, well-anchored supports, etc.) and that the participants are equipped with the proper protective gear (e.g., life vests, helmets, padding, etc.). Other considerations include securing the appropriate permissions and waivers of indemnity from participants. Note that signed waivers will not protect you from negligent behavior. Participation in sports activities should be a pleasurable and rewarding experience. However, participation must never be mandatory, either implicitly or explicitly. As a professional event coordinator, you must always consider options for different levels of participation and/or inclusion as a spectator so that everyone at the main event will enjoy and benefit from the ancillary sports event.

Target Competency Review

Ancillary events held in conjunction with a main event must have a purpose and should be selected based on the needs and objectives of the main event. Companion programs are included to occupy and entertain guests' guests or accompanying persons. They may include indulgent services, self-improvement opportunities, or enriching activities. Scheduling must complement the main event, neither interfering nor conflicting with an attendee's participation in or obligations to the main event program. Special care must be exercised in organizing children's programs and child care facilities.

Optional sightseeing tours and pre- or postevent tour packages offer opportunities to take full advantage of an event destination. They should highlight and offer access to indigenous and unique cultural, environmental, and entertainment attractions. They can become part of the purchase decision for the main event and provide the mechanism to enhance and extend the main event experience. Mini-events, from parades to special exhibits, are often held in conjunction with a main event to enhance, promote, and/or create added value for the main event. They may be educational, recreational, promotional, charitable, or interactive. Whether planned or impromptu, mini-events will be connected with the main event in the audience's mind, so they must be carefully controlled to ensure that the proper message is communicated and that they serve the goals and objectives of the main event.

Sporting activities are included in an event to provide recreation and healthy competition for participants seeking adventure, athletics, or amusement. The professional event coordinator may need to organize participatory and/or spectator options and opportunities for attendees and accompanying persons. Tournaments need organization, which should be delegated to professionals with experience in the specific sport. Teambuilding activities are popular mechanisms for achieving specific growth objectives and should be both challenging and entertaining.

All ancillary activities must be coordinated impeccably and carefully considered, from a risk management perspective, in regard to liability and safety issues, proper insurance coverage, and professional providers. Participation in these activities and mini-events should never be mandatory, but should be designed to attract and include participants of various abilities and demographics.

EXERCISES IN PROFESSIONAL EVENT COORDINATION

Outline and describe the companion programs, trips and tours, mini-events, and sports activities you would select and present at the following events. Explain the logistical requirements associated with these programs and how they will be incorporated into your overall event plan and budget.

1. The Association of Water Treatment Analysts will be having its annual convention in your city. There will be 2000 delegates, most

of whom bring their entire families along, recognizing an opportunity to combine this convention with a vacation. The convention is four days long and takes place in early summer.

2. The Big Bucks Corporation and Consolidated Industries have just completed a merger of their two companies, and you are coordinating a six-day strategic planning meeting that will bring together their upper management teams, approximately 250 executives, to determine the structure of the new organization. Because of the length of this meeting, many will be bringing along their spouses.

3. Your community is celebrating its centennial, and you have been asked to join the planning committee to design a three-day festival that will attract both tourists and residents.

CHAPTER 13

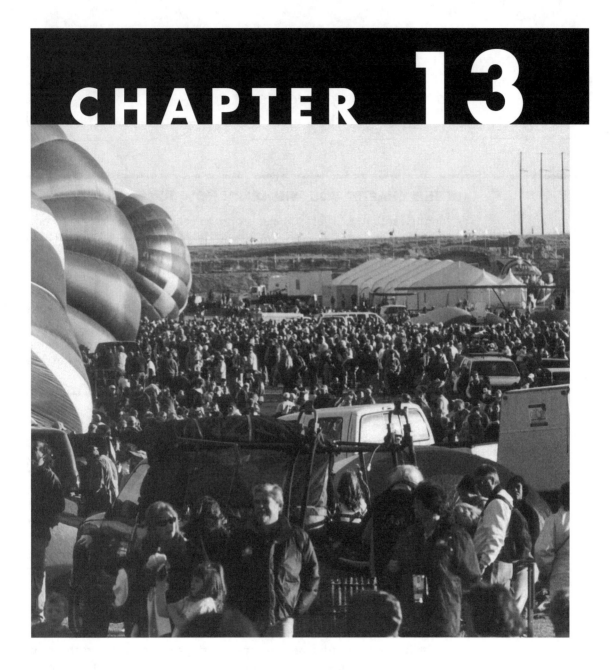

Vendors and Volunteers

The deepest principle of Human Nature is the craving to be appreciated.

—WILLIAM JAMES (1842–1910)

IN THIS CHAPTER YOU WILL LEARN HOW TO:

- Identify, solicit, and select the appropriate vendor partners for an event.
- Develop successful recruitment programs and collateral materials for procuring volunteers and support staff for an event.
- Design and deliver effective orientation and training programs that prepare personnel to shape the success of the event.
- Utilize, motivate, and reward personnel in a manner that benefits both the individual and the event.
- Monitor and manage voluntary, paid, and contracted personnel, using sound supervisory techniques, performance reviews, and appropriate conflict resolution and disciplinary procedures.

The event coordinator was meeting with her various department leaders and committee chairpersons after the event they had all been working on, to discuss the overall staffing for the event. One of the department leaders said that he had had some "real dead wood" in his group—people who did not do their jobs but spent most of their time complaining about the event organization. The event coordinator suggested the department leader talk with these people to find out why they had volunteered and what their frustrations were and to determine whether any of them had constructive suggestions for improving the organization. The event coordinator pointed out, "Sometimes dead wood is just dead wood and it needs to be cleared out, but sometimes it can be the kindling for a great idea."

Everyone who works on an event, whether paid or volunteer, part-time or full-time, vendor or participant, brings a lifetime's worth of experience and expertise that can contribute to the success of the event. The professional event coordinator must incorporate the appropriate mechanisms to take advantage of that wealth while meeting the needs and expectations of those providing it. The process begins with finding the right people and providers for the event, based on the needs of the event operations and the resources available to fill those needs, followed by sharing the vision and requirements of the event with all involved personnel and providers, ensuring that they fully understand what is expected of them and what they will be provided with in return. Finally, the professional event coordinator must supply the tools and training necessary for them to be successful in whatever capacity they serve the event, within a motivational environment that recognizes the value each individual brings to the event. Communication is the foundation of success in all these tasks.

Vendor Selection

Virtually every event or event organization, no matter how big or small, will at one time or another purchase goods and/or services from a variety of vendors (see Figure 13-1). The types of goods and services required will depend on the type and scope of the event as well as its fiscal, organizational, geographical, and logistical parameters. The professional event coordinator must set up an equitable method for soliciting, evaluating, and selecting the right vendors for the event project at hand. This may be accomplished by establishing a purchasing program that streamlines the process through a systematic approach relying on sound assessment criteria. In the world of project management, a purchasing system is referred to as Procurement Management, illustrated in Figure 13-2.

ANALYZE YOUR NEEDS AND RESOURCES

The professional event coordinator must specify the needs to be filled and the resources available to fill them. For many products and/or services, there is a broad range of product types and quality levels available to meet a particular need—for example, paper plates versus designer china or stick-on paper badges versus Smart Cards. In determining the resources available for the event, the professional event coordinator must consider time, money, and humanpower. There may be a sufficient budget but very little time or few personnel to handle certain aspects of the event. There may be plenty of volunteers but very little money. These resources must be allocated effectively and efficiently, which may dictate that certain tasks or products must be outsourced rather than handled or produced in-house.

Once you have determined the needs to be filled by outside vendors, you must itemize the goods and services required and locate the potential vendors or suppliers qualified to provide them. You might search directories, such as a telephone directory and membership directories, for organizations such as the International Special Events Society (ISES), Meeting Professionals International (MPI), convention and visitor

❑ Administrative Staff	❑ Ground Transportation	❑ Set Design/Construction
❑ Advertising/PR Agency	❑ Guides	❑ Shipping Services
❑ Alcohol Provider/Servers	❑ Hosts/Hostesses	❑ Sound Engineers
❑ Audiovisual Equipment	❑ Ice Sculptors	❑ Souvenir Merchandise
❑ Audiovisual Services	❑ ID/Credentials Systems	❑ Sign Makers
❑ Balloon Decorator	❑ Insurance Broker	❑ Speakers
❑ Bridal Accessories	❑ Invitation Designer	❑ Special Effects Services
❑ Cake Makers	❑ Labor Hire Agency/Union	❑ Sponsorship Consultant
❑ Casino Equipment	❑ Laser Providers	❑ Sports Professionals
❑ Caterer	❑ Legal Counsel	❑ Staffing Services
❑ Child Care/Crèche Services	❑ Lighting Designer	❑ Staging Company
❑ Coat Check Service	❑ Lighting Equipment	❑ Technical Director
❑ Communication Systems	❑ Media Consultant	❑ Technical Production
❑ Cooling/Heating Services	❑ Medical Services	❑ Telecommunication
❑ Costume/Mask Providers	❑ Parking Services	Services
❑ Custodial Staff	❑ Performers	❑ Tent/Marquee Provider
❑ Décor Company	❑ Photographers	❑ Ticketing Agency
❑ DMC/PCO	❑ Power/Distribution	❑ Ticket-Taking Staff
❑ Emcees	Provider	❑ Tour Operator
❑ Emergency Services	❑ Portable Toilet Provider	❑ Traffic Consultant
❑ Entertainment Agency	❑ Printers	❑ Traffic Director
❑ Equipment Rentals	❑ Production Company	❑ Trainers
❑ Exhibit Contractors	❑ Protocol Consultant	❑ Translation Services
❑ Fencing Provider	❑ Pyrotechnics Provider	❑ Transportation Consultant
❑ Florist	❑ Registration Staff	❑ Trash Disposal Services
❑ Formalwear Rental	❑ Risk Manager	❑ Uniform/Apparel Providers
❑ Games Provider	❑ Salespeople	❑ Ushers
❑ Graphic Designer	❑ Security Staff	❑ Video Production

Figure 13-1
Typical Event Vendors

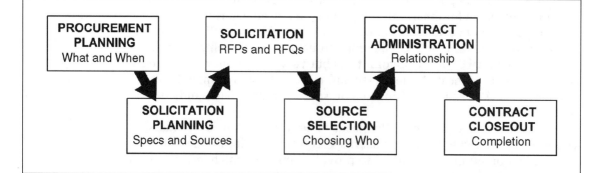

Figure 13-2
Procurement Management Process

bureaus, or chambers of commerce; look through periodicals such as *Special Events* magazine or *Event Solutions* magazine (both of which publish annual resource guide issues); network with colleagues; and search the Internet. You should continually seek out new vendor resources to build an ongoing database of qualified suppliers.

On-Site Insight

Steve Kemble of Steve Kemble Event Design in Dallas, Texas, produces events all over the United States for his clients, sometimes even producing simultaneous events in different cities. Recently he had events for different clients in Dallas, San Francisco, and New York City, all on the same day. Consequently, because he cannot possibly be in several locations at the same time, Kemble regularly contracts with local suppliers for these events, often hiring a local coordinator or designating one vendor as the lead person for an event when he is unable to oversee the event in person.

Kemble says he relies on his *ISES Membership Directory* a great deal to locate ISES members in a particular area, both as potential suppliers and as colleagues with whom he can discuss his project and get referrals to local resources.

It's important to have a lot of vendors in each discipline from which to choose, because each one has different capabilities and different strengths. I will call a colleague I know in a city, or one who has worked in that location, and ask for suggestions and recommendations for suppliers he or she has worked with, based on the specifications for the particular event I am working on. I will also call local vendors I have worked with for recommendations within their disciplines when we both know this particular project isn't suitable for them. They know their competition's strengths and weaknesses better than I do.

Kemble contends that team communication—always keeping all his vendors copied on all the event plans—allows him to delegate and manage projects efficiently.

Since I charge a straight management fee for my services, I don't have to keep my vendors from talking directly with my client. I think it is more professional and illustrates the value of

(Continued)

> *the service I provide—the creativity and coordination—and it allows me to introduce my client to all my vendors. I want my vendors and clients to be able to talk with each other. It's so much more efficient. Of course, I trust my vendors not to try to "back door" me and approach my clients independently for future business. They know that will end our relationship and they will not get any future business from me—I have lots more clients than that one event or that one client.*

DETERMINE SELECTION CRITERIA

The specifications for each product or service to be purchased, outsourced, or contracted must be determined, as well as the criteria to be used to evaluate bids and proposals. Specifications may include brand names, dimensions, features, qualities, quantities, and any other specification important to the success of the event. The more detailed and precise you are with the specifications, the more quality control you will have because such precision will lessen the possibility of receiving inferior materials or services. You must remember that you are now the *customer*.

Evaluation criteria may be objective (e.g., lowest price or holds a specific license or certification) or subjective (e.g., creative approach or demonstrated experience with similar events) and may include such assessment factors as capabilities, creativity, delivery systems, design, equipment, experience, features, financial stability, geographic proximity, price, qualifications, quantities, and/or staffing levels. Depending on your event organization or your client's corporate structure, you might also include such criteria as payment schedules (e.g., payment upon delivery or net 60 days), special preferences given (e.g., women- or minority-owned companies), professional affiliations, environmental programs, Total Quality Management (TQM) initiatives, and so forth. You might create a screening system wherein certain specifications may be established as minimum criteria that must be met for a bid or proposal to be considered (e.g., applicable licenses, insurance coverage, or scope of experience).

SOLICIT BIDS AND PROPOSALS

Once you have determined the specifications and qualified sources, you must prepare the procurement documents and solicit bids and proposals from prospective sellers. Although the terms *bid* and *proposal* are often used interchangeably, in project management these are distinctly different, as specified by the Project Management Institute. "The terms *bid* and *quotation* are generally used when the source selection decision will be based on price (as when buying commercial or standard items), while the term *proposal* is generally used when other considerations, such as technical skills or [creative] approach, are paramount." The standard procurement documents for event products and services include the Request for Proposal (RFP) and the Request for Quotation (RFQ).

Many event professionals recommend that all projects or purchases should be put out for three bids every time to ensure competitive pricing. For many products or materials, the event coordinator may simply call various suppliers for a price quote based on the precise specifications you have established. However, if there is significant latitude in the levels of quality combined with service and/or creative approaches, it is wise to issue an RFP or RFQ. When creating an RFP or RFQ, the professional event coordinator should include certain information in the procurement documents in order to secure complete and comparable responses:

- Specify the scope, expectations, and outcomes.
- Outline the specifications, requirements, and restrictions.
- Put the project in context.
- Identify the budget parameters.
- Define the selection criteria and deadlines.
- Ask for (and check) references.

It is important to include sufficient time in the schedule to solicit and evaluate bids or proposals to select the best vendors for the event, so that this process may be conducted in a comprehensive manner and will not be flawed because of time pressures.

ASSESS CAPABILITIES, COMPETITION, AND COMPLIANCE

Prepare an evaluation instrument that allows you to quickly assess the capabilities of a seller, and compare the strengths and weaknesses of the bid documents or proposals submitted in a manner that minimizes personal preference or prejudice. Your objective is to select reputable, dependable, and competitive vendors or suppliers. You must confirm the seller's ability to deliver the products and/or services proposed in the qualities, quantities, and manner in which you need them. You must make certain the bid includes all costs associated with the delivery and implementation of the product/service, and you must make certain the seller is qualified legally and ethically to provide the product/service.

The evaluation instrument should have the various criteria weighted in relation to their priority in the decision-making process so that you will be able to rank the bids or proposals submitted. For example, if price is most important, it should be weighted more heavily than the quality of equipment or the quantity of staffing proposed, but, as noted throughout this book, using the lowest price alone is rarely a sound strategy for selecting suppliers and can be more costly in the long run. By making price just one of several criteria, you will be able to select the best products and/or services at the best price. The evaluation instrument is used to select a supplier or prepare your negotiation sequence based on the rank order of the proposals received.

ISSUE AND MANAGE CONTRACTS

Once a vendor has been selected, the professional event coordinator must issue and manage the appropriate contractual documents, which may include a contract, letter of understanding, engagement agreement, purchase order, change orders, and seller invoices. These documents must specify the deliverables and schedules, as well as the terms and conditions of the buyer-seller relationship. These must be integrated into the overall event plans and timelines.

When the event is over and/or the products or services have been delivered, you must administratively close out the contracts (secure final invoices, issue final payments, and finalize documentation) and evaluate the vendor's performance as well as the buyer-seller relationship. Would you use this vendor again? Why or why not? The more information you can include in your review and your database, the easier it will be the next time you are seeking qualified vendors, and you will have a better idea of what to expect from this vendor in future dealings.

Volunteers and Support Staffing

The professional event coordinator uses many of the same strategies included in the procurement process or purchasing system when staffing an event with paid and volunteer human resources: planning, sourcing, soliciting, selecting, and evaluating performance. Depending on the type and scope of the event, the event coordinator may be using a handful or hundreds or thousands of people to bring an event to life, and his or her ability to identify staffing needs and the needs of those who will meet those staffing needs will result in a rewarding experience for everyone involved.

ITEMIZE YOUR NEEDS

Large jobs are accomplished by completing small tasks. The professional event coordinator must identify the tasks to be accomplished by internal support staff and volunteers, as well as the number of personnel needed for each task area or team. This calculation will depend on the balance of other resources (time, money, space, etc.) and the types of tasks to be accomplished. These needs should be grouped into task areas within the organizational chart (as discussed in Chapters 2 and 6), then the current volunteer leaders or staff supervisors should be asked to estimate their human resource needs, based on past performance, strengths and weaknesses, and the scope of work to be done. In regard to the size of a volunteer corps, James S. Armstrong, CFRE, author of *Planning Special Events,* notes, "Consider building size and redundancy [because] the work almost always expands beyond the original scope, and some volunteers will leave the project or disappoint in other ways." *The Convention Industry Council Manual,* edited by Susan Krug, recommends scheduling "at least 30 percent more volunteers than needed to cover the assigned tasks."

Stuffing envelopes is different from decorating, and selling tickets is different from data entry. Some people are better at and prefer paperwork, and others prefer "people work"—interacting with event guests or visitors. Determine the skill sets required by those who will fill task area needs, such as administrative skills, organizational skills, manual skills, technical skills, and interpersonal skills. The advantage of this approach is flexibility to allocate people according to their abilities and preferences and to create cross-functional teams using comparable skill sets plus cross training.

CREATE JOB DESCRIPTIONS

It is nearly impossible to effectively allocate your human resources, either paid or volunteer, until you have job descriptions for the various tasks and task areas. A job description should include the job title, a summary of the duties, the required qualifications or skill sets, the hours of work or time commitment, and, if appropriate, the compensation, including benefits and/or entitlements. It should also identify the level of responsibility and authority and the specific conditions or constraints applicable, such as minimum qualifications, security checks, or grooming and dress codes. Alan S. Horowitz, author of *The Unofficial Guide to Hiring and Firing People,* advises that job descriptions should be realistic definitions of what you want and need, not wish lists, and that they must include goals and priorities, not just a list of tasks.

VOLUNTEERS VERSUS PAID STAFF

Event organizations utilize volunteers to fill the jobs that might otherwise be staffed with temporary employees or laborers, but, as discussed earlier, it may be more effective to hire temporary staffing for certain menial task areas and use volunteer resources in other more meaningful (personal or event-specific) task areas. In an article on volunteers and events in the August 1998 issue of *Event Solutions,* Jamise Liddell noted, "Cost-effective and generally more caring and committed than employees hired from temporary agencies, volunteers come when called and sincerely want to be involved." Jo B. Rusin, author of *Volunteers Wanted,* says that people volunteer for many reasons, from personal interest to professional development.

- They **care**—about the cause or the event.
- They want to **contribute**—to make a difference and see results.
- They are **capable**—they have a skill they wish to use.
- They are **curious**—there is a skill that they are interested in developing.
- They want **challenge**——seeking achievement unavailable elsewhere.
- They are **connected**—their friends or family are volunteers.
- They want **connections**—meeting new people and making new friends.
- They are **constituents**—they have something to gain from the outcome.

The professional event coordinator must understand these motives and allocate or assign volunteers so that their needs and desires are met, providing a community atmosphere that supplies connection, participation, and camaraderie. As Dr. Joe Jeff Goldblatt, CSEP, and Frank Supovitz note in their book *Dollars and Events: How to Succeed in the Special Events Business,* "The care and feeding of volunteers puts them somewhere between staff and guests."

FINDING AND RECRUITING VOLUNTEERS

As you look at the reasons people volunteer, you should be able to envision places where these people might be found: the membership of an affinity group or professional association; donors to a charitable organization; schools, retirement communities, recreation centers, clubs, community service groups; on-line communities or interest groups; participant or stakeholder groups, sponsoring organizations, business associates (customers or suppliers); and, of course, the friends and family of current volunteers. Considering that the population as a whole is aging but remaining active and in better health, you should also consider senior citizen centers because they provide a gathering place (and often training). Events that have specific constituencies such as members, participants, fans, or supporters should begin with those constituencies, then identify the demographic profile of the groups and expand their target marketing outward concentrically from those demographics. Events without specific constituencies or first-time events will need to develop target market profiles based on the skill sets and task assignments to be filled.

On-Site Insight

Janet Landey, CSEP, joint managing director of Party Design in Johannesburg, South Africa, and founding president of the South Africa chapter of ISES, cautions event organizers to remember that not all volunteers are people of means with time on their hands—excellent volunteers can be found in any and every socioeconomic strata. "For many civic, political, sports, or cause-related events, many volunteers are enthusiasts or fans who want to participate or support the event, yet they may not have the financial means to even pay for the bus to get to the event or cover the costs of refreshments while working on the event. If event organizers do not take this into consideration they may be losing a valuable work force and the event becomes exclusionary rather than inclusionary."

Landey notes that many people volunteer to get the practical experience that can lead to meaningful employment in a new field, or even employment in any field. "People learn valuable technical and life skills when working on an event that will translate to many different employment contexts. They learn planning skills, organizational skills, communication skills, and teamwork, plus they gain an incredible sense of self esteem." Landey's experience with South Africa's Tourism Learnership Project National Certificate in Tourism: Event Support—a Level Four National Qualifications Framework (NQF) certificate for entry-level event management—and her involvement on the training committees for the World Summit on Sustainable Development, held in Johannesburg in August 2002, and World Cup Cricket in 2003, has allowed her to witness phenomenal results. "You see the most amazing transformation. You would weep with joy. I have to tell you that every day I work with the learners and volunteers, I say, 'This is a miracle.' "

To recruit volunteers effectively, you must have a mechanism for joining the organization or volunteer ranks, usually a volunteer application or enrollment form (similar to a job application form) made available through a variety of portals and/or recruitment events. This application or enrollment form should be designed to collect information regarding the applicant's skills, schedule availability, and interests and to communicate the types of positions and task assignments to be filled and the time commitment required for each (developed from the job description). Such forms should also ask prospective volunteers to indicate their first, second, and third choices of volunteer assignment. Many events include volunteer information, solicitations, and applications in their printed and electronic marketing materials. You might also consider conducting open volunteer recruitment events as a kickoff to your event marketing campaign, as well as during your volunteer thank-you event in anticipation of the next event (inviting each volunteer to bring prospective volunteers as guests).

Temporary Staffing

The employment of temporary or part-time staff must be approached from a traditional human resources perspective, including hiring and firing practices, wage scales and benefits, and employment and workplace standards. All employment situations are subject to various federal, state or provincial, and/or municipal laws regarding personnel. In the United States these may include, among other personnel laws:

- Age Discrimination in Employment Act (ADEA)
- Americans with Disabilities Act (ADA)
- Fair Labor Standards Act (FLSA)—minimum wage, overtime pay, record keeping, and child labor
- Family and Medical Leave Act (FMLA)
- Immigration Reform and Control Act
- Occupational Safety and Health Act (OSHA)—workplace safety regulations
- Title VII of the Civil Rights Act—prohibiting discrimination because of race, color, religion, sex, or national origin
- Workers' compensation requirements

You may acquire these paid human resources through commercial or governmental employment agencies, temporary or contract employee services, or union organizations. You may also find community service groups that will provide temporary workforces in return for a donation or fee. You should also consider your existing internal human resources, perhaps promoting or transferring existing staff or employing individuals who have served as volunteers or interns with your organization. In addition, you might advertise in the employment or "help wanted" sections of local newspapers, on community bulletin boards, in organizational newsletters or publications, and through higher education or continuing education departments of academic institutions in the area.

COMMUNICATION—THE KEY TO SUCCESS

From the planning and sourcing phases to the soliciting and selecting phases, from the initial interview through the orientation and training program, from the job description to the performance evaluation—communication will be the key to success in dealing with your human resources—your human assets. You must be clear about your expectations, clear about the responsibilities and remuneration, and clear about the purpose and outcomes necessary for a successful event and event organization. You must provide the mechanisms for open and interactive communication between leaders and workers and throughout the entire framework of the workforce (see Figure 13-3). You must create an atmosphere of trust, teamwork, and respect, and one that communicates appreciation for a job well done.

Technology Tip

Events utilizing large numbers of volunteers or staff may wish to set up an on-line community with a dedicated Web site linked to the event's Web site. This "team members only" Web site may deal with pertinent issues and information about working on the event and provide chat rooms and message boards accessible only to team members via an identification number and/or password. Staff or volunteers can be instructed to check the Web site for important announcements regarding event plans and updates and invited to submit questions, participate in surveys or polls, or communicate with one another electronically before, during, and after the event. The Web site should include a schedule of important dates, such as training sessions, volunteer or staff kickoff events, and celebratory events, and may be used to profile various team leaders or outstanding volunteers and for other recognition mechanisms. It may include feature articles and behind-the-scenes information just for staff and volunteers, giving them "insider information" about the event, which can be designed to reinforce training on many customer service issues. It might even include on-line training programs and serve as an electronic version of the employee or volunteer instruction/policy manual.

❑ Agendas	❑ Employee Handbooks	❑ Organizational Chart
❑ Announcements	❑ Evaluations	❑ Photographs
❑ Applications	❑ Faxes	❑ Policy Manuals
❑ Banquet Event Orders	❑ Feedback Systems	❑ Posters
❑ Briefings	❑ Fill-in Forms	❑ Pre-Con and Post-Con Meetings
❑ Brochures	❑ Floor Plans	❑ Production Schedules
❑ Bulletin Boards	❑ Flyers	❑ Progress Updates
❑ Cassette Tapes	❑ Guidelines	❑ Publications
❑ CD-ROMs	❑ Handouts	❑ Purchase Orders
❑ Change Orders	❑ Illustrations	❑ Questionnaires
❑ Charts	❑ Incident Reports	❑ Reports
❑ Chat Rooms	❑ In/Out Boards	❑ RFPs/RFQs
❑ Checklists	❑ Instruction Manuals	❑ Speeches
❑ Confirmations	❑ Interviews	❑ Suggestion Boxes
❑ Contact Lists	❑ Intranets	❑ Summaries
❑ Contracts/Agreements	❑ Invoices	❑ Surveys
❑ Conversations	❑ Job Descriptions	❑ Team Meetings
❑ Correspondence	❑ Memos	❑ Telephone Calls
❑ Directions	❑ Meeting Minutes	❑ Time Lines
❑ Directories	❑ Newsletters	❑ Training Manuals
❑ Duty Rosters	❑ Notices	❑ Videos
❑ E-mail	❑ Operations Manuals	❑ Web Site

Figure 13-3
Typical Event Organization Communication Tools

Personnel Management

The professional event coordinator must understand the scope and techniques of human resources management, which is an ongoing and circular process, as illustrated in Figure 13-4. To effectively allocate and coordinate an event's human assets, it is important to establish the guidelines for managing human resources, outlining and defining policies and procedures, roles and responsibilities, communication mechanisms, and performance evaluation techniques. An event's personnel should be utilized to its and their best advantage. They must be provided with the appropriate information and direction so they can perform the tasks required. There must be procedures that allow them to contribute their experience, expertise, and insights to the success of the event, and ways to reward those contributions. The event coordinator may be directly involved throughout the process or responsible for only certain aspects,

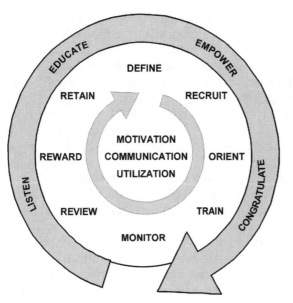

Figure 13-4
The Silvers Circular Model for Human
Resources Management

but he or she must ensure that the people serving within the event
organization are given the appropriate tools, training, motivation, and
recognition.

RECRUITMENT AND SELECTION

Recruitment is actually the first component of a training program. In the
May 1999 issue of *The Event Professional,* a newsletter tracking news
and information for the event industry, Tom Norton, director of recruiting and training at the American Golf Corporation in Santa Monica, California, advised, "A good working relationship begins before the person
is hired. Everything you say during the selection process is just as important and memorable as what you tell [people] when they are hired."
Your recruitment materials, presentations, and personnel must demonstrate the attitude, appearance, and actions expected of people working
on your event or within your event organization.

You might advertise positions on an ongoing basis or hold large recruiting events at which you process dozens, hundreds, or thousands of
applicants at once. Use application forms that collect the necessary and
legally appropriate information, and screen those applications for areas

of job interest and qualifications. Conduct interviews that allow the applicant to learn as much about your event organization as you learn about the applicant's personality and skills, using questions that are open-ended and legally allowed. You are looking for attitude and aptitude, people who exhibit enthusiasm and flexibility; they are looking for opportunity, challenge, and growth. If necessary, include content experts (e.g., technical production, customer service, or food and beverage directors) when interviewing applicants for skill-specific jobs. Always thank the applicant for coming, and let him or her know when the selections will be made.

Select your candidates by reviewing and rating applications, prioritizing and checking the references of the applicants you wish to consider. Make an offer to suitable candidates (and negotiate an employment agreement for paid staffing positions) and welcome them to the event organization. Be certain you notify unsuccessful applicants promptly, but without explanations that might open your organization to discrimination liability. A certain all-volunteer arts and crafts show event organization was involved in a lengthy and costly lawsuit when a potential exhibition judging panelist was told that she was not chosen because the jury selection committee didn't like her own artwork.

Bring a new employee or staff member onto the event team administratively, creating a personnel file or record for the individual. Make certain you have current contact information and that all the appropriate tax forms are completed. You may need to have volunteers sign a Volunteer Liability Waiver if they are not covered under your insurance policy, and confidentiality agreements if event information is sensitive. At the 2002 Olympic Games, volunteers and staff involved in the opening and closing ceremonies were required to sign a confidentiality form to ensure that the production design remained secret. Issue any credentials and equipment necessary, conduct orientation sessions, and provide training as appropriate for the scope and operations of the event.

ORIENTATION SESSIONS

Orientation sessions may be conducted one-on-one, in small groups, or in large group settings. These sessions should introduce new staff members or volunteers to the culture of your event organization and to their coworkers and supervisors. You should discuss the mission and vision of the event, the organizational structure, and the scope of the work to be done, as well as the operational requirements, administrative procedures, accreditation system, emergency procedures, and opportunities for personal/professional development. Although much of this information may be included in an employee manual or volunteer handbook, it should be reiterated verbally in an atmosphere of enthusiasm and interaction to reinforce its content as well as the team spirit.

Many human resource experts recommend creating a program theme or slogan to serve as a framework for the orientation, training, and motivation of employees or volunteers. For example, Team 2002, the volunteer corps for the 2002 Olympic Games in Salt Lake City, used the acronym CHARGE! (Committed, Helpful, Adaptable, Respectful, Gracious, Enjoy!) for its program. Organizers used these six words to introduce and expand on important training concepts and event systems throughout their multilevel training program and training materials. Each word served as an umbrella for the important lessons and instructions they needed their volunteers to remember and practice while working at the Games.

INSTRUCTION MANUALS AND HANDBOOKS

Instruction manuals and handbooks are efficient means of providing your employees and volunteers with the information and regulations that will govern their employment or involvement with your event organization. Depending on the size and complexity of your organization and the paid or volunteer status of the individual worker, you may have a simple instruction sheet or a volume of polices, procedures, and practices. For contracted temporary employees, you should confirm that your policies are compatible with the contracting agency's employment policies. You may wish to, or need to, create different manuals for employees and volunteers (see Figure 13-5), but both should contain the practical instructions and relevant policies or legislated compliance requirements that your employees and volunteers may use and reference to ensure a positive working relationship with your event organization. Always consult with your legal counsel about all applicable employment laws and regulations and the written policies in an employee manual; do not use language in your employee manual that promises or could be construed to promise employees a job as long as they follow your rules.

TRAINING PROGRAMS

Training programs provide the tools necessary to prepare your human resources to deliver a consistent level of service (because services cannot be separated from the person providing them) and to be successful contributors to the success of the event. For training to be effective, the event organization, as well as the trainee, needs to recognize its benefits and commit sufficient resources to the training program. These benefits include improved customer/guest service, increased productivity and skill levels, reduced absenteeism and stress, opportunities for advancement, enthusiasm, event ownership, enjoyment, and a greater commitment to teamwork. You may be providing overall event training as well as job-specific training. You may be training individuals one-on-one on the

Employee Manual	Volunteer Handbook
Introduction Company Mission and Vision; History; Goals, Values, and Beliefs; Terminology Glossary	**Welcome** Event Purpose and Vision; History; Event Overview and Components; Terminology Glossary; FAQs (Frequently Asked Questions)
Employment Practices Equal Employment Opportunity; Employment Status (Permanent, Temporary, Seasonal, Part-time, Full-time, Commissioned, Intern); "At Will" Employment; Outside Employment; Nepotism; Probationary Periods; Personnel File Information Updates	**Administrative Issues** Organizational Structure; Contract Lists; Purchasing and Reimbursement Policies; Documentation Procedures; Volunteer Contact Information Updates
Regulatory Compliance Age Discrimination in Employment Act; Americans with Disabilities Act; Fair Labor Standards Act; Family and Medical Leave Act; Immigration Reform and Control Act; Occupational Safety and Health Act; Title VII of the Civil Rights Act; Workers' Compensation	**Operational Issues** Site Plan; Transportation and Parking Instructions; Equipment Operation; Accreditation System; Communication Protocols; Applicable Legislation (Liquor, Health and Safety, etc.)
Compensation and Benefits Payment Periods and Policies; Overtime and Comp Time; Vacations and Holidays; Travel and Business Expense Policies; Insurance Benefits (Medical, Dental, Life, Disability); Educational Assistance; Pension and Profit-Sharing Plans; Employee Discounts; Good Idea Incentives	**Volunteer Benefits** Volunteer Events; Event Tickets; Rewards; Coupons; Meals; Lounges; Volunteer Discounts; Newsletter; Presentation of Benefits upon Completion of Assignment
Work Practices and Attendance Policies Hours of Operation, Shifts, and Break Policy; Attendance Requirements; Punctuality; Timekeeping Procedures; Leave and Approved Absences; Absence/Late Arrival Notification Procedures; Use of Company Equipment and Vehicles; Data Practices; Destruction of Records	**Schedule and Shift Instructions** Event Time Line and Schedule; Training Sessions; Check-in/Checkout Procedures; Credentials and Passes; Importance of Punctuality; Absence/Late Arrival Notification Procedures

Figure 13-5
Employee Manual and Volunteer Handbook Content Comparison

Employee Manual	Volunteer Handbook
Dress Code Apparel Restrictions; Uniform Issuance and Care Instructions; Hazardous/Inappropriate Accessories and Adornments; Grooming and Hygiene Regulations; Protective Equipment; Identification Badges	**Appearance Instructions** Apparel and Weather-Specific Recommendations; Uniform Issuance and Care Instructions; Sponsor Insignia Integrity Protection; Hazardous/Inappropriate Accessories and Adornments; Importance of Grooming and Hygiene
Health and Safety Safe Work and Manual Handling Procedures; Hazard Identification and Reporting; Fire Safety Procedures; Emergency Procedures; Sanitation Requirements; Accident/Incident Reporting Procedures; Restricted Items, Actions, Areas; Prohibited Items, Actions, Access	**Health and Safety** Safe Work and Manual Handling Procedures; Hazard Identification and Reporting; Fire Safety Procedures; Emergency Procedures; Sanitation Requirements; Accident/Incident Reporting Procedures; Restricted Items, Actions, Areas; Prohibited Items, Actions, Access
Standards of Conduct Confidentiality (Processes and Personal or Proprietary Information); Data Protection Obligations; Conflict of Interest; Smoking Policy; Usage of Phone and Mail Systems; Electronic Policies (E-mail, Internet Access and Usage, Software Usage); Gifts and Gratuities Policy; Media Contact	**Behavior Expectations** Smoking Policy; Onstage/Offstage (Front-of-House and Back-of-House) Behavior; Guest Relations; Confidentiality (Personal or Proprietary Information); Customer Service Attitude; Personal Calls/Visits While on Duty; Media Contact; Celebrity Contact
Discipline and Termination Corrective Disciplinary Guidelines and Procedures; Voluntary and Performance-Related Termination; Misconduct-Related Discipline/Termination (Violence, Weapons, Theft, Sexual/Physical/Mental Harassment, Alcohol/Drug Use, Misuse of Company Property, Information Tampering, etc.); Termination and Separation Procedures	**Unacceptable Behavior** Harassment; Violence; Theft; Disorderly Conduct; Unauthorized Computer Access; Information Tampering; Possession of Unauthorized Firearms, Explosives, or Other Weapons; Assisting in Illegal Access to Event; Disregard for Safety; Alcohol/Drug Use; Obscenity or Offensive Language/Behavior
Dispute and Grievance Procedure Complaint (Discrimination, Sexual Harassment, Programs, Staff) Procedure; Reporting Procedure; Dispute Resolution Process; Retaliation Prohibited; Employee Relations	**Conflict Resolution Strategies** Handling Visitor/Guest Complaints; Sexual Harassment or Staffing Complaints; Reporting Procedures

Figure 13-5
(Continued)

Employee Manual	Volunteer Handbook
Performance Evaluations Wage and Salary Review Policy; Merit Increases; Frequency, Cycle, and Process; Performance Probations; Feedback Systems	**Volunteer Evaluation Survey** Job Satisfaction; Training Received; Value of Rewards; Areas of Concern; Workload; Recommendations
Acknowledgment of Understanding Signature Declaring Employee Has Read and Understands Policies and Procedures	**Volunteer Letter of Understanding** Signature Declaring Volunteer Has Read and Understands Policies; Volunteer Waiver; Confidentiality Agreement

Sources: The Management Assistance Program for Nonprofits *(www.managementhelp.org);* HR-Guide *(www.hr-guide.com);* Employment Law Infonet *(www.elinfonet.com);* HRnext *(www.hrnext.com/tools/index.cfm);* Online Women's Business Center *(www.onlinewbc.gov/Docs/manage/hrpolicy1.html); Deborah Borsum and Robert Sivek, "Communicating Employee Policies,"* Seminar presented at The Special Event 2003; *Joe Goldblatt (2002);* Course One: Amusement and Attraction Human Resource Management *(Alexandria, VA: The International Association of Amusement Parks and Attractions in cooperation with the George Washington University Institute of Tourism Studies).*

Figure 13-5
(Continued)

job or in large groups prior to the event. Some event organizations combine the orientation session with a training session, and others hold progressive training sessions over a period of time; it all depends on the scope and complexity of the training required.

You must determine the training subjects required, the measurable objectives for training and evaluation measurements, and the time, place, trainers, and method of delivery for the training program. Training must employ multiple communication mechanisms that permit trainees to internalize and understand the information and instructions given (see Figure 13-6). Personnel must be given an opportunity to practice procedures at a pace appropriate for them, and these should be practiced in an environment similar to the event conditions in which they will be performing. You should always encourage your staff and volunteers to ask for additional guidance and training as needed.

SCHEDULING AND ASSIGNMENTS

Paid and volunteer staff must be scheduled so that all tasks are accomplished in a timely manner and all functional areas are sufficiently staffed. It is important to assign people to jobs that will satisfy their motives and interests (and that let them use the brains you hired them for),

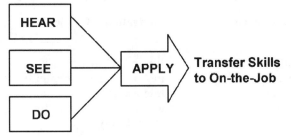

Figure 13-6
The Multiple Dimensions of Effective Training

rather than ask volunteers to do something you wouldn't be willing to do. Never leave individuals without the tools or resources to accomplish their duties, and make certain that they are not stranded at their posts if their replacements do not show up. It is a good idea to have volunteers check in and check out to ensure that they have completed their shifts.

You must promote teamwork and encourage cooperation and mutual support within your entire workforce. Steve Buchholz and Thomas Roth, authors of *Creating the High-Performance Team,* identify the phases of team development: (1) the collection of individuals for the work group, (2) the development of a group identity, defining their roles, directed by a leader, and (3) the development of a purpose-centered team with shared responsibilities. You want to create an atmosphere of teamwork, but you must be careful that functional divisions or teams do not become fiefdoms. It is important to eliminate the distinction between paid and volunteer positions in terms of their value or importance—they are both critical to the success of the event—and you should recognize both team and individual achievements.

EVERYONE NEEDS A STANDING OVATION—MOTIVATION, RECOGNITION, AND RETENTION

The professional event coordinator should establish a motivational environment using rewards and incentives, both tangible and intangible. The work of psychologist Frederick I. Herzberg challenged assumptions that people are motivated solely by money and other tangible benefits. His research showed that employees need to feel that they are achieving something, that they are responsible for their work, and they are allowed to work with minimal supervision (see Figure 13-7). In an article on meeting psychology in the October 1998 issue of *Corporate Meetings and Incentives,* David Rich reported, "According to world-renowned psychologist Nathaniel Branden, there is no more important psychological need than self-esteem."

Job Satisfaction Factors*	Job Dissatisfaction Factors*	Motivational Factors
Achievement Recognition Work Content Responsibility Advancement	Policies and Administration Supervision and Technology Salary Interpersonal Relationships Working Conditions	Personal Growth Inclusion in a Community Intellectual Stimulation Meaningful Contribution Opportunity

Source: Frederick I. Herzberg (1966), "The Motivation-Hygiene Theory," Work and the Nature of Man (World Publishing Co.)

Figure 13-7
Job Satisfaction Factors and Intangible Motivational Factors

Motivation is an inner state that causes a person to act in a way that ensures satisfaction through accomplishment. There are four "people principles" of motivation:

1. All people are motivated.
2. People motivate themselves.
3. People do things for their reasons, not yours.
4. People want and need recognition.

The professional event coordinator must develop recognition systems that link performance directly to rewards. Tangible rewards and incentives should be something of value to the recipient and may need to be held in reserve until the task or assignment has been completed. Recognition (intangible rewards) should be given publicly and whenever appropriate, preferably directly following an achievement to provide positive reinforcement. You might institute such recognition systems as a Wall of Fame with photos of top performers, Event Bucks (coupons given out by supervisors that may be exchanged for prizes or paid time off), or impromptu standing ovations.

Monitoring and Evaluating Performance

Performance monitoring and assessment are important components of any human resources management process. The process begins with clearly stated job descriptions and objectives, followed by appropriate orientation and training, continues with control through monitoring checkpoints and effective feedback systems, and, finally, is refined by conducting performance evaluations that promote the growth and development of the individual as well as the improvement and success of the event organization. People want to do a good job. They want to succeed. They want to know how well they are doing and how they can do things better. The professional event coordinator must implement a systematic approach that fosters two-way communication and a commitment to improvement.

CHECKPOINTS AND COACHING

The professional event coordinator should incorporate monitoring checkpoints into the event timeline and operations plan that ensure that staff and volunteers have sufficient tools and training to complete their assignments successfully. Robert Heller, author of *Effective Leadership,* advises, "Check regularly and informally on progress of delegated tasks. It is important to talk to people regularly about their jobs and how you and they think performance could be improved." Elizabeth A. Wiersma, CSEP, and Kari E. Strolberg, authors of *Exceptional Events: Concept to Completion,* suggest Zone Management with Zone Leaders for events to make certain volunteers feel that they have someone to ask questions of and that there is someone to check on them.

You must institute feedback systems that allow workers to seek guidance and additional training as well as contribute suggestions. In his book *Communicate Clearly,* Heller contends that feedback is essential to communication. "How feedback is transmitted, and what happens in response to it, is basic to effective communication." Ask your workers if they have any questions or concerns and where they are experiencing challenges; their answers can help you identify areas in which your training needs improvement. Then coach and conduct rather than control your workers. Refocus and redirect their efforts as needed. Keep in mind the Law of Buoyancy—let go and they will rise.

DEVELOP EVALUATION CRITERIA

In order to conduct effective performance reviews, the professional event coordinator must establish appropriate evaluation criteria (see Figure 13-8). In *The Basics of Performance Measurement,* author Jerry L. Harbour notes that performance measures are used to establish a baseline measurement, measure performance level changes over time (trending), ensure that performance is staying within tolerance limits (controlling), determine problem areas (diagnostic), and predict future performance (planning). Performance should be measured against the job requirements and the qualities important to the event operations, such as customer service abilities or compliance with safety procedures. As with

❑ Attendance	❑ Flexibility	❑ Problem Solving
❑ Attitude	❑ Grooming	❑ Productivity
❑ Communication	❑ Independence	❑ Punctuality
❑ Cooperation	❑ Initiative	❑ Quality of Work
❑ Customer Service	❑ Job Knowledge	❑ Safety
❑ Decision Making	❑ Policy Compliance	❑ Teamwork
❑ Error Frequency	❑ Presentation Skills	❑ Technical Skills

Figure 13-8
Typical Personnel Performance Evaluation Criteria

criteria for evaluating vendor proposals, more weight can be assigned to certain criteria than to others, but it is important to consider a broad scope of criteria encompassing knowledge, skills, and attitude.

CONDUCT PERFORMANCE REVIEWS

Performance reviews should be conducted one-on-one with employees in a scheduled and logically consistent cycle of frequency, such as at the conclusion of an introductory or probationary period, annually, biannually, seasonally, or at an event-specific point in time. Let people know what they will be evaluated on and why. Performance reviews may be linked with advancement or salary/wage increases, but they should also be structured to encourage achievement. Performance reviews or appraisals are conducted to allow both you and the individual you are evaluating determine areas in which improvement may be made and those in which additional training is required.

Performance assessments should be a mutual (between employee and evaluator) identification and review of the individual's strengths and weaknesses and should be approached as a constructive critique rather than criticism (errors are rarely due to malice). In conducting the evaluation, you should seek input, feedback, and discussion regarding the job requirements and challenges. You should establish agreed-upon plans for improvement within a specified period of time and create opportunities for people to set their own goals. A staff performance review should always be documented in writing, with the employee given an opportunity to review the comments and add his or her own comments, then signed by both evaluator and employee. The performance of individual volunteers should be reviewed and evaluated internally by staff and supervisors, perhaps using the same criteria used for employees, with recommendations as to appropriateness for further involvement recorded for future reference.

DATA MINING THROUGH EVALUATIONS

Just as its external customers (the audience) are asked to evaluate an event, which is discussed further in Chapter 14, its internal customers (volunteers, staff, suppliers, and other stakeholders) must be asked for their reviews of the event and its operations. Volunteers should be asked to evaluate their involvement in the event, including such areas as satisfaction with their assignments, the training received, the workload, and the value of the rewards or incentives. You should also seek feedback on any areas of concern, recommendations for improvement, and interest in repeat involvement. These evaluations, which should be scheduled directly following an event, may include surveys, one-on-one interviews, or group discussions. The 80-20 Rule (80 percent of your sales comes from 20 percent of your customers) applies to cause and effect as well— 80 percent of effects usually comes from 20 percent of the possible causes. Therefore, it is imperative to mine your evaluations for data that will reveal those causes that have significant positive and negative effects on your event operations and human resources.

Conflict Resolution, Discipline, and Termination

In dealing with human beings, conflict is inevitable. In requiring human beings to perform in specific ways, disciplinary measures are often required. In managing human resources, termination may be necessary. Not all conflict is bad—it is often simply a difference of opinion, which may be the catalyst for innovative solutions. As Alan S. Horowitz notes, "assumptions are confronted, decisions questioned, and better choices often result." Disciplinary measures should be designed as corrective actions with specific consequences rather than purely punitive measures. And, when necessary to terminate or separate an employee from the event organization, such actions must protect the dignity of the person being terminated.

PREVENTION IS BEST

Conflict and unacceptable behavior most often result from unclear instructions and ill-defined expectations. Creating an atmosphere of open and effective communication will allow the professional event coordinator to prevent many disputes as well as avoid the destructive aspects of conflict. Blocks to effective communication include the timing (e.g., too early, too late, insufficient repetition), the method (verbal messages must be reinforced with written messages and vice versa), the environment (e.g., too noisy, too busy, interruptions, etc.), and emotions (e.g., hurt feelings, personality conflicts, wishful listening—hearing only what you want to hear). You must establish your expectations in writing in vendor contract language, job descriptions, and instructions, and in published policies and procedures, based on experience, fairness, and regulatory requirements. Many event organizations create a formal grievance procedure that permits staff and volunteers to register complaints through a systematic hierarchy that ensures that grievances will be heard, investigated, and responded to.

CONFLICT RESOLUTION STRATEGIES

Dudley Weeks, author of *The Eight Essential Steps to Conflict Resolution,* contends, "Conflict is an outgrowth of diversity and differences. Conflicts are not always limited to battles between interests and desires. Needs, perceptions, power, values and principles, feelings and emotions, and internal conflicts are critical ingredients of our relationships and the conflicts that punctuate relationships." Weeks advises that rather than trying to find a quick fix or pretending the conflict doesn't exist (typical but ineffective approaches to conflict resolution), one must clarify each individual's perceptions, build shared positive power, and develop action steps that are mutually beneficial. The work of Phillip L. Hunsaker and Anthony J. Alessandra, authors of *The Art of Managing People,* suggests that you must understand transactional styles so that in a conflict with another person, you are interacting as equals (adults) rather than in a parent-child ego state, and that you must look for root problems so that you can ultimately resolve the causes of the conflict rather than simply the symptoms. Conflict resolution techniques include the following:

- **Stop, look, and listen**—Think before you act; identify the nature of the conflict; do not discount the importance of the conflict to the individual(s); recognize the emotional and functional needs of the conflicting parties—people need to be heard.
- **Separate from the situation**—Postpone discussion to a different time (cooling-off period) or place (neutral territory); handle the situation in private; refer to the applicable policies, procedures, and provisions of contractual, collective, or waiver agreements.
- **Be understanding but objective**—Remain calm; do not "take sides"; empathize but stay focused on the goals and objectives of the event.
- **Be reasonable and respectful**—Focus on behavior rather than personality; point to solutions instead of pointing fingers; do not shame; allow people to retain/regain their composure and integrity.
- **Seek solutions**—Solicit and suggest possibilities; prepare to compromise or to relocate an individual; seek agreement on the change and its timeline.

- **Follow up**—Refer to the appropriate entity (e.g., grievance committee or management); record the details and document discussions; follow up on the agreed-upon solutions.

DISCIPLINARY MEASURES

The professional event coordinator must, first and foremost, make certain that staff members are aware of and understand all rules, regulations, policies, procedures, and expectations, and must use positive reinforcement and behavior modeling (displaying the desired behavior) to sculpt desired behavior. If incidents and infractions occur, they should be reported to the proper management authorities and progressive disciplinary measures employed as necessary to correct behavior rather than as punishment. Progressive discipline involves successive warnings with attendant consequences, coupled with corrective training and agreed-to levels of improvement. Any incidents or infractions, as well as the disciplinary measures employed, should be recorded in the employee's personnel record or file.

You may wish to establish a table of offenses and penalties that will make perfectly clear the consequences of certain actions. This listing can include the offense (e.g., unauthorized absence from the job) and the penalties for the first, second, and subsequent offenses. The penalties may include oral admonishments, written reprimands or warnings, suspensions (e.g., 5 to 30 days with or without pay), and removal/termination. You may also need to establish which infractions or conduct will result in automatic removal/termination (e.g., violence, possession of weapons, theft, sexual harassment, alcohol/drug abuse, misuse of company property, information tampering, etc.).

TERMINATION PROCEDURES

No one wants to fail, no one wants the event to be a failure—including the employees of the event organization. Sometimes, however, it is necessary to remove an individual from the event organization because of unacceptable performance levels or behavior. When termination is necessary, Alan S. Horowitz advises, "you can't hide from your responsibilities, but you can help create an atmosphere that makes the process as minimally stressful and as little humiliating as possible." The professional event coordinator charged with firing an employee (or volunteer) must implement a sensitive yet succinct procedure, preferably one that has been established within a written policy.

- **Do it in private**—Safeguard the person's self-esteem.
- **Be straightforward**—Tell the person exactly why he or she is being fired, but conveyed in general terms, preferably with reasons in

writing. (Be prepared to support these reasons with documentation.)

- **Listen but do not argue**—Allow the person to talk, but let him or her know the decision is final.
- **Be clear about immediate expectations**—Explain what the person needs to do next to complete the discharge (e.g., clean out desk now, return property, do not return, etc.).
- **Be discreet**—Tell only those people who need to know and tell them only what they need to know.

Throughout the process of planning, sourcing, soliciting, selecting, and evaluating the vendors and human resources that will come together to create, operate, and deliver the event, the professional event coordinator must remember that it is the people who make an event a success. Each person is an *individual,* with individual needs and expectations as well as talents and limitations. Each person deserves respect and recognition for his or her contribution to the success of the event. Each person is a distinct and distinctive part of the event team. No one should be anonymous.

Target Competency Review

The professional event coordinator must work with a broad variety of people to bring an event to life, including vendors, volunteers, participants, and temporary, part-time, and full-time personnel, all coming together as a team. Finding and securing the right people and providers is dependent on a systematic and equitable approach that matches the needs of the event with the needs of the individuals. Procurement policies and processes should be employed to identify the goods and services to be outsourced and the sources best qualified to provide them, then the best products and services should be secured at the best prices, based on the criteria most important to the achievement of the goals and objectives of the event.

Recruiting and acquiring volunteers and support staff should be approached in the same systematic manner, including planning, sourcing, soliciting, selecting, and evaluating performance. Identifying tasks and skill set requirements forms the basis for job descriptions, and establishing reasonable policies and procedures forms the basis for employee manuals or volunteer handbooks, both of which serve as important communication tools to assist personnel in becoming effective members of the event team.

The professional event coordinator must implement a comprehensive and progressive approach to human resources management that ensures that the personnel serving the event organization have the appropriate tools, training, motivation, and recognition. Recruitment events, orientation sessions, and training programs are all opportunities to establish and reinforce the culture of the event organization, which may be more effective when incorporated within the framework of a program theme promoting teamwork and commitment.

Monitoring and performance evaluation activities provide the feedback mechanisms to promote the growth and development of the individual and the improvement of the event organization's programs and processes. They must be planned carefully to ensure that checkpoints and coaching opportunities are timely and constructive. Effective communications will form the basis for these activities, as well as any conflict resolution, disciplinary measures, or termination procedures that become necessary. The professional event coordinator must create an environment of respect and recognition for the important human assets that bring the event to life.

EXERCISES IN PROFESSIONAL EVENT COORDINATION

Describe the planning, sourcing, soliciting, selection, and performance evaluation of vendors, volunteers, and support staff you would conduct for the following events. Explain the logistical requirements associated with these steps and how they will be incorporated into your overall event plan and budget.

1. You have been hired to coordinate the annual fund-raising event for the Animal Humane Society—the "Doggie Dash"—a fun run and walk for people and their canine pets, which will conclude with a large breakfast and fête for participants, including numerous sponsor displays and pet-related activities.

2. You are coordinating an elegant wedding with a dinner/dance reception for a couple, both with large families who wish to be very much involved in the event yet will not be available until the day before the ceremony.

3. You have been put in charge of the district soccer championship for secondary schools, a four-day event attracting ten school teams within a 60-K radius. You expect not only the teams, but a large attendance of parents, families, and student supporters as well.

CHAPTER 14

Knowledge Management

Knowledge is an organized body of information.

—*The American College Dictionary*

IN THIS CHAPTER YOU WILL LEARN HOW TO:

- Develop and implement efficient record keeping systems and data processing procedures, utilizing technology for the acquisition, storage, retrieval, and security of information.
- Create comprehensive Production Books to facilitate on-site operations and communications.
- Conduct effective evaluation activities to gain valuable information and analysis to direct future event operations and marketing efforts.
- Prepare reports that facilitate the timely and efficient distribution of information to event stakeholders.
- Collect and archive the documentation, documents, records, physical evidence, and historical information that provide examples, proof, or support of actions and activities important to the future success of an event or event organization.

The exhausted event team was sitting at a bare table surrounded by the residue of a huge party that had ended just an hour ago. The party had been the culmination of a multiday convention involving dozens of large events for a group of five thousand delegates. Everyone had been working at peak performance levels for more than a month and just wanted to sleep for a week. In an apologetic but cautionary tone, the event coordinator advised her team, "No job is over until the paperwork is done."

Paperwork, and the information included therein, is a crucial component of professional event coordination. As a professional event coordinator, you will plan, organize, allocate, direct, and control resources to achieve goals and objectives; in these efforts, information is an incredibly valuable resource. You will amass tremendous amounts of information throughout the event coordination process, and without organizing and handling that information appropriately, you will not be able to utilize that profusion of data to achieve the goals and objectives of your event and event organization. The management of information is vital to acquiring the *knowledge* you require to coordinate the events for which you are responsible. You cannot expect to keep all this information in your head, and unless it is on paper or electronically stored, you cannot transfer your knowledge effectively to others on your event team or in your event organization. Sound administrative procedures for bookkeeping, correspondence, database maintenance, and other record keeping and reporting activities must be integrated throughout your event operations.

Information Management

Throughout the event coordination process you will generate, receive, collect, seek out, send out, sort, analyze, and store a broad range of information. This information directs the production of your event, from the research and design stage, through planning and implementation, and, finally, to evaluation of the event. To effectively manage information and implement efficient record keeping, you must understand what types of information you have, what types of information you need, and what information you must keep and why, and then develop systems and procedures for handling and keeping it.

There are three things done with all this information—assessing, organizing, and controlling. Your assessment will include an inventory and review of all the documents and paperwork pertaining to your event operations to identify paperwork redundancy and gaps in the types of documents needed to efficiently and effectively conduct the business of your event. You then conduct a functional analysis to determine how these documents support your event operations. In addition, you will want to ensure that your documents—from correspondence to reports, checklists to memorandums—are designed in such a way that they are easy to comprehend, are economic and effective in style, and project the image and identity of your organization.

Organizing your documents and information will include establishing filing systems, storage methods and materials, plus tracing and tracking systems for efficient retrieval. Many of these functions are best accomplished utilizing standard or specialized computer software programs. Controlling information involves establishing standard operating procedures to deal with communications, record keeping, documentation, reference and archive materials, and security issues. You need a "paper trail" of everything connected with the event—get everything in writing, and keep it where you can get at it.

ANALYZE YOUR INFORMATION SYSTEM

Information and document assessment and analysis are critical to the success of your information management strategy. Look at all the items listed in Figure 14-1 (which is by no means complete) and consider the

❏ Agendas
❏ Agreements
❏ Applications
❏ Archives
❏ Audits and Analyses
❏ Banquet Event Orders
❏ Blueprints
❏ Books
❏ Briefings
❏ Brochures
❏ Budgets
❏ Business Cards
❏ Calendars
❏ Catalogs
❏ Certificates of Insurance
❏ Change Orders
❏ Charts
❏ Checklists
❏ Confirmations
❏ Contact Lists
❏ Contracts
❏ Conversations
❏ Customer Profiles
❏ Diaries
❏ Directories
❏ E-mail
❏ Employee Records
❏ Equipment Orders
❏ Estimates
❏ Evaluations
❏ Facts and Figures
❏ Faxes
❏ Financial Statements
❏ Flyers and Circulars
❏ Forecasts
❏ Fill-in Forms

❏ Guidelines
❏ Handouts
❏ Incident/Accident Reports
❏ Inquiry/Interview Forms
❏ Instructions/Directions
❏ Insurance Policies
❏ Inventory Lists
❏ Invoices
❏ Job Descriptions
❏ Leases
❏ Letters/Correspondence
❏ Licenses
❏ Lost-Business Reports
❏ Magazines
❏ Mailing Lists
❏ Manifests
❏ Manuals
❏ Maps
❏ Meeting Minutes
❏ Memos
❏ Mileage Logs
❏ Newsletters
❏ Newspapers
❏ Notes
❏ Notices
❏ Order Forms
❏ Organizational Charts
❏ Outlines
❏ Patron Lists
❏ Permits
❏ Photos
❏ Plans
❏ Policies and Procedures
❏ Portfolios
❏ Press Clippings
❏ Press Releases

❏ Price Lists
❏ Proceedings
❏ Production Orders
❏ Production Schedules
❏ Proposals
❏ Publications
❏ Purchase Orders
❏ Questionnaires
❏ Registration Forms and Lists
❏ Regulations
❏ Reports
❏ Research
❏ Resumes
❏ Reviews
❏ RFPs/RFQs
❏ Sales Leads
❏ Site/Floor Plans
❏ Sketches/Illustrations
❏ Specifications
❏ Sponsor Packages/Kits
❏ Spreadsheets
❏ Statistics
❏ Suggestion Cards
❏ Surveys
❏ Tax Records
❏ Timelines
❏ Time Sheets
❏ Training Manuals
❏ Transaction Records
❏ Updates
❏ Vendor Lists
❏ VIP Lists
❏ Volunteer Lists
❏ Waivers
❏ Web Sites
❏ Worksheets

Figure 14-1
Typical Event Records and Information Resources

fact that many of these types of documents and information come in a variety of forms and serve numerous functions. Some apply to a specific event, others to your event organization or business. You must develop an understanding of how and why each piece of information and documentation affects and supports your event coordination processes and procedures.

To assess your information resources, assemble and review the documents you use within your event operations and identify the documents that are generated internally, such as memos and proposals, and those that are generated externally, such as permits and regulatory forms. Conduct a "gap analysis" (reviewing your procedures to identify any missing components or functions) to determine what internally generated information or documents are nonexistent or inadequate for your operational requirements. Consider the effort that will be required to gather together all these documents. Next, review all internal documents for style and content. Your documents should reflect your image and branding objectives as well as serve their functional purpose. Do they say what you need them to say in clear and compelling language? Are they economical, simple in style? Are your forms and checklists comprehensive and easy to use?

Carefully analyze the function or functions of each document and each type of information required for your event operations. Analyze how and why you use each in your day-to-day operations. How does each piece of paper impact your ability to research, design, plan, implement, and evaluate your events and event organization? This analysis will help you develop standardized communications and documentation and to determine the best strategies for organizing and controlling paperwork and information.

DESIGN DOCUMENTS FOR EFFICIENCY AND CLARITY

Well-designed documents will improve your efficiency and effectiveness and reinforce your image branding objectives. You must understand who will be using or reading a document, the purpose of the document, and the action required of the recipient. Review your event coordination processes, start to finish and threshold to threshold, to formulate your standard correspondence, memorandums, proposals, reports, and the like. Establish a format and style that includes an effective layout of information, graphics, key branding images, and language style (see Figure 14-2). Remember that image influences perceptions.

Once you have your standard formats defined and refined, use them consistently. Create templates in your word processor for your frequently used documents and routine correspondence, including proposals, time lines, budgets, contracts, job orders, and others. Design your documents to be integrated into your information management systems, collecting the information you require in a format that will function within your procedures, so that you can reduce the number of times you must collect or record information such as names, contact information, dates, and other data. Design checklists and forms that will facilitate your information-gathering requirements and reduce redundancy of effort, including site inspection checklists, client or employee interview forms, evaluation

❏ Purpose of the Document	❏ Lists and Line Items
❏ Message to be Communicated	❏ Dates and Deadlines
❏ Information to be Collected/Disseminated	❏ Contact Information
❏ Action Required	❏ Branding Images and Logo Policies
❏ Options or Choices Available	❏ Confidentiality Considerations

Figure 14-2
Document Design Considerations

instruments, and numerous other documents. These must be easy to use and must be used consistently to be effective. Understand what information you are gathering, why it is required, and how it will be used.

On-Site Insight

Robert Sivek, CSEP, CERP, and Deborah Borsum, CSEP, CMD, owners of The Meetinghouse Companies, Inc., in Elmhurst, Illinois, have what they call "the Rainbow Book"—a series of standard operating forms that are printed on pages of different colors, called "Rainbow Sheets," for different types of jobs and job duties. Sivek notes, "We have a form for everything from checklists to worksheets. These help our event producers make sure they ask all the right questions, and it reduces the 'Oh, I forgot!' These forms provide the checks and balances throughout our administrative and event production operations." Borsum says that those checks and balances are critical to the organization's marketing objectives as well as its management operations. "Since Robert and I own the company, every event our company produces is a reflection on us because our name is on it. We use the Rainbow Sheets as a quality assurance instrument."

UTILIZE INFORMATION TECHNOLOGY TO DEVELOP SYSTEMS AND PROCEDURES

For virtually all information management functions, there are computer software programs to help you (see Figure 14-3). Many of these are completely integrated, allowing you to consolidate information in a single system and transfer information from one application to another with a

❑ Accounting	❑ Project/Event Management
❑ CAD (Computer-Aided Design)	❑ Registration
❑ Catering	❑ Rental/Inventory Management
❑ Database	❑ Scheduling
❑ Desktop Publishing	❑ Spreadsheet
❑ Graphics	❑ Word Processing

Figure 14-3
Typical Computer Software Used for Event Coordination

click or a keystroke. Robert Sivek, CSEP, CERP, notes that his company's rental inventory control software interfaces directly with its accounting software, which streamlines financial operations, from pricing and bid preparation to billing and forecasting cash flow. In everything from inventory tracking, to human resources management, to working with client lists, vendor lists, and venue lists, using your computer to its fullest potential will increase your efficiency. For example, Ginger Kramer of Classic World Events, Inc., in San Jose, California, developed a costing system for calculating catering bids using Windows Excel that has cut a six-hour cost analysis down to 20 minutes.

Word processing software allows you to create document templates to quickly generate reports, contracts, and production orders. Database software allows you to manage lists of information, ranging from inventory to contact lists. Registration-specific software provides integrated registration and reporting operations, and multipurpose meeting management software programs or suites often include relational databases that automatically record or change one piece of information (e.g., telephone number or address) marked as a sort field throughout the system on all documents or records using that sort field. Spreadsheet software allows you to manipulate numbers and automatically calculate percentage markups for your bids, as well as grouping information into table formats, which provides the function of automatically changing all tables, no matter where they are, when you change something in the original table in the spreadsheet function. Accounting software allows you to categorize and tabulate your revenues and expenditures, automatically calculate payroll taxes, and write checks.

Scheduling and project (or event) management software helps you plot out your plans and planning timelines, with automatic reminders or deadline triggers included to ensure that contracts, orders, and invoices are managed in a timely manner. Computer-aided design (CAD) floor plan diagramming software automatically calculates space and plots in tables, chairs, stages, and so forth, but you could do this manually in a simple graphics-based program. Desktop publishing software assists you in designing and developing attractive newsletters, brochures, and other internal and external marketing pieces, as well as employee or volunteer handbooks, a variety of checklists, order forms, and questionnaires that reflect your corporate culture and image.

You must remember, however, that software is a tool, not a panacea, and it requires a significant investment of human capital in addition to the financial capital needed to purchase the software. In an article on implementing event management software in the September 2002 issue of *Event Solutions* magazine, Betsy H. Newman advises that you must "allow time for learning the system, gathering your operation's resource and service information, entering the data into the new system, understanding how the information you entered interacts with each area of the software, developing and conducting staff training, and being available for continued staff support." That data entry and staff training can become expensive, but may be worth the cost in the long run—you must evaluate the software products available and their potential return in terms of efficiency and productivity.

Technology Tip

Although specialized software is available for many event coordination tasks such as budgeting, registration, room diagramming, scheduling, and so on (plus many more applications sure to be developed), the purchase of off-the-shelf software may be a cost-effective approach. Considering the relatively small price of bundled packages such as those Microsoft offers (MS Word, Access, Excel, Outlook, and PowerPoint), as compared with that of an integrated management suite or customized program developed specifically for your operations, as well as their overwhelming popularity and usage, adapting off-the-shelf software to your particular needs may be faster, easier, and more cost-efficient. You may also wish to investigate Web-based products (actually services) that offer an "always on/access anywhere" platform, which may be rented, based on actual use, rather than purchasing a software package.

For a comprehensive listing of industry and technology links including industry-specific software, visit Corbin Ball's "Corbin's List" at www.corbinball.com/tips.list.corbinslist.htm, or purchase his book, *The Ultimate Meeting Professional's Software Guide,* published by MPI.

ORGANIZE AND CONTROL INFORMATION

Once you have assessed and analyzed the documents and documentation that will be required for your event coordination operations and responsibilities, you must organize the information in those documents in a manner that suits your procedures and your work style. Organization is a very personal matter; no one system or strategy will serve the specific needs of all the varied types of events and event organizations. Understand *how* you do *what* you do, then develop the systems and procedures for organizing the information and documentation required for *your* operations. Design these systems to facilitate your needs, while ensuring that these systems are functional for other individuals in your event operation as well.

The best filing system, storage equipment, or document designs will not be effective unless procedures and protocols for their use are established and enforced. Whether you are a one-person operation or part of an event organization employing hundreds of people, you must develop mechanisms for controlling the information you have. Michael E. Gerber, author of *The E-Myth Revisted,* contends that you should become "systems-dependent," not "people-dependent," so that your information management strategy remains efficient and effective regardless of who is involved in the process. Gerber suggests that systems should be designed to be operated by people with the lowest possible level of skill applicable to your organization. Your system design should also anticipate the departure of personnel, ensuring that important information does not exit or disappear into the void when someone leaves the organization. For functions such as acquisition of information, communications, archival operations and the like, set up procedures that outline the actions to be taken with each type of information included in your event coordination process, based on the required flow of information, incoming and outgoing, as well as your legal, ethical, and fiduciary responsibilities.

CONSIDER TRACING, TRACKING, AND RETRIEVAL REQUIREMENTS

The reason information is such a valuable resource within professional event coordination is that it rarely applies to only a single event. Therefore, you must be able to quickly locate information that will be useful to you and critical to the success of your event and event organization. You may be preparing numerous versions of a proposal until the final negotiation has taken place; you need to know which version is which. You might be managing numerous event projects simultaneously, handling numerous contracts that must be tracked for timely execution, or monitoring numerous committees and departments whose reports and meeting notes must be collected, reviewed, distributed, and acted upon to make them worthwhile. For each type of information, a system must be established for efficient tracing, tracking, and retrieval.

Filing systems are typically organized alphabetically, numerically, or chronologically, but may also be organized geographically, categorically, or according to a color coding system applicable to your operations. Tom Hindle, author of *Manage Your Time,* says, "It is helpful to have a system that indicates immediately, by means of color or typography, the level or classification of each file." Also consider your legal obligations regarding information in your files; tax requirements may dictate chronological records by tax period. You should cross-reference your filing systems to increase their functionality. Organize the files in your computer the same way you would in a filing cabinet. You can store vast amounts of information and files within your computer, making it available at your fingertips, but it is critical to remember to back up your files on a systematic and regular basis.

PROTECT YOUR INFORMATION

Filing systems should facilitate easy retrieval, yet you may need to control access to them. Information is not only power; it has fiscal, logistical, and competitive value, and you may have specific ethical and legal responsibility to protect certain types of information. As event coordinator, you must consider the safety and security of information materials. Important documents and records, particularly confidential records, should be stored in filing cabinets with locking mechanisms, and you should use passwords for computer access and change those passwords periodically. What would happen if there was a fire or flood? You may need to invest in fireproof cabinets and consider a storage location other than your business premises where you keep critical original documents or backup copies. After a specific time period, depending on your financial and legal requirements, almost all records should be put in storage or disposed of. Carefully consider the confidentiality and proprietary nature of information and establish the appropriate precautions and protection devices.

The Production Book

The Production Book, or Operations Manual, as it is referred to in the meetings industry, is your on-site reference and guidebook covering every important facet of an entire event. It should include anything and everything required for smooth operations at the event site, even if you are not able to be there. (Remember the Big Truck theory—if you get run over by a big truck, someone else can take over and run the event.) All key information and documents related to the planning and operations of the event, as well as any documentation required to comply with governmental regulations, should be included in the Production Book. (See Figure 14-4.)

The contents of the Production Book should include schedule, directory, and verification documents and documentation important to the event coordination process. Most professional event coordinators use three-ring binders for their Production Books. This book will become your event bible, a compendium of the documentation pertaining to your event operations. Information included in the Production Book must be cross-referenced several ways in order for it to be an effective tool. Organize the Production Book as best suits your needs, and clearly tab each section so you can quickly locate specific sequential or categorical information. Distribute copies of the book (or customized versions) to the key personnel on the event team.

SCHEDULE

The Production Book should include a complete schedule of all event components and activities. This schedule should be in at least two formats—chronological in sequence and alphabetical by activity (e.g., President's Lunch, Resource Room, Winery Tour) or component (e.g., audiovisual, catering, décor, entertainment) or both, depending on the scope and complexity of the event. The chronological schedule will help you monitor the progress of the event, and the alphabetical schedule will help you locate individual components. Create a "Program-at-a-Glance" overview chart of the entire event as a cross-reference tool, showing day, date, times, and site/room name. Sandra L. Morrow, author of *The Art of*

❏ Arrival/Departure Manifest	❏ Floor/Site Plans	❏ Production Schedule
❏ AV Specifications	❏ Instructions	❏ Program Agenda
❏ Banquet Event Orders	❏ Insurance Certificates	❏ Proposals
❏ Billing Arrangements	❏ Lease Agreements	❏ Room Setups
❏ Change Orders	❏ Letters and Memos	❏ Scripts
❏ Charts and Checklists	❏ Licenses	❏ Seating Charts
❏ Confirmations	❏ Orders and Invoices	❏ Staffing Schedules
❏ Contact Numbers	❏ Organizational Charts	❏ Timelines
❏ Contracts	❏ Permits and Waivers	❏ Vendor Lists
❏ Entertainer Riders	❏ Policies and Procedures	❏ VIP Lists

Figure 14-4
Typical Contents of a Production Book

the Show, suggests that the individual vendors and contractors will have their own scheduling forms, and you should include copies of these for comparison and confirmation purposes.

DIRECTORY

Create a contact list of all vendors and key stakeholders, including names, all possible telephone numbers (i.e., office, home, cellular, pager, hotel phone, and room numbers), and mailing and e-mail addresses. Do not forget to include your own contact information, and make certain that all the appropriate members of your staff have copies of this list. Include your organizational chart and staff schedules and instructions. In addition, cross-reference your vendor lists by name and service.

VERIFICATION

All documents, including your proposal, the final contract, correspondence, vendor agreements and purchase orders, floor plans, confirmations, invoices, licenses, and certificates of insurance, should be at your fingertips in case a question or dispute arises on-site. If allowed, put copies of all permits and waivers in your Production Book and keep the originals in a safe place in your office. You might also include copies of pertinent policies and regulations that you can present should there be a question about what will and will not be allowed or what should or should not be done.

Evaluations

You must remember that you cannot control results, only actions, but the better you control actions, the more likely it is that you will have the results you want. Evaluations and research give you the information required to devise and implement effective practices and controls that lead to good results, and this is a circular process (see Figure 14-5). As the event coordinator, you must determine what is to be evaluated and why, when and where evaluations will take place, how evaluations will be conducted and the methods to be used, then integrate the investments of time, money, human resources, and space into the event's overall operational plans.

BEGIN WITH THE END IN MIND

In *The Basics of Performance Measurement,* Jerry L. Harbour states, "Upfront design equals downstream performance." To conduct effective evaluations and evaluative research or situation analyses, the professional

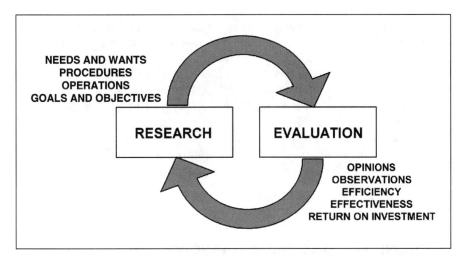

Figure 14-5
The Silvers Research-Evaluation Continuum Model

event coordinator must determine what knowledge or information is needed and why (its purpose and eventual usage). Evaluations may be either proactive (seeking information to facilitate improvements) or reactive (seeking information to validate assumptions or justify actions). They may be performance reviews or customer satisfaction ratings. They can be used to gather statistics or develop a customer profile. They may be used to determine the value of an event component, examine procedures, or define future goals. Evaluation instruments should deal with issues that are relevant and important to the event operations and the event's stakeholders. The goals and objectives of evaluations must be linked directly to the goals and objectives of the event or event organization (review the goals and objectives list in Chapter 2).

On-Site Insight

Dana Zita, CSEP, of a N d Logistix, Inc. in Toronto, Canada, regularly conducts evaluations, collecting and compiling delegate comments, as a service for her clients, but she also has a rigorous and comprehensive internal evaluation strategy. "We generate a client evaluation form that is tracked from the first contact

(Continued)

to the final evaluation. It includes headings linked to our critical path planning points and all the items that are important to our quality control. In addition, we maintain an ongoing list of comments and recommendations that is updated weekly throughout the planning process." Zita notes that each client evaluation is customized with categories specific to each project and indicating whether the client is a first-time or repeat customer. These internal evaluation techniques allow her to mine the data collected to develop comprehensive client profiles, track performance, and implement improved client services.

EVERYONE AND EVERYTHING IS INVOLVED

Evaluations and performance reviews must be designed to gather information and measurements about the entire event coordination process, including the research conducted, the designs and plans developed, the implementation procedures, and even the evaluation instruments and activities employed. As a professional event coordinator, you must evaluate the business plan, marketing plan, communications plan, operational plan, risk management plan, and the on-site activities. You may be evaluating your procurement procedures, vendor performance, and budget controls. You may be seeking audience opinions on the length or location of the event, the facilities or accommodations, the quality of the speakers, and/or the meal functions and special events. You may be conducting evaluations and quantifying the results to match the sponsorship opportunity evaluations that current and potential commercial sponsors of the event are conducting. You may be conducting a gap analysis to identify any gaps between customer expectations and the service or experience actually received.

MEASURE YOUR SUCCESS AND IDENTIFY YOUR CHALLENGES

Evaluations provide both qualitative information—attitudes, opinions, preferences, and perceptions—and quantitative information—those factors capable of being measured or counted, such as demographics, resource allocation, popularity, improvements, or return on investment (see Figure 14-6). The professional event coordinator must remember that in order to quantify evaluation results, rather than collect evaluative research data, there must be a baseline measurement against which to compare or measure differences or variances. This baseline measurement

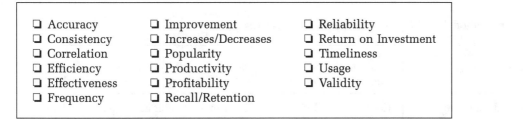

❑ Accuracy	❑ Improvement	❑ Reliability
❑ Consistency	❑ Increases/Decreases	❑ Return on Investment
❑ Correlation	❑ Popularity	❑ Timeliness
❑ Efficiency	❑ Productivity	❑ Usage
❑ Effectiveness	❑ Profitability	❑ Validity
❑ Frequency	❑ Recall/Retention	

Figure 14-6
Typical Event Evaluation Measurements

may be based on assumptions (what was expected or assumed) or previously collected data (historical or comparable data).

It has been said that every complaint is a gift. You should not simply seek out data or opinions that reinforce your current operations or objectives. You must provide the mechanisms for both positive and negative feedback. You should also strive to solicit feedback from those who did not choose to attend the event or chose not to use your event coordination services. Lost-business reports and surveys directed at nonattendees can help in determining how purchase decisions were made and what the influencers were.

EVALUATION INSTRUMENTS AND TECHNIQUES

The professional event coordinator may employ numerous methods for evaluations and evaluative research (see Figure 14-7). The most commonly used instrument is the survey questionnaire, sometimes referred to as an "opinionnaire," conducted either in a written form or through a verbal interview, and administered either on-site or off-site. Louis M. Rea and Richard A. Parker, authors of *Designing and Conducting Survey Research,* assert that surveys can provide descriptive data, identify behavioral patterns, and collect attitudinal information about societal preferences and opinions, from which, through a random sample survey process, the information derived from a small number of people can be an accurate representation of a significantly larger population. Surveys are typically used at events to collect demographic data, preferences, satisfaction levels, and specific feedback.

Most evaluation surveys include both quantitative and qualitative components in the form of closed-ended questions with fixed response alternatives (see Figure 14-8) and open-ended questions asking the respondent for other comments or opinions pertinent to the topic. Rea and

Evaluation Method	Technique and Typical Uses
Advisory Panels	A representative group of customers offering advice; often used to identify current and future issues important in the marketplace.
Coding and Counting	Coding included as or on instruments such as coupons, advertisements, tickets, and other bounce-back items are used to determine outlet usage.
Ethnographic Observation	The observation of actual behaviors by a trained field observer followed up with the collection of the observed individual's demographic information, often used to develop user- or population-specific behavioral profiles.
Examinations/Tests	A written or oral series of questions used to test recall and retention; often used at the conclusion of training programs or sessions.
Feedback/Suggestions	A card or form allowing individuals to provide positive or negative comments and ideas; often included within surveys as "venting" questions.
Focus Groups	An open discussion with group of 8–12 people with similar demographics and a trained moderator in a friendly environment; used to discover attitudes, opinions, usage situations, and conscious/subconscious motivations.
Key Informant Interviews	A one-on-one interview with targeted informants with a high level of expertise, used to elicit expert attitudes, opinions, and preferences.
Lost-Business Reports	An informational tool to determine why business was lost and to whom that business went; used to analyze marketing weaknesses or threats.
Monitors/Secret Shoppers	Individuals provided with specific agendas posing as attendees that observe and record experiences with practices and procedures.
Opinion Polls	A survey interview or questionnaire used to elicit preferences, satisfaction levels, and expectations; often used to provide popularity guidance.
Post-Con Meetings	A face-to-face meeting with client, staff, and/or suppliers to verbally review what actually happened and solicit feedback.

Figure 14-7
Typical Evaluation Methods, Techniques, and Uses

Evaluation Method	Technique and Typical Uses
Survey Interviews	A series of verbal open-ended and closed-ended questions, usually asked of attendees either via intercept, exit, or telephone interviews.
Survey Questionnaires	A series of written open-ended and closed-ended questions used to collect attitudes, opinions, expectations, preferences, demographics, and behaviors; distribution format may be on-site, mail-out, electronic, or Web-enabled.
Verbal Reviews	One-on-one conversations with individual customers or personnel that reveal experiences or incidents told in the individual's own words.

Sources: Louis M. Rea and Richard A. Parker (1992), Designing and Conducting Survey Research *(San Francisco: Jossey-Bass); Joe Jeff Goldblatt (1997),* Special Events: Best Practices in Modern Event Management, *2d ed. (New York: Van Nostrand Reinhold); Joe Goldblatt (2002),* Special Events: Twenty-first Century Global Event Management, *3d ed. (New York: John Wiley & Sons, Inc.); Ron Zemke and John A. Woods, eds. (1998),* Best Practices in Customer Service *(New York: HRD Press, AMACOM).*

Figure 14-7
(Continued)

Parker advise that a survey should include a "series of unbiased, well-structured questions that will systematically obtain the information required," and survey questions must be carefully crafted to ensure a reliable response. The factors to consider include the following:

- **Formatting of questions**—Closed-ended questions with sufficient and logical alternatives, screening questions to qualify or disqualify respondents, appropriate levels or types of measurement, and open-ended and/or "venting" questions.
- **Phrasing of questions**—Using suitable vocabulary level, using neutral bias wording and phrases to solicit and welcome all points of view, avoiding ambiguity or inappropriate emphasis, and avoiding multipurpose questions.
- **Sequencing of questions**—Introductory questions should elicit uncomplicated opinion or factual information, sensitive questions (e.g., affiliations, ethnicity, etc.) should be placed late in the interview or questionnaire to limit participation rejection.
- **Categories of questions**—Appropriate grouping of questions into topics, issues, or objectives with headings.

As a professional event coordinator, you should use a variety of written, verbal, and visual methods to provide a viable and valuable evaluation. You must collect data. You must ask for opinions and observations.

Alternative Response	☐ Male ☐ Female (e.g., if collecting gender for demographics) ☐ Yes ☐ No ☐ No Opinion (e.g., if collecting preferences)
Multiple Choice	How often have you attended the XYZ Festival? ☐ Once ☐ Twice ☐ Two to Four Visits ☐ Five Visits
Multiple Responses	Which attractions did you attend at this XYZ Festival? *Please check all that apply.* ☐ Artist Demonstrations ☐ Craft Booths ☐ Band Concert ☐ Dance Performance ☐ Carnival Rides ☐ Food Court ☐ Children's Activity Area ☐ Photography Exhibit ☐ Cook-off Competition ☐ Poetry Reading
Likert Scale	There are plenty of food choices available at the XYZ Festival. ☐ Strongly Agree ☐ Agree ☐ No Opinion ☐ Disagree ☐ Strongly Disagree
Rating Scale	How was the entertainment at the XYZ Festival? ☐ Poor ☐ Fair ☐ Good ☐ Very Good ☐ Excellent
Semantic Differential	In general, what did you think of the event staff at the XYZ Festival? Very Unfriendly Very Friendly ☐ ☐ ☐ ☐ ☐ ☐ ☐ ☐

Figure 14-8
Quantifiable Fixed Response Types

You should listen to everyone. Deborah Borsum, CSEP, CMD, noted that her organization received some of its most important evaluation data at one of its events from the parking personnel who received and overheard guest comments as they were departing the event. Asking for comments and listening to the answers is a kind of dialogue, and dialogue is critical to effective communications as well as customer service.

To get a good return ratio of responses, the survey or other evaluation instrument must be short and simple, with a logical flow and varied format. It must be administered at the right time to the right population in the right place. Dr. Joe Goldblatt, CSEP, in *Special Events: Twenty-first Century Global Event Management,* advises that conducting surveys both before and after an event "helps event organizers close gaps between overpromising and underdelivering." You must also resist the temptation to include too much in a single survey instrument. Don't ask for data you don't need, and avoid peripheral, extraneous, or tangential questions that do not directly relate to the primary purpose of the evaluation.

VISIONARY ANALYSIS

Once you have all the necessary evaluation data, you must analyze, quantify, and qualify the information and then compile it into useful reports that will serve your current obligations and contribute to your future endeavors and forecasting activities. Know your numbers, create a cost-benefit analysis, capture the statistics, track trends, analyze and cross-reference your findings, and connect the data to the goals and objectives of the event. Incorporate this business and institutional intelligence into the vision for your future events and event endeavors.

The Power of Reports

Reports constitute a significant component of communications as well as knowledge management, including information acquisition and distribution. Reports and reporting procedures, which facilitate the timely and efficient circulation of information to those who need it, may include budgets, evaluations, incident reports, meeting minutes, progress reports, recaps and reviews, and other information. However, no one wants or needs a useless report. You must understand how and when reports should be prepared, who needs them, and why. Use reports to confirm and justify your decisions and decision-making processes. Use reports to monitor planning timelines and performance standards. Use reports to validate your value to your client, your employer, and event stakeholders. The point is—use them, don't let them languish in a drawer. Remember, no report should be generated just to generate a report. The quintessential book on parliamentary procedure, *Robert's Rules of Order,* outlines the best way to organize a detailed report, which can serve as guideline for preparing your reports:

1. A description of the way in which the reporting body undertook its charge
2. The facts uncovered or information obtained
3. The findings or conclusions derived from the facts or information
4. The resolutions or recommendations based on the findings or conclusions

VERIFICATION AND STATUS REPORTS

Status reports and updates are used to monitor and verify the progress of plans throughout the event coordination process. They are also used to detect variances between estimated and actual performance of scheduling, costs, and/or personnel, and they allow the timely implementation of controls and corrective actions as well as help to develop future planning strategies. Progress reports let the event team know the status of activity and the upcoming actions, or as Dana Zita, CSEP, puts it, "Where we are and what's going to happen within the week or the next 30 days." The methods of reporting (e.g., written, electronic, conference call, etc.) and the frequency of preparation and presentation must be established at the beginning of the planning process, with status reports linked to the critical junctures or milestones of the planning process.

CREATING VISIBILITY AND VALUE

Reports are communication mechanisms that provide not only visibility of the event operations during the event coordination process, but also visibility of the event team to external stakeholders. They should also be used to illustrate the value of the investment in the event and in the services of the professional event coordinator. They may be used to illustrate the achievement of goals to clients or upper management, sponsors, the public and public officials, volunteers, and other important stakeholders (or stockholders in the case of corporate entities). Although you may want the event operations to be invisible to the guest ("Oh, you do parties. What fun!"), you want your client or upper management to realize the full scope of your duties, responsibilities, and abilities.

The professional event coordinator will often have responsibility for reporting the final results of an event to stakeholders, which can include financial reports, attendance reports, and executive summaries reviewing performance and cost-benefit analyses. Depending on the recipient, final reports should review performance, processes, and outcomes using anecdotal, statistical, and empirical data. Use percentages to illustrate growth, impact, and the allocation of resources. For example, an increase of 100 attendees over the previous year's 1,000 attendees would be a 10 percent increase, but over the previous year's attendance of 10,000 would be only a 1 percent increase—simply reporting the 100-attendee increase does not tell the whole story. Tell your story with graphs and graphics that show the meanings associated with the measurements and raw data (see Figure 14-9), but make sure they are clear, consistent, and relevant.

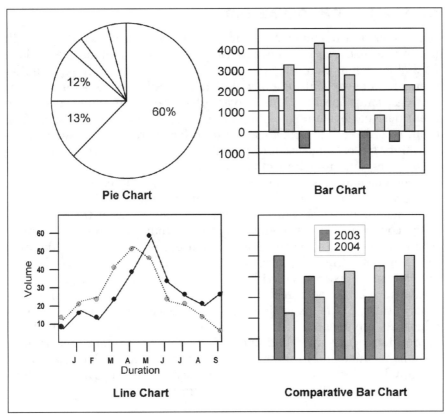

Figure 14-9
Typical Data Analysis Charts

Documentation and Archives

Information and data collected and generated is only part of a knowledge management system. In *Corporate Event Project Management,* authors William O'Toole and Phyllis Mikolaitis contend, "Knowledge is now viewed as a major factor in creating a competitive edge; therefore, the event library, with all of the documentation related to an event, must be protected, as it is both historically and currently valuable." The professional event coordinator must ensure that information is captured correctly and saved in a manner that puts the data to productive and profitable use.

THE PURPOSE OF DOCUMENTATION

Documents and documentation provide the historical records you will use in your research for an event. You will look at previous events done for a client when planning a new one for that client, and look at similar events for a new event for a new client. You will want to review various costings, venue specifications, and assorted evaluations when creating an event design, developing a site plan, or preparing a bid document. The event records and materials may be used for reference, comparisons, inspiration, forecasting, feasibility analyses, tracking growth, illustrating capabilities, and numerous other functions.

Documentation is also evidentiary. You may need to trace your decision-making process or demonstrate your experience. Photographs and other materials may serve as objective evidence in either the boardroom or the courtroom. This evidence may trigger your memory—for example, by allowing you to view room setups and props used—or provide proof in defense of billing disputes, claims, or lawsuits. Certain records must be retained in accordance with tax regulations and other legal requirements, such as financial records, personnel records, accident or incident reports, safety or fire inspection reports, and legal correspondence, among others. As professional event coordinator, you should confirm, with the appropriate legal counsel and/or certified public accountant, what records must be retained and for how long. For an overview of what to keep and for how long (per U.S. laws), visit www.sbaonline.sba.gov/gopher/Business-Development/Success-Series/Vol1/Prof/prof11.txt.

DOCUMENTATION PROCEDURES

First and foremost, the professional event coordinator must make documentation a standard operating procedure—it must be part of the routine, a habit. Write things down, or as Cal Kennedy, CSEP, says, "Log it!" Use conversation diaries to document phone calls and discussions, and follow up with a written review or confirmation. Save everything from the first notes to the final reports. Maintain a chronological perspective by making certain all documents are dated and stored in chronological order, using copies if necessary. Make certain the originals of legally pertinent documents are stored safely. Be sure to retain all electronic records such as e-mails as well.

Archival materials from an individual event should be stored together, including numerous copies of all brochures, flyers, advertising specialties, and posters, plus press clippings and other materials. Photos should be cataloged by event and perhaps also by subject matter. You may wish to digitally scan key photos for your marketing purposes, or all your photos for efficient storage. Photographs, slides, videocasettes, CD-

ROMs, and other media must be stored correctly according to the specific recommendations for each medium. Reference and resource material, such as catalogs, periodicals, and price lists, should be organized and stored so you can access them easily. Tim Hindle recommends that you keep essential reference material separate from your other documents and papers.

ARCHIVES—THE LEGACY OF INFORMATION

It has been said that good judgment comes from experience, and experience comes from bad judgment. The history of an event and its operations is part of an event organization's institutional memory. It provides important insight into its practices, policies, and priorities, which is invaluable in conducting feasibility studies, strategic analyses, and administrative audits. Digital or paper documents, photographs, videotapes, audiotapes, and advertising specialties may all be used to shape and refine future designing, planning, coordination, marketing, evaluation, and risk management activities. Press clippings might be used to plan a public relations strategy. Committee rosters might identify potential volunteer leaders. Event brochures might be used in sponsorship solicitations. Pictorial portfolios might be used to illustrate your capabilities or show clients possible theme ideas. Spreading out all the old advertising specialties and event keepsakes might be the starting point for a brainstorming session. The uses are endless, but none of them are possible unless you have the records and materials saved and accessible.

On-Site Insight

In February 2002, the International Olympic Committee (IOC) launched an Olympics-related knowledge service program known as Olympic Games Knowledge Services (OGKS) to provide knowledge management services to host cities and bidding cities, as well as to offer advice, support, and knowledge services for organizers of other major international events.

The OGKS, a Switzerland-based company, whose partners are the IOC and Monash University in Melbourne, Australia, has grown out of the IOC's Transfer of Olympic Knowledge (TOK) Program. The TOK was initiated by the IOC during preparation for the 2000 Sydney Games in conjunction with the Sydney Organizing Committee for the Olympic Games (SOCOG)

(Continued)

as part of the host city contract deliverables—the preparation of an official report (known internally as the Post Games Report). It was instituted to formalize the transfer of knowledge and information assets from one Games host to the next, passing on "how we did it here" to the organizing committees in Salt Lake City and Athens.

Craig McLatchey, CEO of OGKS, said that the program "will provide event hosts key information and systems to help them stage these major complex events; through this we will increase host organizations' efficiency by transferring know-how from one event to another to avoid reinventing the wheel" (www.ogks.com/ogkspublic/controller/home.htm). Kristine Toohey and Sue Halbwirth, formerly with SOCOG, reported that the Sydney 2000 Games information system, referred to internally as "Athena" after the Greek goddess of wisdom and knowledge, went live on June 30, 1998 (more than two years prior to the Games), encompassed nearly 40,000 documents in more than 90 different functional areas, and supported a public information call center operation that received more than 2.2 million calls (www.sprig.org.uk/seminar2001/toohey.pdf).

Target Competency Review

In the field of event coordination, knowledge management is the acquisition, organization, and control of the information resources and records associated with an event and an event organization. The professional event coordinator must assess and analyze these resources in order to develop effective systems for managing them. The use of computer technology and document design techniques will facilitate efficient data processing procedures, including the tracing, tracking, retrieval, and protection of the valuable documentation that supports the entire event coordination process. All such documentation is included in the Production Book, which should contain schedule, directory, and verification materials pertinent to the on-site event operations and communications.

The professional event coordinator must plan for and utilize evaluation techniques to gather the measurements, opinions, and feedback that contribute to the research-evaluation continuum used to define and direct activities, efforts, and priorities. Evaluation activities and instruments must be designed to link directly with the goals and objectives of an event and the event organization, and must be conducted in a comprehensive, system-wide manner. The data collected must be analyzed carefully and compiled into reports that will be used throughout the event coordination operation to improve practices and increase the return on the investment of future event resources.

Other reports are used throughout the event coordination process to verify the status of plans and the effectiveness of procedures, as well as acquire and distribute necessary information to event stakeholders in a timely manner. This important aspect of the overall event communications plan provides visibility for the event project and personnel and should be used to communicate the value of the project and the personnel. Systematic documentation practices must be established as standard operating procedures to ensure that the collection and distribution of information is automatic and consistent. The library of data captured and archived provides the historical and evidentiary records that constitute the institutional memory of the event organization. These archives provide a legacy of information that may be used to ensure the growth and sustainability of the event and to ensure that the event organization can profit from its own experience.

EXERCISES IN PROFESSIONAL EVENT COORDINATION

Outline and describe the information management plan you would employ for the following events, including the procedures for acquisition, distribution, and storage of pertinent event information. Explain the evaluation activities you would conduct and how you would use their results.

1. A national financial firm has been losing market share as a result of its antiquated systems. You have been hired to coordinate a training session on new tax preparation software for the 3000 accountants recently employed by the company.
2. The International Special Events Society has hired you to coordinate a hospitality reception at a major industry convention for the purpose of increasing its membership.
3. You are serving as the events coordinator for the political campaign to elect your candidate as mayor of your city. The campaign events will include 15 fund-raising receptions, 25 scheduled special appearances at media events, and the election day event at campaign headquarters to await the results.

CHAPTER 15

Strategies for Success

Success is a journey, not a destination.

—BEN SWEETLAND, I WILL, *1978*

IN THIS CHAPTER YOU WILL LEARN HOW TO:

- Understand the integration of professional event coordination within the entire scope of event management.
- Recognize the importance and impact of industry standards and credentials.
- Develop a regimen for achieving a competitive advantage through continuing education and professional development.
- Advance your career and the industry through membership in professional associations.

An event is an experience, one that is carefully crafted by bringing together a broad spectrum of goods, services, and the people that provide them in a specific space and at a specific time. This event experience carries multiple meanings and varying levels of importance for those in attendance and those hosting it. For the professional event coordinator and all those people brought together to stage it, it carries with it an awesome responsibility. This responsibility is not to be undertaken lightly; it must be embraced with a diligent zeal for excellence.

An Integrated Discipline

Professional event coordination is just one facet of event management, which encompasses administrative, marketing, and risk management competencies as well. These four areas of expertise are inextricably connected and woven together, each one affecting and relying on all the others. As discussed throughout this book, the professional event coordinator has administrative duties to perform in bringing together the right event elements and service providers, must deal with the marketing influences that permeate every aspect of the event experience, and has risk management responsibilities associated with absolutely every component. These abilities and responsibilities simply cannot be segregated—they must be completely integrated.

The professional event coordinator may or may not be responsible for directing strategic planning or policy development for an event organization, creating the marketing plans for an event, managing the financial and/or human resources, or formulating the risk management plans, but he or she will, at the very least, need to be a contributor to and a participant in these processes and procedures. The professional event coordinator must strive to fully understand and master each discipline to become a better (and more valuable) partner in the success and sustainability of the event and the event organization. This becomes exponentially more important as a practitioner seeks advancement within this profession.

On-Site Insight

Deborah Borsum, CSEP, CMD, notes that many people enter the event industry because they think it is fun and creative, which it is, but they fail to realize that it is, first and foremost, a business. "Event professionals are entrusted with large budgets and important objectives. You must recognize the responsibility and take it seriously. The credibility of and respect for the industry is on the line." She advises you must continually demonstrate and illustrate your competence and capabilities, always delivering the best and exhibiting the highest standards of the profession.

Industry Standards and Credentials

It has been argued that the event industry has not yet become a true profession because licensing, certification, or a recognized degree is not required as a condition of practice or employment. Many segments of the industry do require specific licenses to conduct business, particularly those that serve other market segments such as food service and transportation. Some governments have codified and adopted national occupational qualifications and standards for the event industry (notably, however, *not* the United States). Although adherence to most such standards is primarily voluntary and serves as a competitive distinction, as consumer protection legislation is more widely developed and demanded, regulatory standards for the industry may become statutory. The trend is toward standardization, particularly outside the United States, as organizations such as the International Organization for Standardization

	Certification Title	Program Administered By:
CAE	Certified Association Executive	American Society of Association Executives (ASAE) www.asaenet.org/main/
CDME	Certified Destination Management Executive	International Association of Convention and Visitors Bureaus (IACVB) www.iacvb.org/
CEM	Certified in Exhibition Management	International Association for Exhibition Management (IAEM) www.iaem.org/
CERP	Certified Event Rental Professional	American Rental Association (ARA) www.ararental.org/
CFE	Certified Festival Executive	International Festivals and Events Association (IFEA) www.ifea.com/
CHME	Certified Hospitality Marketing Executive	Hospitality Sales and Marketing Association International (HSMAI) www.hsmai.org/
CITE	Certified Incentive Travel Executive	Society of Incentive and Travel Executives (SITE) www.site-intl.org./
CMP	Certified Meeting Professional	Convention Industry Council (CIC) www.clc-online.org/
CMM	Global Certification in Meeting Management	Meeting Professionals International (MPI) www.mpiweb.org/
CPCE	Certified Professional Catering Executive	National Association of Catering Executives (NACE) www.nace.net/
CSEP	Certified Special Events Professional	International Special Events Society (ISES) www.ises.com
DMCP	Destination Management Certified Professional	Association of Destination Management Executives (ADME) www.adme.org/
PBC	Professional Bridal Consultant	Association of Bridal Consultants (ABC) www.bridalassn.com/

Figure 15-1
Event Industry Certification Programs

(ISO) develop and conduct conformity assessments whereby a product, process, service, or system is evaluated against specified requirements.

Although various industry sectors have identified the knowledge domains pertinent to their specific occupational practices, as the global economy advances, globally harmonized occupational standards will be developed for this emerging profession. These standards will encompass the specialized skill sets, a common vocabulary, assessment and accountability measures, and agreed-to ethical principles. These standards will form the basis for standardized academic curriculas, and they will likely eventually be adopted by governments throughout the world as the basis for legislation and enforceable regulations with which they can protect the public health and safety.

In the meantime, certification programs offered by the various event industry sectors provide the external validation and demonstrable indication that one has the knowledge, training, experience, judgment, and ability—the qualifications—to be a practitioner in a particular field. Certification is becoming a baseline expectation of discriminating clients, and clients are becoming more discriminating every day. For the professional event coordinator, the Certified Special Events Professional (CSEP) designation, offered through the International Special Events Society (ISES), is the primary certification credential to be acquired because it encompasses the competencies that form the foundation for most event industry–related certifications (see Figure 15-1).

The CSEP credential is earned based on a balance of practical experience, education, industry leadership and service, and successful completion of a three-part examination, which consists of a portfolio presentation, an objective multiple-choice portion based on the vocabulary of event management, and an essay portion requiring the candidate to apply the principles and competencies of event management to an event case study. Contact ISES at www.ises.com for enrollment information. If you are interested in finding out whether you have the practical experience to take the CSEP exam, you may e-mail me at julia@juliasilvers.com for a Personal Assessment Questionnaire that will help you evaluate your readiness.

Embrace Lifelong Learning

One of the key components of the various certification programs offered is the requisite of and commitment to continuing education and professional development. True professionals recognize that exploration, study, research, and investigation are an integral part of their duties. You must be hungry for knowledge, constantly seeking out more in-depth understanding of all the current and emerging technologies, applications, and implications pertaining to this multifaceted industry. Cultivate the joy of lifelong learning. Lifelong learning encompasses theoretical study and practical experience, as well as gleaning knowledge from every corner of the world around you.

Technology Tip

As noted in the preface, many of the hundreds of topics covered in this book represent industry segments and occupations that are supported by countless resources of information and experience. Many of these resources are accessible via the Internet, as evidenced by the Web site addresses provided throughout. The hardest part of writing this book has been editing it down to a reasonable size, which necessitated leaving out page after page of fascinating facts and in-depth information—each topic truly deserves its own book. Much of the research I did was via the Internet, gathering data and insights, charts and explanations, experiences and opinions, technical and practical advice. Take advantage of this incredible resource and explore each and every topic—your hunger for more will never subside.

Take advantage of the continuing education and professional development programs and opportunities offered by academic institutions, professional associations, and other organizations. These need not be specific to the event industry; everything you learn can be applied to your endeavors in professional event coordination. Take classes in computer systems, financial management, leadership, time management, psychology, writing, public speaking, flower arranging, cooking—anything that piques your interest. Also seek out event industry–related courses in administration, coordination, sales and marketing, risk management, CPR/first aid, project management, travel and tourism, entertainment, adult learning principles, fund-raising, and the individual event genres.

READ, SEE, AND DO

Read everything you can get your hands on. Invest in your future by subscribing to industry and nonindustry magazines, newsletters, and newspapers. Read every book and publication you can on every event genre and the event industry. Purchase them, borrow them from a lending library, or spend a few glorious hours reading them in an academic research library. See everything you can see. Attend the theater and concerts. Go to the movies or rent films and watch them at home. Search out informative programming on television. Participate in events in and for your community. Volunteer your time and talents for events for charitable, political, or other organizations you support. Attend the events held in your community as well as those you encounter in your travels. You will collect hundreds of ideas and note hundreds of precautions to apply to your future events.

THE POWER OF THE PROFESSIONAL COMMUNITY

You must also develop relationships with the others in your professional community. When asked what advice they would give to those who would read this book, virtually all the people I interviewed recommended that you join a professional association in the industry, go to the meetings, and become involved. This is where you will meet the people who will help you to continually improve your abilities and connect you with the resources you will need. This is also where you can become an active participant in shaping the future of this industry, this profession.

On-Site Insight

Dana Zita, CSEP, advises, "There is constant change, and you must constantly keep current. Turn your head from side to side to see the options."

Connie Riley, CSEP, recommends, "Get out and see as much as you can. Learn more about the business by seeing it."

John J. Daly Jr., CSEP, contends that the best thing that happened to him was that he started as a delivery person for a florist and learned how to pack a truck first. "You need to get education and experience in all aspects of events."

Steve Kemble, event designer, suggests that you intern with a large event company for a while to find out what you really want to do, what part of the industry you want to specialize in. "Pick what you do best—that's what you will become known for."

Target Competency Review

As you travel through your career in professional event coordination, you must always be a seeker as well as a giver. Seek out the people, education, and technologies that will help you get better and better at what you do. Give of yourself to others in this industry and those who are preparing to enter it. Give to yourself by investing your time and money in continuing education and professional development, as well as certification. And make the commitment to always bring honor, integrity, and innovation to the profession.

EXERCISES IN PROFESSIONAL EVENT COORDINATION

Write a 1500-word essay (approximately five double-spaced typewritten pages) describing your professional event coordination career to date, including your professional development activities, areas needing improvement, and your plans for filling the gaps in your education and practical experience.

Sample Client Interview Form

This Client Interview Form may serve as a preplanning checklist as well as a tool for consultative selling practices. Check to make certain you have included each of these items in the research and design processes of your event. You should adapt this checklist to meet the needs of your organization and the types of events you are coordinating.

Date:
Referred By:

Host or Client Profile

☐ New Client
☐ Repeat Client

Contact Name: _____

Company: _____

Address: _____

City: _____ State/Province: _____

Zip/Postal Code: _____ Country: _____

Phone: _____ Fax: _____

E-mail: _____ Web URL: _____

Organization Type: _____

Organization's Function: _____

Number of Years Hosting This Event: _____

End Client Contact Name and Number:_____

Reporting Structure: _____

Key Influencers and Stakeholders: _____

Support Personnel Available (check all that apply):

☐ Committees   ☐ Performers   ☐ Temporary Staff
☐ Family/Friends   ☐ Sponsors/Cosponsors   ☐ Vendors
☐ Participants   ☐ Staff/Employees   ☐ Volunteers
☐ Patrons/Supporters   ☐ Students/Interns
☐ Other (explain): _____

Event Specifications

Function Type: _____

For Whom:_____

Date(s): _____
　　　　✓ Fixed or Flexible:

Duration: _____
　　　　✓ Start Time:
　　　　✓ End Time:
　　　　✓ Agenda:
　　　　✓ Flash Points: (important highlights)

Location: _____
　　　　✓ Preselected:
　　　　✓ Fixed or Flexible:
　　　　✓ Preferences:
　　　　　　◆ Geographic Site (proximity, destination, access)
　　　　　　◆ Environment (climate, urban, rural, remote)
　　　　　　◆ Facility (hotel, conference center, museum, unique, etc.)
　　　　　　◆ Interior/Exterior
　　　　　　◆ Requirements (features, handicapped access, amenities)
　　　　✓ Where has this event been held before? (past 3 to 5 years)

Expected Attendance: _____
　　　　✓ Highest Number:
　　　　✓ Lowest Number:
　　　　✓ Desired Number:

1. Position of the event within the overall schedule of events:

2. Other known concurrent/competing events:

3. Arrival/departure pattern:

4. Specific activities or elements that must be incorporated:

5. Special requests:

6. Special requirements:

7. Specific theme selected/preferred:

8. What marketing materials will be based on event design?

Event Objectives

1. What is the purpose of the event? (Check all that apply)

☐ Advertising/promotion   ☐ Entertainment   ☐ Problem resolution
☐ Appreciation   ☐ Governed mandate   ☐ Product introduction
☐ Cause-related support   ☐ Hospitality   ☐ Product positioning
☐ Celebration   ☐ Idea exchange   ☐ Recognition
☐ Circulation   ☐ Image enhancement   ☐ Recruitment
☐ Commemoration   ☐ Incentive/reward   ☐ Revenue generation
☐ Competition   ☐ Motivation   ☐ Sales
☐ Decision making   ☐ Networking/interaction ☐ Teambuilding
☐ Education/training   ☐ Policy development   ☐ Tourism/visitors
☐ Other: (please explain) _____
Comments:

2. What are the specific objectives for the event?

☐ Attendance   ☐ Membership   ☐ Return on investment
☐ Contributions   ☐ Participation   ☐ Revenues
☐ Guest satisfaction ☐ Patrons/supporters   ☐ Sales
☐ Image perception   ☐ Performance increase ☐ Sponsorship
☐ Learning outcomes   ☐ Publicity   ☐ Tourism inquiries
☐ Other: (please specify) _____
Comments:

3. Measurements to be used to indicate successful achievement of each of these objectives?

4. How and by whom will measurements be collected?

5. What other areas are to be evaluated?

6. What evaluation criteria will be used?

7. How and by whom will evaluations be conducted?

Audience Profile

1. Who is the audience?
   ✓ Male/female ratio
   ✓ Age range

✓ Spouse/companion attendance
✓ Children in attendance/age range
✓ Position or profession
✓ Income level
✓ Educational level/background
✓ Where are attendees coming from?
✓ Cultural background or restrictions
✓ Previous attendance at similar events
✓ Group Personality

☐ Participatory/Active	☐ Spectator/Passive
☐ Mature/Conservative	☐ Fun/Interactive
☐ Adult-Oriented	☐ Family-oriented
☐ Luxury/Opulence	☐ Rugged/Outdoors
☐ Adventurous	☐ Serious
☐ Sophisticated	☐ Competitive

✓ Special Needs or ADA Accommodations

2. What are *the attendees'* expectations?
   ✓ What has been done before?
   ✓ What did they like?
   ✓ What did they *not* like?

3. What are *your* expectations?
   ✓ What did you like?
   ✓ What did you *not* like?

4. How do you want attendees *to feel* after the event?

5. What do you want them *to think* after the event?

6. What do you want them *to do* as a result of the event?

7. Why do *they* attend this event?

8. Do you have supporting research/evaluation data?

Budget

1. What expense budget range are you considering?

2. What does this expense budget include?
   ☐ Invitations/Marketing Materials
   ☐ Travel/Transportation
   ☐ Venue
   ☐ Décor
   ☐ Food and Beverage
   ☐ Entertainment
   ☐ Technical Production (lighting/sound/AV)
   ☐ Gifts and Amenities

3. Do you have any vendors already contracted for these items?

4. If so, who and for what aspects?

5. Are there revenue expectations?

6. If so, what are the revenue sources?

7. Are there any mandated payment procedures?

8. Who has authority to sign facility and supplier contracts?

9. What insurance coverage is in place?

Event Design

1. Anticipation
- ✓ Advertising/Promotions/Public Relations
- ✓ Invitations/Brochures/Registration Materials
- ✓ Printing and Postage
- ✓ Mailing Lists
- ✓ Other: _____
- Comments:

2. Arrival
- ✓ Travel Arrangements
- ✓ Meet and Greet
- ✓ Ground Transportation
- ✓ Parking Services
- ✓ Admissions/Credentials
- ✓ Registration
- ✓ Attendee Services
- ✓ VIP/Celebrity Security
- ✓ Other: _____
- Comments:

3. Atmosphere
- ✓ Décor
- ✓ Lighting/Soundscaping
- ✓ AV Equipment
- ✓ Special Effects
- ✓ Furnishings
- ✓ Seating Setup
- ✓ Staging Requirements
- ✓ Special Storage Requirements
- ✓ Signage Requirements (sponsor recognition)
- ✓ Telecommunications Needs
- ✓ VIP Areas/Accommodations
- ✓ Other: _____
- Comments:

4. Appetite
- ✓ Food Service Scope
- ✓ Menu Preferences/Requirements
- ✓ Menu Restrictions

✓ Dietary Requirements
✓ Specialty Items/Desserts
✓ Service Style Preference
✓ Seating—Reserved or Open
✓ Beverage Service Scope
✓ Beverage Preferences/Restrictions
✓ Service Style Preference
✓ Brand Preferences/Specialty Drinks
✓ Host Liability Insurance
✓ Special Waitstaff Attire
✓ Other: _____
Comments:

5. Activity

✓ Live Music
✓ Recorded Music
✓ Dancing
✓ Headliner Act/Celebrity
✓ Multimedia Production
✓ Theatrical/Dance Production
✓ Speakers
✓ Ceremony
✓ Exhibits/Demonstrations
✓ Interactive/Games
✓ Sport Tournaments
✓ Tours
✓ Parade
✓ Music Licensing Fees
✓ Other: _____
Comments:

6. Amenities

✓ Prizes
✓ Gifts
✓ Awards
✓ Logo Merchandise
✓ Programs
✓ Collateral/Conference Materials
✓ Other: _____
Comments:

Proposal Specifications

1. Why are you soliciting proposals?
    ✓ How many other companies are submitting proposals?
    ✓ Are any of them already favored to get the project?
    ✓ If so, why are you putting the event out to bid?

2. What should be included in the proposal?
- ☐ Preliminary creative concepts/treatments
- ☐ Cost estimates
- ☐ Special requirements/capabilities documentation (per purchasing practices)

3. In what format would you like the proposal presented?
- ☐ In person
- ☐ Mailed
- ☐ Faxed
- ☐ E-mailed

4. When do you need the proposal?

5. If presented in person or mailed, how many copies of the proposal do you need?

6. What criteria will you use to evaluate the proposal?

7. Are these criteria weighted, and if so, how?

8. Who will be making the final selection?

9. When will the final decision be made?

APPENDIX 2

Sample On-Site Change Order Form

The professional event coordinator should prepare duplicate copies of all change orders and give the client a copy upon execution.

Job Code/Contract #: _____ Date: _____

Client Name: _____

Event: _____

Event Coordinator: _____

Authorization for the following changes and/or additional services:

_____

_____

_____

_____

_____

The estimated cost for the above changes will be $ _____

I am authorized and agree to pay for the above changes and/or additional services as agreed upon in my contract and this change order.

_____
Name (Please Print)

_____
Signature

_____
Company

_____
Date

APPENDIX 3

Event "Survival" Kit

The following items may be assembled and kept in a large toolbox or carton and should be brought on-site at every event. The inventory should be replaced promptly after it is used.

- ☐ Aspirin/analgesic
- ☐ Bar of soap
- ☐ Batteries (assorted sizes)
- ☐ Bottle opener
- ☐ Carpet tape
- ☐ Clear shipping tape
- ☐ Clothespins
- ☐ Dental floss
- ☐ Duct tape
- ☐ Electrical tape
- ☐ Extension cord
- ☐ Facial tissue
- ☐ First aid kit
- ☐ Flashlight
- ☐ Floral wire and tape

- ☐ Hammer
- ☐ Markers, pencils, pens
- ☐ Masking tape
- ☐ Matches and lighters
- ☐ Moist towelettes
- ☐ Nails and screws (assorted)
- ☐ Pad of notepaper
- ☐ Paper clips
- ☐ Paper towels
- ☐ Phillips screwdriver
- ☐ Picture-hanging wire
- ☐ Pliers
- ☐ Pushpins/tacks
- ☐ Rubber bands

- ☐ Safety pins
- ☐ Scissors
- ☐ Scotch tape
- ☐ Screwdriver
- ☐ Shower hooks
- ☐ Stapler and staples
- ☐ Staple remover
- ☐ Straight pins
- ☐ Three-prong adapter
- ☐ Toothpicks
- ☐ Trash bags
- ☐ Twist ties
- ☐ Umbrella
- ☐ Window cleaner
- ☐ Wire cutters
- ☐ Ziploc plastic bags

For Wedding Planners, add:

- ☐ Airline "sick" bag
- ☐ Black men's socks
- ☐ Black shoelaces
- ☐ Bobby pins (assorted colors)
- ☐ Bow ties (black, white)
- ☐ Breath mints
- ☐ Cough drops
- ☐ Crochet hook

- ☐ Cuticle scissors
- ☐ Disposable razor
- ☐ Disposable toothbrush
- ☐ Earring backs
- ☐ Elastic
- ☐ Emery board
- ☐ Hair barrettes and combs
- ☐ Hairbrush

- ☐ Hair spray
- ☐ Lint brush
- ☐ Moleskin
- ☐ Nail polish remover
- ☐ Panty hose (ivory, black)
- ☐ Pearl head corsage pins
- ☐ Ribbon (white, blue)
- ☐ Sewing kit

- ☐ Shoe polish (black, white)
- ☐ Silk boutonniere
- ☐ Small bag of fake rings
- ☐ Small hand mirror
- ☐ Smelling salts
- ☐ Spot remover
- ☐ Static Guard
- ☐ Stick-on fingernails
- ☐ Superglue
- ☐ Tampons/panty liners
- ☐ Toothpaste
- ☐ Toss garter
- ☐ Velour pipe cleaners
- ☐ White envelopes
- ☐ White string

Sample Site Inspection Checklist

This sample site inspection checklist focuses primarily on hotel properties and should be customized to include the selection criteria and specifications important to the particular event to be held and the type of venue under consideration.

Site Inspection Conducted By: _____ Date: _____

Venue Name: _____

Address: _____

Contact Person: _____

Main Telephone: _____ Direct Line: _____

Fax: _____ Toll-free Reservations: _____

E-mail: _____ Web URL: _____

Property Location
☐ Major Transportation Ports (Air, Rail, Water, etc.)
☐ Airport, Station, Pier Condition
☐ Distance and Travel Time to Airport, Station, Pier
☐ Distance to Area Attractions
☐ Ground Transportation Options and Costs
☐ Complimentary Hotel Shuttle Service, Hours of Operation, Schedule
☐ Car Rental and Return Convenience
Assets:
Liabilities:

Surrounding Vicinity
☐ Adjacent Hotels
☐ Appearance

☐ Attractions
☐ Recreation Options
☐ Restaurants
☐ Safety
☐ Shopping
Assets:
Liabilities:

Accessibility
☐ Access to Public Transportation
☐ Traffic Concerns/Considerations
☐ Parking Facilities; Private, Public, Covered, Open, Gated, Security Patrolled, Number of Spaces Available
☐ Parking Services and Fees; Self-park, Valet
☐ Loading Docks; Truck Clearance, Maximum Truck Size and Height Limits, Charges/Fees
☐ Freight Elevators; Number, Dimensions, Weight Limits, Proximity and Route to Function Space
Assets:
Liabilities:

Property Description
☐ Access to Function Rooms (Stairs, Escalators, Elevators)
☐ ADA Compliance
☐ Condition and Cleanliness
☐ Congestion
☐ Décor and Furnishings
☐ Elevators; Number, Capacity, Speed
☐ Entrances
☐ Environment; Well-lighted, Fresh-smelling, Acceptable Noise Levels
☐ Grounds
☐ Hallways
☐ Lobby Areas
☐ Public Telephones; Number and Locations
☐ Public Toilets; Locations, Décor, Maintenance
☐ Registration/Front Desk Areas
☐ Service Passages
☐ Signage
☐ Storage Areas; Secured, Luggage Capacity/Control
Assets:
Liabilities:

Property Amenities
☐ Bars/Lounges; Hours of Service, Capacities
☐ Business Center; Hours of Service and Price List
☐ Concierge; Hours of Service
☐ Gift Shop; Hours of Service

☐ Golf/Tennis On-property; Hours of Service and Price List
☐ Health Club/Fitness Center; Hours of Service and Price List
☐ Pool; Indoor/Outdoor, Hours of Service
☐ Portage Fees
☐ Restaurant Outlets; Hours of Service, Capacities, Selection, Price Range
☐ Room Service; Hours of Service
☐ Spa Services; Hours of Service and Price List
Assets:
Liabilities:

Function Space
(Create an inspection checklist for each function room.)
☐ Fire Marshal–Approved Capacities
☐ Number of Rooms Available
☐ Rental Rates
☐ Acoustics; Air Walls, Soundproofing, Internal/External Noise
☐ Ceiling Height
☐ Computer Hookups
☐ Condition and Cleanliness
☐ Décor
☐ Dimensions
☐ Distractions
☐ Doorways; Dimensions, Number, Egress to
☐ Dressing Rooms
☐ Electrical Outlets/Hookups, Capacities
☐ Flooring/Carpeting
☐ Floor Load Limits
☐ Intercom System
☐ Temperature Controls; In-room
☐ Lighting and Controls; In-room, Dimmers
☐ Obstructions
☐ Prefunction Areas
☐ Proximity to Public Telephones
☐ Proximity to Toilets
☐ Security Features
☐ Smoke Detector
☐ Sprinkler System
☐ Windows; Capable of Blackout Covering for Projection
Assets:
Liabilities:

Catering
☐ Food and Beverage Selection, Presentation, Prices, Sample Menus
☐ Food and Beverage Variety, Creativity, Willingness to Divert from Menus
☐ Gratuity Percentage
☐ Liquor Laws
☐ Service Charges; Typical Ratio Between Guests and Service Staff

☐ Serviceware and Equipment Rental Costs
☐ Decorations Available and Costs
☐ Guarantees Needed by:
☐ Overset Guarantee by ____%
☐ Outside Caterer Allowed; Recommended Caterers
Assets:
Liabilities:

Kitchens
☐ Adequate Staffing
☐ Cleanliness
☐ Equipment Capabilities/Condition
☐ Preparation Areas
☐ Proximity to Function Areas
☐ Sanitation Practices
Assets:
Liabilities:

Equipment (and Fees If Applicable)
☐ Coatracks
☐ Dance Floor
☐ Decorations
☐ In-room AV Equipment; Screens, Sound System, Microphones, Flip Charts, etc.
☐ Lecterns; Number, Dimensions, Description
☐ Preferred Rental Companies
☐ Shipping/Receiving
☐ Staging and Risers
☐ Tables and Chairs
☐ Tents/Marquees for Outdoor Functions
Assets:
Liabilities:

Guest Rooms
☐ Number per Type (Single, Double, Double/Double, King, Suites, Handicapped Accessible, Smoking, Nonsmoking)
☐ Rates per Type
☐ Concierge Level; Amenities and Services
☐ Check-in/Checkout Times, Express Checkout Available
☐ Proximity to Function Space
☐ Amenities (Toiletries, Minibar, Iron/Ironing Board, In-room Safe, Television/In-room Movies, Coffee/Coffeemaker, Hair Dryer, Newspaper Delivery)
☐ Cleanliness
☐ Closet Space
☐ Comfort
☐ Desk/Work Space
☐ Multiple Telephone Lines, Data Ports, Voice Mail, Internet Access, Access Surcharges

☐ Sitting Areas
☐ Security Features
☐ Smoke Detector
☐ Sprinkler System
Assets:
Liabilities:

Services (and Price Lists)
☐ AV Services
☐ Child Care Providers
☐ Cleaning
☐ Coat Check
☐ Currency Exchange
☐ Dry Cleaning/Laundry
☐ Exhibit Service Contractor
☐ Florist
☐ Furniture
☐ Local Doctors/Dentists
☐ Photography
☐ Safety Deposit Boxes
☐ Self-Service Laundry
☐ Telecommunications Equipment, Outside Lines, T1, ISDN, etc.
☐ Translation Services
Assets:
Liabilities:

Personnel
☐ Bellmen/Porters
☐ Chef and Banquet Staff
☐ Convention Services Manager
☐ Engineering
☐ General Manager (length of time with this property)
☐ Housekeeping
☐ Registration/Front Desk Staffing
☐ Security
☐ Sales/Account Representatives
☐ Recent/Anticipated Franchise Ownership
☐ Staff Turnover Rate and Frequency
☐ Attitude, Demeanor, and Customer Service Training
Assets:
Liabilities:

Policies
☐ Booking Deposit Fee Structure and Deadlines
☐ Complimentary Room/Rental Policy, Ratio
☐ Date(s)/Hours Availability
☐ Drayage Policies

☐ Exclusive Vendors, Preferred Vendors
☐ Insurance Carried, Insurance Required
☐ Licenses/Permits Required
☐ Low/Shoulder/Peak Seasons
☐ Move-in/Move-out Allotments, Overtime Charges
☐ Planned Renovations/Construction
☐ Promotional Material Availability
☐ Refund/Cancellation/Attrition Policies and Fees
☐ Reservation Policies; Reservation Cutoff Dates, Rate Availability after Cutoff Date
☐ Sample Contract
☐ Signage Restrictions; Interior and Exterior
☐ Simultaneous/Contiguous Groups Booked; Same-day Functions
☐ Special Restrictions; Alcohol, Decorating, Electrical, Music, Membership Requirement
☐ Taxes; Sales Tax—Guest Room, Sales Tax—Food/Beverage, Bed/Lodging Tax
☐ Union Requirements, Union Contract Renewals
☐ Utility Usage Surcharges
Assets:
Liabilities:

Risk Management
☐ Backup Generator in Case of Power Failure
☐ Elevator Inspections
☐ Emergency Exits; Well Marked, Battery Lighted
☐ Evacuation Plan/Instructions
☐ FEMA Number (U.S.—Federal Emergency Management Agency certification that property is in compliance with the Fire Safety Act)
☐ Fire Extinguishers; Placement, Visibility
☐ First Aid Capabilities/Equipment
☐ Key Type and Issuance Procedure; Guest Rooms and Function Rooms
☐ Health Department Rating
☐ Hotel Staff Trained in CPR, Heimlich Maneuver, First Aid
☐ Nearest Medical Facility
☐ Restricted Access to Guest Room Floors
☐ Security Cameras/Patrols/Personnel
☐ Security Requirements for Events
Assets:
Liabilities:

APPENDIX 5

References and Reading List

Chapter 1

Event Solutions 2002 Fact Book: A Statistical Analysis of the Event Industry. Event Solutions Magazine, p. 20.

Goldblatt, Joe Jeff (1990). *Special Events: The Art and Science of Celebration.* New York: Van Nostrand Reinhold.

Goldblatt, Joe Jeff (1997). *Special Events: Best Practices in Modern Event Management.* 2d ed. New York: Van Nostrand Reinhold.

Goldblatt, Joe (2002). *Special Events: Twenty-first Century Global Event Management.* 3d ed. New York: John Wiley & Sons, Inc.

Lewis, Robert C. (1997). *Instructor's Manual to Accompany Cases in Hospitality Marketing and Management.* 2d ed. New York: John Wiley & Sons, Inc., p. 7.

Shone, Anton (2001). *Successful Event Management: A Practical Handbook.* London: Continuum, p. 223.

Sullivan, Louis. (1947). "The Tall Office Building Artistically Considered." In *Kindergarten Chats (revised 1918) and Other Writing,* ed. I. Athey, pp. 202–213. New York.

Toffler, Alvin (1970). *Future Shock.* New York: Random House, p. 203.

Visser, Margaret (1991). *The Rituals of Dinner: The Origins, Evolution, Eccentricities, and Meaning of Table Manners.* New York: Penguin Books, p. 171.

Chapter 2

Augustine, Norman R. (1997). *Augustine's Law.* 6th ed. Reston, VA: American Institute of Aeronautics and Astronautics.

Berlonghi, Alexander (1990). *The Special Event Risk Management Manual.* Dana Point, CA: Berlonghi.

Covey, Stephen R. (1989). *The Seven Habits of Highly Effective People.* New York: Fireside.

Doran, George T. (1981). "There's a S.M.A.R.T. Way to Write Management Goals and Objectives." *Management Review* (November): 35–36, cited in Joseph W. Weiss, and Robert K. Wysocki (1992). *5-Phase Project Management: A Practical Planning and Implementation Guide.* Cambridge, MA: Perseus Books, p. 13.

Forsberg, Kevin, Hal Mooz, and Howard Cotterman (2000). *Visualizing Project Management: A Model for Business and Technical Success.* New York: John Wiley & Sons, Inc.

Lewis, James P. (1997). *Fundamentals of Project Management.* New York: AMACOM, p. 105.

Middleton, Robert (2002). "Socially Unacceptable Questions." *More Clients eZine* (February 19) (www.actionplan.com, mailto: robmid@actionplan.com).

Project Management Institute, Inc. (2000). *A Guide to the Project Management Body of Knowledge (PMBOK Guide).* Newtown Square, PA: PMI, p. 127.

Tarlow, Peter (2002). *Event Risk Management and Safety.* New York: John Wiley & Sons, Inc., p. 42.

Thomsett, Michael C. (1990). *The Little Black Book of Project Management.* New York: AMACOM, pp. 14, 88.

Chapter 3

Armstrong, James S. (2001). *Planning Special Events.* San Francisco: Jossey-Bass, p. 52.

Event Solutions 2002 Fact Book: A Statistical Analysis of the Event Industry. Tempe, AZ: Event Solutions Magazine, p. 21.

O'Toole, William (2002). *The Event Project Management System* (www-personal.usyd.edu.au/~wotoole/EPMS_Planning/Function_areas/site_venue-map/event_map.html).

Polivka, Edward G., ed. (1996). *Professional Meeting Management.* 3d ed. Birmingham, AL: PCMA Education Foundation, pp. 386–397.

Tarlow, Peter E. (2002). *Event Risk Management and Safety.* New York: John Wiley & Sons, Inc., p. 210.

U.S. Department of Justice, ADA Information Line, 800-514-0301 (voice), 800-514-0383 (TTY) (www.usdoj.gov/crt/ada/adahom1.htm).

Chapter 4

Anderson, Kristin, and Ron Zemke (1991). *Delivering Knock Your Socks Off Service.* New York: Performance Research Associates, Inc., AMACOM, pp. 17, 74.

Axtell, Roger E. (1993). *Do's and Taboos Around the World.* 3d ed. New York: John Wiley & Sons, Inc.

Boehme, Ann J. (1999). *Planning Successful Meetings and Events.* New York: AMACOM.

Briggs, Susan (2001). *Successful Tourism Marketing: A Practical Handbook.* 2d ed. London: Kogan Page Limited, pp. 94, 149–150.

Goldblatt, Joe, and Kathleen Nelson, eds. (2001). *The International Dictionary of Event Management.* 2d ed. New York: John Wiley & Sons, Inc., p. 4.

Hoyle, Leonard H. (2002). *Event Marketing: How to Successfully Promote Events, Festivals, Conventions, and Expositions.* New York: John Wiley & Sons, Inc.

International Events Group (1985). *Banking on Leisure Transcripts: Event Marketing Seminar Series.* Chicago: IEG, p. 76.

Kotler, Philip, John Bowen, and James Makens (1999). *Marketing for Hospitality and Tourism.* 2d ed. Upper Saddle River, NJ: Prentice-Hall, p. 584.

McCaffree, Mary Jane, and Pauline Innis (1989). *Protocol: The Complete Handbook of Diplomatic, Official and Social Usage.* Washington, DC: Devon Publishing, p. 2.

Middleton, Victor T. C. (2001). *Marketing in Travel and Tourism.* 3d ed. Oxford, U.K.: Butterworth-Heinemann, p. 285.

Morrison, Terri, Wayne A. Conaway, and George A. Borden (1994). *Kiss, Bow, or Shake Hands: How to Do Business in Sixty Countries.* Holbrook, MA: Adams Media Corporation, p. x.

Morrow, Sandra L. (1997). *The Art of the Show.* Dallas, TX: International Association of Exposition Management Education Foundation.

Polivka, Edward G., ed. (1996). *Professional Meeting Management.* 3d ed. Birmingham, AL: PCMA Education Foundation, pp. 129–131, 668.

Price, Catherine H. (1999). *The Complete Guide to Professional Meeting and Event Coordination,* 2d pub. Washington, DC: George Washington University Event Management Program, p. 269.

Shock, Patti J., and John M. Stefanelli. (2001). *On-Premise Catering.* New York: John Wiley & Sons, Inc.

Shone, Anton (2001). *Successful Event Management: A Practical Handbook.* London: Continuum, p. 216.

Swartz, Oretha D. (1988). *Service Etiquette.* 4th ed. Annapolis, MD: Naval Institute Press, pp. 478–481.

Tarlow, Peter E. (2002). *Event Risk Management and Safety.* New York: John Wiley & Sons, Inc.

Zemke, Ron, and John A. Woods, eds. (1998). *Best Practices in Customer Service.* New York: HRD Press, AMACOM, pp. 41, 81.

Chapter 5

Carless, Jennifer (1992). *Taking Out the Trash.* Washington, DC: Island Press.

Catherwood, Dwight W. and Richard L. Van Kirk (1992). *The Complete Guide to Special Event Management: Business Insights, Financial Advice, and Successful Strategies from Ernst & Young, Advisors to the Olympics, the Emmy Awards and the PGA Tour.* New York: John Wiley & Sons, Inc., pp. 6–7.

Craven, Robin E., and Lynn Johnson Golabowski (2001). *The Complete Idiot's Guide to Meeting and Event Planning.* Indianapolis, IN: Alpha Books, p. 182.

Getz, Donald (1997). *Event Management and Event Tourism.* New York: Cognizant Communications Corporation, pp. 86–89, 351.

Hildreth, Richard A. (1990). *The Essentials of Meeting Management.* Englewood Cliffs, NJ: Prentice-Hall, p. 84.

Jennings, Gregory D., and Ronald E. Sneed (1996). *Water Quality and Waste Management Glossary.* North Carolina Cooperative Extension Service (www.bae.ncsu.edu/bae/programs/extension/publicat/wqwm/ebae144_90.html).

Journal for Municipal Solid Waste Professionals Glossary (www.forester.net/mw_glossary.html).

Kotler, Philip, John Bowen, and James Makens (1999). *Marketing for Hospitality and Tourism.* 2d ed. Upper Saddle River, NJ: Prentice-Hall, pp. 656–658.

Reis, Marilyn J. (2001). *The Receptive Operator.* New York: M. J. Lark Publishing, pp. 63–64.

Chapter 6

Berlonghi, Alexander (1990). *The Special Event Risk Management Manual.* Dana Point, CA: Berlonghi, pp. 199–201, 251–252.

Emergency Management Australia (1999). *Safe and Healthy Mass Gatherings: A Medical, Health and Safety Planning Manual for Public Events.* Australian Emergency Manuals Series, Manual 2. Commonwealth of Australia. (www.health.sa.gov.au/pehs/PDF-files/ema-mass-gatherings-manual.pdf).

Goldblatt, Joe, and Kathleen Nelson, eds. (2001). *The International Dictionary of Event Management.* 2d ed. New York: John Wiley & Sons, Inc., p. 172.

National Fire Protection Association Glossary of Terms (www.nfpa.org).

Tarlow, Peter (2002). *Event Risk Management and Safety.* New York: John Wiley & Sons, Inc.

U.S. Department of Transportation (2000). *North American Emergency Response Guidebook* (hazmat.dot.gov/erg2000/erg2000.pdf).

Chapter 7

Davis, Marion L. (1980). *Visual Design in Dress.* Englewood Cliffs, NJ: Prentice-Hall, p. 11.

Mackenzie, John K. (2000). "Meeting Themes: And Other Psycho-Syntactic Issues." *A Meeting Masters' Memo.* Vol. 1, no. 11. The Writing Works Web site (www.thewritingworks.com).

Pine, B. Joseph, and James Gilmore (1999). *The Experience Economy.* Boston: Harvard Business School Press, pp. 49–52, 213.

Whiting, Frank M. (1954). *An Introduction to the Theatre.* New York: Harper & Brothers, p. 210.

Chapter 8

Boulanger, Norman C., and Warren C. Lounsbury (1992). *Theatre Lighting from A to Z.* Seattle: University of Washington Press, p. 75.

Campbell, Drew (1999). *Technical Theater for Nontechnical People.* New York: Allworth Press, pp. 71, 129.

Fraser, Neil (1989). *Lighting and Sound.* 1st American ed. New York: Schirmer Books, p. 92.

Moxley, Jan (1995). *Advance Coordination Manual.* Boulder, CO: Zone Interactive, pp. 387, 255–256.

Simonson, Lee (1932). *The Stage Is Set.* New York: Harcourt, Brace and Company, Inc. p. 358. Also quoted in Frank M. Whiting (1954). *An Introduction to the Theatre.* New York: Harper & Brothers, p. 257.

Uram, Ted (1999). "Say It with Style: Attention Grabbing Special Effects for the New Millennium." *Event Solutions* (June): 34–38.

Walters, Graham (1997). *Stage Lighting Step-by-Step.* Cincinnati, OH: Betterway Books, p. 7.

Whiting, Frank M. (1954). *An Introduction to the Theatre.* New York: Harper & Brothers, p. 208.

Chapter 9

Allen, Judy (2000). *Event Planning: The Ultimate Guide to Successful Meetings, Corporate Events, Fundraising Galas, Conferences, Conventions, Incentives and Other Special Events,* Etobicoke, ON: John Wiley & Sons Canada Limited.

Brenner, Alfred (1980). *The T.V. Scriptwriter's Handbook.* Cincinnati, OH: Writer's Digest Books, pp. 52–62.

Catherwood, Dwight W., and Richard L. Van Kirk (1992). *The Complete Guide to Special Event Management.* New York: John Wiley & Sons, Inc.

Jackson, Robert (1997). *Making Special Events Fit in the 21st Century.* Champaign, IL: Sagamore Publishing, pp. 28–30.

Kupsh, Joyce, and Pat R. Graves (1993). *How to Create High Impact Business Presentations.* Lincolnwood, IL: NTC Business Books, p. 25.

Moxley, Jan (1995). *Advance Coordination Manual.* Boulder, CO: Zone Interactive.

Pine, B. Joseph, and James H. Gilmore (1999). *The Experience Economy.* Boston: Harvard Business School Press, p. 61.

Chapter 10

Hansen, Bill (1995). *Off-Premise Catering Management.* New York: John Wiley & Sons, Inc.

Krug, Susan, ed. (2000). *The Convention Industry Council Manual: A Working Guide for Effective Meetings and Conventions.* 7th ed. McLean, VA: CIC, p. 250.

Loken, Joan K. (1995). *The HACCP Food Safety Manual.* New York: John Wiley & Sons, Inc.

Shock, Patti J., and John M. Stefanelli (2001). *On-Premise Catering.* New York: John Wiley & Sons, Inc.

Sloan, Elizabeth A. (2002). "The Top 10 Functional Food Trends: The Next Generation." *Food Technology* 56(4):32–56.

Tarlow, Peter (2002). *Event Risk Management and Safety.* New York: John Wiley & Sons, Inc.

Visser, Margaret (1991). *The Rituals of Dinner.* New York, Penguin Books, p. 2.

Chapter 11

Chapman, Edward A., Jr. (1987). *Exhibit Marketing, A Survival Guide for Managers.* New York: McGraw-Hill, pp. 161–162.

Devney, Darcy Campion (1990). *Organizing Special Events and Conferences.* Sarasota, FL: Pineapple Press, p. 82.

Freedman, Harry A., and Karen Feldman (1998). *The Business of Special Events: Fundraising Strategies for Changing Times.* Sarasota, FL: Pineapple Press, pp. 27–28.

Getz, Donald (1997). *Event Management and Event Tourism.* New York: Cognizant Communications Corporation, pp. 207–208, 215–216.

Graham, Stedman, Joe Jeff Goldblatt, and Lisa Delpy (1995). *The Ultimate Guide to Sport Event Management and Marketing.* Chicago: Irwin Professional Publishing, pp. 223, 225.

Hoyle, Leonard H., Jr. (2002). *Event Marketing: How to Successfully Promote Events, Festivals, Conventions, and Expositions.* New York: John Wiley & Sons, Inc., p. 46

Kaatz, Ron (1989). *Advertising and Marketing Checklists.* 1990 printing. Lincolnwood, IL: NTC Business Books, p. 113.

Korza, Pam, and Dian Magie (1989). *The Arts Festival Work Kit.* Amherst, MA: Arts Extension Service, University of Massachusetts, pp. 35–36.

Underhill, Paco (2000). *Why We Buy: The Science of Shopping.* New York: Simon & Schuster, Touchstone Books.

West, Edie (1996). *201 Icebreakers.* New York: McGraw-Hill Trade.

West, Edie (1999). *The Big Book of Icebreakers: Quick, Fun Activities for Energizing Meetings and Workshops.* New York: McGraw-Hill Trade.

Chapter 12

Byl, John (1990). *Organizing Successful Tournaments.* 2d ed. Champaign, IL: Human Kinetics, pp. 2–4, 162, 173.

Goldblatt, Joe, and Kathleen Nelson, eds. (2001). *The International Dictionary of Event Management.* 2d ed. New York: John Wiley & Sons, Inc., p. 139.

Michaels, Jon (2002). "Building the Better Team: Innovative and Educational Teambuilding Enhances Communication, Commonality and Morale." *Event Solutions* (October): 24–30.

Morrow, Sandra L. (1997). *The Art of the Show.* Dallas, TX: International Association of Exposition Management Education Foundation, pp. 383, 386–390.

Reis, Marilyn J. (2001). *The Receptive Operator.* New York: M. J. Lark Publishing, pp. 93, 104.

Chapter 13

Armstrong, James S. (2001). *Planning Special Events.* San Francisco: Jossey-Bass, pp. 75, 80.

Buchholz, Steve, and Thomas Roth (1987). *Creating the High-Performance Team.* New York: John Wiley & Sons, Inc., p. 15.

Goldblatt, Joe Jeff, and Frank Supovitz (1999). *Dollars and Events: How to Succeed in the Special Events Business.* New York: John Wiley & Sons, Inc., p. 253.

Goldblatt, Joe (2002). *Course One: Amusement and Attraction Human Resources Management.* Alexandria, VA: The International Association of Amusement Parks and Attractions in cooperation with the George Washington University Institute of Tourism Studies.

Harbour, Jerry L. (1997). *The Basics of Performance Measurement.* Portland, OR: Productivity Press, p. 19.

Heller, Robert (1998). *Communicate Clearly.* New York: DK Publishing, p. 64.

Heller, Robert (1999). *Effective Leadership.* New York: DK Publishing, pp. 29, 67.

Herzberg, Frederick (1966). "The Motivation-Hygiene Theory," *Work and the Nature of Man,* World Publishing Co., Chapter 6, pp. 71–91. Also cited in *Organization Theory: Selected Readings,* ed. D. S. Pugh (1971). Baltimore, MD: Penguin Books, pp. 324–344.

Horowitz, Alan S. (1999). *The Unofficial Guide to Hiring and Firing People.* New York: Macmillan, pp. 81, 131, 307–325.

Hunsaker, Phillip L., and Anthony J. Alessandra (1986). *The Art of Managing People.* New York: Simon & Schuster, Touchstone Books, pp. 70, 230.

Jablonski, Joseph R. (1992). *Implementing TQM,* 2d ed. Albuquerque, NM: Technical Management Consortium.

Krug, Susan, ed. (2000). *The Convention Industry Council Manual: A Working Guide for Effective Meetings and Conventions.* 7th ed. McLean, VA: CIC, p. 137.

Liddell, Jamise (1998). "Volunteers and Events: A Winning Combination." *Event Solutions* (August): 58–61.

Norton, Tom (1999). "Three Steps to Getting and Keeping Staff." *The Event Professional* (May): 3.

Project Management Institute, Inc. (2000). *A Guide to the Project Management Body of Knowledge (PMBOK Guide).* Newtown Square, PA: PMI, pp. 115, 147, 153.

Rich, David (1998). "The Psychology of Meetings, Part Two." *Corporate Meetings and Incentives,* (October): 71–72.

Rusin, Jo B. (1999). *Volunteers Wanted: A Practical Guide to Finding and Keeping Good Volunteers.* Mobile, AL: Magnolia Mansions Press, pp. 37–40.

Weeks, Dudley (1992). *The Eight Essential Steps to Conflict Resolution.* New York: Tarcher/Putnam, Penguin Putnam, pp. 16–28, 61, 70.

Wiersma, Elizabeth A., and Kari E. Strolberg (2001). *Exceptional Events: Concept to Completion.* Weimar, TX: Chips Books, p. 98.

Chapter 14

Gerber, Michael E. (1995). *The E-Myth Revisted.* New York: HarperCollins, HarperBusiness, p. 100.

Goldblatt, Joe Jeff (1997). *Special Events: Best Practices in Modern Event Management,* 2nd ed. New York: Van Nostrand Reinhold.

Goldblatt, Joe (2002). *Special Events: Twenty-first Century Global Event Management.* 3d ed. New York: John Wiley & Sons, Inc., p. 56.

Harbour, Jerry L. (1997). *The Basics of Performance Measurement.* Portland, OR: Productivity Press, p. 65.

Hindle, Tom (1998). *Manage Your Time.* New York: DK Publishing, pp. 35, 48.

Marrow, Sandra L. (1997). *The Art of the Show.* Dallas, TX: International Association of Exposition Management Education Foundation, pp. 385–389.

Newman, Betsy H. (2002). "Surviving the Implementation of Event Management Software." *Event Solutions* (September): 48–53.

O'Toole, William, and Phyllis Mikolaitis (2002). *Corporate Event Project Management.* New York: John Wiley & Sons, Inc., p. 59.

Rea, Louis M., and Richard A. Parker (1992). *Designing and Conducting Survey Research.* San Francisco: Jossey-Bass, p. 16.

Robert, Henry M. (1970). *Roberts Rules of Order, Newly Revised.* Glenview, IL: Scott, Foresman, p. 420.

Zemke, Ron, and John A. Woods, eds. (1998). *Best Practices in Customer Service.* New York: HRD Press, AMACOM.

Chapter 15

Sweetland, Ben (1978). *I Will.* North Hollywood, CA: Wilshire Book Co.

Index